BARNSLEY PUBLIC LIBRARY

BARNSLEY LIBRARIES

GW01513794

06. MAR 93

14. APR 94

13. DEC 94

18. 11.

18. 11.

21. 04. 97

2 040699 01

The Nationalized Transport Industries

In series with this book
The Nationalized Fuel Industries
G. L. Reid, Kevin Allen and D. J. Harris

The Nationalized Transport Industries

A. W. J. Thompson
L. C. Hunter

Heinemann Educational Books
London

Heinemann Educational Books Ltd

**LONDON EDINBURGH MELBOURNE AUCKLAND
TORONTO HONG KONG SINGAPORE
KUALA LUMPUR IBADAN NAIROBI
JOHANNESBURG NEW DELHI**

ISBN 0 435 84855 0
paperback ISBN 0 435 84856 9

© A. W. J. Thompson, L. C. Hunter 1973
First published 1973

Published by Heinemann Educational Books Ltd
48 Charles Street, London W1X 8AH

Printed in Great Britain by
Richard Clay (The Chaucer Press) Ltd, Bungay, Suffolk

Contents

1 Introduction   1
- I   The Background to Nationalization, *3*
- II The Rationale of Nationalization, *9*
- III The Emergence of Economic Issues, *14*
- IV The Position of Nationalization in the 1970s, *26*

2 The Air Corporations   35
- I   Introduction, *35*
- II General Background, *37*
- III British European Airways, *53*
- IV British Overseas Airways Corporation, *75*
- V   Three Problems of Nationalization, *92*
- VI Conclusions, *115*

3 The Railways   124
- I   Introduction, *124*
- II Historical Background, *125*
- III Demand, *141*
- IV Costing and Pricing, *157*
- V   Efficiency, *181*
- VI Conclusions, *200*

4 Road Haulage   214
- I   Introduction, *214*
- II Development of the Industry, *216*
- III Regulation of the Industry, *222*

	IV	The Structure of the Industry, 227
	V	Demand, 236
	VI	Costs, 238
	VII	Pricing, 241
	VIII	Technical Efficiency, 245
	IX	Labour, 249
	X	Profitability and Investment, 251
	XI	Conclusions, 255

5 Road Passenger Transport — 266

    I Introduction, 266
   II History and Development of the Industry, 267
  III Structure of the Industry, 271
   IV The Licensing System and its Effects, 276
    V Demand, 281
   VI Costing and Pricing, 289
  VII Profitability and Investment, 296
 VIII Productivity and Industrial Relations, 300
   IX The Role of State Ownership in the Bus Industry, 306
    X The Future of the Industry, 308

6 Transport Policy — 316

    I The Concept of Co-ordination, 316
   II Co-ordination in Practice, 324
  III Conclusion, 342

Index — 349

Preface

The nationalized industries have, from their inception, been the cause of much debate among politicians and academics, but in spite of, or perhaps even because of, the scrutiny to which they have been subjected, the problems which they raise are far from completely solved. For this reason, together with the size and strategic position of the nationalized sector, we feel that not too much justification is required for adding to the already extensive literature. However, while much work has been done, it is slightly curious that no major attempt has been made to look at the economic problems of the nationalized industries *as industries*, or to consider the ways in which the economic character of the industries has become interwoven with the context of nationalization. This is the particular objective of the present study, which seeks to explore this inter-relationship for each of the major industries, against the background of the overall economic policy for the transport and fuel sectors.

This is one of two volumes, designed as companion works, which were made possible by a generous grant from the Carnegie Trust for the Universities of Scotland to a working group at the Department of Social and Economic Research at the University of Glasgow. The group itself comprised Professor L. C. Hunter, G. L. Reid, K. J. Allen, A. W. J. Thomson and D. J. Harris, and while the authorship of the volumes has been allocated to those who were assigned primary responsibility for the various chapters, all greatly benefited from a continual interchange of views within the group. In the present volume, all chapters except that on the Air Corporations (contributed by L. C. Hunter) have been written by A. W. J. Thomson. Outside the group, others within the University freely gave assistance and advice; J. F. Sleeman of the Department of Political Economy must especially be mentioned in this context.

Co-operation is also gratefully acknowledged from those in the nationalized industries who gave assistance to members of the group. Even though there is more published material available about the nationalized industries than about firms within the private sector, discussion with people inside the industries was enormously helpful in gaining perspective. It goes without saying that neither the industries nor the individuals are in any way associated with any of the comments or judgments contained. Dr M. R. Bonavia and Mr F. T. Sykes of British Railways Board, Mr D. W. Glassborow, Mr D. E. Done and Mr B. Barrett of the National Bus Company and Mr J. R. W. Graham at the Board of Trade (and now of British European Airways) must be singled out of those who gave assistance, since they also read and made comments on at least one of the chapters in draft form. Next, but not least in these acknowledgments, we should like to thank our secretaries Mrs E. M. Patterson and Mrs D. Ryder for their patience in typing the several drafts. Miss F. P. Rennie, Miss M. D. Simpson, Miss M. Oliver and Miss E. Fairgrieve also helped in preparing the final typescript.

One point of style which must be mentioned is that in the vast majority of cases monetary values have been converted to their decimal equivalents, even though the original notation was in the old form. This has occasionally led to a slightly clumsy mode of expression, but seems preferable to the confusion which might otherwise result.

August A.W.J.T.
1972 L.C.H.

I INTRODUCTION

This introduction, which also serves for the companion volume on the fuel industries, is about the economics of the nationalized industries. The two themes running through these volumes are the interaction of each industry with its environment, an obvious necessity in any work of industrial economics, and the methods, or rules, by which the industries are guided or controlled by central government policies. Nationalization, in other words, is being examined as an exercise in the economics of control in widely differing environments. However, some elucidation is necessary to delineate what are 'economic issues' and what is meant by the term 'nationalized industries', since neither term is free from ambiguity.

The first differentiation is that between economics on the one hand and politics and administration on the other. In a sense, the two approaches are indistinguishable, since the expression of economic policy requires a political or administrative act. Moreover, nationalization has been a topic of constant political debate in Britain to a greater extent than in any other country. Not only the boundaries of the public and private sectors but also the formulation of economic rules for the operation of public enterprises have been party issues. Indeed one of the continuing economic problems of the industries has been the effect of political uncertainty on morale, customer attitudes, management recruitment, and so on. Unfortunately these political divisions and their effects, although perhaps diminished in recent times, have far from disappeared. But even if the distinction between politics and economics has often been a fine one, most works on the nationalized industries have stressed the former aspect;[1] the present volumes will emphasize the latter.

The second line to be drawn is that defining a nationalized industry, which again is by no means easy. Nationalization involves public ownership, but not all publicly owned organizations are nationalized; many are controlled by local or municipal authorities. Nationalization also involves public corporations as the organizational vehicle, but not all public corporations involve nationalization in its accepted sense. Thus the White Fish Authority, the Arts Council, the Independent Television Authority, and the British Council are public corporations, but they do not operate nationalized industries. In fact there is no absolute dividing line, but merely a continuum between the nationalized industries at one extreme, industries with a measure of governmental control or influence in the middle, and private enterprise at the other extreme.

The definition of industry is also important. There are many offshoots of public enterprise in industries which are predominantly in private ownership, such as the brickworks owned by the National Coal Board or the hotels owned by British Rail. For the most part such offshoots have historical origins, being acquired along with their parent company in another industry, but there are also cases, such as the partial nationalization of Rolls-Royce in 1971 or the continuation of Richard Thomas and Baldwin in public ownership after the 1951 steel denationalization, where special circumstances forced the government's hand. It is clear that these situations do not constitute nationalized industries, but there is a question of the necessary extent of public ownership in an industry before it becomes a suitable subject for study. At the other extreme from incidental involvement, a monopoly of output would be too restrictive a definition. All the 'nationalized industries' have close substitutes over large parts of their range of output and are by no means complete monopolies. Because British Rail controls all traffics running over two rails this by no means gives it a monopoly of the carriage of goods, any more than the NCB has a monopoly of energy because it controls all the coal coming out of the ground. By contrast, the National Bus Company has a monopoly of public transport for many places in the country, even though it represents considerably less than half the bus industry.

The choice of the transport and fuel sectors may therefore be criticized as somewhat arbitrary yet there is no doubt that the public conception of nationalization largely emphasizes the energy and transport sectors and these also make up the greatest proportion of public enterprise by any measurement. Furthermore, those large industries lying outside transport and energy, such as steel and the Post Office,[2] have only recently become fully nationalized industries, and their experiences under the economic rules applied to the nationalized sector have been too short to warrant drawing conclusions from them. Thus while due acknowledgement must be made to the omissions, we have taken the view that more is to be gained by a selective approach than by trying to be comprehensive.

I The Background to Nationalization

A study of the economics of the nationalized industries suggests that there is something rather special about their economic organization and the impact they have on the economy at large. However fundamental this point, it is one which has not yet been satisfactorily investigated. There is one school of thought which says that state ownership must involve different economic criteria from the private sector of the economy, while another holds that it can and should be organized and operated according to the dictates of the market. One of the difficulties in resolving this argument is that economic considerations are not all-important. Political issues as basic as the desirability of private property have played a part in the history of nationalization as important as any technical economic question. And just as the reasons for nationalization have in some measure been non-economic, so too have the expected gains been in other dimensions than the purely economic. The threshold question in a study of this nature is therefore how and why nationalization was introduced in the first place.

State ownership and state monopolies have a very long history, but for our purposes nationalization is a modern concept, aroused on the one hand by the apparent exploitation of labour by capital and on the other by the growing awareness of the limitations of competition in those industries where a natural monopoly seemed to exist. These two strands of nationalization, the one rooted in Socialist ideology, the other in pragmatism, have interacted and overlapped considerably but they can be examined separately in terms of their contribution to the present operation of the nationalized industries.

Nineteenth-century Socialist theory took many forms, from Marx to Bernstein to Bellamy, but all were connected by the notion of exploitation of the workers by the owners of capital, and the need for this injustice to be corrected through the redirection of surplus value was the central linchpin of all policies. In Britain the main developments of the 1880s onwards were provided by the Fabian Society on the one hand and the Independent Labour Party and the trade unions on the other. The early Fabians, while accepting the need for national operation of the Post Office and the railways, for the most part envisaged the surplus value going to more local units such as municipalities or county councils, or communes, as the Fabians called them. Early Fabian efforts were therefore directed at municipal ownership, hence their label 'Gas and Water Socialists'. The ILP and the unions took a less theoretical approach, basing their programmes largely on the demands of unions in industries with particularly difficult industrial relations, such as mining and the railways. However, although a large number of resolutions advocating nationalization were passed at the TUC from the middle 1880s onwards, it could not be said that the TUC as a body was completely committed to nationalization until after 1918.

The First World War not only gave an impetus to nationalization through the centralized industrial controls which it necessitated, it also produced a sharp swing to the left by the unions and the Labour Party. The Labour Party's 1918 Constitution, and its manifesto 'Labour and the New Social Order', were much more positive than hitherto about state ownership. Section 3(d) of the Constitution contained an unequivocal statement of party objectives: 'To secure for the producers by hand or by brain the full fruits of their industry, and the most equitable distribution thereof that may be possible, upon the basis of the common ownership of the means of production and the best obtainable system of popular administration and control of each industry and service.' Now known as Clause 4 this is still the most emotive plank in the Party's Constitution.

The two documents did not intend instant nationalization of all industries. Immediate nationalization was to be reserved for the railways, mines and the generation of electric power (with municipal distribution of the latter). Also proposed was the 'common ownership of the nation's land, to be applied as suitable opportunities occur', and public ownership of canals, harbours, steamships and the insurance industry. Even though the documents were Fabian in origin and tone, they suited the unions and most of the leadership of the ILP, although a substantial body of more extreme opinion remained in the latter group.

There was, however, a considerable gap between theory and practice. When the Labour Party came to power in 1923, it attempted no single measure of nationalization, or, with the one exception of building materials, of state control over industry. Many supporters felt that an effort at least should have been made to nationalize the coal-mines, even if this had invited defeat in Parliament. In the 1929 election, Labour promised to nationalize the mines if it received a clear majority, but made no reference to public ownership of any other industry. Since it did not get a clear majority, and in any case many issues were overshadowed by that of the Depression, the only measure of nationalization attempted in this administration was the London Passenger Transport Bill, based on private Bills introduced before 1929, and even this was left unfinished. Nevertheless, in spite of these failures, it was well established by the middle 1930s that the next Labour programme would include a number of acts of nationalization.

One of the most important early issues in nationalization was the various means by which nationalized industries should be operated. The generally accepted assumption before the First World War was that if state control was desirable, the industries would become government departments, rather as the Post Office was until 1970. There were, however, other possibilities. One important attitude towards nationalization was represented by Syndicalism and Guild Socialism. Essentially these two movements saw the purpose of nationalization as being the benefit of the workers in the particular industry, with the unions as the organizational vehicles. Syndicalism was a revolutionary movement which had a strong following among shop stewards in the First World War, while Guild Socialism was a much more sophisticated gradualist movement largely conceived by G. D. H. Cole. Behind both movements was the belief that state Socialism might be even more remote and bureaucratic than private enterprise; in this it had something in common with the early Fabian interest in democratic municipal control. Although both Syndicalism and Guild Socialism died out in the 1920s, the demand for 'workers' control' remained, and indeed has shown signs of reviving with the current movement for worker participation.

A further organizational possibility, which gained general acceptance in the 1930s was Herbert Morrison's concept of the public corporation. Morrison argued that the best available brains were needed to run the industries, and that it was undesirable that they should represent special interests. The unions, although continuing to fight for direct trade union representation, were primarily concerned with the setting up of adequate consultative machinery and they accepted the principle of the public corporation at their 1932 Congress. Morrison's concept emphasized the commercial aspects of the undertaking's responsibilities, but it had much wider responsibilities as well: 'The public corporation must be no capitalist business ... It must have a different atmosphere at its Board table from that of a shareholders' meeting; the Board and its officers must regard themselves as the high custodians of the public interest.'[3]

Before moving on to other aspects in the development of nationalization, one more issue must be examined. This is the charge that the Labour Party gave very little thought to the actual economic and administrative issues involved in operating the nationalized industries. The extent of this neglect may be judged by the poignant recollections of Emanuel Shinwell as Minister of Fuel and Power in 1945:

> I immediately took up the task of preparing the legislation for the nationalization of the mines ... For the whole of my political life I had listened to the Party speakers advocating State ownership and control of the coal mines, and I had myself spoken of it as a primary task once the Labour Party was in power. I had believed, as other members had, that in the Party archives a blueprint was ready. Now, as Minister of Fuel and Power, I found that nothing practical and tangible existed. There were some pamphlets, some memoranda produced for private circulation, and nothing else. I had to start on a clear desk.[4]

Shinwell's amazement on not finding a blueprint may be somewhat overstated. The New Fabian Research Bureau, a breakaway from the parent organization, had in fact produced proposals covering many of the industries even if not in the detail required. Hugh Dalton's *Practical Socialism for Britain* and Evan Durbin's *The Politics of Democratic Socialism* were other works which tried to shape the Labour Party's view more clearly. In 1935, moreover, an interim report from the Labour Party's Executive Policy Committee had announced that a full plan for the socialization of fuel and power was being worked out in conjunction with the TUC. Yet Shinwell's account is essentially correct. Those writing about reorganization were largely basing their case on abstract principles, very few in the Labour leadership having had any practical experience of industrial management. But if there was uncertainty over issues of organization, questions of economic management were hardly even considered. Issues such as public accountability, policy determination, managerial control, and sensitivity to public needs were much more discussed than those of pricing, costing, the provision of capital, financial responsibilities, or the principles of investment. Part of the answer lies in the limited applicability of economic theory to the details of industrial policy. It must be remembered that the economic principles of the period were largely Marshallian. Keynesian ideas of macro-economic control, the theories of imperfect competition put forward by Robinson and Chamberlin, and even Pigou's development of welfare theory were all in the process of acceptance into the conventional academic wisdom, but as yet were too ill-digested for practical application. Given these factors we should not perhaps be too surprised that the economics of nationalization tended to be relatively neglected. It is therefore understandable that the Party was not adequately prepared for the complexity of the problems, at either the conceptual or the practical level, which ensued from nationalization.

If Socialism was the first and major strand of nationalization, a second was represented by the pragmatic and expedient attitudes of politicians and businessmen outside the Labour Party. The arguments involved were largely those connected with monopoly and size. If an industry appeared capable of operating more efficiently as an integrated entity, if competition could not be made effective, or if a service which was clearly desirable in the public interest could not be adequately provided by private enterprise, there was obviously a case for state control or ownership. As a result a wide variety of institutions appeared in the century before 1945 which covered imposing minimum standards or licensing particular kinds of operation, direct regulation of a wide range of activities or the co-ordination of small units into an integrated whole, state sponsorship of an infant industry, state competition with private enterprise and, at the extreme, outright state ownership and monopoly. No party and very few groups were opposed to state intervention in any form, but how far across the spectrum they might go depended on many factors. The Post Office was accepted from its inception as a clear case for outright state ownership, but less well known is the fact that Gladstone seriously considered the eventual nationalization of the railways when he was President of the Board of Trade in 1844. He did in any case nationalize the telegraph service in 1869. Towards the end of the century the public service industries of gas, water and electricity were clear candidates for municipal ownership or various forms of state control. Thus the first Electricity Act in 1892 laid it down that electricity franchises were to revert to the local authority after twenty-one years, although several years later a further Act doubled the period.

The first major effort of twentieth-century nationalization was the creation of the Port of London Authority by the Liberal Government in 1908. The First World War required a national takeover of the most important national services, and this was achieved without any major arguments about the rights of private property. Indeed after the war there was a serious discussion about the virtues of nationalizing the coal-mines and the railways in which the proponents of nationalization included many from outside the Labour Party.[5] Had either measure been passed, the subsequent history of nationalization might have been different. As it was, several other important measures were passed in the ensuing years. When the Electricity Commissioners, appointed in 1919, were found to lack the necessary powers to integrate services, it seemed reasonable to begin creating a National Grid system under the publicly owned Central Electricity Board in 1926. Two-thirds of the electricity undertakings were in any case under municipal ownership by this time. A public corporation, the BBC, had already been set up to control broadcasting in 1923. Neither of these instances was one of pure nationalization, in that there was no transfer from private to public ownership, but they were nevertheless valuable practical precedents, and helped to swing Labour opinion towards the public corporation. The case of the London Passenger Transport Board was rather different, since it involved the acceptance of Herbert Morrison's ideas by the Conservative-dominated National Government; furthermore, there was in this case a transfer from private to public hands, even if a large part of the services was already owned by the London County Council. This was the first time that the strands of Socialism and pragmatism came together, and Morrison's book on the subject, *Socialization and Transport*, had a wide influence even outside the Labour Party. One economic aspect of the LPTB which was significantly different from the post-1945 schemes was that the new Board was not to be in any way dependent on public funds. It was to raise its own capital, and compensation was to be made in London Transport stock, which was not to be guaranteed by the Government. A further development came in 1938 when the Conservative Government nationalized coal mineral rights, putting them under the control of a Coal Commission. The last of the pre-1945 public boards to be set up was BOAC, which took over from Imperial Airways in April 1940. In this instance the rationalization of the airline into a widespread network was clearly associated with military and imperial objectives. As with their other acts of nationalization, this seemed to the Conservatives to be an exception to Socialist desiderata for nationalization. In fact, however, the reasons and methods used by non-Socialist parties were not far from those of the Labour Party, although the latter wanted to go further and faster.

But if the specific acts of nationalization were carried out for expedient and apparently specialized reasons in each case, it would be wrong to ignore the sizeable body of non-Socialist opinion whose views paralleled those of the Socialists. One strand of such feeling was the optimistic expectation of many businessmen that 'bigger' meant 'better and more efficient'. They had seen the

American trusts and the German cartels take over a large share of what had previously been a British hegemony in world trade, and they regarded Britain's relative fall as being in part due to not taking advantage of potential economies of scale. Implicit in this argument was the Socialist and Marxist view of a continuing trend towards industrial concentration and thus the inevitable death of competition. The creation of such large units as ICI and Unilever in the late 1920s was one manifestation of this trend, but another indication of it was a readiness to accept state ownership if it was the only way of obtaining the promised economies. After all, there seemed to be little between monopoly capitalism and state Socialism except the legal formality of ownership. Perhaps the best example of this was the eagerness with which Lord Ashfield, who had long dominated London passenger transport, accepted nationalization as a means of ridding his undertaking of small competitors. A second facet of the sympathy with Socialism came from a loss of faith in the virtues of private enterprise as a result of the Depression. Thus even a Conservative such as Harold Macmillan could write in 1938: 'The Socialist remedy should . . . be accepted . . . where it is obvious that private enterprise has exhausted its social usefulness or where the general welfare of the economy requires that certain basic industries need now to be conducted in the light of broader social considerations than the profit motive provides.'[6]

The role that promises of nationalization played in Labour's sweeping election victory of 1945 should not be overstated. In the estimate of one close observer, G. D. H. Cole, it was the desire for social security and social justice which brought the electors to vote Labour.[7] Only the miners as a group probably wanted nationalization as an end in itself. Nevertheless nationalization was by no means a bogey-word even to large sections of the middle class by 1945. Other European countries had already nationalized important industries in the inter-war period, so that there was no feeling of setting out into uncharted seas. The Second World War had involved even more centralized administration of industry than the First, and thus there was not so much a transition from private to public ownership as a continuation of central control under a different legal and organizational format.

II The Rationale of Nationalization

Since the historical attitudes towards nationalization were neither completely uncompromising on the Labour side nor completely antagonistic on the Conservative side, it is not surprising to find that the post-1945 Acts were not as controversial in principle as they were in respect of detail. Many of the reasons advanced at the time had a good measure of bi-partisan support, and we shall now briefly examine some of these.[8]

(a) *The Technological Argument of Scale*

As might be expected given the attitudes of businessmen in the inter-war period, the argument that technical economies could be gained only by integration and central control of the public utility industries was not solely made from the Socialist side. The McGowan Report on electricity and the Heyworth Report on gas,[9] both headed by important industrialists, showed the advantages of larger units, and while neither explicitly recommended nationalization, the implied degree of regulation and supervision made outright national operation and ownership seem a simple and reasonable solution. The same argument was true of the railways, for although the 1921 Act, by creating four companies, had cut down the amount of overlapping, the four companies still had difficulties of interchange along their boundaries which could only be solved by single ownership.

(b) *The Wasteful Competition Argument*

A related argument, that of preventing waste rather than positively promoting economies of scale, was raised when more than one industry was considered. The wasteful effects of competition, both within and between industries, had of course been a Socialist argument from the earliest days of the movement. In areas where fixed costs formed a high proportion of total costs it was argued that competition must lead to a wasteful under-utilization of capital equipment. Thus in transport, only common ownership could ensure that there was the correct allocation of traffics between the modes, and long-distance road haulage had to be nationalized in order to enable integration to take place.

(c) *The Social Service Argument*

The nationalization debates stressed the social service benefits that nationalization would bring to those who had previously not benefited from the basic public services. Thus Alfred Barnes, the Minister of Transport, in introducing the 1947 Transport Act said:

The Commissioners have to carry through the task of integrating all forms of transport covered by the Bill and—this I particularly emphasize—to see that all parts of the country are adequately served. By that I mean the inclusion of rural and sparsely populated areas. These districts have never had the transport facilities they need. It is only by a unified system of which the cost can be spread over the whole system, that we shall be able to overcome this state of affairs.[10]

Such a statement, the philosophy of which was also particularly applicable to the electricity industry, was generally acceptable from the point of view of equity, but it was also a direct inducement or even instruction to cross-subsidization, an issue which has since caused a good deal of heart-searching. An analogous point, which also raised the vexed issue of social versus economic costs, was implicit in coal nationalization, namely that the reorganization of the coal-mines would take into account issues of regional unemployment and social immobility as well as profitability.

(d) *The Capital Procurement Argument*

Capital in post-war Britain was desperately short, and it was clear that priorities for investment had to be created. All the industries due to be nationalized had important claims on capital, yet there were severe doubts as to whether this would be forthcoming if the private capital market were the only source. In the case of an industry such as electricity, the sheer amount of capital required was daunting, while in the case of coal and the railways, the industries were in such a rundown state that any returns on new capital were likely to be extremely low. Yet their needs were great. The Reid Committee on coal had found that British mining methods and efficiency compared unfavourably with those of other countries and had made many detailed recommendations which would require a good deal of capital.[11] The railways were visibly rundown after heavy use and net disinvestment during the war. Both industries had also suffered from the fact that private-enterprise capital had not been invested in the inter-war period, in part because of the uncertain political future under nationalization.

(e) *The Larger National Good Argument*

This argument, primarily that some industries were too important to be left in private hands, had both an ideological and a practical side. The latter was frequently stressed in the nationalization debates. Thus the railways had to be nationalized in order to ensure that there remained an adequate framework for national defence purposes, just as in 1940 BOAC had been nationalized partly for imperial and prestige reasons. Similarly, takeover of the fuel industries was justified by the importance of maintaining supplies without requiring to base decisions on considerations of short-run profitability.

(f) *Industrial Relations*

In the inter-war period, the disastrous state of industrial relations in the coal industry had embittered industrial relations in the rest of the economy, and had led directly to the General Strike. Thus by 1945 many people both inside and outside the Labour Party were convinced that nationalization was the only answer to the industrial-relations issue in coal. Coal's labour problem was unique, but in the railways the state of industrial relations was also a consideration. In a sense, this feeling was another manifestation of the attitude that it was the State's responsibility to maintain declining industries.

So far we have dealt with reasons put forward in the nationalization debates for which there was a considerable amount of bi-partisan support. There were of course other reasons which were rooted more deeply in Socialist theory. One was that the capitalist system, with its competitive ethos, was fundamentally unChristian, and prevented the co-operation which Socialism sought to engender. A second was that the ownership of private property gave too much wealth and power in the community to its owners. A third point again connected with the second, was the expectation that nationalization would lead to a redistribution of income and a greater degree of equality. Again, closely connected with this was a fourth point that some industries, by their very nature, occupied such 'commanding heights' within the economy that Socialist government and planning would be impossible unless they were publicly owned. A fifth point, that private cost accounting should not be the sole criterion of whether a service should be operated, has partly been covered by the earlier social service argument. These arguments were not used as explicitly in the nationalization debates as those stated earlier, but their influence on the demand for nationalization should not be underestimated.

Within all these arguments, both Socialist and relatively bi-partisan, there was the assumption that nationalization would be more efficient than private enterprise. This was based more on the end of competition and the esprit de corps which was expected to evolve from a co-operative venture than from expectations of superior economic management, and in fact it sat oddly with the assumption that under nationalization industries would be prepared to behave in a non-commercial way. Nevertheless, increased efficiency undoubtedly was one of the attributes expected from nationalization.

Later Developments

Since the initial period of nationalization, there have been various developments which have changed the extent of nationalization without fundamentally changing its character. The Conservative reaction to nationalization on returning to power in 1951 was relatively modest, namely denationalization of the steel industry (although retaining Richard Thomas and Baldwin and some of the features of central control) and partial denationalization of long-distance road haulage. Thereafter, in spite of misgivings in some sections of the party, the Conservative Governments of the 1951–64 period accepted the fact of ownership and sought ways of improving the efficiency of the industries. This was done partly by administrative reorganization, with decentralization a central feature, partly by setting new financial obligations, and partly by capital controls.

The Labour Party, in its period out of office, did little positive planning for further nationalization. Indeed, there was a considerable 'revisionist' section within the Party which followed C. A. R. Crosland in thinking that 'ownership is not now an important determinant of economic power',[12] although the 'fundamentalist' section continued to regard state ownership as the central point of the Party's credo. The 1964 election manifesto mentioned only steel and water as industries to be nationalized, although those already owned by the state were to be given greater freedom of operation. In practice, steel was nationalized, this time in a form which was intended to make the 1952 type of denationalization impossible,[13] the status of the Post Office was transferred from that of a Government Department to that of a nationalized industry, and a Bill to nationalize the ports failed only due to the timing of the 1970 election.

The new Conservative Government in 1970 seemed at first determined to end the largely bi-partisan policies of the post-war period by thoroughgoing denationalization. 'Disengagement' and 'hiving off' were two frequently used terms. However, the extent of denationalization seems more likely to be limited to the sale of a few peripheral bodies such as Thomas Cook, the state public-house schemes, and Penarth Docks than to include, as some rumours have suggested, all the profitable sections of the corporations owned by the State. Indeed, the Government's overall policy of enforced commercialism was overtaken by events, to the extent that one of the principal victims, Rolls-Royce, had to be nationalized. At the same time the Labour Party, as well as promising to re-nationalize any properties which the Conservatives might denationalize, have shown more interest in further nationalization. Industries which have been mentioned include pharmaceuticals, insurance and airframe. Nevertheless, the net change in the extent of nationalization since 1950 has been minimal,[14] excepting the transfer of the Post Office. On the other hand, the reawakening of the ideological aspects of nationalization, which had been relatively quiescent for the period since 1951, means that the future extent of state control must be more uncertain than it seemed to be in the 1960s.

III The Emergence of Economic Issues

(a) *The Early Years*

During the 1945–50 nationalization debates in Parliament, as in the discussions in the years preceding, very little attention was given to the issues of economic management. The Labour Party was concerned with structure and accountability, the Conservative side with compensation. Outside the most general instructions, no guidance was given, and in any case it was thought such issues should be decided by the new corporations.[15] Even in the early years after nationalization, the industries were primarily concerned with questions of organization. This was only natural in fields such as road haulage where a very large number of separate businesses had to be welded into a single whole. Moreover, in several industries, especially in the fuel sector, the order of the day was production almost without regard to cost. Then, as the immediate pressures of production and organization faded, issues of economic policy emerged which had not been considered at the time of nationalization.

The initial statutory economic and financial obligations imposed on the nationalized industries were far from precise. As we have seen, many of the issues were left for the industries themselves to solve. Financially they were expected to pay their way 'taking one year with another', which implied that there must be a balance of surpluses and deficits over a not unduly prolonged period. In view of the fixed interest nature of the capital some degree of oscillation of surpluses and deficits was necessary. In private industry, of course, equity capital acts as a cushion against economic vicissitudes. As defined in the statutes, items properly chargeable to costs included interest, redemption of capital, depreciation at historic cost and the provision of reserves. Although the last of these items would not normally be included before the calculation of profit, this was less of a barrier to good accounting than the fact that the costing obligations were to relate only to total sums for the whole enterprise, in spite of many different units being involved. Only in the case of the gas industry, where the twelve area boards were treated as separate financial entities, was there any attempt to prevent or forestall widespread cross-subsidization. Indeed, cross-subsidization of the railways by the roads seemed to be one of the objects of creating the British Transport Commission, although of course this was never made an explicit objective.

The service obligations of the industries were phrased in words such as 'adequate', 'efficient', 'economical', 'co-ordinated', and so on, by which was roughly meant that as much as was demanded should be produced at the cheapest possible price, but there was little or no statutory advice on how this was to be achieved. However, Chester has pointed out that the overall effect of the Acts was to push the industries into average cost pricing since most of the Acts had an injunction not to discriminate unfairly which could easily be interpreted in this way.[16] Here was a further inducement to cross-subsidization.

Little guidance was given on either theoretical or practical economic issues. Theoretically, pricing and particularly marginal cost pricing received most attention. That an optimum allocation of resources could best be obtained if prices were equal to or at least reflected marginal cost was fairly well accepted in academic circles, but there was less agreement as to the precise definition or measurement of marginal cost, particularly with respect to the time period involved. These practical problems, to which economists gave quite inadequate attention, take up a considerable proportion of the later chapters. In any case, whatever its theoretical advantages, it could hardly be said that the concept was generally accepted or even appreciated at the level of political determination in the immediate post-war period.

Pricing was also the most immediate practical issue, with the problems in the coal industry the first to claim attention. The amount of coal available was severely limited; rationing was imposed. Since at least some coal was being produced at a loss, and the NCB had by 1952 a cumulative deficit of £14 million, it was clear that coal was priced well below the level which would equate supply and demand. The Ridley Committee in 1952 was equally split between those who would charge marginal and those who would charge average cost.[17] This was followed by a powerful argument by I. M. D. Little for marginal cost pricing as soon as long-run supply and demand could be equated.[18] Pricing was also a key issue in the other industries. The Transport Commission announced its intention to bring price more into line with cost on the railways, but public reaction and the interminable administrative procedures involved in going through the Transport Tribunal were major stumbling-blocks to any realignment. Electricity and gas had more freedom of manoeuvre, but here, as in all the industries, high fixed costs, seasonal and daily fluctuations in demand, and the problems of accurately measuring variable costs created great difficulties in arriving at a soundly based system of charging, even assuming agreement on the theoretical principles. Throughout the 1950s marginal cost pricing gained increasing favour as the theoretical starting-point, although its practical applicability remained dubious.

From the arguments over pricing, and particularly the role to be played by marginalist principles, it was but a short step to two other related areas which caused policy divisions after nationalization, namely investment and the financial obligations of the industries. Again there were both theoretical and practical considerations. The principle of marginal cost pricing raised the theoretical problems of suitable investment criteria, since a return could not be expected from capital which was not taken into account in the pricing decision, and of what to do about deficits in those industries where marginal cost lay below average cost. More important, at the time there were also severe practical problems. Investment in the immediate post-war period was made where shortages seemed to be greatest, without relation to the rate of return. At first this meant concentrating on the electricity and coal industries, but in 1955, with a growing availability of capital, expansion was permitted in several other industries, most notably the railways, where the massive Modernization Plan was to cost well over £1,000 million. This was accepted with a notable lack of scrutiny which soon became apparent as the profitability of many projects was called into question. It thus became clear that a far better system of evaluating projects and for deciding the priorities of projects in different industries was required. This need was exacerbated in 1956 when the Finance Act changed the method of providing fresh capital from the capital market (with Treasury guarantees) to direct borrowing from the Exchequer, which the coal industry alone had done hitherto. Thus even the very limited degree of market appraisal was removed.

The investment issue also had implications for the financial obligations of the industries. An obligation merely to pay their way meant that there was a very low amount of self-financing by the industries, based only on depreciation at historic cost, and the question arose as to whether the nationalized industries were not taking too high a proportion of the total capital available, and whether the low prices made possible by such a minimal financial requirement were not inducing a greater demand both for the services themselves and for still more investment than would have been the case with a higher required rate of return. Another issue, for which there seemed to be no easy answer, was that once the Government had accepted a need for deficit grants on a large scale, as it had done for the railways by the late 1950s, financial obligations no longer acted as any sort of check on costs.

These three problems of pricing, investment and the rate of return were seen as the central issues in the economic policy of the industries not only by academics but, even more pertinently, by the Select Committee on Nationalized Industries, a House of Commons Committee which began operations in the mid-1950s. It soon proved itself a powerful critic of prevailing policy not only through the publicity it could provide for facts which would otherwise have remained hidden, but also because of its bi-partisan approach and its willingness to use economic analysis. There can be little doubt that its reports were influential in forcing the Government to try to clarify the economic principles on which the nationalized industries should operate.

(b) *The 1961 White Paper*

The first attempt to clarify the ground rules came in April 1961, with the publication of a White Paper, *The Financial and Economic Obligations of the Nationalized Industries*.[19] It was primarily concerned with the fact that the financial performance of the nationalized industries had not fulfilled even the relatively limited obligations imposed at nationalization. Indeed, it noted: 'The total retained income of all these industries taken together (including supplementary depreciation provisions, capital redemption funds and reserves) has not been sufficient to provide for the replacement of assets used up in the production process, and this is also the case in most of the individual industries concerned.'[20] The rate of return on capital employed was therefore very low in comparison with private enterprise, and while the White Paper recognized that there could be no direct equivalence between the two sectors, one of its primary objectives was still to redress the balance to some extent. It therefore laid down certain conditions for improvement:

(i) Surpluses on revenue account should be sufficient to cover deficits over a five-year period.

(ii) Provision within revenue should also be made for the difference between depreciation at historical and at replacement cost, and for a contribution towards capital development and other contingencies.

(iii) An overall rate of return would be negotiated with each industry according to its circumstances, which would include the extent to which industries were expected to undertake commercially unprofitable activities. The obligation might be expressed in terms of net or total assets, or even as a surplus on operating account.

(iv) New procedures for investment allocation were set up, based on five-year capital development plans. It was made clear that investments carrying a relatively low rate of return would be very carefully scrutinized.

(v) It was announced that Ministers would continue to interest themselves in pricing policy, but boards responding to persuasion would now be allowed to publish the Minister's instruction.

These rules, while unquestionably a great step forward from what had gone before, went only a limited distance towards answering the problems. Could the economic obligations of these giant, multi-faceted industries be adequately summed up in a single rate of return? Was the determination of the rate of return in any case not based on 'horse-trading' between Minister and industry rather than any objective economic criteria? What happened, as in the case of British Railways, if there was little hope of breaking even, never mind earning a positive rate of return? What happened if, as in the case of the airlines, the Corporations had far from complete control over their prices and could thus only approach the rate of return from the cost side? Moreover, because the White Paper concentrated on end results it gave little indication of how those results were to be achieved. Was it desirable, for instance, that industries with monopoly power should be able to achieve their objectives merely by raising their prices, without necessarily being forced to make better use of their resources? In any case, the pricing instructions were perfectly compatible with average cost pricing, widespread cross-subsidization, or any other system which might mean that price did not reflect true resource cost. The investment policies were also far from clear. Because the financial objectives were expressed as an overall figure, there was no direct indication of the rate of return to be earned on new investment. Nor did the rate of return, except in the long term, reflect the alternative uses to which the new capital might be put. Again, five-year rates of return were of little relevance in evaluating projects which might have a life expectancy of thirty years, and whose rate of return in the first five years might be low relative to its long-term return.

The White Paper, involving the determination of pricing and investment criteria through the rate of return, was criticized for having got things the wrong way round. The argument was that if pricing and investment criteria were economically correct, resources would be efficiently allocated, and the rate of return would become a residual, or possibly even redundant. This is the so-called triangle argument, that if any two of the three sets of control criteria, pricing, investment and rate of return are predetermined, the third follows inevitably from the others as a residual.

(c) *The 1967 White Paper*

The result of this and other criticisms was a further White Paper, *Nationalized Industries: A Review of Economic and Financial Objectives*, in November 1967.[21] The main change was one of emphasis from regulating the end effect—the rate of return—to regulating the means to this end—the pricing and investment criteria. Average target rates of return were still to be set, but they were to reflect correct pricing and investment criteria. Most fundamental was the new approach to pricing. Other than pointing out that the consumer must pay the true costs of his goods, the key instruction was that: 'In addition to recovering accounting costs, prices need to be reasonably related to costs at the margin and to be designed to promote the efficient use of resources with industry.'[22] This was the first time the economic rules had explicitly acknowledged the case for marginalism. Even from the sentence quoted above, however, it was clear that there were limits to acceptance of the doctrine. As critics of the White Paper, and particularly the Select Committee, pointed out, in requiring price to reflect marginal cost and yet be adequate to cover total cost, the Government was trying to have its cake and eat it, and they questioned the extent of the Government's commitment to marginal cost. The result would be a hybrid in which average cost was dressed up to look like long-run marginal cost pricing. If the Government really believed in marginal cost pricing, it should be prepared to accept losses in certain situations.[23]

Even within the White Paper, there were other considerable qualifications of the marginal principle. It was noted that there would 'of course' be exceptions to the general rule and the paper spelled out some of these: where cross-subsidization was justified by wider economic or social considerations; if innovation led to the rapid reduction of long run marginal costs but too rapid a reduction in prices would over-stimulate demand; where the area of unallocable costs is large, such that prices could not accurately reflect the cost of particular services whilst also covering total cost; and, associated with the last point, where it is simply impracticable to cost separately relatively minor operations. Such exceptions could of course be stretched to cover a large range of circumstances, and indeed the pricing instructions concluded with the comment that: 'It will be clear from the preceding paragraphs that there is nothing rigid or doctrinaire about the pricing policy which the industries are expected to follow.'[24] But while this new approach to pricing was far from explicit, it was nevertheless a much closer definition than had hitherto been attempted.

The investment rules were also fundamentally changed. A new concept, the test rate of discount, was introduced, quite distinct from the overall rate of return. It represented 'the minimum rate of return to be expected on a marginal low-risk project undertaken for commercial reasons', and was initially set at 8 per cent on a discounted cash-flow basis; but since it was specifically designed to be flexible, it was no surprise when it was raised to 10 per cent in 1969 to reflect rising world interest rates. However, the rate was not necessarily that which the industries actually paid on new borrowing from the Exchequer, since the borrowing rates reflected Government credit. The White Paper also recognized that social as well as economic costs and benefits must be taken into account, and this might mean undertaking projects with less than the stipulated rate of return. Conversely, the fact that a project promised more than the rate of return was not to guarantee its acceptance. These rules for investment, with the exception of the last two, represented no more than the best practice in private industry, but were clearly a major advance within the public sector.

Several other points were made by the White Paper, of which the most important were: the possible scope for reducing costs was to be carefully examined—with this in mind, all requests for price increases were to be referred to the National Board for Prices and Incomes; and services performed under social obligations were to be separately costed, with the financial responsibility being accepted by the Government.

The 1967 White Paper represents the current economic rules of the nationalized industries, although some refinements have been put forward by the Prices and Incomes Board.[25] There is, however, a large gap between theory and practice. As can be seen from the following chapters, the extent to which the rules are actually followed is far from complete. The task of finding methods of implementing them and ensuring that they are properly applied must remain at the forefront of governmental policy for some time to come, always assuming that the rules or indeed the whole role of the industries does not radically change under the Conservative Government.

(d) *Some Other Economic Considerations*

If the economic issues arising out of the 'triangle' have been of most interest to economists, and they will of course be examined at greater length in the succeeding chapters, there are numerous other economic issues of a more general nature which have had considerable repercussions on the performance of the nationalized industries. There is not, unfortunately, sufficient space to do full justice to all of these, but they must at least be mentioned. First, however, it should be noted in advance that most of them are manifested through the delicate relationship between Minister and industry. The Select Committee, in considering the purposes of Ministerial control, thought two were basic: to secure the wider public interest, and to ensure the efficiency of the industries.[26] Obviously, however, a great deal can be subsumed under these two headings, and much depends on how these things are achieved. The Committee was sympathetic to the conception that the industries should be given overall policy guidelines which they should then be free to follow, but the committee found that the sponsoring Departments were more concerned with detail than with broad policy issues, and worse still that they were confused about the nature of policy, the methods of checking and ultimately the division of responsibility between the Treasury, the Departments and the industries.[27] In practice, in fact, the operation of Ministerial control was the reverse of the theoretical conception. It is in the light of this judgement that the following issues may be better understood.

(i) CROSS-SUBSIDIZATION AS A SOCIAL WELFARE POLICY

One important category of issues has related to the social role of the nationalized industries. How purely commercial should they be? How far should they reflect the 'wider public interest'? There are a number of different issues here. One is cross-subsidization. As we have seen, several of the industries, either statutorily or by the intentions of their sponsors at nationalization, were expected to cross-subsidize in order to provide a reasonable equality of price across the range of services. Clearly there is no sense in extending, say, a transport service to a remote area if costs and prices are so high as to preclude its use. The problem is particularly acute in transport and communications, where costs vary by very large amounts for apparently similar services, and where the public has strong opinions of equitable treatment if there is too much digression from a standard charge. The solution propounded by economists, and also the Select Committee on Nationalized Industries, was a direct subsidy for uncommercial activities, but for price to reflect costs in other situations. Not until the 1967 White Paper did this become official policy, however, and since then the 1968 Transport Act has created a system for governmental payment of the losses of unremunerative railway lines and part of the losses of rural buses. There is still a good deal of cross-subsidization in the nationalized industries, nevertheless, and in practice governmental policy has been far from explicit about the types of case where some cross-subsidization might be justified on social grounds.

(ii) REGIONAL POLICY

Cross subsidization has also played a role in regional policy. Transport and electricity are two fields where the rural population has been subsidized by those in more densely populated areas in that similar prices have been charged although costs differ. Again, the older, high-cost coal mines have generally been in those areas where higher than average unemployment already existed. In order to keep down the rate of unemployment, arguments have been made in favour of policies to permit the older pits to be subsidized by the newer. But there have also been other pressures on the nationalized industries with respect to regional policy. Should a high proportion of new investment go into depressed areas, or should it go where its commercial return is highest? The best example of this sort of pressure comes from the steel industry, where regional interests competed fiercely through their political lobbies for new investment even in the period when the industry had been returned to private ownership, and this has certainly not diminished since renationalization. The 1962 governmentally dictated split of new investment in rolling mills between Wales and Scotland, such that neither plant achieved the full economies of scale, is an excellent example of compromise leading to loss of economic efficiency.

(iii) PRICE CONTROL

Another issue which has considerably affected the freedom of the nationalized industries has been governmental pressure on prices. The nationalization statutes gave Ministers no control over prices, yet at intermittent intervals Governments of both parties have asked the nationalized industries to defer price increases for political and even redistributive reasons, both when price and incomes policies have been in operation and when they have not. Direct pressure was exerted in 1967 when the Prime Minister directed that the Prices and Incomes Board should investigate all price increases by the nationalized industries, and this helped to clarify the considerations involved. Indeed, on occasions the Board told industries that increases have been insufficient for their needs. However, the 1970 Conservative Government has already provided some of the best examples of governmental pressure on the industries. Indeed, in the election campaign the Party announced that it intended to use the nationalized industries as a means of curbing price increases. A particularly significant example of this came in April 1971 when the Prime Minister himself intervened to instruct the Steel Corporation to halve its proposed price increases, even though the Corporation was known to be losing money. This was followed by whole-hearted governmental backing for the summer 1971 CBI initiative to keep price increases down to 5 per cent for a year, such that the nationalized industries were under pressure to conform. The implications of such actions for following the 'rules' are obvious, especially in terms of financial targets, but also for pricing itself.

(iv) INVESTMENT CONTROL

An analogous issue concerns the use of investment in the nationalized industries as a counter-cyclical macro-economic tool, in much the same way as public works expenditure was a favourite remedy during the Depression, except that in the post-war period it has usually been used in a restrictionist rather than expansionist way. The use of investment in this way is perhaps best illustrated by the years following 1955. The year 1955 promised to be something of an *annus mirabilis* as far as the nationalized industries were concerned, since the post-war capital shortage seemed to have come to an end. Nuclear power, steel and, above all, transport in the shape of the Railway Modernization Plan and the authorizations for the first motorways received their first major capital injections. Yet in July 1955, only six months after these measures had been announced, the Government pruned the investment programmes of the nationalized industries. Further cuts followed in February 1956. While the Suez crisis of that year led to a speeding-up of the nuclear energy programme in order to save imported fuels, the September 1957 balance of payments crisis led to further cuts in public sector investment, including a year's delay in the completion of the nuclear programme. With recovery in the balance of payments position and poor performance in the nationalized industries, especially railways and coal, the Chancellor announced in October 1958 that all limitations on public investment were to be removed. These vicissitudes, which occurred in the context of fragmentary investment criteria which have since been improved, were considerably dampened but by no means removed in the 1960s, and recently in the early 1970s another 'cycle' seems to be operating. The 1970 Conservative Government tried initially to make the industries more self-sufficient in capital to help cut public expenditure, but only a year later it was instructing the industries to bring forward proposed expenditure to help create jobs. Whilst the Government must use a wide range of fiscal weapons for deflationary or reflationary needs, it is nevertheless arguable that the nationalized industries have had more than their fair share of intervention in long-term capital planning.

(v) SECTOR CO-ORDINATION

One of the most significant facts about the industries nationalized in the immediate post-war period is that none of them is a complete monopoly. The death of competition, so confidently forecast in the pre-war period, has proved to be a long time coming. Since there are significant cross-elasticities of demand within both the fuel and transport sectors, governmental policy towards one industry could not leave out of account the repercussions for another. Inevitably questions of resource allocation in the industries had to be seen in terms of resource allocation in the sectors; policy had to be not only the minimization of real resource costs in the gas or railway industry, but also minimization in terms of energy or transport. The interaction of the transport industries had been obvious long before nationalization, but in the fuel sector the relationships took time to emerge. Only the most nebulous powers of co-ordination were given to the Minister of Power when the post was created in 1945, and the Ridley Committee in 1952 strongly argued the case for competition between industries without governmental intervention of any sort. However, worries created by the Suez crisis, threatening oil supplies, and thereafter the growing stocks of unsold coal forced the Government to look at co-ordination in the fuel sector also. In transport the opportunities for integration were in fact the main reason for putting the various modes under the umbrella of the British Transport Commission. However, integration was equated at the time with common ownership, and it was some time before it was appreciated that the two were not necessarily the same.

The theoretical answer to the problem of achieving co-ordination has always been the price mechanism. Industries should make their prices either equal to, or systematically related to, marginal cost, and they should also be required to cover their costs, including a minimum return on capital. However, most or all of the social issues mentioned, as well as those created by problems of measurement and the presence of private enterprise, have intervened, and the price mechanism has not been able to operate freely. Thus the co-ordination achieved by means of price competition has been limited, although it should not be underestimated. In place of this type of co-ordination, governments have tried to develop co-ordination by administrative regulation, but even so they have had to react expediently to short-term pressures, both inside and outside the sectors. So detailed and important is this question that a chapter on sector co-ordination has been included in each volume.

(vi) MANAGEMENT

The problem of obtaining and keeping high-calibre management involves both personality and financial facets. Inevitably the nationalization Acts created a new scale of operations which would in any case have strained the capacities of the previous private-enterprise managers, and this was exacerbated by the departure of many able men for ideological reasons or because they were unable to adapt to the new structure. To take the most extreme example, it was expecting a lot for highly independent, individualistic, down-to-earth road hauliers to become junior managers in a massive and, at least initially, highly centralized organization like BRS. The financial facet has been the simple one of low salaries. The railways have provided perhaps the greatest amount of public controversy, first with Dr Beeching's £24,000 salary, and some six years later with the refusal to pay Mr Peter Palmer the £18,000 he sought as prospective chairman. There has always been antipathy in the Labour Party to paying salaries even reasonably competitive with private industry, with the result that the calibre of management at all levels has suffered.[28] The position has improved in recent years, but the nationalized industries still suffer from a poor image as far as a career in management is concerned.

IV The Position of Nationalization in the 1970s

A final section in this introduction must be reflective, to see where nationalization stands in the early 1970s. From the foregoing section, it can be seen that the nationalized industries are very far from operating as self-contained entities according to a set of definitive economic rules, and this will become even more obvious after reading the various industry chapters. Indeed, the reader may well be excused for wondering if the rules have had any function at all, given the difficulties of applying them, to say nothing of the series of financial shortfalls, capital write-offs, administrative reorganizations, institutional constraints, competitive pressures, social obligations and the like about which he will read. That question we must reserve for a little while yet, however, since there are a number of other viewpoints which have a bearing on the matter.

One viewpoint is political. While both the major political parties have changed their attitudes towards certain aspects of nationalization in the last quarter of a century, and in spite of both a good deal of bi-partisanship in trying to make the industries operate more efficiently, and of the several jointly accepted reasons for nationalization in the first place, it is arguable that their fundamental ideological beliefs about the principle of state versus private ownership have not changed. There have remained many in the Labour Party who look upon Clause 4 as the basis of Socialism, while there are others in the Conservative Party who still conceive of state operation not only as being ipso facto less efficient than private enterprise but also as a lost source of potential private profit. While bi-partisanship has been real, it has also been tenuous, ready to be disturbed by a changing balance within one of the parties. Thus while state-owned industry has ceased to be a major political factor in most Western countries, in Britain it remains one of the primary dividing issues. As a result, ideological considerations have always played a part in economic deliberations, and the extent of this has not lessened. Indeed in the early 1970s some widening of the ideological positions of the parties may be observed.

Beyond the political issue, there are various aspects of the role of the nationalized industries which have still not been satisfactorily solved. One such is accountability, which in fact goes much wider than the nationalized industries to the National Health Service, the armed forces, road-building, education and so on, but has been particularly important with regard to the nationalized sector. By definition, the industries cannot be made efficient through normal market processes, although there is in fact far more competition than the concept of a single-firm industry implies. The economic rules are of course one mechanism for ensuring efficiency, and economists have argued that they should be sufficient if properly applied. Nevertheless, since this would involve an unacceptably high degree of autonomy, other controls have been sought in the field of public administration, of which the major one has been the much-criticized system of ministerial control. But this particular issue has been only one facet of the debate. What is the proper role of Parliament? Should there be a Ministry of Nationalized Industries, as the Select Committee suggested? Does the Select Committee itself play a correct role? Should there be some permanent commission, analogous to the Prices and Incomes Board, standing outside the Government? Given the inevitability of overlordship, what should be the division of power and responsibility between the Treasury, holding the purse-strings, and the sponsoring Ministry, holding formal responsibility? Has there been too much supervision in the past? And finally, at a very different level of accountability, how should the consumer make his views known, bearing in mind that many decisions are virtually irreversible and that the right quality of service is often difficult to determine by purely economic criteria? All these, and other, questions are intermittently re-examined, but the right balance between managerial autonomy and public supervision remains elusive.

A second unresolved question about the role of the industries asks how far the nationalized industries can be realistically held aloof from becoming instruments of wider government economic policy. Given the obligation of all governments, domestic and foreign, to pursue overall economic objectives which are, to put it mildly, difficult to reconcile, is it not correct to use all the available tools for managing the economy? Is a self-contained nationalized sector compatible with a prices and incomes policy which is concerned with holding down inflation, especially when its products are such visible and vital consumer goods. It has indeed often been argued that one of the purposes of nationalization is to permit the use of the industries as instruments in the management of economy. To its credit, the Prices and Incomes Board frequently defended the need to raise prices in the nationalized sector, but the very fact that two sets of criteria are being applied—one internal, based upon economic rules implying self-containment and isolation from the rest of the economy, the other external, based on consideration of short-term national policy needs—must inevitably lead to confusion. Worse, it can lead to a tacit ignoring or bypassing of the economic rules. It was, of course, to prevent undue short-term and external influences affecting decisions that the rules were set up in the first place. The Select Committee accepted that some manipulation would be necessary, but agreed that the Minister ought to take responsibility and be accountable. Unfortunately, if the manipulation is constant, the criteria for ministerial accountability become blurred. Throughout the 1960s both parties tried to avoid undue intervention and paid at least some attention to the rules they had created, but the early period of the 1970 Conservative Government, with its concurrent rapid inflation and high unemployment, has tended to be a relapse to earlier days. It is arguable, in fact, that the manipulation of the industries to try to solve these twin problems has thrown the rules for operating the industries into sad disarray. We have already mentioned some contributory occurrences: the stated intention to use the nationalized industries as a means of curbing prices, the consequent instruction to the British Steel Corporation to halve its 14 per cent increase, and the pressure exerted by the Government's backing for the CBI's price control initiative; and on the investment side the change in policy from searching for potential cuts in investment programmes to reduce public expenditure to bringing forward programmes to help provide jobs, especially in the development areas. The effects of policies like these are undoubtedly to make the financial obligations of the industries very much more difficult to achieve, as if inflation had not created problems enough. Most of the major public sector industries are in deep financial trouble as 1971 ends, and several may well have to borrow to make up revenue deficits, thereby storing up higher interest charges in future years. The Government's decision to give grants to the BRB and the NCB at the end of 1971 to enable them to keep down price increases in 1972 recognizes this point, but also serves to highlight the breakdown of financial controls. To point out all these problems is not to criticize the Government but rather to illustrate that trying to solve a larger problem may create other smaller ones.

These last paragraphs prompt the even more far-reaching question, namely whether the same objective of economic control could not be achieved more effectively by some means other than nationalization as it currently exists, with possibilities ranging from the regulatory commissions of the US variety to the injection of private capital, much more public dividend capital, hiving off various parts of the industries, a widespread denationalization. The Labour Government of 1964–70 created a number of new institutions of control, with the Industrial Reorganization Corporation and the Prices and Incomes Board being the most conspicuous, but these have now been wound up. Yet another possibility is the further expansion of 'twilight' nationalization as the Government is forced by its new social and economic responsibilities to extend financial and indirect control to parts of the private sector such as computers (ICL), aircraft (Concorde and Rolls-Royce), and shipbuilding (UCS and Harland and Wolff). Whatever the formal structure, it seems inevitable that the State must be involved in industry, and that this involvement will grow. To this extent, direct ownership may indeed, as Crosland has argued, be less relevant than the fact of control.

The time has now come to return to the point with which we started this section, namely to sum up the record of nationalization and the economic rules as a means of control. So far we have been intent upon the problems of nationalization, the unsolved issues, and the implied failures. However, it would be wrong to present such an uncertain picture without also recording some of the achievements of the industries. Too frequently the popular conception that the state-owned sector is far less efficient than the private sector has been uncritically accepted. Indeed one of the heaviest burdens the industries have had to bear has been the generally negative attitude of the public, which is dispiriting for self-confidence and can all too easily becoming self-fulfilling in its effects. There are of course considerable difficulties in comparing the public and the private sector, and it is only recently that the public sector has received a reasoned economic defence by Pryke.[29] These two volumes are not designed to be comparative, but taken by and large any judgements in them come closer to Pryke's verdict than that of the popular myth.

It is always more difficult to point to positive virtues than to already well-publicized deficiencies, but the nationalized industries have greatly improved their performance, so that far from being the backward problem children of British industry, they now lead the private sector in some spheres. A selection of these changes can be simply summarized:

(i) Annual productivity gains increased dramatically. Pryke has calculated that while in the period 1948–58 the overall annual increase in labour productivity was 1·5 per cent in the nationalized sector and 1·9 per cent in the private manufacturing sector, in the period 1958–68 the position was reversed, with a 5·3 per cent growth in the state sector and 3·7 per cent in private manufacturing.[30]

(ii) In spite of the poor relative salaries, the quality of management improved greatly, fostered by training and development schemes and by the use of management techniques ranging from work measurement and job evaluation through to sophisticated methods of investment appraisal.

(iii) In the area of scientific innovation and development, the industries have had some notable successes, such as British Rail's Advanced Passenger Train, BOAC's Boadicea, or the Gas Council's oil-gasification process. Moreover, in terms of adaptability few industries can equal the gas industry's change from town gas to oil-based gas to natural gas, each of them requiring a different technology, in not much more than a decade.

(iv) The industries have maintained social policies which were generally humane, if sometimes ill-advised in that they added to costs and detracted from financial results. The policies nevertheless saved the Government considerable amounts of expenditure in other forms, and it could be argued that the planned rundown of the coal industry is perhaps the outstanding single achievement by the nationalized sector.

(v) In a similar vein, although the state industries contained some of the traditional black spots for industrial relations, the quality of relationship between the corporations and their employees improved greatly. In some areas, such as consultation procedures and productivity bargaining, they were generally more progressive than most of industry.

(vi) In purely economic terms, the criteria of decision-making became much better. Pricing structures became much more rational, as did investment planning, while the knowledge of costs at last could get beyond global terms.

(vii) Finally, but not least important, the state companies established themselves as full members of the industrial community, which had once distrusted them as extensions of government. Indeed some of the industries showed a taste of entrepreneurship by innovating in areas not directly the concern of their own industry, examples being the Coal Board's hotel booking system and the railways' property development. The nationalized sector has also pleased the rest of industry by its willingness not to be a tame pawn of government, but to develop its own policies.

These are considerable changes, and in evaluating them it is highly significant that the record of improvement, in financial, productivity and organizational terms undoubtedly accelerated in the 1960s as compared with the 1950s. Even Pryke, the most staunch defender of the nationalized sector, has admitted that results in the first decade, particularly in terms of productivity, were disappointing.[31] But whereas he tended to blame the upheaval caused by nationalization,[32] an equally likely candidate was the lack of clarity about objectives or the criteria for action. The industries had to face incompatible public expectations for both commercial and public service standards, for minimum cost and maximum quality, and for accountability without responsibility. It is arguable that when some thought was given to these aspects of operation, performances generally improved and that this improvement continued as better criteria developed into the broad rules laid down in the White Papers. At the very least it can be said that although the rules may not have been, and indeed cannot be, fully applied, they have played a valuable role in clarifying the problems faced by the industries and in sharpening the quality of thinking applied to them.

From this introduction, it will be evident that while economic issues have always been present in the discussion of nationalization, they have not always been the sole consideration and in many cases they have not even been the primary concern. Yet in recent years the economic issues have come increasingly to the fore, and it is with these problems that the two present volumes are essentially concerned. The economic issues have two aspects: first, the basic features of the industries themselves, and the kind of difficulties that characterize them; and second, the economic implications of nationalization as it affects the performance and organization of the industries. In one sense, therefore, the following chapters are essays in industrial economics, in another they are essays in the economics of nationalization. The latter sort of problem very often cannot be properly understood in isolation from the former: in the case of the railways, for example, it is surely not without significance that major railway systems all over the world have experienced serious financial problems, whether publicly owned or not, so that the industry and its difficulties are as important as the fact that in the British case the industry is nationalized. Nationalization may affect the organization of the industry, its objectives, and the ways in which it performs its economic function, but the essential economics of that particular activity also have to enter the picture as part of the constraints and opportunities relating to the industry's operation. These two threads of economic investigation are to be found in the subsequent chapters, all of which have a common aim. But the varying circumstances of the industries preclude the possibility of adopting a standard format for each chapter, and the authors have been left free to develop the structure of each chapter in the way that seems most appropriate to the industry.

NOTES TO CHAPTER 1

1. See in particular Select Committee on Nationalized Industries, *Ministerial Control of Nationalized Industries* (HC371—I, II, III: HMSO, 1968) and the most recent book on the subject, David Coombes, *State Enterprise, Business or Politics* (P.E.P. and Allen and Unwin, 1971).
2. A separate examination of the Post Office is being undertaken by members of the present team.
3. H. Morrison, *Socialization and Transport* (Constable, 1933), pp. 156–7.
4. E. Shinwell, *Conflict Without Malice* (Odhams Press, 1955), p. 172.
5. A Coal Commission under Mr Justice Sankey was set up in 1919 to avoid the threat of combined action by the Triple Alliance of Miners, Railwaymen and Transport Workers. Its subject was primarily that of nationalization, and the Lloyd George Government promised to abide by its findings. There was a unanimous acceptance of public ownership of the coal measures themselves, and even on the critical question of the nationalization of the mines there was a majority, albeit a bare one, in favour of nationalization. However, the majority was split on the question of control, and the Government used this as an excuse for

taking no action, even on the issue of the mineral rights. The railways did not come so close to nationalization, but even here the Government seriously considered state ownership rather than the compulsory reorganization eventually carried out in 1921.
6. H. Macmillan, *The Middle Way* (Macmillan, 1938), p. 239.
7. G. D. H. Cole, *A History of the Labour Party from 1914* (Routledge & Kegan Paul, 1948), p. 465.
8. For a greater amount of detail on the reasons for nationalization see A. H. Hanson (ed.), *Nationalization* (Allen and Unwin, 1963).
9. *Report of the Committee on Electricity Distribution* (HMSO, 1936); *Report of a Committee of Inquiry into the Gas Industry* (Cmnd. 6699: HMSO, 1945).
10. Parl. Deb. 5th Ser. Vol. 431, Col. 1623, 1947.
11. *Report of the Technical Advisory Committee on Coal Mining* (Cmnd. 6610: HMSO, 1945).
12. C. A. R. Crosland, *The Future of Socialism* (Jonathan Cape, 1956), p. 318.
13. The reasons given for the second nationalization were much more specific and economic than for the first. Rather than the needs of national planning, which was the main argument in 1951, in 1967 stress was laid on the inability of the industry to raise adequate capital for expansion, the lack of exploitation of economies of scale, the consequent need for structural rationalization, and a history of restrictive pricing practices in the industry.
14. In 1950 the state-owned industries (excluding steel and the Post Office) accounted for approximately 8 per cent of Gross Domestic Product. Twenty years later the proportion for the same companies was around 7 per cent, or, if steel were added, about 10 per cent.
15. An example of the lack of policy comes from an answer to the question of how transport integration would be achieved by the price mechanism. Mr Strauss, the Parliamentary Secretary to the Minister, replied: 'I cannot say what the new charges system is to be. I can only reasonably forecast that it will not be based, like all recent explorations into this problem, on the need for somehow relating road and rail charges on a profit basis, but on the principles which are best likely to serve the national interest.' This, naturally, was not very enlightening to the House. Parl. Deb. 5th. Ser. Vol. 431, Col. 1982, 1947.
16. D. N. Chester, 'Note on the Price Policy Indicated by the Nationalization Acts', *Oxford Economic Papers*, January 1950.
17. *Report of the Committee on National Policy for the Use of Fuel and Power Resources*, Ridley Committee (Cmnd. 8647: HMSO, 1952).
18. I. M. D. Little, *The Price of Fuel* (Oxford University Press, 1952).
19. Cmnd. 1337: HMSO, 1961.
20. ibid., p. 5.
21. Cmnd. 3437: HMSO, 1967.
22. ibid., p. 9.
23. SCNI, *Ministerial Control*, Vol. I, Ch. V and VI. The White Paper published by the Government in reply did not really answer these criticisms (*Ministerial Control of the Nationalized Industries*, Cmnd. 4027: HMSO, 1969).

24. *Ministerial Control of the Nationalized Industries*, Cmnd. 4027, p. 10.
25. For instance, the Board has tried to evaluate marginal social costs for the coal industry. See NBPI, Report No. 153, *Coal Prices* (Cmnd. 4455: HMSO, 1970).
26. SCNI, *Ministerial Control*, Vol. I, p. 9.
27. ibid., pp. 189–90.
28. The NBPI found the average salary for main board members of the nationalized industries (excluding steel) to be £8,860, whereas that for board members of private companies with assets of more than £250 millions, the nearest equivalent group, was £18,760. The NBPI also found, as might be expected from the above, that the management salary structures in the nationalized industries were unduly compressed, creating problems of promotion, of relating reward to performance, and of recruiting from the outside. (NBPI Report No. 107, *Top Salaries in the Private Sector and Nationalized Industries*, Cmnd. 3970: HMSO, 1969.)
29. Richard Pryke, *Public Enterprise in Practice* (McGibbon and Kee, 1971).
30. ibid., p. 104.
31. ibid., p. 21.
32. There is undoubtedly some truth in this point. The problems of the Post Office and the steel industry in the recent past bear out Pryke's argument about the difficulties of implementing any policies until the organizational structure is right.

2 THE AIR CORPORATIONS

I Introduction

Discussion of the economic problems of the two State Air Corporations, the British Overseas Airways Corporation (BOAC) and British European Airways (BEA), involves two distinct issues. The first is the economics of airline *operation*, including analysis of the demand for different kinds of air transport, the composition of costs and their behaviour with changes in output. The second is the economics of airline *regulation*, which involves public policy towards civil aviation, the controls exerted by government on the Corporations as nationalized concerns, and the institutional regulation by international agencies and agreements of all airlines operating internationally. Government regulation in recent years has given rise to increased interest in the organization of the industry in such a way as to secure the maximum net economic benefit to the country as a whole.

British civil aviation is characterized by a mixture of State and private enterprise. BEA and BOAC together account for about 70 per cent of the British industry's output, measured in capacity ton miles (CTM). The remainder is contributed by a number of smaller, privately owned airlines, some of which at least are direct competitors to the two Corporations. British airline operators, with 90 per cent of their output on international services, are participants in an international market, and the main competition to BEA and BOAC comes from the airlines of other countries. In addition, competition to civil aviation comes from surface operators providing road, rail and shipping services and at the margin there are competing facilities offered by telecommunications and the postal service. BEA and BOAC are not competitive to one another in any real sense since they have historically had quite separate roles, with BEA concentrating on short-haul operations, BOAC on long-haul.

The Corporations' problems have to be viewed against the background of a sustained and rapid growth of world air travel, the market for which expanded at about 15 per cent a year over the 1960s. At the same time, technology has been advancing rapidly, adding problems of premature obsolescence to those of acquiring investment funds simply to keep up with the growth of demand. Under these circumstances, airline operators need a policy that is sufficiently flexible to allow advantage to be taken of new opportunities, while government policy on civil aviation and the institutional arrangements of the industry require to be brought up to date at not too infrequent intervals. Recognition that civil aviation policy in Britain was lagging behind events, and that the structure of the industry and its regulatory machinery were becoming outmoded, persuaded the Government in 1967 to set up a Committee of Inquiry into Civil Air Transport, under the chairmanship of Sir Ronald Edwards. The Edwards Committee's terms of reference were:

> To inquire into the economic and financial situation and prospects of the British civil air transport industry and into the methods of regulating competition and of licensing currently employed; and to propose with due attention to other forms of transport in this country what changes may be desirable to enable the industry to make its full contribution to the development of the economy and to the service and safety of the travelling public.

After eighteen months' collection of evidence and deliberation, the committee presented its report[1] to Parliament in May 1969. From then until mid-1971 considerable uncertainty prevailed. In November 1969 a White Paper was published by the Labour Government, in which many of the Edwards Committee's proposals were incorporated,[2] but the necessary legislation could not be brought before Parliament prior to the General Election of 1970. The incoming Conservative Government quickly indicated that it had rather different ideas for the future shape of civil aviation—notably in the relationship between the private and public sectors of the industry, and preliminary announcements of policy were made in November 1970. The legislative changes necessary were framed in the 1971 Civil Aviation Act, and most of the political uncertainties have now been resolved.

Substantial changes are already beginning to occur in the organization of British civil aviation, roughly but not entirely along the lines advocated in the Edwards Report. This chapter will be concerned with the implications of these changes for the two Corporations, viewed against the background of their general economic

THE AIR CORPORATIONS 37

problems, their recent performance, and the extent to which past obstacles to commercial profitability and efficient operation have been overcome. There are in particular two recurring themes: first, the competitive problems facing the Corporations and secondly, the implications of the closer linking of the activities of BEA and BOAC (which could eventually result in complete merger) foreshadowed in the deliberations of 1969/70.

The remainder of this chapter takes the following form: section II sets out some of the relevant background to the subsequent discussion, describing the civil aviation market and its institutional framework and outlining some of the main economic problems of airline operation. Sections III and IV respectively deal with the main characteristics and recent performance of BEA and BOAC, while section V examines in more detail the critical questions of the future competitiveness and viability of the nationalized sector of the industry. Some conclusions are presented in section VI.

II General Background

By the usual standards, civil aviation is a small industry within the British economy, with 75,000 employees in 1970 and an annual level of gross domestic fixed capital formation averaging less than £50 million in recent years though a sharp increase was recorded in 1970 and higher levels may be expected in the 1970s. Its share of total *domestic* passenger mileage is only about half of one per cent, and its share in freight traffic even less. Yet Britain ranks at least third in importance in world civil aviation, after the United States and the USSR, and the economic importance of civil aviation is much greater than the above figures suggest. In part this is due to rather doubtful arguments (from the economic standpoint at least) relating to national prestige and strategic or defence objectives. More important, however, is the contribution made to the balance of payments —the annual net surplus on the civil aviation account averaged about £40 million in the period 1969–71—and to the movement of passengers and freight over longer distances, especially to Europe and North America. For journeys of the order of 200 to 300 miles, air transport becomes a possible substitute for surface travel, and above 300 miles air becomes increasingly the preferred mode of transport by virtue of reduced journey time. The main problem for the airlines is the amount of 'dead' time in air travel, spent on processing and assembling passengers. On short trips this amounts to a high proportion of total journey time, thus wiping out the benefits of faster speeds on the journey itself. Thus the importance of civil aviation is best seen in its share of long-distance journeys. In the late 1960s, more people were travelling to Europe by air than by sea, and about 85 per cent of passenger movements between Britain and the rest of the world were by air. Internally, too, on trunk routes like London to Glasgow and Edinburgh, air is an important commercial mode for passengers. Recent estimates suggest that on the Glasgow–London route the airline share is 41 per cent, compared with 29 per cent rail. The London–Manchester route, conversely, has 50 per cent travelling by rail and only 9 per cent by air.[3]

The total market for travel has been increasing as a result of growing real incomes, greater intra-country linkages and perhaps above all due to the growth of international communications in business and recreation. The ability of the airlines to capture a bigger share of this market has been due largely to the time savings it makes possible on long journeys, improved safety standards and a relative (and at times an absolute) reduction in the costs of air travel compared with surface transport. It is necessary to explore both the demand and supply aspects in a little more detail.

(a) *Supply and Demand*

At the most general level, civil aviation output is the provision of space for passengers and cargo in aircraft operating over a route or system of routes. The supply of capacity is measured in capacity ton miles (CTM) which reflects both payload capacity and length of haul. There is a great deal of difference between providing one hundred tons of capacity over one thousand and ten thousand miles, and the CTM measure takes into account both elements. (For a single aircraft with payload capacity of ten tons flying 2,000 miles per week the output would be 20,000 CTM.) This is only a measure of supply, for aircraft often fly with empty seats and unused cargo space, reflecting the limited divisibility of capacity. One of the main problems for airlines is to adjust capacity provision to demand on the route network served, in such a way that the proportion of capacity utilized, or *load factor*, remains high enough at existing levels of fares to cover the fully allocated costs of operation and yield some surplus.

The problems of obtaining a load factor above break-even point vary greatly with the type of service under consideration. Aside from the fairly obvious distinctions between domestic and international services and between passenger and cargo services, there is a traditional distinction between *scheduled* and *non-scheduled* operations, deriving from the 1944 Chicago Convention.[4] Scheduled services are openly available to individual members of the public at a fixed price and comprise a systematic series of flights, usually based on published timetables. All other services are *non-scheduled*. Scheduled operation in air, as in other forms of transport, commonly implies an obligation on the part of the operator to provide the public with a regular and reliable service. This frequently results in lower load factors than in non-scheduled operation, where the supplier is freer to adapt his services according to the pattern of demand. Low load factors may, however, be due to other factors as well.

In the first decade after the war the protected position of the scheduled operators was secure and non-scheduled operators provided only a minute proportion of total airline business, but there has since been a major change in the balance and composition of traffic. In particular there have been new types of non-scheduled service, most notably the *inclusive tour* (IT) which involves the sale of package holidays, with air travel and hotel accommodation at an all-in price. These tours are provided by tour organizers to the general public, offering the advantage of a complete holiday abroad at a total cost usually equal to the charge for a normal scheduled air return. According to a resolution of the International Air Transport Association (IATA), member airlines agree not to allow anyone chartering an aircraft for IT purposes to undercut the normal scheduled fare. This resolution has been applied by the British licensing authority under the title of 'Provision One'. However, during the winters of 1970/71 and 1971/72, prices were decontrolled for short holidays in many resorts and often prices were reduced. The economies of the IT depend upon block hotel bookings, often right through the season, and the charter of aircraft capable of being used intensively (or at off-peak times of day or year) at a high load factor, so that average passenger costs can be reduced substantially below those of individually arranged holidays.

Other types of charter operation include the *affinity charter*, in which an aircraft is chartered for a specific journey by an affinity group formed for a purpose other than air travel: for example, student flights during vacations or football supporters travelling to a match abroad. Here again the possibility of achieving high load factors allows the fare to be reduced considerably below the comparable scheduled fare. Affinity charters are excepted from the rules applying to inclusive tours, but have been subject to control by governments and their agencies as a defence against possible erosion of the scheduled tariff structure. These controls have not always been successful, however.

So long as these new developments can be kept quite separate from the market for scheduled services, no difficulties arise. But especially where scheduled operators are providing services to areas abroad that are also served by tour operators, it is almost inevitable that traffic will be partially diverted to the latter. To understand this more fully we have to look at the nature of demand for air travel.

Four principal motives for air travel can be identified: business, vacation, personal and affinity group activities. The last of these is likely to be best catered for by charter flights, while the urgency of personal motives will generally dictate the time and money allocated to the trip. The biggest categories are business and vacation travel, and these afford strong contrasts. Business trips normally imply a specific destination and a short booking period, while in addition demand is relatively price inelastic. The requirement here is for a service offering a fairly wide choice of flights on a regular basis, resulting in a high probability of the passenger being able to travel 'on demand'. In this situation, the airline is reduced to guessing demand. Where adequate service is not provided, travellers will tend to switch to other airlines offering more convenient service, or even to another transport mode. This explains the importance attached by scheduled airlines to achieving a relatively high frequency of service. The tendency, therefore, is for scheduled services to be over-provided, driving down load factors.

In the case of vacation travel on the other hand, the specific destination may be less important than the general area, and demand will tend to be much more price elastic (and more responsive, too, to increases in real income). Also, the lead-time in booking will generally be much longer, the peak booking period for summer holidays abroad occurring in mid-winter.

In planning future services, scheduled airline operators need to find means of cushioning themselves against the low average load factors associated with 'on-demand' business. This need is reinforced by the fact that whereas in recent years the growth of business travel has been modest, in line with the moderate growth of GNP, 'pleasure' travel has been growing rapidly as a result of market-creating strategies on the part of British IT and charter operators who in 1970 carried around three and a half million passengers, compared with a combined figure of about ten million for the scheduled services of BEA and BOAC. The large increase now taking place in average aircraft capacity, which will not be fully compensated by a reduction in service frequencies, has further aggravated the problem of excess capacity. Under the conventional conditions for scheduled service, the operators were not able to differentiate the two types of demand or to adopt a differential fares policy. However, in the face of growing non-scheduled demand, and in view of the need to sell more capacity to cover the higher total costs of operating the new larger aircraft, the scheduled operators have begun to introduce tour and charter groups on scheduled flights.

The key to this differentiation has been the encouragement of various forms of forward booking from those willing to commit themselves to a flight date well in advance—a condition which applies in particular to IT and charter passengers, but not those who require service of the 'on-demand' variety. It has thus become possible for the two sorts of demand to be reconciled, and the scheduled operators have the opportunity to increase capacity utilization while still meeting the obligation of scheduled operation to provide the public with a regular, continuously available service. At the same time the whole basis of the traditional scheduled/non-scheduled distinction dissolves in favour of a new distinction based on differences in the economic character of demand for air travel.

This brief survey of supply and demand considerations has shown up some of the main trends now occurring as a result of changing market and technological factors, and the stress they are putting on well-established attitudes, policies and institutions. This stress helped to form the views of the Edwards Committee and Government on the need for new policies and organization in British civil aviation. But before we proceed to these changes, we must sketch in the main features of the existing institutional framework.

(b) *Civil Aviation and its Regulation*

Stephen Wheatcroft[5] has set out the principal arguments in defence of regulating civil aviation. These diverse arguments cannot be taken with equal weight and include some that are frankly controversial, but may be summarized, without substantial comment, as follows:[6]

(i) Air transport is a quasi-public utility, providing services endowed with a special public interest and forming part of the nation's social overhead capital in transport: lack of profitability may have to be weighed against the external economies generated.

(ii) Air transport raises several questions relating to the national interest, especially the need for high safety standards, but including also defence considerations (a strategic aircraft reserve, trained flying personnel, and the maintenance of a home-based aircraft manufacturing industry).

(iii) Air transport may need to be co-ordinated with other forms of transport to avoid duplication and undesirable competition.

(iv) The 'natural economic characteristics' of air transport are such that if not regulated they would fail to meet the objectives set out in (i) to (iii) above. These characteristics are that it is impossible to envisage air routes being served by more than a small number of airlines—the tendency is towards oligopoly; economies of scale do not act as a natural barrier to new entry; the possibilities of effective product differentiation are relatively limited.

(v) Competition cannot be an efficient regulator because of the effects of route-sharing on unit costs.

(vi) Regulation can be used to achieve certain public policies at minimum direct cost to public funds: by protecting licensees, the Government can impose obligations on them to provide low-profit or loss-making services that are in the public interest.

Perhaps the main reason for regulation is that transport has long been regulated historically where the public interest is in question, and in the case of airlines the public service character of scheduled operations has required that protection should be given to them, while the safety factor has also played an undoubted role in the cause of intervention. Whatever the reason, the fact is that regulation has been and continues to be a prime feature of the industry, both nationally and internationally.

The Chicago Convention of 1944 confirmed the sovereignty of each country over its own air space and thereby enabled countries to trade in air space, granting rights of landing for commercial purposes to other nations in exchange for equivalent rights in these countries. The convention failed in its main objective of reaching a multilateral agreement on the exchange of air traffic rights, but a second conference between Britain and the United States at Bermuda in 1946 resulted in agreement on certain principles that were intended to guide the two countries' relations with one another and with other countries in subsequent negotiations. This agreement was a compromise between the American desire for open competition and the British wish for greater regulation still, these attitudes being a reflection of the strong American and weak British positions as a result of wartime specialization in aircraft production. The Bermuda principles were essentially that capacity and frequency of service on any route between the two countries would not be regulated, nor would the number of airlines operating out of these countries be controlled. The possibility of an ex post facto review of capacity was however allowed in the event of what seemed to be unrealistic capacity provision. In addition, tariffs would be agreed by the airlines through the Tariff Conferences of the International Air Transport Association (IATA),[7] subject to mutual government approval. It is important to recognize that the Bermuda agreement was one between the two *governments*, under which the designated *airlines* themselves were able to arrange services as they thought appropriate.

Although a number of countries accepted the letter of the Bermuda philosophy, only the United States has stuck firmly to the spirit. The vast majority of international air service agreements are much more restrictionist, with frequency of service and capacity determined ex ante, usually with an equal sharing of capacity between the two countries and with a single designated airline from each country. In many cases it is actually stipulated in the agreement that capacity must be shared between the two airlines in terms of a pooling agreement.

Pooling, or as the airlines prefer to describe it, the operation of 'commercial agreements', usually involves an equal sharing of capacity provision and joint revenue, irrespective of traffic actually carried. Regular opportunities for re-negotiation of these agreements are provided in the event of one airline getting its actual traffic seriously out of line with capacity, so that the scope for competition is not ruled out. In practice, examples of redistribution are few. In BEA's evidence to the Edwards Committee, it was stated that between 1960 and 1968 there were five cases of re-negotiation relating to changes in capacity, and in another five cases limitations had been set to pool payments when one partner fell behind. In the opinion of Sir Anthony Milward, formerly Chairman of BEA,

> a pool is a long term affair and one does not vary it merely because for a season or two seasons one side has got to better advantage through aircraft or any other reason.[8]

Since pooling is a condition of operation on certain routes, unilateral abandonment of pooling could lead to the loss of traffic rights and a loss of service to the travelling public. Nevertheless, in the last analysis, pooling is a restrictive arrangement that is likely to militate against innovations in marketing and pricing strategy, and whatever it may do to protect the airline interests of a single nation, it is liable to produce an inefficient allocation of resources on an international basis.

Two further aspects of regulation remain to be considered: governmental designation of airlines as scheduled carriers, and control of domestic air transport. In the immediate post-war period the grounds for the designation of airlines were clearly established. BOAC had been formed as a nationalized corporation in 1939, and was joined in 1946 under the Civil Aviation Act by BEA and British South American Airways (merged into BOAC in 1949). In the White Paper setting out this policy,[9] it was stated that this approach offered

> ... the best guarantee to the public of disinterested expansion of the nation's air services with economy and efficiency. It will make it possible as costs of operation are progressively reduced for the taxpayer to receive some benefit in return for the assistance he is required to provide during the initial period of subsidized operation and, where this is essential, to develop uneconomic as well as profitable services.

The decision to divide responsibilities was based on three arguments: the need for flexibility in meeting international competition, the necessity to develop alternative methods and techniques and to avoid placing sole responsibility in the hands of one managerial group, and the desire to create a pool of knowledge and experience. The three Corporations, therefore, were established with specific geographical territories and no competition between them. The later demise of British South American Airways set the twofold division of operations still present today.

The nationalized Corporations held a complete monopoly of British scheduled services until 1952. In that year, under the Conservative Government, independent operators became eligible to enter into associate agreements with the Corporations to provide scheduled services. The independents were able to acquire some scheduled services not in conflict with the Corporations' established operations and this, together with charter work (including military trooping) which was the mainstay of the private sector in this period, allowed a nucleus of independents to survive until greater competitive freedom was introduced.

This greater freedom of operation came with the Civil Aviation (Licensing) Act of 1960, which also tightened safety regulations and introduced two major innovations. The Act set up the Air Transport Licensing Board (ATLB), a formal licensing authority, to replace the Air Transport Advisory Council. It also eliminated the monopoly right of the Corporations to scheduled services on particular routes, and allowed independent operators to seek licences for scheduled services on their own account. The ATLB was to exercise its functions so as 'to further the development of British civil aviation', although it was given more specific guidance on the criteria to be applied in considering licensing applications.[10] The Board was also charged with the duty of determining domestic air fares.[11] Its powers to develop its own policy were considerable, and one of the main criticisms of its work has been that it failed to develop a sufficiently unambiguous and consistent policy to allow operators to plan ahead. At times, the Board proved unwilling to align its decisions with Ministerial statements of policy and, while appeal could be made to the Minister, this did not make for confidence and stability in an industry which already had problems in this direction. The mounting criticism[12] was summed up in the 1969 White Paper:

> The air licensing system has not worked as well as was hoped when it was set up in 1960. Justified criticism has been made of the system for appeals. The basic weakness has been a lack of clarity about the objectives of civil aviation policy and a lack of suitable machinery for acting positively in their pursuit.[13]

Not surprisingly, the regulatory system is now being reorganized. The immediate point, however, is that during the 1960s the ATLB's decisions to grant licences for scheduled operations to independent operators permitted, for the first time, direct competition between scheduled British carriers. The consequences of this for the nationalized airlines emerge in sections III and IV below.

(c) *Some Problems in Airline Economics*

It is not possible in the present study to undertake a full discussion of airline economics, but a preview of some difficulties underlying the subsequent discussion is necessary.[14] First, we consider some implications of the fact that airline operations involve an interdependent *system* of activities. This has implications for scheduling in the short run, but it also raises questions about the desirable scale of operation and structure of the route network. Some further analysis is required also of the demand for air transport and the alternatives open to the operator in choice of aircraft, mixture of route-types and marketing strategy. Finally, we note some views on the advantages or otherwise of large-scale operations.

In the short run the problem for an airline with a given fleet of aircraft, a given route network and a fixed tariff structure, is to operate a pattern of services at frequencies that will produce the best return on expenditure. An airline comprises a total system rather than a diverse accumulation of aircraft and routes. This implies that alterations and decisions at one point in the system will tend to have repercussions throughout the system: for example, an aircraft delay at one point may have effects on scheduling of aircraft and crews at many other points. As a result schedule planning for the total system is of paramount importance. Such planning must include an analysis of the demand characteristics of the system and its constituent parts, especially those which bear on time of day, day of week or seasonal variations, and the make-up of demand with respect to 'on-demand' and forward-booking requirements. Secondly, the capital tied up in aircraft and ground facilities should be used as intensively as possible. In particular, the periods during which aircraft need to be withdrawn from service for maintenance and repair require to be minimized. Every temporary loss of aircraft from service increases the need for additional standby aircraft to plug the gaps as they arise. Since the cost of aircraft is increasing (around £12 million for the Boeing 747 in 1971) the importance of this point is immediately obvious. Thirdly, there is a need for rapid and reliable turnround of aircraft between flights or stages, although this is a relatively labour-intensive process and the economies of quick turnround must be weighed against the cost of extra labour used only for short and intermittent periods. These points, taken in conjunction with the performance, capacity and operating cost of the available aircraft, give rise to what is essentially a programming problem, for with given tariffs, and limitations imposed by air services or pooling agreements, the scope for short-run flexibility is largely restricted to improvements in scheduling to reduce costs for a virtually predetermined set of operations. Efficient scheduling, combined with good maintenance and turnround performance, can cut the number of aircraft required by a large operator to serve a given network, enabling large capital outlays to be saved. All this applies particularly to scheduled operations, but even in the case of other operations the same sorts of problem arise and the need for maximum utilization of fixed capital is just as vital.

In the long run, major changes in the scale of operations and in the structure of the route network become more possible. What are the important factors for an airline contemplating extension (or curtailment) of its system? Both demand and supply characteristics are important here and we will first consider the demand side.

Routes vary in length and generate different types and densities of traffic. Very broadly, three kinds of route can be identified:

(i) *main trunk routes*, which may be subdivided into long-haul intercontinental routes typified by the transatlantic services, and short-haul regional routes such as the domestic trunks and the principal intra-European services;

(ii) *the second-level routes* (mainly domestic) linking provincial centres and acting as feeders to trunk services from the main metropolitan centres;

(iii) *the third-level routes* which are primarily air taxi services.

In this chapter, concerned as it is with BEA and BOAC, the first of these categories is of greatest importance. For this type of service, the traditional distinction between short- and long-haul operations, based on differences in aircraft economics and standards of service, is rapidly becoming less critical. The important distinction now is between business and pleasure travel. Business passengers generally require higher standards of service and comfort, and greater frequency of service: pleasure travel has proved to be more price elastic but less sensitive to the business cycle.

The characteristics of demand on any prospective route will be of prime importance to the airline. Because of the nature of the airline system as an interrelated complex, this information is critical for various estimates covering an area much wider than that of the particular route in question. Knowledge of the components of traffic on the route will not only be useful for forecasting demand and market shares for that sector, but will also contribute to an understanding of the system effect of the addition: for example, how it will be likely to affect *total* traffic volume and market shares, and what prospects it will afford for improvement in aircraft and aircrew scheduling throughout the system. The need for good market forecasting is therefore of considerable importance, for while the very rapid growth of demand for air travel may seem to reduce the penalties for over-provision, the short-run penalties of excess capacity may be very heavy indeed, as we shall see. The sensitivity of airline business to external events such as Middle East unrest, hijacking activity and restrictions on foreign travel allowances, serves only to exaggerate the problem.

On the supply side, a number of issues have to be considered. Having estimated its own likely share of demand on a particular route in terms of passenger miles, the airline has to decide how the capacity is to be provided. A given number of seat miles per period can be produced in various ways, for example, by altering the number or type of aircraft serving the route (implying changes in speed and seat capacity), while changes in the timing or frequency of services offer further scope for flexibility. The alternatives may have quite different cost implications. Aircraft, in general, are designed to operate at maximum efficiency over specific ranges, with a specified payload. While there is some room for trade-off between payload and range, the optimal performance will be achieved when route lengths and payload lie within the design range. However, whereas it would have been true in the 1950s that aircraft choice would be determined primarily by the length of route on which it was to be used, this is no longer so, despite the view of the Edwards Committee that 'the distinction between long-haul and short-haul aircraft is a genuine economic one'.[15]

Two factors have eroded this distinction: the great increases in aircraft size, and the more flexible performance obtainable from the new types of aero-engines. In the 1950s, over a short stage of 500 miles a long-haul aircraft had a seat-mile operating cost roughly twice that of a short-haul aircraft. By the late 1960s the Boeing 707, designed for long-haul work, had a seat-mile cost almost as low as the short-haul Viscount over a 500-mile stage, while in the 1970s the advent of the Boeing 747 promises to extend still further the cost advantage of greater aircraft capacity, even over such short stages. At the same time, the operating range of 'short-haul' aircraft has been extended, so that they can operate on routes once regarded as more long-haul in character.[16] Because of these changes, the critical factor in aircraft choice is increasingly a matter of route density rather than route length. Historically, the short-haul routes demanded higher frequency of service instead of the same capacity in the form of lower-frequency trips by larger aircraft. But with the growth of traffic on short-haul routes, and an already high daily frequency, the need is for larger capacity aircraft. Given the reduced cost differential per unit of capacity between 'long-haul' and 'short-haul' aircraft, the real choice is that between larger or smaller aircraft.

While there may still ideally be advantages in having a range of aircraft types, each largely specific to a particular route-type on which optimal performance can be achieved,[17] the large capital cost of aircraft makes high utilization essential. To achieve this high utilization, airlines generally have to accept the need to switch aircraft from route to route in accordance with demand. This may result in a technically second-best solution in the sense that aircraft will be used on stages where their cost efficiency is sub-optimal, but the higher seat-mile costs incurred on these stages—which are in any case less important now due to the greater flexibility of modern aircraft—are offset by savings in the number of aircraft required. Aircraft standing charges are thus more widely spread over revenue flying hours, and in addition there may be cost advantages in possessing a more standardized fleet of aircraft.

The Edwards Committee has listed the advantages of a standardized fleet as follows:[18]

(i) reduced holding of spares, thus cutting capital costs;
(ii) higher levels of fleet utilization, minimizing capital costs and insurance costs per flying hour;
(iii) reduced training costs for flight crew, ground handling and maintenance personnel;
(iv) reduced flying crew costs per hour due to the higher degree of crew utilization; flying crew have to be trained to operate each type of aircraft, and are not directly substitutable between types;
(v) reduced ground equipment costs;
(vi) lower maintenance and overhaul costs.

There are, furthermore, benefits to be derived from easier substitution of aircraft in the case of breakdowns. Cuts can be made in the standby fleet, leading to gains in scheduling and generally achieving more work with the same number of aircraft. As an extension of these points it is arguable that airlines would derive the best commercial advantage from a relatively homogeneous network system,[19] rather than a mixture of long-haul, short-haul and local service routes unless, of course, *each* of these can be operated on a scale affording all the available standardization economies. This conclusion, if valid, would be relevant to the existing specialization of BEA and BOAC, but other influences have to be considered, not least the extent to which a mixture of route lengths enables the airline to transfer its passengers directly between main-line services and also between these and feeder routes.

There remains a basic policy decision to be taken by the airline, again relating to aircraft selection. With a given volume of traffic on any route or system of scheduled routes, it will be possible to aim for a higher or a lower load factor, depending on the type of aircraft selected. Either may be a legitimate objective, depending on circumstances, but the essential point is that the load factor is a residual, dependent on a policy decision. While a high load factor may seem a desirable economic objective, this has to be qualified by the fact that the higher the average load factor, the greater is the probability that some traffic is being turned away. Every increase in load factor involves additional risk of overbooking on flights already well filled and those who cannot obtain the required booking may search elsewhere. A high frequency of flights may help to persuade customers to switch to alternative flights on the same line, but there are obvious limits to this on routes with marked daily peaks in demand, and possibly also where pooling agreements are in operation. Here again the importance of efficient scheduling can be seen, for the ability to switch aircraft with different capacities between routes so as to match peaks in demand will go a long way to minimizing the problem. It is worth noting, however, that some airlines, including BEA in particular, have adopted the policy of trying to tie a particular aircraft type to a route but this leads to a loss of flexibility.[20] Here again is an issue which bears on the relationship between BEA and BOAC, and indeed many of the problems just raised recur in a practical way later.

One final matter to be introduced is the economies of scale attainable in airline operation. This matter was examined at some length by the Edwards Committee, whose main conclusions are set out below. We shall return to some of these points, since they are not all equally certain, and problems of interpretation may arise when they are applied to any one airline.

(i) Large airline size may produce significant economic benefits:
    (a) when the route network justifies a large fleet of standard aircraft, and
    (b) when large overall scale is associated with large participation in particular markets, and
    (c) when, as in intercontinental operations, marketing effectiveness demands a widespread geographical coverage of routes and sales outlets.

(ii) Large airline size may not produce significant economic benefits:
    (a) if expansion is based on an operating pattern which requires a variety of aircraft of different sizes and ranges for its optimum exploitation, and

(b) if expansion takes place in markets which require a variety of different standards of service for their optimum satisfaction. In these circumstances it is probable that smaller airlines specializing in particular types of operations and concentrating on particular markets, either in type of traffic or area, may be most effective.
(iii) Large airline size may be a positive disadvantage:
    (a) when efficient marketing requires that there should be very close contact between the carrier and the customer as in the case of IT and other charter operations, and
    (b) when efficient operations require that there should be very close managerial control over the way that each flight is operated, as in the case of air freight charter operations.[21]

The difficulty with such generalizations is that they tend to overlook the extent to which the management structure of the organization may be adapted—for example by devolution of decision-taking in selected areas—to offset some of the disadvantages of the large enterprise engaged in serving specialized or diversified markets.

That completes our review of some of the main operating problems of airlines. The final stage in this background discussion is to summarize the main changes proposed for the structure of British civil aviation.

(d) *The Changing Structure of British Civil Aviation*

Civil aviation has changed rapidly in the course of the 1960s. While the scheduled airlines have been expanding quickly, their growth has been outpaced by the development of non-scheduled operators, especially in the holiday market—indeed some successful non-scheduled operators who had obtained rights to fly some scheduled services have recently withdrawn from them. At the end of the 1960s, difficulties in keeping scheduled and non-scheduled markets separate obliged some of the major scheduled operators to introduce new forms of tariff as a means of more effectively tapping the faster growing sector of the total market. In consequence, the Fares Conferences of IATA in recent years have found great difficulty in reaching agreement on the level and structure of tariffs. The strain then appearing in the existing international framework was aggravated by the appearance of the Boeing 747—the 'jumbo jet'—which more than ever stressed the need for the airlines to sell more seats, and for the IATA to develop policies which acknowledge the presence of greater competition.

Within the United Kingdom there was considerable dissatisfaction with the work of the Air Transport Licensing Board, although this may be explained in part by the absence of an adequate national policy for civil aviation in the developing situation. While in some respects the two nationalized Corporations (and especially BOAC) were operating profitably, there were increasing doubts about their proper relationship both with one another and with the larger independent operators seeking to compete with them on a more equitable basis. There were signs, too, that efficiency was not all it might be. This was the background to the inquiries of the Edwards Committee, and while that committee's report and the subsequent statements from successive governments were concerned with the whole structure of British civil aviation rather than with the public Corporations, the problems for BEA and BOAC can only be seen in the wider context. Despite some major differences between the Labour and Conservative Governments, the Edwards analysis has been largely accepted by both.

Although it advocated a continuing mixture of public and private enterprise, the Edwards Committee saw a need for rationalization in the private sector, as a means to securing sounder financial strength and management. To this end Edwards looked for amalgamation among the bigger independents, leading in the longer term to the evolution of a 'second force' British airline undertaking scheduled work, including some that would involve it in competition with the nationalized enterprises. The Edwards view of large-scale economies did not lead it to recommend outright merger of BEA and BOAC, but the report suggested the establishment of an Airways Board that would have strategic control over both airlines to ensure optimum aggregate results for the economy. Related to this was the wish to develop a regional airline group, to be concerned with 'second-level' routes (mainly those linking provincial centres with one another and with some of the nearer parts of continental Europe). This group would acquire many of BEA's non-trunk routes, would be under the control of the new Airways Board (and therefore part of the public sector) but would also involve private equity participation.

Corresponding with these alterations, Edwards advocated a new authority for civil aviation to take the place of the ATLB but also to be responsible for other matters, including 'the main weight' of international traffic rights negotiations. This latter suggestion was not followed in full either by the Labour or Conservative Government, although both agreed with the idea of a Civil Aviation Authority to replace the ATLB. The Conservative Government's proposal is for the creation of such an Authority in 1972, to take over the functions of the ATLB and a number of other bodies concerned with matters like registration, safety and air traffic control. The Authority will not, however, be directly involved in the negotiation of tariffs or traffic rights. Parliament will be responsible for laying down civil aviation policies, leaving the Authority discretion in implementing them.

The Government's proposals also accepted the need for an Airways Board to control BOAC and BEA and to integrate their activities where possible. In addition, measures were taken to get a major 'second-force' airline into operation, with Government approval for the acquisition of British United Airways by Caledonian Airways. The new airline, Caledonian-BUA, came into being on 1 December 1970 with capital and reserves of about £12 million, 31 jet aircraft and 4,400 staff. It was later renamed British Caledonian Airways. This tie-up between the two largest independent operators was given Government support by the transfer from the State airlines of routes which were generating about £6 million annual revenue. This was bitterly criticized in many quarters but the Government thought it necessary if the second force was to be established on a strong footing. In March 1971 the final package was confirmed, comprising the BOAC routes to West Africa and to Tripoli, plus rights to fly between Gatwick and Paris (Le Bourget). The acquisition of the latter rights involved BEA in relinquishing up to four flights a day in each direction.

Finally, there has not yet been any significant progress towards the creation of a stronger regional domestic airline which Edwards saw as developing from British Air Services, a BEA-controlled subsidiary.

This shake-up in the structure of civil aviation inevitably leads to important questions for the nationalized airlines, particularly on the degree of competition from the second-force airline and the implications of joint operation under the Airways Board.

III British European Airways

This section is concerned with the recent economic performance of BEA, leading up to an appraisal of its current problems. The changing economic and technical environment of civil aviation requires of the organization an ability to reach quick as well as correct decisions. How then has BEA fared in this respect? And what has been the effect of its nationalized status, in which the difficulties of rapid decision-taking on clear commercial lines may be hard to overcome?

(a) *Operational Characteristics and Economic Performance*

BEA is a specialized short- and medium-haul carrier, providing mainly scheduled services on domestic and European routes, according to the division of responsibility laid down in the 1946 Civil Aviation Act. Scheduled operations in recent years have produced about 95 per cent of total revenue, so that BEA has little participation in the fast-growing charter tour market. Domestic services accounted for about one-fifth of BEA's total CTM in 1970/71, most of this being business traffic.

TABLE 2.1
BEA traffic and operating statistics 1960/61 and 1970/71

Traffic	1960/61	1970/71	% change
CTM offered (millions)	237·4	699·0	+194
Load ton miles sold (millions)	154·8	378·6	+145
Overall load factor (%)	65·2	54·2	—
Passengers (millions)	4·0	8·7	+118
Passenger miles (millions)	1,393	3,275	+135
Available seat miles (millions)	2,089	5,425	+160
Passenger load factor (%)	66·7	60·4	—
Mail ton miles (millions)	4·2	7·1	+69
Freight ton miles (millions)	16·6	45·9	+177
Operations			
Unduplicated route mileage	47,016	69,471	+48
Revenue flying hours	195,700	225,832	+15
Mean block speed (mph)	205	283	+38
Average no. of seats available per flight	56·2	94·8	+69
Average stage distance (statute miles)	288	358	+24
Aircraft			
Effective fleet—excluding training, conversion, etc.	92·5	98·2	—
CTM produced per effective aircraft (millions)	2·44	6·69	+174

Source: BEA *Annual Reports*.

Table 2.1 gives details on some indicators of BEA's operations and traffic between 1960/61 (when the Civil Aviation (Licensing) Act was introduced and established a framework for the 1960s) and 1970/71. Output (CTM) rose by 194 per cent, due in part to an increase in the number of aircraft in use, but especially because of the greater block speed of aircraft (up by 38 per cent) and their greater capacity (average seats available rising by 69 per cent). In addition BEA achieved a higher utilization rate of its aircraft in 1970/71.

Over the same period, demand increased less than capacity. The number of passengers rose from 4 million to 8·7 million, while freight ton miles increased by over 177 per cent, the latter being the fastest growing sector but still providing a relatively small proportion of total revenue at about 8·5 per cent in recent years, or 11 per cent including mail. The more rapid increase of capacity, however, caused both the passenger and the overall load factors to decline, from 66·7 to 60·4 per cent and from 65·2 to 54·2 per cent respectively.

A year by year examination of load factors indicates that the first major change came in 1961/62, when both passenger and overall load factors fell by 5 percentage points from 1960/61 levels. This sharp reduction in load factor was caused partly by an unexpected slowdown in the rate of expansion of European traffic, but principally by the introduction of seven Comet and fourteen Vanguard aircraft which boosted average seats per flight from 56 to 68 in a single year. In addition, BEA's competitive position in Europe slumped due to the introduction of new jet aircraft by rival airlines, further emphasizing the need for BEA both to maintain frequencies to avoid further reductions in market shares, and to substitute jet-engined aircraft wherever possible. Between 1961/62 and 1969/70, yearly variations in load factor were small, but in 1970/71 load factors again fell sharply, by 4 percentage points overall and by 2 percentage points for passengers. This decline was largely due to depressed business conditions, though uncertainty in the Middle East and a spate of hijacking probably contributed. The difficulties of forecasting, and the narrowness of the margin between success and failure, are well illustrated by this experience. If the rate of traffic growth had not fallen off sharply between 1966/67 and 1969/70, BEA could well have been caught short of capacity by the latter years of the decade.[22] A continuation of earlier growth experience with existing capacity would have raised load factors to around 70 per cent, which might have brought short-term gains in revenue but could have driven away custom on account of the higher probability of passengers failing to get first-choice bookings.[23] As matters turned out, BEA largely avoided the problem of capacity shortage because of the stagnation of demand, but was faced with the opposite problem of excess capacity in 1970 and 1971, when it was introducing a substantial number of new, larger aircraft, with serious consequences for load factors.

Changes in load factors, whether due to alterations in demand or supply, do not necessarily tell us much about profitability, which depends also on unit costs and unit revenue. Certainly, other things equal, and aside from pooling arrangements, a fall in load factor will mean a reduction in revenue for a given expenditure on the provision of capacity, and in the short run the need to maintain market shares may force the airline to accept many costs as fixed. In the longer run, there is more flexibility in route structure, while costs and revenue over unit may alter because of technical factors and tariff changes respectively. In practice, all these variables have been at work in determining BEA's financial performance. As Table 2.1 shows, total route mileage increased over the period, and average stage distances increased by one-quarter, enabling a greater spread of fixed costs over revenue miles. Additionally, larger and faster aircraft have increased potential aircraft productivity and even although the capital cost of aircraft has been rising, the period is one in which real unit costs could be expected to fall. BEA's unit costs in fact fell from 17·2 p per CTM in 1960/61 to 14·8 p in 1964/65, then rose to 20·3 p in 1970/71. This total increase of 3·1 p in ten years is roughly equivalent to a fall in costs of about one-fifth in real terms. It is,

TABLE 2.2

Aircraft fleet of BEA, March 1961, and March 1971; and seat-mile costs, 1970/71

	Aircraft 1961	Aircraft 1971	Seat-Mile Costs* 1970/71
Comet 4B	7	—	—
Vanguard	6	13†	1·1 p
Merchantman (freighter)	—	6	—
Viscount	62	24‡	1·6 p
Pionair (DC-3)	8	—	—
Hebrides (Heron)	2	2	8·3 p
Islander (DH89)	3	—	—
Pionair/Leopard (freighter)	7	—	—
Trident One	—	21	1·3 p
Trident Two	—	15	1·1 p
Trident Three	—	3	—
Super One-eleven	—	18	1·4 p

* Costs included here are only those directly related to aircraft type and exclude airline and promotional costs such as sales and publicity commission, station and passenger costs and general administrative costs. Costs refer to expenditure after capitalization and write-off of introductory costs.
† Includes two aircraft under conversion to Merchantman freighters.
‡ Includes one aircraft on lease to Gibraltar Airways.
Source: BEA *Annual Reports*.

however, notable that costs per CTM shot up from 15·7 p in 1966/67 to 18·5 p in 1968/69, which raises questions about BEA's operating efficiency during that period.

The favourable overall trend of BEA's unit costs is directly connected with the major changes in fleet composition over the period, illustrated in Table 2.2. In 1960/61 both the Comet 4B and the Vanguard were just being introduced, and 79 per cent of BEA's passengers travelled by Viscount. By 1970/71 the Viscount fleet had been cut by half, the Comet fleet had been sold off and the Vanguard aircraft were being gradually converted to freighting. In their place had been introduced more advanced jet aircraft such as the Trident Two and the Super One-eleven to support the existing Trident One, while twenty-six Trident Three aircraft have been ordered and delivery began in 1971. The new Trident and Super One-eleven aircraft initially meant higher seat-mile costs than for the outgoing Comets, Vanguards and Viscounts, due to lower average utilization of new aircraft in the first year of service and to the writing-off of introductory costs in the early years of an aircraft's life. In line with past experience, this initial disadvantage proved to be temporary, and by 1970/71 the seat-mile costs of the new aircraft compared favourably with those they had replaced.

The labour force and its productivity is also relevant to costs. Table 2.3 reveals an increase of 88 per cent over the period in the number of employees and an increase in labour productivity of just under 60 per cent. An examination of the year to year changes, however, shows a decline in staff productivity between 1966/67 and 1968/69—a reflection of the much slower growth of output in that

TABLE 2.3
BEA staff and labour productivity, 1960/61 and 1970/71

	1960/61	1970/71	Per cent increase
Average no. of employees	13,240	24,868	88
CTM per employee	17,930	28,110	57
Revenue per employee	£3,193	£5,362	68

Source: BEA *Annual Reports*.

period, during which employment continued to expand. Improved conditions in 1969/70 saw a resumption of productivity growth only to be followed by a relapse in 1970/71. Labour productivity is not of course a measure only of the effective utilization of labour, but depends inter alia on the capital employed per man, and in the airline case a great deal depends on the type of operation, the mix of aircraft and other factors. Yet the Edwards Committee was clearly worried by the slow *growth* of BEA staff productivity, and it found also that in 1967 BEA ranked lowest in both CTM per employee and load ton miles per employee out of the thirty largest world airlines.[24] The clear implication is that BEA may be overstaffed, even when allowance is made for the specialized short-haul nature of the airline, which may require a greater labour intensity than other types of operations. This is due for example to the higher proportion of total journey time taken up by bookings, passenger concentration, embarkation and disembarkation, etc. all of which are more labour-intensive activities.

On the revenue side, there have again been important changes. Revenue per load ton mile fell from 27·3 p in 1960/61 to 25·9 p in 1964/65, but rose thereafter to 27·9 p in 1967/68 and to 35·2 p in 1970/71. This latter rise was partly a reflection of the sterling devaluation of 18 November 1967, and partly due to increases in tariffs.

These fluctuations in costs, productivity and revenue are reflected in the financial performance of BEA. In the view of the Corporation itself, the main indicator of achievement is the level of profit.[25] Examples of this are frequently to be found in the evidence given to the Select Committee on Nationalized Industries: for example, according to Mr Kenneth Keith, Deputy Chairman, 'at all levels in

TABLE 2.4
Financial performance of BEA, 1960/61 to 1970/71

	Year ended 31st March					
	1961	1962	1963	1964	1965	1966
Net profit* (Loss) £m	1·54	(1·49)	(0·26)	3·03	1·32	1·28
Rate of return on net assets†	8·0	1·6	4·7	8·9	6·4	6‡
	1967	1968	1969	1970	1971	
Net profit* (Loss) £m	0·71	(1·78)	3·54	6·53	0·52	
Rate of return on net assets†	5·5	3‡	6·5‡	8·5	5·1	

* Net profit refers to profits after payment of interest and depreciation.

† Rate of return on net assets is the gross profit (before payment of interest but after depreciation) for the year expressed as a percentage of the average capital employed during that year.

‡ Estimated, owing to the fact that BEA have not consistently published the rate of return achieved. It is also to be noted that the other figures are taken from BEA *Annual Reports*, and are consistently above those calculated by the Treasury and published elsewhere.

Source: BEA *Annual Reports*.

BEA with which I have dealt, there is a great anxiety to be in the black, that is, to make a profit, and the profit, so far as everyone is concerned, is the profit that appears in the accounts.' This statement is to be taken as referring to profits after interest and depreciation.

The net profit and loss figures for BEA are shown in Table 2.4. After a record level of profits in 1963/64 there was a progressive decline until 1967/68 when a loss was incurred. In 1968/69 and 1969/70 BEA recorded a profit and indeed in the latter year Operating Profit was a record £11 million and the Net Profit was £6.5 million. However, this was achieved with the help of a £4 million transfer from Special Account, and £5 million had been transferred in this way in 1968/69. This account was established as a means of compensating BEA for a Government decision that the Corporation was not to buy American aircraft. See below (pp. 62–65). The financial year 1970/71 was marked by a sharp dip in net profit once again.

Further examination reveals different degrees of profitability within BEA. Table 2.5 shows that whereas, in 1966/67, scheduled

TABLE 2.5
BEA operating results by types of services 1966/67

	Operating revenue £m	Operating expenditure £m	Surplus (deficit) £m
International scheduled services	61·6	56·1	5·5
Domestic scheduled services	22·0	23·3	(1·3)
All scheduled services	83·6	79·4	4·2
IT charters	1·0	1·1	(0·1)
Other charters	1·8	1·6	0·2
Total—all operations	86·4	82·1	4·3

Source: derived from the Edwards Committee Report (Cmnd. 4018: HMSO, 1969), p. 33.

services and 'other charters' operating revenue was well in excess of operating costs, this was not so in the case of IT charters (admittedly a small part of operations). More importantly, there is a marked difference between international and domestic scheduled services. The loss on domestic services is long-standing, and indeed no service within the UK, including the main trunk services, makes an operating profit.[26] The reasons for this are diverse, but important considerations include:

(i) the sparse traffic on the Scottish Highlands and Islands routes which are operated as a social service, with high unit-cost aircraft;

(ii) the highly seasonal traffic on the Channel Islands routes;

(iii) the competition to BEA on domestic services from British Rail, initially on the London–Manchester route but latterly, with the speeding-up of rail services and fares cuts between London to Glasgow and London to Edinburgh, on longer trunk routes as well;

(iv) and the competition from other airlines on trunk routes, from British Eagle (until 1968) and British United Airways (now British Caledonian Airways).

BEA's view in general, is that this competition, by forcing down load factors, has so worsened the economics of operating on these routes that increases in fares were necessary. Other factors, such as the slowdown in business growth, have undoubtedly contributed to this deterioration. In late 1971, however, growing anxiety about the falling load factor, and the effects of a new British Rail scheme, caused BEA (and British Caledonian) to apply to the ATLB for permission to introduce cut-rate fares for off-peak and group travel on the London to Glasgow, Edinburgh and Belfast routes. Shortly after this, BEA announced its withdrawal of first-class accommodation on domestic flights, due to the losses that service was believed to incur.

In contrast, BEA makes a substantial surplus from its European scheduled operations, not least because European fares are much higher than domestic fares for journeys of similar length.[27]

Besides profitability, there is the question of the financial objective set for BEA as a nationalized Corporation. For the five-year period to 1967/68, BEA was set a target of a 6 per cent rate of return on net assets employed, before interest but after depreciation. In addition, the Corporation is expected to balance its accounts, 'taking one year with another' over a period of five years, after providing for interest and depreciation at historic cost. The second line of Table 2.4 shows the success of BEA in meeting the target: over the quinquennium the rate of return as calculated by BEA[28] was 5.7 per cent, so that the objective was not quite met, due largely to a very poor final year, the reasons for which were given earlier. Although the shortfall is not marked, it is clear that there was a steady deterioration in the situation over the period; although it should be noted that all the major world airlines have been experiencing reduced profitability, and BEA's temporary recovery between 1968 and 1970 was counter to the general trend.

The interpretation of these figures depends upon how far the function of the objective and its conceptual basis are accepted as valid. BEA's own view of the objective is one of open scepticism. The Select Committee on Nationalized Industries took BEA to task on this very question, concluding that:

> In view of the value of a financial objective, your Committee believe that there has been a basic and indefensible error in that the Treasury and the Board of Trade have been going to a lot of trouble, in order to agree a financial objective without ensuring that BEA understand, and if possible agree with them about, its purposes and value, however limited.[29]

No doubt the Treasury and the Board of Trade might dispute the inferences to be drawn from this finding, but the immediate point is that the established target was not fulfilled. Despite this, the new objective set for BEA for the period 1968/69 to 1972/73 was raised to 8 per cent rate of return on net assets. Results to date suggest this target is unlikely to be achieved.

While in many ways BEA as a nationalized corporation has very nearly met its objective, several features of its recent performance are suggestive of deficiencies within the organization. The proposed changes in the structure of British civil aviation may help, and we shall be looking at the implications of closer co-operation between BEA and BOAC in section V. There are, however, some issues which are of special importance in an understanding of BEA's present position and these are our immediate concern.

(b) *Current Issues*

It is impossible to make much of BEA's failure quite to achieve its financial objective over the period to 1967/68 without attributing to the financial objective a scientific basis which did not in practice exist. Yet there is a real question whether BEA's record over the 1960s was as good as it might have been, or whether either external events or poor management were responsible for some degree of shortfall in achievement. An examination of BEA's history suggests two areas in which external factors, aside from fluctuations in business, may have been important. These are aircraft procurement and pricing.

(i) AIRCRAFT PROCUREMENT

The importance of securing the right aircraft at the right time has already been stressed. In the past both BEA and BOAC have faced major difficulties over re-equipment, and the problems of BEA are worth illustrating. Over the years BEA has normally followed a 'buy British' policy, but in June 1966 permission was sought from the Board of Trade to buy American aircraft (18 Boeing 727s and 23 Boeing 737s). Permission was refused and BEA were told to 'buy British', despite the fact that the British aircraft on offer at the time were less economical than the proposed American types. Following a re-examination by the aircraft manufacturers and BEA, proposals for modifications of available or planned aircraft were put forward, embodying better economic performance and improved design. The re-equipment programme then proceeded in two phases. In January 1967 a contract was signed for 18 BAC Super One-eleven aircraft—alternatives to the Boeing 737—with an option for 6 more. In February 1967, Board of Trade approval was sought for the purchase of 30 BAC Two-eleven aircraft, to be delivered from 1971 onward. This proposal was finally rejected at the end of 1967, since it was estimated that it would be more costly to the country than the Trident Three, which BEA regarded, however, as being too small for its needs and more costly than the Boeing 727. Approval for the purchase of 26 Trident Three aircraft, with an option for 10 more, was given by the President of the Board of Trade in March 1968.

In economic terms what matters is the reasoning behind particular cases of intervention, and the arrangements by which BEA is to be compensated for being required to act out of line with its commercial interests. The principal reason for interference in procurement policy, of course, is the Government's interests in the aircraft manufacturing industry of the United Kingdom and in balance of payments implications. A number of justifications for government support of the aircraft industry can be advanced, ranging from the purely economic, through the 'defence' argument that a healthy domestic aircraft industry is essential to national interests, to the still less tangible benefits of technological spin-off from advanced aircraft development. If government adopts a policy of support for the manufacturing industry, intervention in the aircraft procurement decisions of home-based airlines, especially nationalized airlines, is a probability. Support can be given either by direct financial aid to the manufacturing companies, or by obliging home airlines to buy British. In practice, government has done both, by paying up to 50 per cent of the launching costs of civil aircraft and by requiring BEA to buy home-produced aircraft.

The issue of government support for the aircraft industry would not arise if the industry could regularly produce aircraft capable of being sold in the world market in sufficient volume to recover the heavy development costs. With some notable exceptions, this has not been so, partly because of BEA and BOAC policies. BEA has sought modifications from the manufacturers in order to adapt the aircraft more closely to its own specialized needs and route network. But every step in the direction of meeting such specialist interests and away from a basic design is likely to reduce the possibility of large world sales. Even with government launching aid, the price of 'tailor-made' aircraft has been higher than if the basic costs had been spread over a longer production run. Although there are signs that the aircraft industry is increasingly less enthusiastic about 'tailor-made' aircraft and more interested in European co-operative ventures, the changes required to give effect to the new attitude are likely to take some time to materialize. In the meantime, there is the very real issue of what compensation should be paid to the airline obliged by government to accept a second-best solution to its re-equipment problems, as BEA was obliged to do in 1967/68.

The policy followed by the Labour Government after its refusal to allow BEA to buy Boeing aircraft may be a guide to future thinking on this issue. No real problem arose over the Super One-elevens, but the Trident Three aircraft would not be available when BEA wished to introduce it into service. This delay threatened to leave BEA short of capacity. To compensate BEA for this, the President of the Board of Trade announced that the terms of compensation:

> will take the form of transferring part of its [BEA's] borrowings from the Government into a special account, which will not bear interest and from which pre-determined amounts will be included annually in BEA's profit and loss account.
>
> In considering the amount to be transferred in this way, I have examined with BEA its forecasts of future financial results. Because such forecasts are subject to increasing margins of error in the later years, and because we cannot at this stage assess the changes that may result from the work of the Edwards Committee, I have agreed with BEA to make assistance available in the form of an initial transfer of £25 million, with the possibility of a further amount of up to £12½ million for consideration later, should this be needed.
>
> In 1972 the Board of Trade will consult BEA on the basis of experience up to then and of the latest forecasts, to determine whether BEA will still need this further sum up to £12½ million

to be transferred for the period from 1st April 1972 to 31st March 1975. The object of this arrangement is to enable BEA to earn a small margin after payment of interest.[30]

This arrangement was not to be regarded as a subsidy, but as a means of compensating BEA generally

> because as a result of Government decisions it could not have the aircraft of the size it wanted at the time it wanted because we said it was not to buy American.[31]

The conclusions to be drawn from this action would thus seem to be as follows:

(a) Government can prevent BEA from buying foreign aircraft;
(b) it can do so without there being any guarantee of compensation even if the airline has to accept what it regards as second-best aircraft;
(c) if, however, government action results in the airline being short of capacity at the requisite time, so that its revenue is liable to suffer, compensation may be payable by government.

Commenting on the steps taken by government in this case, the Edwards Committee did not believe

> it is good either for the airline concerned or the product it has to buy if financial aid is given to the airline. We believe that if aid is required to help improve the sales prospects of a British aircraft, it should be given to the manufacturing industry ... [Then] there is no possibility of the impression being wrongly given that the national airline is being compensated for having to purchase an inferior product.[32]

In fact, BEA *was* purchasing an inferior product (both in the Super One-eleven and in the Trident Three case) at least as far as the airline was concerned. That there is a general case to be made for increased subsidies to the aircraft manufacturing companies is not disputed here, but the consequences for BEA's commercial position resulting from the fact that BEA could not have the aircraft it wanted because of government policy, surely deserve to be considered within the context of BEA's financial framework alone. The course of action followed by the Board of Trade has met this requirement, and has made clear to the public at large the estimated cost of the decision. The main alternative would have been a reduction in the financial objective to be set for the next five years (or whatever period is adopted) with the reason being made fully explicit in the announcement of the objective. This indeed is what seems to have been in the minds of the Treasury at the time: 'When the present target is revised, the new target will reflect among other things any arrangements necessary to enable BEA to operate commercially with its new fleet.'[33]

From an economic point of view, the main requirements to safeguard the public interest are that the costs to BEA (or any nationalized concern) of being required to act against its commercial judgement should be clearly quantified, and that consideration should be given to the consequences of *not* making full compensation. Social reasons, or economic justification on criteria external to the concern, may oblige government to make such decisions from time to time. To make the concern bear the opportunity losses of such decisions is to run the risks that the enterprise will be made to appear less efficient in its use of resources than it really is, that undesirable cross-subsidization will take place within the concern,[34] and that management and staff morale may suffer. Thus there is a strong case for making the costs of the decision clear, and in view of the general obscurity which surrounds the financial objective, a straightforward compensation payment, clearly labelled, may be the best solution. Nevertheless, one wonders how many people, reading of BEA's record year in 1969/70, were aware that 60 per cent of the net profit of £6·5 million was attributable to a transfer from the Special Account and thereby stemmed from a subsidy to the British aircraft industry.

One final point is best stated in the words of BEA's *Annual Report* for 1966–67:

> International aviation, at all times highly competitive, is also a fast moving industry in which . . . delays are unacceptable. The price of being ill-equipped or under-equipped is quickly marked by a rapid decline in competitive ability . . .[35]

This complaint, directed against government delays in coming to decisions on BEA's re-equipment programme, clearly has some justification, in view of the timetable of events in 1966–68 outlined above. There will at times be requests from BEA which raise concerns wider than BEA's own commercial interests, and decisions may have to be delayed until a proper appraisal of these is undertaken, possibly by means of cost-benefit studies. If BEA is penalized in commercial terms by such delays and if the airline is expected to work to a financial objective, the costs of such postponements of decision-taking should clearly be taken into account.

The principle of compensation cannot be taken too far: some risks and some upset plans are part of everyday business. Nevertheless, if BEA is 'to operate commercially' as expected by Government, there is a case for saying that it should not have to encounter difficulties that are foreign to the commercial world. In matters of aircraft procurement, BEA has had to do just that.

(ii) TARIFF REGULATION

A second area where BEA is not free to administer its own policies is that of tariffs. In the domestic sector the role of the ATLB has to be taken into account, and in the international sector the determination of fares through IATA Conferences. We shall come later to the relevance of the Treasury 'ground-rules' for pricing in the nationalized industries.[36]

Examination of tariffs immediately reveals an important difference between the domestic and European sectors of BEA's market, for the average fare per passenger mile on domestic routes is lower than on European routes. The Edwards Committee quoted a figure of 6·6 cents passenger yield per passenger mile on domestic flights compared with 6·8 cents on European routes, but the figures of the ATLB, comparing tourist-class return fares on international and domestic routes of similar distance, show much higher fares on the former.[37] This, together with the higher passenger cost per seat mile on domestic as opposed to European services (4·2 cents compared with 3·9 cents) has meant that domestic services have been much less remunerative. The higher average cost per seat mile on domestic services is largely due to the shorter stage distances and the low density of traffic on some of the regional services. That the problem is well understood by BEA is shown in their statement to the Select Committee on Nationalized Industries that

> It should be able to bring the domestic services as a whole into a break-even position in two to three years by progressive adjustment of fares levels. The present average domestic rate per mile can be considerably increased without causing hardship to the public or turning away appreciable traffic.[38]

In the event this expectation has proved to be ill-founded. Substantial increases in domestic fares were made in 1967 and 1968. In a further application to the ATLB (initially rejected but later allowed on appeal) for higher domestic fares in November 1970, BEA's traffic and sales manager stated that the loss on domestic services in 1970/71 was expected to be over £2 million; and the 6–10 per cent increase sought in basic fares would still have left the airline with a loss in 1971/72 of £700,000 on domestic services. The slow growth of the economy has assuredly exaggerated the problem but the possibility cannot be overlooked that BEA has consistently taken too optimistic a view on the price elasticity of demand for domestic air travel.

What are the reasons for the different average fare levels in Europe and on domestic routes? It is not simply that different levels are dictated to BEA, for as the largest European operator BEA has a strong bargaining position in the IATA fares conference while on the domestic front BEA has *generally* been able to obtain the increases it has sought—if occasionally with some delay. A more likely explanation lies in the different market structure of the two sectors.

On its European routes, BEA works in pool and under the IATA cartel arrangement one may assume that average fares will tend to be set rather above the level that would result from open price competition. Conversely, internal services—although still not subject to price competition in respect of basic fares, which has been ruled out by the ATLB—are more competitive in a number of ways. First, since 1963/64 BEA has had to contend with rival services on the domestic trunk routes from British Eagle[39] or British United Airways (or both) and now from British Caledonian, although this competition has itself been controlled. Although there is no pooling agreement on domestic services, BEA has been subject to no restrictions on service frequency, while the independents have been strictly limited in the number of weekly flights by licensing decisions of the ATLB. Since higher service frequency means a better quality of service to the passenger by giving greater choice and probably greater reliability, the threat to BEA's share of the trunk traffic has been muted. However, at the end of 1970 it was announced that from April 1971 British Caledonian would be able to offer unrestricted frequencies on these routes, and the airline promptly publicized an increase in the number of flights per week.

Despite the frequency restrictions in the period up to 1970, the independent operators still succeeded in making inroads into BEA's traffic share, principally by the introduction of jet aircraft on the trunk routes at a time when BEA had counted on being able to use the turbo-prop Vanguard for some time to come. The Corporation was obliged to introduce Comet 4B and Trident One jets on these routes and these aircraft were more expensive per seat mile than the BAC One-elevens used by the independents, and much more costly than the Vanguards they replaced. This rise in costs brought about applications from BEA for fares increases, so that between 1965/66 and 1967/68, trunk fares rose on average by 30 per cent, compared with a fall of 4 per cent over the previous six years.

Secondly, competition for domestic services is due not only to the presence of other airlines, but also to the availability of road and rail services, as well as private transport, which are all likely to be more important alternatives for domestic than for European journeys. Here price competition *does* enter the reckoning, and given the continuing improvement in performance in rail and road transport due to new capital and track, and extended motorway mileages, BEA has increasingly had to consider the effect of rising fares on passenger choice of mode. This has been so particularly on routes like London–Manchester, and is becoming more important elsewhere, with the completion of plans for improving both rail and road services between London and Glasgow, and London and Edinburgh.

It would be misleading, of course, to overlook competitive pressures on the European air-routes, where the development of IT traffic has undoubtedly had effects on the growth of BEA's scheduled business. To combat this, BEA has for many years been offering reduced excursion fares to groups travelling on scheduled services, and IATA airlines generally have been extending this facility, no doubt partly in response to IT competition but also in the knowledge that the wide-fuselage aircraft now being introduced make it imperative to adopt more flexible pricing if the investment is to be justified. In addition, BEA has recently—and perhaps belatedly—begun marketing its own brand of inclusive tours.

The future structure of scheduled service tariffs depends on the maintenance of Provision One—the British version of the IATA regulation which keeps the price of package tours from falling below the fare for a scheduled return flight on that route—which has been increasingly attacked by tour operators on the ground that it keeps the price of certain IT holidays unnecessarily high: particularly for winter holidays, short-duration tours and long-distance tours, where the scheduled fare is high relative to the average cost of a chartered seat. In fact some relaxations of Provision One on European inclusive tours have recently been introduced [40] and in 1969 the Labour Government's White Paper, *Civil Aviation Policy*, expressed a sympathetic view towards relaxation, requiring only that

> the structure of prices for inclusive tours ... should be internally coherent and that their levels should be no higher than is neces-

sary to give adequate protection to competing scheduled services *for which there is a genuine need.** [41]

Thus there are already signs of increasing competition on BEA's European services, and as this intensifies—for example by extended relaxation of Provision One or as a result of continuing excess capacity among the scheduled operators—the average revenue per seat mile may fall, or at least increase less quickly, relative to costs. At the same time, apart from the general rises in costs over the economy, the heavy capital costs of new aircraft and the expenses attributable to anti-hijacking measures have added to the burden. The prospects then are for a continuing 'squeeze' on the surplus BEA has been accustomed to earning on international services; and it is this surplus which has allowed BEA consistently to carry the losses on domestic services, while still coming close to meeting its financial objective.

It is questionable, therefore, whether BEA can long continue to operate a policy of cross-subsidization from its international to its domestic traffic, as it has apparently been prepared to do—with the explicit sanction of the ATLB. In its 1967/68 *Report*, the ATLB recognized this cross-subsidization and went on to say that

> with the prospect that this surplus [from European operations] was about to disappear, we were obliged in July 1967 to approve substantial increases in domestic fares . . . [42]

Thus the Board seemed to be prepared indefinitely to set domestic tariffs in such a way that cross-subsidization would be maintained, and losses accepted on domestic routes as long as enough profit was made on international services—a rather odd view, to say the least! And again in December 1970, the Board turned down applications from a number of airlines for fare rises on domestic services: the losses of BEA on these routes were noted

> But not withstanding the views we have often expressed about cross-subsidy, we think they [the losses] should be met for the time being out of the profits being made on international routes.[43]

How BEA can extract itself from this difficulty is less easy to see. Other things equal, it is to be expected that average seat-mile costs on domestic services will be higher than those on international routes, simply because higher costs are normally incurred on short-stage flights, and the average flight on BEA's domestic services is only 212 miles compared with 439 miles on international services. If fares were

*Italics are mine—L.C.H.

based directly on costs, we would expect the average fare per mile to be higher on domestic than on international services, whereas at present the reverse is true. To raise domestic fares so substantially would almost certainly reduce demand, especially with the steady improvement in road and rail services. If that analysis is valid, the main alternative is likely to be a reassessment of the pattern of domestic services.

It is indeed questionable why BEA should have continued, in the face of steady losses, to operate domestic services on the present scale. The passive acceptance of cross-subsidization by the ATLB and government has no doubt encouraged BEA to adopt the line it has. Another part of the answer may lie in BEA's acceptance of something like a common-carrier obligation in respect of domestic services, although its only real 'social-service' obligation is the operation of the Scottish Highlands and Islands Services, comprising all internal services on the Scottish mainland and to the islands, but excluding services between Scotland and other countries.[44] BEA has made a consistent loss on these services since 1946 and does not expect them ever to be profitable, partly because of the low density of traffic and the lack of a suitable aircraft. But the importance of this group of operations in the total domestic network is small. The average losses between 1966 and 1970 have been around £300,000 a year,[45] and in any case the Board of Trade stated that, in the setting of a financial obligation in 1963, account was taken of the loss from this service, and that to the Scilly Isles, without which the target might have been one-half per cent higher. Additionally, BEA is required to produce in its Annual Report and Accounts a separate profit and loss account for internal Scottish services, so that the effect on the overall position of the Corporation can be seen clearly: inevitably, it does not in fact reflect the true economic costs and returns of the service. Apart from problems of allocating joint costs it is likely that these services act as a feeder to BEA's main routes and attract to the airline passengers wishing to terminate their journeys in the remoter parts of Scotland. The extent of this is not known.

As for the remainder of the domestic services, which are by far the greatest portion, it may be that BEA has hoped that in the long run they will generate enough traffic to make operations profitable. If so, these expectations must have been progressively diminished as a result of the licensing of additional operators, their resort to jet aircraft and the improved service from surface operators—to say nothing of the latest removal of restriction on British Caledonian trunk-route frequencies.

It must be asked, therefore, whether BEA ought not now to consider some rationalization of its domestic services. In the absence of tariff increases which would at least cover costs—and the demand constraints may well preclude this for some time to come—the best hope may lie in an increase in cost efficiency, which could require the curtailment or abandonment of certain services. This kind of solution was evidently in the mind of the Edwards Committee when it recommended the hiving off of non-trunk domestic routes to a more powerful regional airline based on British Air Services (BAS), leaving BEA to run the main trunk services only. Certainly there is greater chance of long-term profitability on the latter, and in any case the profitability or otherwise of the trunk routes cannot be looked at in isolation from the European services, for which they act as feeders and distributors.

This would still leave a problem of losses in the regional airline (BAS has been undergoing difficulties and other carriers have left the secondary network altogether) but the longer-term prospects might nevertheless be more hopeful. Once separated out from the rather different trunk-route and international operations of BEA, the real dimensions of the secondary network problem will become clearer. There will certainly be more pressure towards rationalization of these services, and the scope for more flexible pricing and adjustment of standards of service will be enhanced. On this latter point, BEA has always held back from setting more economical standards on its secondary services, on the grounds that the overall image of the Corporation would be damaged. Furthermore, it would then be more possible to see how far and in what particular areas some form of direct subsidy was justified—a point taken sympathetically in the Labour Government's White Paper of 1969,[46] on the assumption that route rationalization and other economies would be undertaken. It remains to be seen how the Conservative Government regard the problem of these regional services.

In conclusion, the arguments against cross-subsidization should not be pressed too far, particularly in the case of airlines, where accounting losses on certain services may not reflect true economic costs and returns, due to the role of certain routes as feeders and distributors. Cross-subsidization may also be legitimate while a service is building up to a level of traffic at which profits can be made. But in the present case, the long-term deficits on domestic services, which have only been sustainable through the surplus earned on European services, have become such a permanent feature that the continuation of this policy must now be criticized on economic grounds as almost certainly leading to resource misallocation. If, as argued here, the raising of domestic fares is unlikely to bring a long-term solution, the attack must be made on the cost side, for example, by means of a reduction in the standard of service, though BEA is unwilling to accept this. Apart then from the main trunk routes, which are properly to be seen as part of the European city-pair airline network, there seems a strong case for developing a 'utility' standard of service parallel with a more flexible fare structure. If that cannot be made profitable overall, even with rationalization by a specialist regional carrier, the case for subsidy on any particular service should be made in the light of social-service needs and of alternative transport opportunities.

(iii) CONCLUSION

This review of procurement and pricing leaves the general impression that BEA has not suffered unduly from its lack of independence in these matters. It is true that in the matter of aircraft selection it underwent agonizing delays and reversals of policy, but in the end there has been ample provision in the way of compensation. Indeed, some might regard it as over-generous since the slower growth of demand in the late 1960s made the requirement for additional capacity less urgent than if previous growth rates had continued. On the tariff question, the administrative procedures have arguably had less to do with the level of fares than the underlying competitive structure of the markets, while the losses on social-service provision have been relatively small and in any case have been taken into account in the setting of a financial objective.

There remains a question, therefore, whether BEA has in other ways been less efficient in the management of resources at its disposal than might be expected. There are several issues on which such a conclusion seems justified.

In the first place, there is evidence to suggest that BEA has not planned operations on the basis of the total 'system' approach described in section II above. We have already commented, for example, on the tendency of BEA to operate particular aircraft on a given route, whereas real savings can often be derived from a more flexible 'systems' approach whereby aircraft can be shuffled between routes to match variations in demand on these routes. This relative inflexibility in the use of aircraft (which is in contrast to the policy of BOAC and other airlines who use complete systems methods of aircraft allocation) tends to lead to piecemeal solutions of day-to-day problems, the effect of which is to increase the number of aircraft required to provide a given level and range of service.[47] The lack of a systems approach is reflected also in the 'profit-centre' organizational structure introduced in BEA in 1967 in place of a 'functional control' structure.[48] This change created four profit-centred units covering Traffic and Sales, Operations, Engineering and Scottish activities. In 1971 the number of units was increased to ten, based mainly on individual aircraft fleets and geographical route groups. While this may offer advantages over the alternative system in defining managerial objectives and identifying high-cost activities, it does rather run against the interrelated system conception of the airline, in which decisions at local level have to take into account repercussions throughout the system.

Secondly, there may be doubts about the choice of aircraft by BEA. Allowing for the difficulties imposed on BEA by government control over procurement there are several instances where BEA has been caught in an unfavourable position. For example, the Corporation was put at a competitive disadvantage by having committed itself extensively to the turbo-prop Vanguards for introduction in the early 1960s, at a time when the first real impact of jet aircraft was about to be felt. Again, in ordering the Trident One, BEA acquired a sophisticated aircraft, but since it incorporated much advanced equipment it was also expensive compared with available competitors. It is also arguable that BEA has consistently sought aircraft which have been rather too small for the requirements of a growing market although in the end any real disadvantage was minimized by the slow growth of traffic towards the end of the 1960s.

Closely connected with this is the tendency for BEA to commit itself to bulk purchases of aircraft, no doubt largely because of the pressures put on the Corporation to 'buy British' and thereby provide support for the British aircraft manufacturing industry. A more usual approach for airlines is to acquire aircraft in fairly small numbers at a time, thereby enabling them to add progressively to their fleet, to adjust to changing market circumstances and to take advantage of newer versions becoming available. This is possible only so long as the airline is prepared to engage in a more or less continuous process of buying and selling aircraft, and is willing and able to purchase standard aircraft coming off a long production run. This BEA has either been unable or unwilling to do, with the result that changes in fleet composition have been discrete and somewhat inflexible.

On a rather different tack, BEA has not been noticeably active until recently in developing its share of the fast-growing inclusive tour market. It is true that BEA has in the later 1960s been moving increasingly into IT operations, hotels and the provision of related travel services, but it was only in 1969 that the decision was taken to establish a subsidiary company to compete in the IT market. Tardy adaptation to the changing character of the scheduled and non-scheduled sectors of the air-travel market may mean that BEA will find it difficult to capture a proper share of the growth market, and in the interim there are likely to have been costs in under-utilization of aircraft, especially at night when European tour operations on a more extended scale might have done much to raise aircraft productivity and reduce overall unit costs.

A further problem exists in the failure of BEA to contain the growth of its labour force, with the observed result that despite substantial changes in technology which should have led to corresponding increases in labour productivity, there has been a surprisingly small productivity growth in the later years of the decade. BEA has for some time been participating in productivity bargaining both at industry-wide levels through the National Joint Council for Civil Air Transport and at sectional level, and clearly the problem of productivity is one now recognized by management.

The final point concerns management itself. The Edwards Committee Report gave substantial weight to the quality of management in civil aviation as a primary determining factor in industrial efficiency. Some doubts about the appropriateness of the organizational structure have been raised above and other criticisms carry implications of management weakness, though any conclusive judgement would require a much more intensive investigation than is appropriate here. Two brief points may nevertheless be made. First, until very recently the senior management in BEA (as in many other airlines) has had a very high representation of staff whose backgrounds are in flight operations rather than in management and organization, with the result that policies have tended to be flight dominated and given to overemphasize technological, relative to market and organizational considerations. Secondly, there is the problem of the failure in nationalized industries in general to offer sufficiently high salaries to the chairman and board members to allow sufficient head room for those below that level, and the consequent difficulties of establishing a salary structure capable of providing incentive and reward for performance and responsibility. This problem was studied by the National Board for Prices and Incomes, which recommended progressive increases to leave more room for manoeuvre.[49]

THE AIR CORPORATIONS 75

In conclusion, there are sufficient symptoms of weakness in BEA's position to justify a judgement that whatever problems may have been thrust upon the Corporation by external events and by government intervention, some of the difficulties of BEA are due to internal factors, and to the pursuit of policies that may not be in the airline's best long-term commercial interests and certainly not in the overall interests of British civil aviation. This raises questions of control which are, however, best postponed until section V.

IV British Overseas Airways Corporation

The format for this section follows that for BEA. We consider first the main operating characteristics of BOAC, and proceed to a review of some of the main problems.

(a) *Operational Characteristics and Economic Performance*

BOAC is a long-haul airline with a high proportion of scheduled operations in its total output. It operates services from London and some provincial centres to three broad geographical regions: the West, including the United States and Canada, the Caribbean and on to Australia and the South Pacific; the South, principally the African countries; and the East, including the Middle East and stretching to Australia and New Zealand by the 'eastabout' routes. In recent years roughly one-third of its revenue has accrued in Britain, another third in the sterling area and a quarter in the dollar area.

Further details of traffic and operating statistics for the period 1960/61 to 1970/71 are given in Table 2.6. The years 1960/61 to 1962/63 were very poor trading years for BOAC, by far the worst year being 1961/62. In 1970/71, the trading situation was again poor, following a good run in the late 1960s.

Output rose over the period by a factor of 2·4 despite a reduction in the size of BOAC's fleet. The average size of aircraft had virtually doubled and the average speed had risen by 30 per cent, while in addition average aircraft utilization rose from 7·79 to 11·77 hours per day over the period. Demand rose less rapidly, resulting in a 6·3 percentage points fall in average load factor. The number of passengers more than doubled, but the fastest growth was in the transport of freight which rose by 500 per cent to account for more than a quarter of capacity sold (but only one-seventh of total revenue).

TABLE 2.6
BOAC traffic and operating statistics, 1960/61 and 1970/71

Traffic*	1960/61	1970/71	Per cent change
CTM offered (millions)	577·4	1,974·3	+242
Load ton miles sold (millions)	321·7	974·8	+203
Overall load factor	55·7%	49·4%	—
Passengers (millions)	0·794	1·846	+132
Passenger miles flown (millions)	2,445	6,617	+171
Available seat miles (millions)	4,181	12,270	+193
Passenger load factor	59·8%	53·9%	—
Mail ton miles (millions)	30·1	53·7	+72
Freight ton miles (millions)	43·7	258·8	+500
Operations			
Total flying hours (thousands)	201(1961/62)	230	+14
Mean block speed (mph)	347	451	+30
Average aircraft capacity (tons)	10·4	20·1	+93
Aircraft			
No. of operational aircraft	74	54	—
CTM produced per aircraft hour on scheduled operations	3,612	9,045	+150

* Traffic statistics relate only to scheduled routes. In 1970/71 non-scheduled services accounted for 1·1 per cent of total CTM, about 2·2 per cent of revenue and 2·5 per cent of passengers carried.
Source: BOAC *Annual Reports*.

Although the data available for BOAC are not fully comparable with those for BEA, a number of contrasts between the airlines emerge—in many ways reflecting the key characteristics of short-haul and long-haul airlines.

BOAC carried only about one-fifth the number of passengers of BEA in 1970/71 but flew twice as many passenger miles, illustrating the much longer average stage distances on BOAC's routes: 358 miles for BEA against about 1700 miles for BOAC. BOAC's aircraft were roughly one-third larger than BEA's in seating capacity—a reflection of the greater frequency of service and correspondingly smaller aircraft that typify the short-haul specialist (though it is not necessarily implied that the actual aircraft size is ideal). The advantage of the long-haul operator in having less aircraft time spent on the ground in turn round between flights is illustrated by a comparison for 1970/71 of the average utilization of aircraft in the two airlines: 2,170 hours for BEA against about 4,200 for BOAC.

On the whole, therefore, BOAC would seem to have a number of 'built-in' advantages, compared with BEA, which is reflected in a much lower operating cost per CTM (9·5 p in 1970/71 against 20·3 p for BEA). BOAC's overall operating costs per CTM fell by about 20 per cent between 1961/62 and 1970/71, mainly due to a fall in the operating costs of aircraft. In real terms, the cost savings are much more substantial.

This cost improvement is largely the result of changes in fleet composition, and due especially to the conversion to all-jet aircraft after 1960/61, which brought advantages of speed, size and greater overall operating efficiency. In 1960/61 BOAC was in the middle of a re-equipment programme involving the introduction of a completely jet-powered fleet. The Comet 4 had just entered full service and the Boeing 707 was being introduced. This change, involving a substantial rise in capacity and an expensive investment outlay, coincided with similar re-equipment on the part of rival airlines and also with an unexpected stagnation in the growth of demand, with the result that BOAC underwent a period of major financial crisis. At the end of the decade, BOAC was again starting a new stage in its development in which re-equipment problems once more loomed large, with the introduction of the Boeing 747 (the jumbo jet) and possibly, later in the 1970s, of supersonic aircraft. Details of fleet composition at the start and finish of the 1960s are shown in Table 2.7.

TABLE 2.7
BOAC's aircraft fleet in 1961 and 1971*

Aircraft type	1961	1971
Boeing 707	15	27(+2†)
Comet 4	19	—
Britannia 312	17	—
Britannia 102	14	—
DC 7C	8	—
DC 7C Freighter	2	—
VC-10	—	11
Super VC-10	—	16
Boeing 747	—	6(+6†)

* 1970 figures as at 31 March.
† On order.
Source: BOAC *Annual Reports*.

A further factor contributing to the favourable cost trend is the behaviour of employment and productivity. Table 2.8 shows the changes between 1960/61 and 1970/71.

Whereas BEA's labour force increased by three-quarters over the period, BOAC employment fell from 21,660 in 1961/62 to 18,845 in 1965/66, since when it has gradually increased again to a figure only 18 per cent above the earlier peak. This overall containment of employment growth bears witness to BOAC's concern for manpower

TABLE 2.8
BOAC staff and labour productivity, 1960/61 and 1970/71

	1960/61	1970/71	Per cent change
Average no. of employees	19,896	23,478	+18
CTM per employee	33,532	85,006	+154
Traffic revenue per employee	£4,425	£8,328	+88

Source: BOAC *Annual Reports*.

economies and productivity performance. (In the same period BOAC staff costs as a percentage of total operating costs rose from 31 to 36 per cent, compared with a rise from 38 to 48 per cent in the case of BEA.) Table 2.8 also shows a labour productivity growth of over 150 per cent though this is attributable in part to capital factors as well as improvements in labour utilization: again BEA shows up less well with an increase of 57 per cent. Finally, revenue per employee has increased substantially more than in the case of BEA. Overall, BOAC stands relatively much higher in the labour productivity rankings of the world's largest airlines, but as the Edwards Committee Report observed, BOAC's staff productivity level in 1967 was only two-thirds of the American giants, Pan American and TWA.[50] If BOAC is relatively much better placed than BEA, more might yet be done.

While operating costs were falling in the 1960s, revenue per unit of output remained roughly static after an initial dramatic fall from 13·2 p per CTM in 1960/61 to 9·9 p in 1962/63. Thus BOAC now

TABLE 2.9
Operating results of BOAC, 1960/61 to 1970/71
£ million

Year	Traffic revenue	Operating surplus (deficit)	Group profit (loss) before interest and tax	Group profit (loss) after interest and tax*	Dividend on Exchequer dividend capital
1960/61	88.0	4·3	—	(2.0)	Inapplicable
1961/62	92·7	(10·5)	(43·4)	(50·1)	Inapplicable
1962/63	92·4	(4·7)	(6·3)	(12·9)	Inapplicable
1963/64	103·8	8·7	(2·7)	(10·4)	Inapplicable
1964/65	114·4	16·8	17·9	8·9	Inapplicable
1965/66	124·7	20·7	11·8	8·1	3·5
1966/67	137·4	23·3	27·1	23·9	5·3
1967/68	150·3	19·9	25·3	22·5	10·0
1968/69	169·6	21·9	35·7	21·7	12·5
1969/70	198·0	31·1	36·9	19·3	13·0
1970/71	195·5	5·9	10·6	3·4	4·9

* Attributable to BOAC after profit to minority shareholders in subsidiary companies.
Source: BOAC *Annual Reports*.

has a much larger surplus per CTM over costs than BEA, and its financial position has improved out of all recognition over the decade—as indeed it had much need to do.

The trend of profitability over the period is shown in Table 2.9. Traffic revenue more than doubled, and in nine years an operating surplus was achieved. The Group Profit figures show a much more serious picture, with four consecutive years showing a cumulative loss after interest on borrowings and taxation of about £75 million. This period was followed, however, by seven years of overall profitability, amounting to £108 million after interest and tax. In the last six of these years, under an experimental structure,[51] BOAC was able to pay to the Treasury a dividend averaging £8 million a year. This was possible with the help of a financial reconstruction involving, inter alia, a write-off of £110 million of BOAC's accrued liabilities.

As well as overall profitability, there is the financial obligation of the Corporation to be considered. The difficulties facing BOAC in the early 1960s delayed the setting of a target as outlined in the 1961 White Paper on the *Financial and Economic Obligations of the Nationalized Industries*.[52] Only in 1966/67, when about two-thirds of its liabilities had been written off, did BOAC begin to operate with an established target, of $12\frac{1}{2}$ per cent return, before interest but after depreciation at historic cost, on average net assets.

BOAC's view of this target is not dissimilar to that of BEA, though less vehemently argued. Sir Giles Guthrie, Chairman of the Board of BOAC from 1964 to 1968, stated to a Select Committee in 1967 that 'from BOAC's own standpoint . . . a target is of very little value' and that its only function could be to guide government as to what the Corporation might achieve.[53] Despite this, over the period 1966/67 to 1970/71 the yield on net assets was 13·6 per cent—rather above the target which was set for a six-year period. The somewhat disturbing fact remains that in both airlines, a financial objective has been set without its purpose being properly understood; or, if understood, ignored. It may also be that not enough has been done by the Corporations to try to persuade government that their point of view may be legitimate.

In summary, BOAC has managed to regain a secure financial footing after a disastrous period at the start of the 1960s. To maintain this performance in the early part of the 1970s will be much more difficult, as the poor trading results now being returned by most of the major world airlines already indicate. There is more uncertainty about the growth of demand, particularly in scheduled operations. On the supply side, the introduction of the jumbo jet is giving rise to problems of excess capacity and it may be some time before demand expands sufficiently to take up the slack. In the middle 1970s the proposed introduction of Concorde will raise further problems both on the operational and on the investment side. This combination of circumstances, in terms of demand, planned additions to world long-haul capacity and technical advance, is disturbingly similar to the conditions in 1960. However, many other aspects of BOAC's position have altered in the interim and it may be much better placed now to withstand a leaner trading situation than in 1960.

(b) *Current Issues*

This discussion of BOAC's current problems takes up two main issues. The first is the changing competitive situation faced by BOAC, especially in the North Atlantic, and the Corporation's response to it. The second issue is the growing investment programme required by BOAC and the new financial arrangements adopted to prevent additional drain on Exchequer resources.

(i) THE COMPETITIVE POLICIES OF BOAC

There are a number of reasons for the heightened competition now being faced by BOAC. In the first place, the introduction of the jumbo jet by the largest airlines has meant a surge of capacity much greater than demand—which in any case grew less rapidly than expected. Secondly, as in BEA's European operations, there are increasing competitive pressures from the non-scheduled operators. And thirdly, the presence of a strong second-force airline in Britain may provide additional competition on long-haul routes, quite apart from the Conservative Government's decision to reallocate routes bringing in about £6 million gross revenue, from the public Corporations (largely from BOAC) to British Caledonian.

Each of these factors is particularly important for the US–UK routes, where pooling arrangements are not in force and where BOAC already competes with a great many national airlines. Elsewhere, BOAC is mainly in a partnership agreement[54] and its problems are similar to those of BEA, so that we need add little on that aspect. Indeed, BOAC's problems may be rather easier since there is less competition to the pool partners from IT and other charter operators over the long-haul intercontinental routes than within Western Europe, though this may become less true as higher incomes, greater leisure time and falling real costs encourage people to travel further afield for holiday purposes.

Our main interest then is in the North Atlantic market, which is the world's biggest international market: in 1968 traffic between Europe and the UK and the United States produced a revenue of £250 million from passengers and £60 million from freight, and traffic is expected to double by 1973. BOAC has until now[55] been the sole British scheduled operator in the UK–US sector of the market while the US has long allowed two carriers (Pan American and Trans World Airlines) to operate, and has more recently added a third. The situation is made especially difficult for BOAC by the fact that the UK (and London in particular) has been adopted by the US carriers as the main 'gateway' into Europe, to the extent that in 1969 177 out of 369 direct flights per week by American airlines from the US to Europe passed through the UK. BOAC's flights per week in the same market totalled only 57. In addition, BOAC has to face competition from other scheduled airlines using fifth-freedom rights to break US–Europe journeys in London to set down and pick up passengers.[56] While the fifth-freedom operators in combination do not occupy a dominant position in UK–US traffic their share (under 10 per cent in recent years) is likely to mean some loss of traffic to BOAC. Finally, it has to be noted that the transatlantic market is a large and growing field for the non-scheduled airlines operating IT and charter services who had a market share of around 20 per cent in 1967 but who have been steadily increasing their portion of the growing market since then.

Both for BOAC and for the prosperity of British civil aviation in general, it is desirable that Britain should obtain a proper share of this very important market, but BOAC, under the pressure of competition from these various sources, has suffered a reduction in its share of the market. To understand this, it is necessary to analyse the market itself a little further. The North Atlantic market can be divided into three components: (a) traffic between the US and Europe;[57] (b) traffic between the UK and the US; and (c) traffic between the UK and Europe. The last of these, (c), is at present largely supplied from the British side by BEA, while BOAC caters for the second, (b). But the largest sector of the total market, between Europe and the US, is to all intents and purposes left out of account by the two Corporations, though BOAC has a very small share, perhaps of the order of 2 per cent. Since the American airlines in particular make much use of the UK gateway to Europe and thereby provide through-services to Europe for passengers wishing to break journeys in the UK, it follows that the British operators with their specialist roles cannot properly offer a competitive service in this sector of the total market and it must be asked whether this can be afforded in the light of the growing pressures from other directions. This would require a change in the organizational structure, which is a matter for later consideration.

A second part of the problem lies in the declining share of BOAC in the UK–US scheduled market itself, in the course of the 1960s, from about 38 per cent in 1961/62 to only 25 per cent in 1969, the gain going to the US carriers.[58] In part this was the result of deliberate BOAC policy rather than lack of competitiveness. The roots of BOAC's difficulties in the early 1960s[59] lay mainly in the accidents to the Comet 1 which led to the withdrawal of the aircraft in 1954. This set BOAC on a path that was to lead to the introduction of too many new types of aircraft in a short space of time, involving high introductory costs and the need to accelerate the writing down of capital costs. By 1960/61, BOAC was introducing both the Comet 4 and the Boeing 707, at a time when the international air traffic market temporarily ceased to grow and when all major airlines were embarked on a major expansion of capacity. BOAC was following a policy of trying to retrieve lost market shares, especially on the North Atlantic, and planned to increase capacity by one-third in *each* of the years 1960/61 and 1961/62, after which it was intended to reduce the pace to a more sedate 10 per cent per annum. This plan was to achieve for BOAC, by the mid-1960s, a network big enough to occupy its fleet fully, including not only 15 Boeing 707s for the North Atlantic, but also 35 VC-10 aircraft ordered in 1957 for the mid-1960s, which were the motivating force for the expansion. At one time, in 1960, BOAC had agreed to order 10 additional VC-10 aircraft, making a total of 45, of which 30 were to be the Super VC-10, an improved and larger version.

The story here is familiar: BOAC wanted an aircraft designed for its own specialist requirements, the British manufacturers had to be given a sufficiently large order to proceed with production, and BOAC began thinking in terms of expanding the market to use up aircraft rather than acquiring aircraft to meet market requirements. When BOAC's expansion plans coincided with a slowdown in traffic growth, the overall load factor fell by 10 points to 46 per cent and an operating loss of £10 million was supplemented by losses through accelerated depreciation of obsolescent aircraft and interest charges so that the total group loss in 1961/62 amounted to £50 million.

Following thorough investigation culminating in the famous (but unpublished) Corbett Report, a shake-up of top management and a financial reconstruction involving inter alia the writing off of £110 million of accrued liabilities, BOAC set about a process of rationalization and consolidation. A number of services were cut back or dropped altogether, including some services to the United States, and it was mainly this which caused the reduction in BOAC's share of the North Atlantic market.[60] By pursuing a policy of lower market shares during most of the 1960s, BOAC was able to restore morale and profitability, though it may at the same time have reduced the benefits accruing to the British balance of payments. However, as demand increased on previously sub-marginal routes, and with the impending arrival of the jumbo jet, capable of lower seat-mile costs and reduced break-even load factors, a more expansionist policy seemed essential to BOAC; and there were no doubt pressures in this direction arising from balance of payments considerations.

A number of problems had to be faced, however. First, as we have seen, BOAC has little opportunity to offer through-services to Europe due to the special responsibilities of BEA in that region. However, BEA *does* gain some traffic by reason of its non-participation in the transatlantic market, having an agreement with Pan Am and TWA which gives BEA rather more favourable terms on traffic switching to BEA in London; and in addition the American operators are prepared to give preference to BEA in booking passengers through to Europe. Secondly, whereas the American operators can provide through-services from points behind the main American gateways to the North Atlantic by linking up regional and international services, this is not open to BOAC. Thirdly, because of a prolonged pay dispute with the pilots, BOAC was unable to bring into service its first jumbo jets, acquired in 1970 but not flown commercially until well into 1971, ten months later than planned. Since these were intended for the North Atlantic market, and since other airlines were able to bring their aircraft into service, BOAC's share of the market again suffered. Fourthly, this delay in introducing the Boeing 747s postponed BOAC's plans to increase frequency on established routes and reintroduce services from which it had withdrawn in the retrenchment of the early 1960s.

These obstacles to the expansion of BOAC's market share on the North Atlantic are further compounded by the fact that in the current situation of excess capacity among the world's airlines, disputes have arisen within the IATA on fares policy: the North Atlantic routes occupy a specially important place as they often set the standard for tariffs in other international sectors. The competitive pressures from group charter operators, offering return fares over the Atlantic for as little as one-third the standard tourist rate, forced the scheduled operators to retaliate. Many of them, including BOAC, set up their own charter subsidiaries to compete with the charter operators on their own terms. BOAC also helped to pioneer competitive fares along two different lines.

The first of these involved the sale to travel agents of blocks of seats on scheduled flights. These bulk purchases were then retailed to the general public with a combination of package elements. Such experiments were first carried out with success on cabotage routes (between two points in the territory of the same state or its dependencies) which were not subject to IATA regulations but came under the authority of the ATLB. But BOAC also sought to have such tariffs introduced on IATA routes, and achieved some success at least as an interim measure, though it is unlikely to prove a complete solution to the threat of charter competition. Even with the 'packaged holiday' traveller paying only about £60 for air travel, the other package elements usually brought the total cost to about twice that figure, and while that compared favourably with the £180–£200 fare for an economy class round-trip on the North Atlantic routes, it was still much higher than the fare on most affinity group charters.

Another approach, again pioneered by BOAC on cabotage routes, is the 'Earlybird' scheme, based on substantially reduced fares for bookings well in advance of the flight. This scheme avoids the need for prospective travellers to be members of an affinity group, and it does not require them to buy a complete package which may not suit their needs. All that is necessary is that they should be prepared to make their travel plans several months ahead. BOAC's pressure for the adoption of this form of promotional fare resulted in an 'open rate' situation on the mid-Atlantic routes to the Caribbean: that is, operators were able to fix their own fares rather than conforming to a scale agreed at the appropriate IATA conference. Having succeeded in extending the Earlybird idea, BOAC announced its intention of seeking the introduction of the scheme on the more important North Atlantic routes by the summer of 1972. This was expected to bring BOAC a further 400,000 passengers and an increased revenue of £10 million a year.

However, the increasing anxiety of airlines engaged on the North Atlantic routes, on the score of overcapacity, led to a breakthrough at the IATA Conference in the autumn of 1971. This development has to be seen against a background of uncertainty prevailing since

1968. A temporary open-rate situation—greatly disliked by the IATA operators because of the cut-throat competition it can generate—developed in November 1969, after four separate fares conferences over an eighteen-month period had failed to produce agreement. This was replaced by a phase in which the previous economy-class fare between New York and London—the basis of the whole structure—was upheld, although certain reductions were allowed for extended stay overseas and for group travel. Finally, after the collapse of negotiations, a last-minute agreement was reached in November 1971, involving a series of fares cuts of up to 26 per cent: the individual economy excursion fare between New York and London, for example, was reduced from £113 to £83 (off-peak). This solution fell short of a package which had almost been agreed earlier, and which would have involved the principle of advanced purchase excursion rates—the principle adopted by BOAC for its Earlybird scheme. It remains to be seen whether the new fare structure will suffice to attract sufficient custom to the scheduled operators or whether still further modifications will prove necessary.

One further source of help to the scheduled airlines may be forthcoming from the tightening up of affinity charter regulations. Accusation by the scheduled operators that charter airlines were breaking the rules led to the US Civil Aeronautics Board seeking the suspension of a number of charter licences in 1970, while more recently the Department of Trade and Industry has indicated that under the new Civil Aviation Act of 1971 more effective control and scrutiny of charter operations will be introduced. The more successful these controls are, the less will be the competitive pressures on BOAC and other scheduled airlines from the charter side; and to the extent that this pressure is reduced, the less will be the need for the IATA operators to contemplate further cuts in scheduled tariffs.

Similar problems of capacity utilization exist in the freight market, which now accounts for about 15 per cent of BOAC's traffic revenue and is growing rapidly. BOAC already operates a number of scheduled all-freight services, but the possibilities of major expansion in this direction seem limited in the immediate future, particularly in view of the additional cargo space available on passenger aircraft with the introduction of the jumbo jets. The problems of finding complete freight-loads for such large aircraft are likely to prove severe for some time to come, and even the task of obtaining adequate loads for the cargo space of larger passenger aircraft—which of course provide a useful source of additional operating revenue at a low marginal cost—will be difficult. Steps are however being taken by BOAC and other airlines to improve the infrastructure required for the handling of cargo on a larger scale and to develop the market for air freight by adopting new pricing policies designed to attract business from other types of transport.

In conclusion to this discussion, it is evident that while BOAC has recovered much growth that was lost in the retrenchment of services in the 1960s, the task of expanding its share of the transatlantic market on a profitable basis remains formidable. In this market above all, with the extent of competition from other scheduled operators and from charter and IT services, and with the prestige attaching to operations on these routes, the difficulties of making headway are huge. In recognizing this, we have to note two important implications. First, to the extent that what is at stake here is a concern for expanding the share of British civil aviation in this market, it may be that British Caledonian Airways will be granted scheduled services on the Atlantic routes, on the grounds that while some traffic may be diverted from BOAC more will be attracted away from foreign operators, bringing a net balance of advantage to UK operators as a whole. British Caledonian have already indicated their intention of seeking rights in this sector. Secondly, there is the question whether the separation of BEA and BOAC is working to the best advantage of British civil aviation as a whole, particularly in the constraint it imposes on tapping the important market between the USA and continental Europe. The prospects for merger are discussed in section V below.

(ii) FINANCIAL PROBLEMS

Many of the questions raised above have implications for the financial situation of BOAC. The re-equipment necessary for BOAC to remain in effective competition in many areas of the world market, and especially on the North Atlantic, will involve the Corporation in a large investment programme. How large is this programme in fact, and how is it to be financed? Secondly, how appropriate are BOAC's present financial arrangements as the Corporation enters a period certain to be characterized by increased competition and major changes in technology?

At the end of March 1965 the Corporation's liabilities stood at £176 million, about 70 per cent of which was in the form of advances by the Minister of Aviation, the remainder being BOAC stock. The accumulated deficit was then £82.5 million. Under the financial reconstruction announced by the Minister on 1 March 1965 and implemented in the Air Corporations Act of 1966, it was agreed to write off £110 million of existing liabilities, extinguishing the deficit and establishing a contingency reserve. The new capital structure took the form of £31 million loan capital advanced by the Minister of Aviation, bearing a fixed interest rate of 4 per cent per annum, and a further £35 million Exchequer Dividend Capital (later termed Public Dividend Capital) which was to be remunerated out of profits. The immediate effect of this was to reduce BOAC's interest payments in the first year of the reconstruction from £8·3 million to £1·24 million. During the debate on the Second Reading of the 1966 Air Corporations Bill, the Minister of Aviation argued that this arrangement ensured

> that the incentive to make a surplus is not dulled by the knowledge that, once made, a surplus will be more than swallowed up in interest on dead capital.[61]

The financial reconstruction and associated rationalization brought BOAC to the end of a period in which it had made losses in seven out of eight consecutive years. It also marked the end of BOAC's reliance on Exchequer Advances for financing its investment programme. As Table 2.10 shows, between 1965/66 and 1970/71 the Corporation was able to finance its investment, make appropriate repayment of loans and make dividend payments on its Public Dividend Capital to the extent of over £44 million without further recourse to government sources. A futher dividend of £4·9 million was paid by BOAC for the financial year 1970/71 making a total of £49·2 million in all. In addition, reserves were built up from £8·4 million in 1965 to £77·8 million in 1971 and £30 million has been added from reserves to the Corporation's Public Dividend Capital, bringing it to a total of £65 million.

Together with the fact that BOAC exceeded its financial objective in all but one of the years (1970/71) since it was first set in 1967, this is very much a success story. The real question, however, is whether this can be continued in the future. Table 2.11 shows the first-year investment programme of BOAC, as set out in 1968, and the intended sources of finance.

On average, BOAC was to invest about £80 million per year until 1972/73, a substantial increase on the figures for 1965–68. Fixed investment would rise from around £16 million per year on average to over £50 million, reflecting the greater cost of new aircraft and the extensive complementary investments required in providing ground-handling, terminal and reservation facilities, yet the

TABLE 2.10

BOAC: Sources and dispositions of funds, 1965/66 to 1970/71

£ million

	1965/66	1966/67	1967/68	1968/69	1969/70	1970/71
Sources:						
Profit (excluding proceeds from sale of assets)	8·1	20·5	21·3	17·8	31·9	3·9
Obsolescence and depreciation	10·4	14·7	15·5	18·0	17·5	20·3
Amortization of training and development expenditure	2·2	1·1	1·1	1·7	1·6	1·3
Increase in provision for joint pension scheme liability	4·4	3·0	—	—	—	—
Other items	—	3·9	1·1	2·3	1·8	1·5
Sale of assets	2·7	3·7	2·3	2·3	2·3	44·5*
Net decrease in investments in subsidiary companies	1·9	—	—	—	—	—
Loans	—	0·9	6·3†	14·8†	18·6†	51·8†
	29·7	47·8	47·6	56·9	73·7	123·3
Disposition:						
Aircraft and spares	10·6	8·2	15·0	26·8	27·4	61·9
Other fixed assets	3·2	4·3	6·1	14·4	15·3	18·2
Training and development	1·3	0·5	0·7	1·7	1·6	2·8
Other items	0·6	11·5‡	—	—	—	4·3
Repayment of borrowings	2·8	2·8	2·8	4·0	4·5	23·1
Funds temporarily invested	11·2	17·0	17·8	—	12·4	—
Gross dividend	—	3·5§	5·2§	10·0§	12·5§	13·0§
	29·7	47·8	47·6	56·9	73·7	123·3

* Includes £43·3m from realization of temporary investments.
† US dollar and other foreign loans to finance American aircraft purchases and other projects.
‡ Purchase of Cunard interest in BOAC-Cunard Limited.
§ For previous year.
Source: BOAC *Annual Reports*.

Corporation was confident that this could be achieved without recourse to government finance.

It is evident from Tables 2.10 and 2.11 that a new element has entered into BOAC's financial position since 1967: the resort to dollar (and more generally foreign) loans. Since 1956 BOAC has been allowed by government to buy American aircraft, though not entirely without conditions, as we saw in the example of the VC-10 purchases. It was recognized in 1965 that from 1969 onwards there

TABLE 2.11
BOAC: Projected investment programme and sources of finance, 1967/68 to 1972/73

Capital Investment		£m
Aircraft and spares		198
Land and buildings		34
Plant and machinery		9
Equipment		25
Repayment of Borrowings		47
Other		88
	Total	401
Sources of Finance		£m
Profits and sale of assets		84
Obsolescence and depreciation		150
US dollar loans		167
	Total	401

Source: BOAC *Annual Reports, 1967/68*.

would be a need for substantially larger aircraft, with seating capacity in excess of 250: this requirement had to be met from American manufacturers, in the shape of the Boeing 747. BOAC's initial order for six 747s was announced in 1966. Twenty per cent of the purchase price was to be provided from BOAC's internal resources, but the Corporation was obliged by government to seek the main finance by means of dollar loans raised abroad. In November 1967 approval was given for the order of a further five 747s (for delivery in 1972), the *whole* finance of which was to be raised through overseas borrowing to ease the burden on the UK balance of payments.

This has been a matter of some dissatisfaction to BOAC, for several reasons. BOAC is a major dollar earner and yet is neither allowed to use these dollar earnings to buy American aircraft nor to purchase official dollars for aircraft finance. Because of the Treasury constraints, an estimated $300 million would have to be raised over the period 1967/68 to 1972/73, by means of foreign loans, building up the sterling funds in BOAC's hands while incurring longer-term dollar liabilities. BOAC feels that it is being unduly discriminated against, since the independent airlines, apparently because of their lesser requirements and less serious impact on the balance of payments, are allowed by government to pay by means of official dollars.[62]

On the other hand, were BOAC to be given capital by the Government to buy official dollars for the purchase of American aircraft, government itself would have to borrow that money, probably at an interest rate higher than that obtainable by BOAC through the Export–Import Bank in New York. By raising finance abroad, therefore, BOAC is easing the burden on Government and on the total cost of a given equipment programme—a fact which may put BOAC in a relatively advantageous position when investment plans are being put forward for approval.

So far we have not commented upon the introduction of an element of Public Dividend Capital, for an experimental period of six years commencing in April 1965, and now extended for a further five years. As already observed, BOAC started in 1965 with £35 million in Public Dividend Capital and under Treasury instruction has subsequently increased the amount to £65 million. The dividend on the capital (payable to the Government) can be varied according to each year's financial results, if necessary no dividend being paid in a poor year. The dividend for any year is proposed by the Corporation, but is subject (like the allocation of profits to reserve) to the approval of the sponsoring department and the consent of the Treasury. In the terms of the Act, the power to determine the dividend and the allocation to reserves rests with the Minister acting 'with the approval of the Treasury and after consultation with the Corporation'. In practice this does not seem to have led to any real difficulties.

BOAC was regarded as being especially suitable for this kind of experiment for a number of reasons. Because of its financial reconstruction it was able to make a fresh start without any accumulated debt. It was free of social-service obligations in respect of unremunerative services and was engaged in a highly competitive and risk-prone area of business. Perhaps most importantly, it was operating in a commercial sector that was subject to considerable annual variations in activity, and the flexibility allowed by this form of capital was thought especially appropriate in such cases. So far, the experiment appears to have worked well. In the first five years of its operation, BOAC paid dividends totalling almost £50 million. In the absence of a Public Dividend element of capital there is no saying what alternative approach would have been adopted, but on the supposition that Public Dividend Capital had been replaced by a conventional loan capital amount at the 4 per cent interest set on the remainder of BOAC's capital liabilities at the time of the reconstruction the return to the Exchequer would have been far below that actually achieved. This device can be regarded as one means of giving a nationalized concern some of the trappings of a fully commercial business particularly in the form of some financial discipline and a motivation that may be more real than the financial objective, at least for staff and management.

This concludes our review of BOAC at the present time. The Corporation has made a remarkable recuperation since the dark years at the start of the 1960s, thanks largely to a sensibly limited marketing policy and a financial reconstruction which relieved it of a sizeable interest debt. In many respects BOAC appears to the observer to have made more progress than BEA in solving its problems, though that may be unfair to BEA which, after all, managed to avoid the problems that beset BOAC. Since 1965, BOAC has markedly improved its public image. It has been prepared to adapt its policy on growth and market shares on the basis of realistic market analyses, and has shown more signs of working on a systems approach to management than has BEA. Since the VC-10 episode, it has been prepared to accept standard aircraft and has pursued an aircraft procurement policy which has added progressively but in small doses to the established fleet, rather than committing itself to large orders. It has also shown a progressive outlook on fares, as shown by its advocacy of bulk market tariffs, first on cabotage then on international routes. The growth of productivity has been favourable, and considerable efforts have obviously been made to check the growth of employment.

All this is not to say that BOAC's problems are over. The recent history of labour relations has been less happy, especially in the protracted dispute with the pilots over the introduction of the jumbo jet. It might also be argued that the successes of the last five years simply derive from the elimination of gross inefficiencies which should never have been allowed to develop in the first place, and that now this task is complete the problems of making further progress may be substantial. Again, the wisdom of pursuing an expansionist policy at a time when the new aircraft arriving on the scene are producing world excess capacity is yet to be proven. The effectiveness of the Corporation in providing a competitive service in the jumbo jet (and later, the supersonic) era remains to be seen. The ability of the Corporation to finance its increased investment requirements has still to be fully tested in the long run, when bad trading years break up the string of successes between 1965 and 1970. Above all, perhaps, there is the question of the new relationship to be forged with BEA under the proposed new Airways Board. Some aspects of this, together with further questions that are of common concern to both the Air Corporations, are more fully discussed in the following section.

V Three Problems of Nationalization

At this point, having looked at the two Corporations separately, we move on to an examination of some problems they have in common. First, we take up the problems of the future relationship between BEA and BOAC in the light of the Edwards Report and the subsequent policy statements. Secondly, further attention has to be directed to the problems of the airlines in the context of the Treasury prescriptions on pricing, investment and financial objectives. And thirdly, deriving from these two questions and much of the earlier discussion, there is the issue of the relations between government and the two Corporations.

(a) *A Merger between BEA and BOAC?*

The debate about the relationship between BEA and BOAC is a long-standing one. In the 1945 White Paper[63] there were explicit reasons for developing separate long-haul and short-haul airlines—reasons which were probably very sound in the economic and technical situation of the time. The Ministry of Aviation 1963 White Paper, *Financial Problems of BOAC*, returned to the issue when BOAC's financial difficulties were at their most critical. Its conclusions are worth quoting in full:

In favour of merger it can be argued, for example, that:

(i) the two Corporations have many common functions (e.g. engineering, catering) and merger would give scope for overall economies;

(ii) the size of a merged Corporation would be no greater than that of certain other major airlines;

(iii) overlapping services could be eliminated and through-traffic from North America to Europe would be increased.

Against merger, it can be argued that:

(i) differences in the composition of the fleets make it more efficient to have two specialist organizations as at present;

(iii) any gains on through-traffic to Europe would be more than offset by losses of inter-line sales at present enjoyed by BEA;

(iii) BOAC and BEA are in very different financial circumstances.

The arguments for and against are finely balanced. Nevertheless, neither of the Corporations is in favour of merger at the present time. BOAC considers that it would not solve its immediate problems, BEA that it would destroy its singleness of purpose and *esprit de corps*.[64]

At this time it was again decided to leave the organizations separate, although rather more collaboration between them was sought by means of appointing the chairman of each as a part-time member of the board of the other.

Inevitably, the issue arose once more during the Edwards Committee's investigations. The report noted the growth of co-operation between the two Corporations, especially in the fields of medical services, pilot and engineering training and pensions, but these are peripheral to the operational questions. The Edwards Committee saw the argument as depending on two main points: first, whether common services are as extensive as possible, and secondly, whether the two airlines in their concern for autonomy might be allowing overall national interest to take second place. Despite its finding that closer working could bring advantages that were not being achieved under the existing arrangement, the committee stopped short of recommending outright merger, seemingly on 'judgements about the behaviour and the reaction of human beings' which, for the committee, meant that 'no organization should be made larger than it needs to be to secure the major economies of scale and specialization.'[65]

While one would not wish to quarrel with the *basis* of the committee's recommendation, so stated, it is less clear (at least on the evidence of the report) that the 'major economies of scale and specialization' were fully investigated in concrete economic terms, and that all the possible factors were taken into consideration. There may indeed be some recognition of this in the decision both of the Labour Government in its White Paper,[66] and of the Conservative Government in 1970, to set up a single Airways Board stronger than that envisaged by the Edwards Committee. In both cases it was the explicit objective to have the Airways Board exercise 'strategic control' over the state airlines and there is no room for doubt that further integration of the airlines' activities is a major aspect of this.

The Edwards Committee examined a number of areas in which there seemed to be possible economies from closer working of the two Corporations: these areas included information handling, engineering maintenance and engineering design, terminal facilities and hotel investment, but above all marketing. It was the need to secure further collaboration on such matters that persuaded the Committee to recommend the linking of the two airlines under a 'Holdings Board'.[67] Leaving these opportunities for benefit on one side for the present, we have to note the relative absence of concrete discussion of operating economies likely to result from merger. Yet one might expect, on *a priori* grounds, that merger could produce net gains in operating expenses, not least perhaps in relation to fleet requirements. Let us consider, then, some of the possibilities of merger on the operating side.

The new airline would in the first instance have a route network comprising the existing networks of BEA and BOAC, and to serve these would have a fleet made up of the essentially long-haul aircraft that were BOAC's and the short- to medium-haul aircraft that were BEA's. A number of questions, some of them complex in themselves, then arise.

(i) In so far as BOAC is typified by long-haul routes, how far can short-haul aircraft be used effectively on its routes?

(ii) In so far as BEA is typified by short-haul routes, how far can long-haul aircraft be used effectively on its routes?

(iii) How far does BEA possess routes that are not 'typical'? And similarly for BOAC?

(iv) What scope is there for integration to reduce the number of aircraft required in total (a) in the short run; (b) in the longer run?

These are not, in themselves, questions about the scale of operations and the economies or diseconomies of changes in scale, although a merger leading to increased enterprise scale would also raise that sort of problem. They are rather questions about the operating conditions which would obtain under a merger, and to that extent they might only be once-and-for-all gains (or losses), although as we shall argue later, there are likely to be implications for future investment and hence the flow of capital costs into the future.

Questions (i) and (ii) relate to a general issue that has run through the course of British civil aviation policy to date. It has traditionally been argued that the economics of short- and long-haul operations are so different as to make any significant substitution of the two types of aircraft either impossible on technical grounds or inefficient for economic reasons. As we argued earlier,[68] however, the strength of this argument is now much diminished, while other difficulties in the transferability of aircraft have also lessened.

The factors which gave economic point to the initial specialization of BEA and BOAC have so altered, therefore, that at the start of the 1970s the separatist solution is now much more open to doubt. European traffic densities are now adequate to justify using large aircraft to provide at least part of the service. Runway length is much less of a problem. Above all, a situation has come about where not only are seat-mile costs lower for long-haul than for short-haul aircraft when each is operating over its optimal range, but also where the *total* operating costs of some long-haul types (like the Boeing 707 and even the 747) over short stages lie below those of aircraft such as the Trident 1 and Trident 2 which are essentially medium-haul aircraft. This is only partly to be explained by the fact that many of the existing Boeing 707s have been in service for some time and their capital costs have been largely written down, while aircraft such as the Trident are experiencing heavy introductory costs. The new generation of wide-fuselage aircraft, powered by improved engines, is proving itself capable of such flexibility in performance over different ranges without significant cost penalties, that even total operating costs are below those of the more conventional type of aircraft. When consideration is given to the much higher seating capacity available on such aircraft as the Boeing 747, even on short stages of between 200 and 500 miles, the non-depreciated wide-fuselage aircraft is capable of seat-mile costs significantly below those of non-depreciated conventional short- to medium-haul types such as the Boeing 737 and Trident 3B.

Such cost comparisons are already beginning to render obsolete the distinction between long- and short-haul aircraft, and indeed the market for large aircraft with a maximum range of 750 to 1,000 miles is virtually defunct, the preference now being for aircraft with a capability of 2,000-mile stages yet not subject to major cost disadvantages over shorter ranges. In consequence the really significant issue for airlines (except for special cases) is that of possessing aircraft of the right *size* for given routes.[69] Given adequate traffic on any short-stage route, the airline will often find it advantageous to use the larger aircraft, at least at peak periods, rather than risk turning away custom by running smaller aircraft at high load factors or having to increase the service frequency of these smaller aircraft (which implies additions to the fleet if existing aircraft are already being utilized at levels near to the maximum).

In short, the critical factor in the decisions about aircraft procurement and deployment is increasingly that of the density of the market. There are undoubtedly many routes served by BEA which do not generate enough traffic to warrant the use of larger aircraft even at peak periods. In 1968 BEA had over a hundred services with less than forty passengers per day—although some of these were holiday routes operated on a once or twice per week basis which does not altogether preclude the use of large aircraft. Equally certainly, there are some routes which could sustain the use of such aircraft, and as traffic volume grows, the number of these is likely to increase also. At present, BEA operates on all four of the highest density routes in

Europe, but has no capability of serving these with large-capacity aircraft as we have seen from the earlier discussion of fleet composition. This may seem surprising, but it has to be appreciated that while a relatively specialized airline may not in itself be able to justify acquisition of such large-capacity aircraft until a sufficient scale of activity and purchase is achieved, an expanded airline with a balance of route lengths and route densities may well be able to gain by transferring aircraft between routes with different characteristics. It is only fair to add that there is likely to be a 'core' of routes which can only be effectively served by specific aircraft types—and this would not be confined only to sparse routes such as BEA's Highlands and Islands services.

Two questions have then to be asked: first, whether BOAC has any spare capacity which might be used on BEA routes justifying the deployment of the larger aircraft; and second, whether the advantage would lie solely in the use of large aircraft on short-haul stages or whether there might be some reciprocal transfer. (This latter question in fact puts question (iii) above in a different form.)

BOAC already achieves a high utilization rate on its aircraft, including the Boeing 707 which seems the most likely candidate for use on selected BEA routes.[70] This is not to say, however, that the Boeing 707 could not be used effectively either during winter on inclusive tours or in the way of 'tail-end' flights into Europe after crossing the Atlantic. Again, with the progressive introduction of the Boeing 747, some Boeing 707s will either become redundant to BOAC or will be less highly utilized, and this would open up the possibility of using these aircraft on appropriate services within Europe. The advantages would be those of increased capacity (for scheduled services the Boeing 707 would seat about 150 compared with just over 100 on the Trident 3B) and hence reduction in the risk of losing custom, and lower operating costs per seat mile (on any reasonable assumption about depreciation and renovation costs).

An additional possibility under an integrated organization is that some of the routes now served by BOAC's larger capacity aircraft might be served by BEA's aircraft, thus setting free some additional BOAC capacity for use in Europe. An examination of BOAC networks shows that roughly one-quarter of its weekly frequencies operated involve stages of less than 600 miles.[71] In other words, although the median stage-length in the two airlines is quite different, there is a significant portion of BOAC's operations which is more characteristically short-haul. At least on some of the frequencies operated on these routes, sparsity of traffic may make it economic to use smaller aircraft, despite their higher *average* seat-mile cost. Certainly this is not practicable at present, with independent scheduling by the two airlines, but with integrated scheduling the prospects of making available suitable aircraft at the time they are wanted are likely to be more favourable.

There are good reasons, therefore, for believing that some reciprocal transfer of aircraft between BEA and BOAC routes would be possible under an integrated organization. Admittedly, this would be rather limited in the early stages for a number of reasons. First, as we have seen, BOAC's Boeing 707s are already highly utilized. Secondly, the two airlines operate different systems of aircraft deployment, BOAC operating a basic 'first in, first out' method, which gives at least two 'standby' aircraft to cover each departure, while BEA operates mainly by having aircraft committed to routes well in advance, with departures covered by 'permanent' standby aircraft. The need to maintain adequate standby cover on BOAC routes would reduce the scope for transfer. Thirdly, whatever spare capacity exists in either fleet may not be available at times when it could be advantageously used on the route system of the other airline. Fourthly, the possibility of transferring BEA aircraft to BOAC short stages will depend on their geographical location and also on the ability of the smaller aircraft to cope with demand at existing frequencies. These are, however, essentially short-term difficulties, which would diminish, though not disappear, as integration of scheduling began to take effect. An integrated airline would also be expected to adopt a common approach to the standby aircraft problem. In addition, we have observed the possibility that BOAC's Boeing 707 fleet may become less heavily used, while, on the assumption that recent growth rates continue, several of BEA's present European routes could well sustain *some* regular and rather more frequent 'tail-end' use of Boeing 747s by the mid-1970s. Obviously, however, the opportunity cost of using Boeing 747s in this way would have to be carefully scrutinized.

This brings us to question (iv) above, the short- and long-run potential for reducing aircraft requirements through integration. In the short-run, the merger would bring together under a single management two sets of route networks and two sets of aircraft, related capital equipment and personnel which will be relatively specific to the airline to which it originally belonged. It is perhaps doubtful whether any substantial savings would be achieved until a start had been made on operating schedules which utilized the possibilities of economy in the integrated route system that would replace two separate, specialist systems, planned independently. However, even with a given network system and given aircraft, the above discussion suggests that as schedule planning is revised to take into account the new potential for switching, it will be possible to cut the number of aircraft required to provide existing services at present frequencies, while allowing additional operating economies to be achieved. By itself that might not seem to matter greatly, since it would mean only that a small number of aircraft could be sold off in the second-hand market, the gain from which might be slight since the capital costs of such aircraft would already be largely written down. Yet in a growth market such as civil aviation, the possibility of using more fully and efficiently a given fleet of aircraft, enabling it to cope with an expansion of demand, would represent a substantial saving in capital costs even in the short run.

One of the critical factors in modern airline economics is precisely this ability to achieve high utilization rates for expensive aircraft, and while BOAC at present do well in this respect, BEA (even allowing for the generally acknowledged lower levels of utilization attainable on short-haul operations) have some margin of spare capacity, especially between the hours of 7 pm and 8 am, when roughly one-third of BEA's effective fleet is not in use. The existence of spare capacity in the aggregate over a whole fleet may of course be misleading. Some of this will be absorbed by routine maintenance and some may be explicable in terms of restrictions on night flights. Even then there is still a question whether one or more aircraft can be transferred temporarily out of the system and returned to it without disrupting that system, yet ensuring that it is out long enough to make a contribution. A working rule would be that an aircraft must be made available for eight hours at a stretch. Solutions to this sort of problem are likely only to be overcome in the medium term, when integrated scheduling is well developed, and it becomes possible to arrange schedules to satisfy the need to make spare capacity available in usable portions.

Larger gains would seem to be feasible in the longer run, for it then becomes possible to adapt both the network, and investment in new aircraft and facilities, to take advantage of the more varied system. So long as two separate systems co-exist, the total aircraft requirement is likely to be higher than under an integrated system, fully adjusted to allow for high aircraft utilization rates and substitution. The expected continuation in the growth of air travel and hence the higher density of demand on many routes is likely to increase the prospects for substitution—and we have suggested that these already exist on a scale adequate to permit *some* savings to be achieved. Nor can we reasonably expect this growth to be met by increases in frequency of service, for constraints exist in the inability of many airports to handle greater frequencies, the impracticability of switching the extra traffic wholly to off-peak services, and the disadvantageous operating cost situation when two small aircraft have to be substituted for one larger aircraft, even if the latter has to operate at a moderate load factor.

In the longer run, too, some of the problems of transition will disappear. The merging of the BEA and BOAC fleets at the present time would bring together nine main types of aircraft, which is certainly too many, and which represent different vintages of aircraft technology, requiring specialist maintenance, specially trained crews, and to some extent specific facilities. To be fully effective, the merger would have to reduce the number of aircraft types, perhaps moving towards a situation, now increasingly common in other airlines, in which one 'family' of aircraft from the same manufacturer is adopted, simplifying problems of maintenance, crew training, terminal facilities and stocking of spares. This might have serious implications for the British aircraft manufacturing industry, but would nevertheless be a highly rational policy for an integrated airline of the size envisaged.

The above arguments imply a prima facie case in favour of merger from the point of view of operating economies. At first, merger might produce relatively few economies, due to the time required to draw up an integrated scheduling programme capable of yielding the possible economies in aircraft substitution between routes. In the medium term, the introduction of interdependent scheduling over the enlarged total system would result in improved utilization of aircraft, giving benefits in terms of costs, and possibly also in revenue, due to more appropriate deployment of aircraft in relation to passenger demand. In the longer term still, when it becomes possible for new investment in aircraft, flight systems and other facilities to adapt to the new situation, there are further prospects of gain. In particular, opportunities should exist for serving an integrated system at a given standard of service and frequency with a reduced number of aircraft, compared with fleet requirements for two subsystems of the same total size but subject to independent scheduling. Greater scope would also exist for building up an aircraft fleet based on a limited number of standard types, possessing as far as possible common characteristics such as flight systems, training and maintenance; and in this way greater standardization would add to the available economies.

When these arguments are placed alongside the Edwards Committee's case for closer co-operation in certain areas, the advantages of merger appear stronger still. As matters now stand, the Government has charged the British Airways Board with the duty of exercising 'strategic control' over BEA and BOAC, and with securing 'the gains and economies which would result by treating the resources and the route networks of BOAC and BEA as a single system'.[72] The Government has thus stopped short of outright merger, though in many respects the proposed solution comes close to it, and the possibility of further action is explicitly left open.

The 1971 Civil Aviation Act, establishing the Board, specified as one of the first duties of the Board 'a review of the group's affairs for the purpose of determining whether the carrying on of the activities of the group is organized . . . in the most efficient manner'.[73] As matters now stand, most of the benefits of merger, as discussed above, are capable of being achieved. The advantage of stopping so little short is perhaps that the names of the two corporations will remain intact, which may be important for staff morale and for marketing. It may also make allowance for the Edwards Committee's fears about the 'behaviour and reactions of human beings' in such a large enterprise as would be created by this merger.

There are four points that can be made in answer to this last item. First, the size of the merged enterprise, either in employment or in assets, would not place the Corporation in the 'giant' category, and its business would be characterized by vertical rather than by horizontal integration of the conglomerate type, the economies of which are often open to question. Secondly, much will depend on the organizational form of the enterprise: provided that is adapted to the needs of the airline business as discussed above,[74] problems of bureaucracy and top-heavy administration should not be serious. On organization, too, it remains to be seen whether BEA will be relieved of some of its domestic responsibilities, leaving it only with the main trunk routes—such a step would simplify some of the problems and give a less heterogeneous route network. Thirdly, the changing attitudes of government, following the Prices and Incomes Board Report on Top Salaries, should make it more possible to secure the appropriate top and middle management expertise for an organization of this sort. And finally, it should not be forgotten (as it often is in discussions of managerial diseconomies of scale) that the technology of management is subject to innovation and development in just the same way as plant and product technology. In the airline business particularly, considerable scope exists for the application of computer technology, operational research and related techniques to the systems problems that are central to air transportation.

(b) *The Air Corporations and the Financial Objective*

Both Corporations have financial objectives, set by the Treasury in conjunction with the sponsoring department. Two questions have to be asked here. First, in view of the Treasury's own conception of the financial objective as a target which should be achieved if rational pricing and investment policies are followed, can the desired relation between pricing, investment and objective be expected to hold in the air corporations—however appropriate it may be elsewhere? Secondly, aside from this consideration, is there a role for a financial objective in the case of the air corporations which are engaged in international competition and so have to match up to standards that are not necessarily present in other nationalized industries?

The basis for the first of these questions is best stated in Treasury evidence to the Select Committee on Nationalized Industries:

> The Treasury considers that financial objectives will continue to be necessary so that the success or failure of management over a period may be assessed; but believes that it is essential that the new objectives should provide some definite guidance for the industries over their investment and pricing ... the new objectives should be a good deal more than the result of negotiations centring round a projection of recent performance. The financial objective should be a simple reflection of what the industry might be expected to achieve on the basis of:
> (a) undertaking investments which show a satisfactory rate of return or which the Government considers are justified on grounds of social policy;
> (b) pursuing sound pricing policies related to the circumstances in which individual services and products are supplied;
> (c) achieving a progressive improvement in efficiency and productivity over the target period.[75]

This statement clearly implies that the objective should be a result of sound investment and pricing procedures, as elsewhere defined, rather than being itself a target to be met by manipulation of pricing and investment.

The tenets of pricing policy in the nationalized industries were further discussed in the 1967 White Paper.[76] In the short run, the object was to be that of persuading customers to make use of spare capacity or to reduce demand where it exceeded capacity: in the long run, the basis of pricing was to be the long-run marginal cost of providing a service. Unless pricing policies were devised with reference to production costs, including replacement costs and a satisfactory rate of return on capital, there would be a risk of cross-subsidization and resource misallocation, and cross-subsidization was to be countenanced only where some wider and properly identified consideration was relevant.

On the pricing ground-rules, the Air Corporations would be expected to identify the long-run marginal cost of each of its 'operations' and to base fares on that cost: the price charged for any 'operation' should be just able to cover the addition to the airline's total costs attributable to that operation. Yet there are serious practical as well as conceptual difficulties to be encountered in the pursuit of such a policy.

On the practical side, we have seen that international fares are set by the various IATA conferences. These fares are the result of multilateral negotiations which are likely to be influenced as much by political as by purely economic considerations, and the cartel arrangement is unlikely to produce a fare structure reflecting the differing costs, technology and efficiency of the member airlines. The fact that on many routes only two airlines may be operating does not really help, for the fares on that route are normally closely related to the whole structure of fares obtaining in the traffic region, and the scope for real variation appears slight. A further complication arises from the prevalence of pooling agreements, which again make for uniformity of tariffs irrespective of cost of production differences.

Domestic fares may offer slightly better prospects, since neither the cartel nor the pooling conditions are present. But while in this context cost considerations might be made to play a greater role in price-setting, there are no real grounds for supposing that the administrative process of fixing tariffs is likely to result in fares accurately reflecting the costs of providing the service. The willingness of the ATLB to accept the principle of cross-subsidization, and the failure to explore seriously the possibility of allowing competing airlines on domestic routes to charge different fares despite their use of different capital equipment with divergent cost characteristics, would not give much ground for optimism in this connection—

though the new Civil Aviation Authority could gradually bring about changes.

From a purely practical point of view, then, it may seem quite unrealistic to embark on a discussion of the implications of pricing on the basis of long-run marginal costs, but there are some important issues for the economics of nationalization to be raised in this context. Where, for example, the relationship between prices and costs at the margin in the provision of air and alternative transport services (by road or rail) is widely divergent, resources in the transport sector will be inefficiently allocated in the sense that, say, rail services may be over-expanded compared with road or air services. Likewise, we have observed the difference in the cost–price relationship between domestic and international air fares, with the consequent cross-subsidization from the latter to the former.

While we cannot fully explore the conceptual problems in this area, it is important to indicate some of the difficulties. An immediate problem is that of defining the marginal unit itself. Four main possibilities can be identified:

(i) the incremental passenger
(ii) the incremental frequency on a route
(iii) the addition of an aircraft to the airline fleet and
(iv) the addition of a further route to the existing route system.

The change in total airline costs incurred as a result of each of these marginal changes will be different, and the problem is to know which is most relevant for the purpose of pricing policy. The first point of clarification is that in air transport the smallest effective unit of output is the plane journey. Commercial aircraft normally have upwards of fifty seats, while the norm is about twice that figure and the new generation of wide-fuselage aircraft possess seating capacity much in excess of that. As in other forms of commercial transport, the unit of pricing—the passenger journey—is not the same as the lowest unit of output. To avoid the difficulties that would arise from charging the first passenger on any flight the full cost of that flight and the remainder a zero (or almost zero) fare since they add nothing (or very little) to total costs, it will be preferable to disregard the cost changes resulting from the marginal passenger, and to take the plane-load as the lowest unit of output.

Each of the three remaining concepts of marginal cost (ii, iii and iv above) relates to different questions: will the airline derive economic advantages

(ii) from adding an additional frequency to a route;
(iii) from increasing the number of aircraft; and
(iv) from extending the route system?

Question (ii) is probably best regarded as a short-run problem, involving the rescheduling of the existing fleet, but both (iii) and (iv) involve investment decisions, and of these (iv) is likely to be the longer-term decision since it will normally require greater preparatory investment in infrastructure. On that basis we might *provisionally* adopt (iv)—the additional route—as the marginal unit of output for purposes of pricing policy. Then on the assumption that each route can be regarded as an independent unit for operating purposes (so that there is no transferability of resources between routes) the additional costs to the total route system arising from the inclusion of that route can be determined. By a simple process of averaging, it would then be possible to derive a cost per flight or per passenger on that route and this might be used as the basis for pricing.

Such an averaging process would, however, be too simple an approach, for in practice flight costs would vary and short-term imbalances of demand and supply would necessitate some form of differential pricing if peak-load problems were to be tackled and if cross-subsidization among passengers was to be minimized. There would, almost inevitably, be a need for costing exercises for individual flights to provide the basis for such differential pricing.

But there is another, more serious difficulty in this proposed solution—the assumption that each route can be regarded as an independent unit.[77] In practice this is not the case. Aircraft and personnel can be readily interchanged between routes and we have already stressed that the efficient operation of an airline network will depend on its being treated as an integrated system, within which the ability to redeploy resources in response to changing conditions will be of the utmost importance. Once this condition of interdependence is admitted, as it must be, it becomes much more difficult to identify the costs attributable to serving a particular route. Aircraft, for example, now become capital jointly shared by a number of routes and the allocating and scheduling of aircraft can no longer be planned on a route-by-route basis. Instead, the problem in the short run would have to be restated as one of determining the effect on total system costs of a very large number of possible variations in the deployment of a given quantum of aircraft and personnel. Any one change in deployment might theoretically require a complete rescheduling of flight frequencies and the reallocation of aircraft and personnel among routes, with the total cost implications having to be worked out each time for an optimal solution to be reached. In the longer run, one must move away from the conception of a fixed quantum of resources to a consideration of the effects on total system costs of changes in the volume and structure of assets—for example in the size of the aircraft fleet. In the short run the problem can be regarded as one of meeting given commitments with given resources at minimum system costs, in which case the solution lies in efficient scheduling: whereas in the long run, the problem is rather one of determining the optimal network and investing in aircraft and route infrastructure capable of servicing that network efficiently at the desired levels of frequency. Aircraft are, however, the main item, since the infrastructure costs are relatively low compared with rail, for example: this is due primarily to the absence of track costs in the airline case.

The nature of the difficulties can now be more succinctly stated. If by marginal cost is meant the change in total system costs incurred by the introduction of a new route or new aircraft to the system, the greater will be the averaging of costs over the travelling public and the greater the artificiality of the exercise as a result of departing from the interrelated character of the system. But by acknowledging interrelatedness and moving the measure of marginal output closer to the individual unit of travel (the plane journey or ultimately the passenger journey), we increasingly encounter difficulties of cost apportionment. Because of the high proportion of fixed costs over the system as a whole, it is difficult to determine how these can be systematically allocated among relatively small units of output in a way that will reflect their net impact on the system. Admittedly, this sort of problem is now much more amenable to solution with the aid of operational research and computer techniques and to some extent the airlines are already engaged in a similar kind of exercise to solve the *scheduling* problem. But a great deal of additional information would be needed if the cost consequences were to be fully assessed in the detail required for a comprehensive policy of relating prices to marginal costs in a consistent fashion. Likewise the use by the air corporations of DCF methods of investment appraisal relating to decisions such as the introduction of new routes or new aircraft must incorporate data about the effects of these changes on system traffic, costs and revenue. While that information—particularly on price elasticities of demand— may not be so refined as would be required for the objective of relating fares to marginal costs, it does illustrate the existing need for the corporations to take into account the kind of considerations mentioned above.

At this stage in the argument the institutional regulation of air tariffs again becomes relevant. The particular form taken by this regulation has until now been accepted by Government as a normal condition of the industry and there has been no apparent pressure for the Corporations to begin moving to marginal cost pricing in any explicit form. In a situation where price competition has been effectively ruled out by institutional regulation, the airlines have resorted to quality and service competition. This has normally meant that, for a given price, competing airlines have vied with one another to adapt flight frequencies and timing of flights to suit the customer, and to improve the standards of passenger service, especially in-flight service. It is quite possible in such circumstances that the pursuit of long-run cost reductions (from technological innovation, for example) might take second place to such considerations as maintaining or increasing market shares, or maximizing sales. And indeed there are signs in the international civil aviation industry that these types of objective are given much weight.

However, two main constraints set limits to this deviation from the pursuit of short-term profits. First, where the airlines face direct competition from surface operators they are normally at a cost disadvantage, while the other (non-price) advantages of air travel have been partially offset by quality improvements in surface travel. Secondly, rival airlines have commonly tried to differentiate their products by 'selling' the merits of their respective aircraft. This has been especially important when fundamentally new types of aircraft have become available: for example, when the jet-engined aircraft began to replace the turbo-prop or when the jumbo jet was introduced as a replacement for the conventional airliner of the 1960s. This appetite of the airlines for new technology, which is not always due solely to cost considerations, has undoubtedly contributed to the rate at which seat-mile costs have been reduced.

This technical form of competition, together with the cost advantage of surface transport, has assuredly offset in part, if not absolutely, the tendency of the cartelized market to pay less attention than in a freer market to the problem of long-run cost reduction. The decline in seat-mile costs in both Corporations, as the scale of activity has grown over the last decade, adds weight to this assessment, and might further be taken as a very crude indication of a declining trend in long-run average (and marginal) costs for each of the two airline systems taken as a whole. If this is so, then the expectation would be for a continuing reduction in average passenger fares where fares are related to long-run costs—aside from short-run variations in fares designed to remedy temporary imbalances in demand and supply. How far this will materialize will depend on such factors as the continued yield of cost reductions from increases in the scale of operations and aircraft made possible by advancing technology, and the extent of the airlines' desire to engage in competition in ways that make available to the air traveller the benefits of technical progress.

There is little doubt that a greater share of the benefits of available cost reductions is likely to accrue to the passenger in a more openly competitive market situation than is presently the case. The really important question here is whether, given that greater competition, the market would show greater signs of instability (in the form of wide fluctuations in fares, erratic scheduling and unreliable service, for example) that would act to the detriment of the travelling public. Historically, the main justification for public ownership (in addition to various forms of governmentally approved regulation of the industry at large) has probably been the need to provide a stable basis for a young and developing industry to which much international prestige is attributed. At present, some of this historical justification lingers on, though it is arguable that direct governmental backing of airlines is less necessary than it was even ten years ago. In the stage of development now attained, the strongest need is for a continued effort to meet, at an acceptable level of cost to the Exchequer, the public demand for various types of service that now exist, and to extend that effort in line with the natural evolution of the industry at international level. It may be that public ownership is now no longer necessary to secure this objective, or that in a competitive environment, less constrained by control of prices and capacity provision, a reduced role for the State would be practicable: the Government might for example identify certain routes as unlikely to attract fully commercial operators, but it could still set certain standards of service for these and offer them for tender on these terms, probably with a direct subsidy for the route in question.

Under such a modified system of public ownership or public intervention in the industry it would be possible to specify more closely governmental objectives in civil aviation. Such an approach would without doubt give more explicit recognition to the radically different types of business which exist within the civil aviation market, and in that respect there would be implications for pricing policy, for it would then be more feasible than at present to adopt differing approaches to pricing in the various sectors. This would be preferable to the current situation where the applicability of the Treasury rules for pricing in nationalized industries is slight, due to the rules being conceptually in advance of the techniques available for implementing them and to the irreconcilability of their practical application with the present machinery for tariff determination. In qualification of this, one interesting aspect of the recent discussion and experimentation on the question of advanced purchase fares, at substantial discounts on the standard rate, is that this may be seen as a step towards closer relations between price and marginal cost. This involves yet another view of marginal cost not yet considered, depending on the differences in cost imposed on the airline by passengers booking at different times up to the flight itself.

To meet the requirements of the 'on-demand' passenger, the airline has to plan sufficient capacity for any route to be fairly certain of meeting the demand: if it falls short, it runs the risk of turning away traffic to competitors. Almost inevitably this means excess provision on average, practically reflected in the moderate load factor achieved on scheduled operations, and the addition to total system costs on this account will usually be substantial. In contrast the IT operator is able to achieve much higher load factors and achieve savings on total costs by tailoring capacity provision to a demand that is known well in advance: in practice, planned flights not attracting adequate custom are frequently cancelled, perhaps with compensation to the disappointed passengers. That solution, by definition, is not really open to the scheduled operator.

More generally, the addition to system costs will become progressively greater the shorter the interval between booking and flight time. The greatest part of this cost will derive from the need to possess, and to commit, aircraft in advance of knowing capacity utilization, but some additional costs will also stem from the overhead expenditures attaching to the more complicated scheduling and booking apparatus required by the scheduled operator. If this is so and if there were to be developed a spectrum of fares for any route, increasing step-by-step as the flight-date approached, the result would be an increased correspondence between price and marginal cost in the sense now defined.

This need not of course mean *equivalence* of marginal cost and price, but the general shape of the relationship would be right. Many of the problems discussed earlier would still exist, of course, in that the relationships between the 'standard' fare and the cost of providing the service would have to be determined by other methods. In practical terms, too, the airlines are still some way from accepting the concept of advanced purchase fares, although one IATA conference in 1971 came close to accepting it as part of a compromise package. Clearly, however, it is a possible solution to some of the problems of fares structure, and if it does gain acceptance it will offer some scope for an approximation to one interpretation of the Treasury pricing rules.

This aspect aside, however, the overall situation is such as to suggest that it may be better if the rules are recognized for the fiction they are—in this industry at least—and to devise a system which relates to the realities of the situation, while providing the necessary safeguards against instability or socially unacceptable standards of service. The pricing problem, in short, is not in the last resort a separate issue from that of the organization of the industry and the Government's objectives for it.

We turn now to the second main question raised at the start of this section, whether there is a useful role for a financial objective in the nationalized airlines which have to compete in an international market. In terms of the nationalized industries as a whole, it is difficult to know whether a financial objective of $12\frac{1}{2}$ per cent for BOAC and 8 per cent for BEA is reasonable, and whenever the British Airways Board is given its objective the combination of the two enterprises under one organizing authority will make this problem doubly acute. However clearly the Treasury conception of the derivation of the financial objective may be set out as an expected result of 'proper' pricing and investment policies, there is no doubt that in most cases (including the airlines) the establishment of the objective does not at present proceed in that way. Little is publicly known about the way in which the financial targets actually get determined, and the evidence on this in the investigation of Ministerial control by the Select Committee on Nationalized Industries is not at all reassuring as to whether there is any systematic economic basis for fixing objectives.

Given this, we might ask whether the financial objective should not be eliminated in the air corporations' case, in favour of a systematic comparison of performance with other airlines providing similar services. Allowance would of course have to be made for differences in route structure, aircraft mix and other operational features, as well as in financial structure, the extent of State aid and the effects of State intervention on commercial behaviour.

Both Corporations are substantially engaged in an international and competitive market and are supposed to be doing so on a fully commercial basis. If the airlines compete successfully in this market without undue reliance on State assistance or protection, could that not in itself be regarded as a reasonable criterion of efficiency? If, on broadly comparable operations and with common fares, the Corporations achieve cost figures as good as, or better than, their competitors, is that not adequate evidence of efficiency?

Add to this the two following considerations. First, the Corporations do not have direct control over prices either in the domestic or international market. The prices so set are more likely to be a compromise based on average airline costs than on the costs of any individual airline, still less on any basis such as marginal costs however defined. In consequence, even if investment decisions are taken on marginal criteria, the difficulties of ever getting to a position where the financial objective would be determined as a resultant of prescribed pricing and investment rules are so immense as to render the whole principle unrealistic. Second, what would be implied by a Corporation doing very much better than just meeting its objective over the appointed period? Would it mean that the target was set too low? Was it set on wrong assumptions about costs, tariffs or traffic growth? Was the airline able to increase its efficiency beyond the most optimistic expectation? Does 'over-achievement' mean that a stiffer target should be set for the following period? The general inference from these points is that financial objectives, at least in the case of the airlines, are unnecessary or impossible to operate in any meaningful fashion.

Yet, on reflection, the arguments may not be all in one direction. While comparisons with other airlines may be instructive, the fact that, say, BOAC does better than most of its foreign counterparts does not tell us whether BOAC is efficient in anything but a relative sense, and presumably the concern in this case is one about efficiency in absolute terms—or at least about the efficiency of the Air Corporations relative to that of other public enterprise. Again, if one accepts the rationale of having such objectives for the nationalized industries in general, something may be said for applying the principle to all the industries. Much depends also on whether the objectives are viewed as a managerial tool for the airlines or as an aid to Government in the allocation of resources. On the evidence of earlier sections, the objective has *not* worked as a managerial tool.

Even so, may not the setting of such a target act as a guide to government in the allocation of public funds for investment and related purposes, for which some economic principles have to be applied? While an independent control already exists over new investment, by means of the test rate of discount and detailed scrutiny of investment programmes, a case can also be made out for some additional measure of the overall efficiency of a nationalized enterprise, taking into account its use of existing as well as newly acquired assets, and the particular circumstances of demand, technological changes and other special factors which bear on the industry's performance. Unfortunately, it is not at all evident that the measures used to state the financial objectives (for all nationalized industries) really meet this requirement, for the measures adopted are based on accounting convention rather than on economic standards of efficient resource utilization.

More generally, what are the directions in which a solution to the efficiency measurement problem might be sought? Familiarity with the many available measures of efficiency and productivity suggests that there is no unique approach. Efficiency is not a simple concept, but one which embraces complex relationships and the results of multiple activities. It seems more appropriate, therefore, to identify certain critical measures which will each relate directly to performance in areas explicitly recognized as vital to the commercial success of the enterprise. For example, in the airlines case it will be valuable to have a battery of measures (many of them already calculated) such as output per employee and per aircraft by type, costs per CTM, costs per flying hour, perhaps further subdivided by aircraft type, together with additional productivity measures in financial terms. By itself, each measure will help to answer particular questions about performance: together they add up to a varied and much more complete picture of the organization's effectiveness. Furthermore, comparisons will often be possible, both between units of the organization, and between different airlines. Comparison is only a first step, however, for the important issue is that the *causes* of different levels of performance should be thoroughly investigated. This aspect is conspicuously absent from the present form of the financial objective. Some variations may be found to be justified by real differences of function or structure but others may shed light on sources of inefficiency and misutilization of resources within the enterprise. In the international airline business, there is undoubtedly a good deal that can be done in this direction, provided the proper measures are chosen.

If the use of such 'economic' approaches to efficiency estimation could be further developed in this way as an internal managerial tool, there would still be a problem in relation to the Government's own surveillance of the industry. A solution already exists for new investment, through the procedures discussed above, although the return on new investment will depend on pricing—which we have seen to be somewhat removed from the approved principles. In the past, too, the annual investment review has involved an examination of forecasting and efficiency, as obvious complements to the appraisal of investment. While this is normal practice it is not statutory, but could well be made so in future legislation. Alternatively, a strong case may be made for having a more independent body perform this function, and here the precedent of the former National Board for Prices and Incomes is relevant. For the Board undertook, for some of the nationalized industries, very much the kind of 'efficiency audit' which is implicitly under discussion here, embracing aspects of the enterprise's performance in pricing, investment and forecasting in relation to effectiveness in the use of resources. Such a procedure would seem to provide a reasonable check on the plans and internal efficiency of the enterprise without unduly interfering with its overall commercial freedom, although as we shall now see, such a view might not be accepted by the Corporations themselves.

(c) *Government's Relations with the Corporations*

The final question is that of the relations between the Corporations and government and in particular the nature of governmental control. We shall look at this issue fairly briefly, because it is a matter more of political and administrative rather than economic significance, and because the working of the new organizational structure has not been tested at the time of writing.

The nature of the airline business brings both BEA and BOAC into direct competition with the airlines of other countries. No matter how institutionalized this competition in certain respects—or perhaps because of that—competitive forces consist largely of attempts to differentiate the product, not least by improvements in aircraft type to increase passenger appeal. Thus the ability of the airline to raise capital for frequent re-equipment and expansion of capacity, to choose freely the type of aircraft it judges the best commercial proposition for its route structure, and even its capability of influencing aircraft and flight-system design, are matters of major importance to the market prospects and long-term commercial viability of the enterprise. In the case of nationalized corporations, the nature of the control exercised by government is particularly critical.

Until the time of writing the relations between the Corporations and government have been conducted mainly by the Department of Trade and Industry (formerly the Board of Trade).[78] This Department as the 'sponsoring department' of both Corporations exercised a number of statutory functions. The formal powers of the Minister ranged from the appointment (and dismissal) of the chairman and board of the Corporations, through a series of financial and presentational matters (including borrowing and investment) to authority to issue general directives and to redefine the Corporations' powers in the national interest. In practice, however, the really important powers have been those relating to investment and procurement—although BEA felt it had been 'directed' on one occasion, over the issue of aircraft procurement in 1966.[79]

In seeking to manage their businesses on strictly commercial lines in full competition with rival airlines, the Corporations recognize the ultimate responsibility of Parliament on matters subject to statutory definition, but BEA in particular more than once expressed the view that its relations with the (then) Board of Trade were not satisfactory. The Board of Trade was a complex department with many responsibilities other than civil aviation, with the result that there was felt to be less personal contact than previously obtained under a separate Ministry of Civil Aviation. It is difficult to tell whether what really mattered was the political contact or the more detailed business contact with the civil service. The latter should not have been a problem, given the existence of a specialized civil aviation branch within the Board of Trade.

The views taken by BEA and the Department about the proper nature of their relationship were not identical. The view expressed by BEA through its Chairman in the course of evidence to Select Committee in 1967/68,[80] was that the Corporation should be allowed to manage its own affairs within the limits of borrowing voted by Parliament, with failures in management being penalized by dismissal of the chairman of the Corporation or members of his board. However, the Department of Trade and Industry, through its control over the financial affairs of BEA, was able to exert a close and continuing influence on matters which BEA regarded as virtually day-to-day management and certainly not the proper function of the 'sponsoring department'.[81] BOAC has been much less critical, possibly because of its greater freedom in the recent past to purchase American aircraft—though it should also be remembered that BOAC has been obliged by government to raise finance abroad. From the Department's point of view, detailed information was regarded as necessary if it was to fulfil its function of answering Parliamentary questions on the Air Corporations' efficiency and performance.

It remains to be seen whether matters will be improved under the new arrangements introduced by the 1971 Civil Aviation Act. The individual autonomy of the Corporations will be reduced as they come under the authority of the British Airways Board, which has the power 'to control all the activities' of BOAC and BEA and 'to give to the Corporations or either of them such directions as the Board thinks fit'.[82] The Board in turn will have to face up to some of the difficulties hitherto encountered by the Corporations, for it will be subject to direction from the Secretary of State if the national interest or other prescribed circumstances make this desirable. The Board will also have a financial objective, probably in the form of a rate of return on net assets, and will be subject to limits on borrowing powers in the same way as the Corporations individually have been.

But while, inevitably, governmental control must be expected to influence the Board's work from time to time, the replacement of the ATLB by a more powerful Civil Aviation Authority may reduce the discomfort created by surveillance from Whitehall. Certainly, it has been stated that the Authority is intended

> to relieve Whitehall of detailed regulatory and operational functions which for the most part have hitherto been carried out by Government Departments.[83]

How far this will extend to the relationships between the Aviation Authority and the Airways Board must remain a matter of speculation until the new organization becomes operational. The terms of reference of the Authority are more positive than those of the ATLB. It has to carry out its various functions in such a way as to ensure that all substantial categories of public demand for air services are provided 'at the lowest charges consistent with a high standard of safety . . . and an economic return to efficient operators', to secure that at least one major British airline other than those controlled by the Airways Board is given opportunities to participate in the provision of charter and other services, to encourage the air transport industry to increase its contribution towards a favourable UK balance of payments, and to further the reasonable interests of users of air transport services.[84]

The specific reference to efficiency and economic return suggests that the Authority is likely to investigate more deeply the economics of particular services and airline operators. This could mean either that the Corporations become subject to a *further* type of investigation, or it could mean that some of the work now done by the Department of Trade and Industry will be transferred to the Authority. On the other hand, the shift of responsibilities from the Department to the Authority in respect of such matters as navigation services, airworthiness and air traffic control must have the effect of reducing some of the problems created by the Department's wide range of interests in civil aviation and this should be beneficial.

The balance of advantage or disadvantage to the Corporations will become clear only when the Authority begins to give its own practical expression to the guidelines it has been given. In this, particular importance may attach to the interpretation placed on the responsibilities to provide opportunities for the development of British Caledonian (which must be regarded as the major airline outside the Airways Board's control) and to improve the balance of payments situation.

VI Conclusions

One of the main objectives of this discussion has been to show in what respects nationalization has influenced the Corporations in their attempts to solve their economic problems. But there is a very real question over and above this, namely whether nationalization has had a different sort of effect from that which could have been achieved by other forms of government control over industries of major public importance. In short, is there anything that has been done in the name of nationalization which could not have been done by other means of control?

The environment of the whole civil aviation industry in the United Kingdom we have seen to be one of close regulation, not only in the domestic sphere through the ATLB but also internationally through the IATA. In addition, government has considerable influence over the domestic aircraft manufacturing industry, and over the purchase of foreign aircraft. In this environment, the real freedom of action for any major airline, whether state owned or not, is likely to be limited.

It certainly *does* matter that BEA and BOAC are the major British flag-carrying airlines on short- and long-haul operations respectively. It matters that both airlines should have been firmly supported by government in advancing their views on tariffs at the appropriate conferences. Government action in negotiating air traffic rights is also vital to the Corporations. It has certainly mattered in the past—in the case of BOAC—that the Corporation could be rescued from a serious financial situation and set on a more secure financial footing (although conversely, it could be argued that had BOAC not been nationalized it might not have got into the position of attempting to expand its operations to make use of aircraft it was pressed by Government to accept).

It is not clear, however, whether these important matters would necessarily be different in the absence of nationalization. Nationalization is not a necessary condition of an airline being a designated carrier, nor of its being assured of strong governmental support in negotiations, nor even of it being rescued in the event of a financial crisis. It is arguable, therefore, that all these benefits to the Corporations could have accrued in the absence of nationalization.

On the obverse side of the coin, BOAC and BEA have both been influenced in their activities and policies by being subject to direct ministerial pressure; in the matter of aircraft procurement, for example. This pressure has not been applied by means of formal ministerial directives (as would be possible under nationalization), but has rather been exerted behind the scenes so that changes in policy have not been publicly seen as resulting from ministerial intervention through the channels offered by nationalization. Again, BOAC has been obliged to raise foreign loans to finance a major part of its investment programme, whereas a private concern would possibly have been more able to use its own dollar earnings for this purpose. In these ways, nationalization has undoubtedly made it easier for the Corporations to be 'steered' than if they had been under a different form of ownership. In fact, the occasions on which intervention has been used have been few but none the less important.

The presence of reserve powers in the hands of government is likely to have an effect on the economic performance of nationalized industry itself. From the national point of view, much may be said for having direct means of control over the economic (and, on occasion, social) policies adopted by industries. From the enterprise's standpoint, the resort to intervention, either formally or informally, may be regarded as an undesirable interference with management's views on what is in its best commercial interests. In civil aviation, both Corporations, but especially BEA, take the view that they should be allowed to follow their commercial instincts, subject to the condition that management is to be held responsible for errors. The main difficulty of this approach, which is otherwise justifiable if state corporations are to be regarded as 'fully commercial', is that by the time mistakes are discovered, the damage to the public purse may have been done and dismissal of the key figures responsible will not make adequate amends. In the last resort, the existence of reserve powers will almost certainly have an indirect influence on the behaviour of the industry.

Although the economic performance of the two Corporations has varied, they have over the last five years or so broadly achieved the objectives asked of them, though there is no certainty that these objectives are in any way 'optimal', either in the sense that they have done as well as they might for themselves, or in the sense that they have *together* produced the maximum aggregate benefit for the industry or the economy as a whole. They have, in addition to the purely financial achievement, managed to establish for themselves a reputation for technical innovation and leadership which is not always associated with public enterprise. They have also diversified into related fields such as hotels and catering, though they are not free from criticism in having been slow to follow the lead of the independents in developing the IT and charter sections of the market. In the course of the 1960s the two Corporations have managed to sort out—or have had sorted out for them—some of the problems deriving from their nationalized status and the resulting controls exercised over them, although not all these problems are fully resolved.

As for the future, much will depend on the success of the revised policy for civil aviation and the new structure of the industry. There is no doubt that the ATLB was due for replacement, not altogether for reasons of its own making and certainly in part because of the lack of confidence of the industry over its functioning. The Edwards Committee in its appraisal found sufficient reasons to believe that closer co-operation between the Corporations was necessary in the overall interest of the industry and the economy, and we have added further considerations indicating that more or less complete merger may come about under the British Airways Board. In addition, steps have been taken to tidy up some loose ends which have a bearing on the adequacy of the industry's structure in the 1970s; and from a purely structural viewpoint (including in this the ability of the industry to adapt to changing requirements and opportunities), the industry and the two major Corporations are in a much improved position in comparison with that in the mid-1960s.

There remain, however, issues of more purely commercial importance. It is yet too early to predict the long-term effect of the jumbo jet on the relation between capacity provision and demand. The consequences of this for the nature of the competition between the world's airlines, and for the future structure of air tariffs, will be critical for the financial circumstances of the airline over the next few years. In the next year or two, the advent of Concorde will require important decisions from the major long-haul airlines before the full commercial implications of supersonic commercial air travel are known. Changes in the technology of surface transport, and especially the improvement of motorway travel and the Advanced Passenger Train, will pose further problems for the airlines, this time primarily in the domestic sector where the future of regional air services is still far from clear. In the face of all this, it will be of immense importance for the Corporations, as presently constituted, to be able to secure the necessary finance for investment and to select the right mix of aircraft for their requirements. These questions underline the importance of matters discussed above: the fleet requirements of a single corporation as opposed to those of two independently operating organizations, the problem of pricing, and the nature of the control exerted either directly or indirectly by government.

There is no sign of a respite for the public sector of the British aviation industry. Although in many respects 1970 was a major watershed in the lives of the two Corporations, both from a technical and from an organizational point of view, many problems remain to be resolved, as is perhaps only to be expected in a fast-growing, technologically advanced industry. In this kind of environment, the main requirement is perhaps that the participants should be quickly adaptable to change. We have seen that this characteristic is only partly within the control of the Corporations themselves, since they must often rely on equally rapid responses to change on the part of the responsible branches of government. In the end, it may be the latter's speed of reaction, as much as the actions and policies of the Corporations themselves, which determines their success over the next decade.

NOTES TO CHAPTER 2

1. *British Air Transport in the Seventies* (Cmnd. 4018: HMSO, 1969). (Subsequently referred to as the Edwards Committee Report.)
2. *Civil Aviation Policy* (Cmnd. 4213: HMSO, 1969).
3. *The Times*, 14 September 1970.
4. This convention was the result of an international conference at which fifty-two nations were represented, the objective being to devise an international policy for civil aviation. Though failing in some of its objectives, it did establish important rules and set up the International Civil Aviation Organization (ICAO), a body which is now an agency of the United Nations, whose function is to secure continuing collaboration among countries on matters of international civil aviation.
5. S. Wheatcroft, *Air Transport Policy* (Michael Joseph, 1964).
6. Some of the arguments are more fully discussed below in the context of the two Corporations.
7. IATA is an international body comprising most of the world's scheduled airlines. One of its major activities is the organization of rate-fixing conferences for international scheduled services, and in this it serves as an inter-governmental agency.
8. Select Committee on Nationalized Industries, *British European Airways* (HC273: HMSO, 1967), p. 213.
9. *British Air Services* (Cmnd. 6712: HMSO, 1945).
10. These criteria included the applicant's competence to operate the proposed service, his experience, financial resources, equipment, organization and staffing; his insurance arrangements; the fairness of the conditions of employment offered, relative to other operators; the actual or potential need or demand for the proposed service; the extent of any likely duplication or material diversion from other services; expenditures or financial commitments incurred by the applicant or other operators; and any objections or representations made by interested parties.
11. For fuller discussion of this, see K. M. Gwilliam, 'Domestic Air Transport Fares', *Journal of Transport Economics and Policy*, May 1968, pp. 203–17; also M. H. Cooper and A. K. Maynard, *The Price of Air Travel*, Hobart Paper No. 53 (Institute of Economic Affairs, 1971).
12. For examples, see Wheatcroft, op. cit.; K. M. Gwilliam, 'The Regulation of Air Transport', *Yorkshire Bulletin*, May 1966; and the Edwards Committee Report.
13. loc. cit., p. 6.
14. For more thorough discussion of airline economics in general, see especially R. E. Caves, *Air Transport and its Regulators* (Harvard University Press, 1962, Cambridge, Mass.); Wheatcroft, op. cit.; A. H. Stratford, *Air Transport Economics in the Supersonic Era* (Macmillan, 1967); and M. R. Straszheim, *The International Airline Industry* (Washington: Brookings Institution, 1969). The Edwards Committee Report makes its own contribution, especially in chapters 6 and 7.
15. loc. cit., p. 105.

16. For fuller discussion, see pp. 95–6.
17. For further discussion, see SCNI, *British European Airways*, Annex 2 to BEA written evidence, pp. 306–8.
18. Cf. Edwards Committee Report, pp. 67–70, for fuller discussion.
19. It has been suggested that airlines with a 'star-shaped' system of routes (radiating from a central point) may have slightly higher costs than one with a more 'circular' network shape which gives rise to more flexible scheduling possibilities.
20. This view is reflected in the statement that in BEA's experience 'one gets more traffic if one maximizes one's frequencies with a somewhat smaller aircraft than one does if one is landed with too large an aircraft to fly at all the times that traffic is offering'. (SCNI, *British European Airways*, p. 17.) This does not seem to admit of the possibility of shuffling aircraft between routes according to variations in demand. In addition, there may be costs (e.g. in more frequent re-equipment) in having aircraft basically too small to cope with market growth. A further confirmation of this policy may be observed in BEA's decision to operate all domestic air services with aircraft specifically allocated to these routes, rather than use aircraft also deployed on European operations. (Reported in *Financial Times*, 7 January 1972.)
21. loc. cit., pp. 77–8.
22. Between 1966/67 and 1969/70, traffic growth measured in load ton miles grew by less than 20 per cent, compared with an average *annual* rate of growth of 16 per cent in the previous seven years.
23. This possible difficulty, from which BEA escaped, was due to the problems faced by the airline in getting the aircraft it wanted—a matter discussed more fully later in the chapter.
24 Edwards Committee Report, Table 3.4 and pp. 24–6.
25. SCNI, *British European Airways*, p. 238.
26. See BEA's written evidence to the Select Committee on Nationalized Industries. SCNI, *British European Airways*, pp. 294–5. It is however surprising that not even the trunk routes break even and part of the explanation may lie in the way costs are allocated for the purposes of making this calculation.
27. See p. 66 ff.
28. See notes to Table 2.4. The Treasury figure would almost certainly be lower than the BEA estimate.
29. SCNI, *British European Airways*, p. xxxiii.
30. *Hansard*, Vol. 768, 10 July 1968, cols. 522–6.
31. ibid., col. 526.
32. Edwards Committee Report, p. 199.
33. SCNI, *British European Airways*, Appendix to Minutes of Evidence, p. 284.
34. In the case of BEA, a distortion in costs resulting from such a decision may fail to be reflected in prices which are the subject of bilateral negotiation or of adjudication by the Licensing Board.
35. loc. cit., p. 47.
36. Section V, pp. 101 ff.

37. The following figures are typical:

Routes (London to:)	Distances from London (miles)	Normal tourist fare International	Normal tourist fare Domestic
Lille	158	£21·00	
Manchester	164		£12·90
Paris	209	£20·90	
Brussels	211	£23·20	
Tees-side	226		£14·50
Cologne	325	£29·40	
Belfast	338		⎫
Edinburgh	344		⎬ £19·30
Glasgow	348		⎭

Source: Air Transport Licensing Board, *Annual Report 1967/68* (HC417: HMSO, 1968), p. 19.
38. SCNI, *British European Airways*, p. 296.
39. British Eagle ceased trading in November 1968.
40. In February 1971 the Government announced changes in the control of minimum prices for IT holidays to resorts in Southern Europe and North Africa. For an experimental period between October 1971 and March 1972 IT prices to these resorts would be virtually free from control provided the holiday was less than 7 days, while some reduction in the minimum would also be possible for more extended holidays.
41. loc. cit., p. 22.
42. ATLB, *Annual Report 1967/68*, p. 8.
43. 'BEA plea to raise home fares fails', *Financial Times*, 12 December 1970.
44. This is BEA's own view. Sir Anthony Milward in evidence to the Select Committee on Nationalized Industries in 1967 said that 'there is only one [item] which occurs to me which possibly is not strictly commercial, though even that might be arguable, and that is the Highlands and Islands Services, a very small part of our business'. Select Committee on Nationalized Industries, *Ministerial Control of the Nationalized Industries* (HC371—II: HMSO, 1968), Vol. II, p. 281. The Board of Trade also included the services between Penzance and the Scilly Isles. SCNI, *British European Airways*, p. 286.
45. The loss in 1970/71 rose to £459,000.
46. *Civil Aviation Policy*, pp. 24–5.
47. However, the *Annual Report 1969/70* reports that 'a more advanced version of the Mark II Fleet Simulation Model is now being used by the Schedules Planning Office to test proposed aircraft cycles for the purpose of disclosing and eliminating weaknesses in the schedule that might lead to operational disruptions and impunctual operations'. (HC46: HMSO, 1970), p. 35.
48. See BEA, *Annual Report 1967/68* (HC362: HMSO, 1968). This is not of course to say that the original system was preferable.
49. National Board for Prices and Incomes, *Top Salaries in the Private Sector and Nationalized Industries*, Report No. 107 (Cmnd. 3970: HMSO, 1969). The first step towards this was taken in 1970, with an increase in the Chairman's salary to £15,000, as compared with £11,000 in 1968.
50. Edwards Committee Report, p. 25.

E

51. This scheme is discussed on p. 90.
52. Cmnd. 1337: HMSO, 1961.
53. SCNI, *Ministerial Control of the Nationalized Industries*, Vol. II, p. 197.
54. Among the most important of these are the following: the BOAC–Air India–Quantas agreement in the London–Tokyo–Australia triangle of routes: the BOAC–Quantas agreement on the 'westabout' routes from London to Australia and New Zealand (in which Air New Zealand also participates): there are also agreements with a number of other national airlines including Air Canada and several African airlines.
55. It remains to be seen whether British Caledonian will obtain rights to fly on North American routes. Early announcements after the merger indicated Caledonian's desire to enter this market, though not until 1972.
56. Fifth-freedom rights allow designated carriers of country A to pick up and set down in country B traffic destined for or originating in country C. These rights are the result of negotiation between A and B in the total context of traffic-rights exchange.
57. 'Europe' in this context refers to continental Europe.
58. BOAC is aiming at a 36 per cent share of this market by 1974, according to a statement by BOAC's chairman in April 1971.
59. For a full account, see Select Committee on Nationalized Industries, *British Overseas Airways Corporation* (HC240: HMSO, 1964), Vol. I.
60. A number of other changes cannot be ignored, however. For example, Pan Am and TWA introduced non-stop services to London from Chicago and Washington, linked up with domestic services (sometimes run by other domestic carriers) which act as feeders from cities behind these gateways themselves. The greater range of the modern jet aircraft has made possible non-stop services to Europe and the United States, including cities lying well inland. The impact of charter operators has also been mentioned above.
61. *Hansard*, Vol. 721, 22 November 1965, col. 32.
62. See BOAC *Annual Reports, 1966/67, 1967/68* and *1968/69* for comments on this. However, since 1969/70, purchases of several Boeing 707 aircraft have been made, financed in part from BOAC's own resources.
63. *British Air Services* (Cmnd. 6712: HMSO, 1945). Cf. p. 12 above.
64. *Financial Problems of BOAC* (HC5: HMSO, 1963), pp. 13–14.
65. Edwards Committee Report, p. 132.
66. *Civil Aviation Policy*.
67. For fuller discussion of these points, see Edwards Committee Report, chapter 10.
68. Cf. pp. 48–50 above.
69. Cf. p. 50 above.
70. On BOAC's figures the costs per CTM of the VC-10 (Standard and Super) are inferior and these aircraft are possibly less flexible in use over different ranges than the 707. It is also worth noting that operators on many European and US domestic services use 707s to provide some services, the proportion of capacity provided in this way sometimes exceeding 50 per cent.

71. Roughly one-sixth of BEA frequencies per week involve stages of more than 600 miles, but the point here is not the length of the flight-stage but the ability to use to advantage larger capacity aircraft.
72. Statement by Mr Michael Noble, Minister for Trade, in the House of Commons, 24 November 1970.
73. loc. cit., pp. 44–5.
74. Cf. pp. 48–9 above.
75. SCNI, *Ministerial Control of the Nationalized Industries*, Vol. II, p. 7.
76. *Nationalized Industries: A Review of Economic and Financial Objectives*, (Cmnd. 3437: HMSO, 1967), pp. 8–10. See also chapter 1 above.
77. A further difficulty of a more conceptual nature may be noted at this point. The treatment of the route as the marginal unit takes us very far from the conditions required for the valid application of the conventional welfare theorem on marginal cost pricing. The addition or subtraction of a route normally involves a major and discrete change in the output function rather than the very small change envisaged in the theorem. It is arguable that where large changes such as route additions are involved, the consequent discontinuities will render the exercise of little value either in practical or in welfare terms.
78. The Department also exercised general authority over the private sector of the industry. In addition, both the Treasury and the Ministry of Technology have had some influence on the Corporations—the former through examination of future investment programmes to ensure that they are in line with government policy for the industry and the economy, the latter through its relations with the aircraft manufacturing industry, where decisions on airframe and engine development may have important consequences for the airlines themselves. It was announced in April 1971 that this latter function was to be vested in the Department of Trade and Industry.
79. BEA was also 'directed' on an occasion in 1947 on a minor technicality.
80. SCNI, *Ministerial Control of the Nationalized Industries*, Vol. II, pp. 289–90.
81. Sir Anthony Milward, in evidence to the 1967 Select Committee, spoke as follows: 'In practice, in order to satisfy themselves that capital is required for the right purposes and ought to be approved by the Board of Trade, there is naturally a tendency to ask for a great deal of information. Sometimes we have the feeling that they ask for too much information and that through this power of approval of capital, we feel they may lay themselves open to the charge of taking powers unto themselves which take the management from the hands of the Corporation and put it in the hands of the Board of Trade.' SCNI, *British European Airways*, p. 21.
82. *Civil Aviation Act* 1971, ch. 75, p. 44.
83. Statement in the House of Commons by Mr Michael Noble, Minister for Trade, 24 November 1970.
84. *Civil Aviation Act* 1971, ch. 75, pp. 2–3.

3 THE RAILWAYS

I Introduction

The apparently inexorable decline of the railways is to many people a puzzling and dismaying feature of the twentieth century. In part this reflects a nostalgic association of the railways with Britain's industrial pre-eminence in the Age of Steam, but it also appears strange in an era which seems to worship size for its own sake that the railways, for long the symbol of large-scale organization, should have decayed rather than thrived. In view of this paradox there is a tendency to blame misconceived policies and inefficient management. It is worth emphasizing, however, although international comparisons are beyond the scope of this chapter, that railways are in deep financial trouble almost everywhere in the industrialized world. Thus, although policy or management should not be ruled out as contributory factors in the railways' decline, it is apparent that many other causes lie deep in the economic and technological structure of the railways.

For almost a century from the late 1830s, the railways held an unchallenged domination of inland transport. The coming of road competition dramatically changed this situation. Excepting the atypical circumstances of the World Wars, the railways carried their highest tonnage in 1913, their greatest number of passengers in 1920, and achieved their best profits in 1922. Now the railways carry just over 10 per cent of all tonnage, very much less than 10 per cent of all passengers, and have mounted up a net loss of some £1,700 millions since nationalization.[1] Drastic reorganization, not only of the railways themselves but of other forms of transport, has failed to halt the downward spiral. The latest attempt, the Transport Act of 1968, is also the most far-reaching, but it is as yet too early to say whether it will be successful in reversing the process.

II History

(a) *The Pre-Nationalization Period*

Many of the problems which currently face the railways have their roots deep in the past.[2] In particular, part of the legacy of the nineteenth century was the social (and for a long time legal) obligations which the railways were forced to accept as a consequence of their virtual monopoly of transport, the unsophisticated methods of costing and the elaborate and excessively rigid structure of prices (both of which were also a function of the lack of any external competitive challenge), and a system which even when it was built was too large and widespread for the available demand and duplicated far too many of its facilities. The twentieth century has further compounded these difficulties, not least because attitudes engendered in a period of monopoly were unable to change when road competition finally broke the railway hegemony. The refusal to recognize and react to a changed situation has been most culpable in railway management, of course, but successive governments and the public themselves must also bear part of the blame.

The early history of the railways was one of haphazard development with periodic building booms, reckless speculation and the amassing of great fortunes. Naturally the early trunk lines followed the main traffic flows, but the network soon developed beyond these. The capital cost of building was high, since under the procedure by which the railways had to buy land, landowners could hold out for large sums of money. Railway capital per route mile in the United Kingdom averaged £54,000 (£64,000 in England and Wales) as against £21,000 in Prussia and less than £13,000 in the United States. Thus from the early days the railways had to carry a burden of high capitalization. In some areas there was fierce competition between companies and many overlapping lines were built as much for strategic reasons in inter-company fights as for commercial reasons. The companies often showed little respect for public convenience or interest, forcing traffic to go by longer routes to keep it on their own tracks.

In other areas monopolies developed either by amalgamation or natural growth. The need for through and connecting facilities between lines was met by the creation in 1842 of the Railway Clearing House, and the co-operation thus necessitated was a considerable factor in the latter decline of competition.

The technical superiority of the railways made traders and passengers heavily dependent on them and very alert to any efforts at exploitation. Political pressure produced volumes of regulatory legislation: in all there were some 200 regulatory public Acts before 1930, a figure which takes no account of the private Acts required to build particular lines. The public Acts covered a wide variety of issues. Some were concerned with construction standards and safety; others with controlling the financial returns, organization and amalgamation of the companies; but their chief concern was the private control of a monopoly power. Gladstone's 1844 Railway Act gave the Government the option of purchasing newly formed companies after twenty-one years, but these powers were never exercised. However, less far-reaching but nevertheless extremely important controls were placed on the railways in their activities vis-à-vis the public.

Regulation of charges began with the fixing of maximum rates in the enabling Acts, but gradually became more comprehensive and uniform as a result of the anti-discriminatory Railway and Canal Traffic Act of 1854 and the appointment of a Railway Commission to implement it in 1873, and finally culminated in the years 1888–93 with the drawing up of a standard freight classification and of the fixing of schedules of maximum charges for each type of traffic. The primary criterion for charging was the value of the goods transported, not the cost of transporting them. Effective machinery for the supervision of rates and facilities came into being in 1888 when the Railway Commission gave way to the Railway and Canal Commission, with extended powers to deal with complaints and decide whether charges and services were reasonable. The Railway and Canal Traffic Act of 1894 had the effect of freezing freight charges at the existing levels, for it placed on the companies the onus of justifying any increases before the Commissioners. This meant that they were reluctant also to reduce rates, in case they were not allowed to raise them again later if circumstances changed. The freezing of existing rates also implied the continuance of built-in cross-subsidization, for it was not possible to raise rates where costs were high and reduce them where they were low, even if the companies had wished to do so.

As time went on the railways acquired other obligations of a social-service nature. The Act of 1844 had required the provision of one service a day on each line on which passengers were carried at a fare of a 0·41 p per mile, but this obligation was ended when the Cheap Trains Act of 1883 placed on the companies a general obligation to provide workmen's tickets at reduced rates, in order to encourage workmen to move from congested areas to more salubrious neighbourhoods further from their place of work. These developed into a system of return tickets at very low prices issued to those who began their journeys before an early hour in the morning. Meanwhile, suburban development around London and other large cities had induced the granting of cheap season tickets for regular daily travel. These were originally aimed at promoting traffic, but since they had the effect of producing a one-way flow at the peak period, the twentieth century inherited a position whereby traffic which cost more to carry was being carried at concession rates. As the way of life of suburban communities came to be based on cheap season tickets, what started off as legal obligations thus acquired the status of social necessities.

Rate control was only one and perhaps not the most important control on railway autonomy. By the time that road competition became significant in the 1920s, the railways had the following legal requirements from which their rivals were free:

(i) to publish their fares and charges
(ii) to carry all goods under their statutory conditions—often loosely called the 'common carrier obligation'
(iii) to afford 'reasonable facilities'
(iv) to afford facilities for the through conveyance of traffic
(v) to show no undue preference
(vi) to provide facilities for workmen and members of the armed forces at reduced rates
(vii) to submit to statutory regulation of wages and conditions of service
(viii) to submit accounts and returns in the prescribed form.[3]

It is only fair to point out that the railways often took these obligations more seriously than was strictly warranted; nevertheless until they were abolished in the 1950s and 1960s, they were undoubtedly inimical to the railways' competitive position.

Railway policies on pricing and costing were in part a consequence of their legal and social limitations. Thus it was only natural that if maximum prices were set externally under a system which prohibited discrimination and allowed apparently endless appeals against any change, the price structure would be rigid, for even if a large proportion of traffic passed under negotiated 'exceptional' rates, these in turn tended to become fixed. Furthermore, because maximum prices were based on factors such as mileage, and not on cost, which might vary greatly between routes with different densities of traffic, there was inevitably much cross-subsidization. Yet in part their policies were a result of the monopoly situation. There always was a monopoly in those towns served only by a single company, and as the nineteenth century wore on competition over duplicated routes diminished as amalgamations between both complementary and competitive companies produced ever larger groups.[4] Thus there was little need for the companies to consider the revenue of each service in relation to the cost of operating it. There were, as there still are, obvious difficulties in calculating specific costs due to the high proportion of fixed costs, but it tended to be too easily assumed that calculations could not be done. If the company's total revenue exceeded total cost by a satisfactory amount, however, this was considered a sufficient test of economic efficiency.

This widespread averaging of prices and lack of interest in cost categories cost the railways dear with the onset of road competition. It was ironical that the standard freight classification resulting from the 1921 Railways Act, which was based on the value of the commodity carried and an assumption of continuing railway monopoly, should be introduced in the same year, 1928, as a Royal Commission was appointed to examine the implications of road competition. Although by no means the whole reason for the growth of road transport could be blamed on the railways' charging system, the system made undercutting easy for the road interests. By charging according to the cost of carriage, which their small-scale, flexible nature enabled them to do, road operators could take over those traffics for which the railways were charging far too much in relation to cost. The fact that the railways had to publish their charges was a further aid to the road haulier.

Since the pricing systems of rail and road did not have the same basis, competition between them did not ensure that traffic was carried by the most economical means. The railways lost some traffic which they could have carried more cheaply in real terms had they matched their cost advantages in handling bulk traffics over long distances by suitable charges. They also retained much traffic which it did not pay them to carry, particularly the short-distance station-to-station goods transported in less than full wagon loads, and the carriage of passengers in stopping trains.

A third problem originating in the nineteenth century and exacerbated by the coming of road competition was the question of surplus or duplicated capacity. As road took over part of the railways' traffics, the amount of surplus capacity on the railways grew, producing a very low overall utilization of their assets.

By the end of the 1860s the basic framework of the British railway system was complete. What was built thereafter tended to have less economic justification, although, for instance, the extension of the suburban networks around the large cities was clearly necessary. But excess capacity also existed where competing main lines had been built or where company boundaries existed, and particularly where each company had its own facilities. A classic example was Carlisle, where seven different companies built nine different freight depots and marshalling yards, thus necessitating a good deal of intricate manoeuvering and delay for through traffic. Once such facilities had been established, rationalization tended, at least until recently, to be postponed indefinitely. Part of the difficulty, of course, was that there were no accurate costs of the inefficiency which duplication and excess capacity caused.

The experience of the First World War, during which the railways were centrally run by the Railway Executive Committee comprising the general managers of the ten largest companies, convinced railwaymen and politicians that considerable economies of scale were available through further amalgamation.[5] In the immediate postwar years, moreover, profitability dropped almost to vanishing point because charges were frozen while wages were rising, and this provided an additional reason for a radical reshaping of railway structure. Hence, after nationalization of the system had been rejected, the 1921 Railways Act brought into existence four new groupings out of the 120 separate companies then extant. Had this been done half a century earlier many of the worst problems of duplication and excess capacity might have been avoided which is not to say that many anomalies did not remain after the Act.

When the railways were faced with road competition in the 1920s, their reaction was largely defensive. Capital was short, since the companies in the inter-war period never managed to earn the 'standard revenue' which the new pricing structure had been expected to achieve, and there was consequently little investment—little of which was in new methods of operation.[6] Changes in the pricing structure under the 1921 Act merely produced still more millions of 'exceptional' rate reductions to compete with the road hauliers. It would be wrong to say that there was no attempt to re-examine the role of the railways in this period; indeed there was a good deal of heart-searching, but the solutions were not able to provide panaceas. One response was to buy into road operations, with the result that the railways were by far the biggest road hauliers and bus operators by the outbreak of the Second World War, although in the first category their holdings were a small proportion of the total and concentrated in the ancillary function to rail of collection and delivery. Another response was to appeal for their road competitors to be given similar legal obligations. This question was examined by the Royal Commission on Transport, 1928–30. The result was the Road Traffic Act of 1930, which created a bus licensing system, and the Road and Rail Traffic Act of 1933, which created a goods haulage licensing system. Both of these Acts will be examined more fully in the two ensuing chapters although it needs to be noted here that they did little to improve the position of the railways. Yet the primary question put to the Royal Commission, which was how best to co-ordinate transport, elicited no practical suggestion. This was scarcely surprising, since in the context, how to 'co-ordinate' meant how to save the railways from competition with rivals more flexible, more up to date, and frequently offering both better prices and better quality. One last point about the inter-war period is that in 1938/9 the railways, in the 'Square Deal' campaign, reversed their position that road transport should have legal constraints, and themselves requested freedom from legal obligations, but although the Government of the day accepted this view, the Second World War prevented such a change.

(b) *The Railways in the Post-War Period*

During the Second World War, the railways, already suffering from net disinvestment in the inter-war period, were strained to the utmost by the war effort. Although they performed extremely well both financially and in amounts carried, their physical condition was very poor by 1945, and it was clear that large amounts of money needed to be spent on modernization. The only obvious source of this finance was the State itself in spite of the money accumulated in the arrears of maintenance funds set up by the wartime agreement.

For this reason, nationalization might have been necessary whatever the Government, but the election of a Labour Government made it certain. Public ownership of the basic services had long been Labour Party policy. But equally important, integration was the keynote of the Labour Party's transport policy, based on Herbert Morrison's successful creation of the London Passenger

Transport Board in 1933. Integration, it appeared, could only be achieved by common ownership, which meant state ownership. The Transport Act of 1947 therefore brought not only the railways, but also long-distance road haulage, parts of road passenger transport, London Transport Board, the Inland Waterways, and many docks and harbours under a new overland body, the British Transport Commission, which was to have five Executives for day-to-day operating. The BTC was envisaged as a policy-making and strategic planning body, but in practice much of its time was spent on day-to-day decisions.

Little attention, however, was given to the nature of integration or how it was to be achieved. There seems to have been some feeling that nationalization would do it automatically. In effect this problem was handed by the Government to the BTC. Moreover, during the passage of the Bill, two changes fatal to the success of freight integration of any administrative kind were permitted by the Government. In the first place users were to be allowed to choose their mode of transport, and second, traders' own account lorries were excepted from coverage. The rapid growth of own account transport in the immediate post-war period was a logical consequence of these decisions.

If the Government gave little guidance on the economic principles to be followed in integration, the Conservative Opposition did not pursue this point either since it was preoccupied with the question of compensation for the railway and other shareholders. Eventually, for the public companies, Stock Exchange valuations in the immediate post-war period were used as a base. However fair this might have been, it meant that because the future earning capacity of the railways in particular was not reflected in a valuation which primarily resulted from their good war-time performance, the BTC was over-capitalized and overburdened with interest payments.

The Act laid down as an operating objective the provision of 'efficient, adequate, economical, and properly integrated' transport. As a financial objective the BTC was told to ensure that its revenue was sufficient to meet all expenses properly chargeable to revenue, taking one year with another. Although this clearly meant that the Commission was to break even, the time period involved and the items chargeable to revenue were not made explicit. Nor was there any injunction that each separate part should break even; indeed the concept of integration almost inevitably involved some cross-subsidization, and this in practice meant cross-subsidizing the railways from the profits of the other operations. Finally, no guidance was given in the eventuality that the operating objective conflicted with the financial objective, as rapidly proved to be the case.

A last point about the Act concerns its protection for the consumer against any arbitrary actions of the new monopoly. New bodies, the Transport Users Consultative Committees, were set up on an area basis but, much more unfortunately, the whole paraphernalia of legal regulation over both road and rail transport was left in existence, although the BTC was excused from haulage licensing. Of particular importance was the maintenance of the Railway Rates Tribunal, although its name was changed to the Transport Tribunal and its functions widened. All railway schemes for charging had to go through this body, with rights of objection to anyone adversely affected.

In its early years, the BTC tried to work out means of integrating the various services, in spite of its preoccupation with immediate problems. The price mechanism was the logical way of doing this, so the Commission set in action a review of both passenger and freight prices on the railways. To try to further commercial and technical integration it also initiated an experiment in common road-rail services in East Anglia. However, the Road Haulage Executive argued that if it was to provide profits for the BTC, it should not be further interfered with in the name of integration, and this undoubtedly retarded any move to integration. In any case, before integration could show any results, the 1951 election brought the Conservatives back into power. It was rapidly made clear that the notion of co-ordination through physical integration was to be replaced by 'co-ordination through the interplay of natural forces', and that the trend towards increased centralization was to be vigorously reversed. The Transport Act of 1953 abolished all the Executives except London Transport, denationalized much of the road haulage, and set up six Area Boards to administer the railway system. Though the Commission retained central control over major policy questions, the Area Boards were to formulate policy at the area level under a theory which might be called competitive emulation. It was also hoped to produce regional accounts, but this proved impractical due to the high proportion of traffic which moved between regions. In practice, moreover, decentralization meant some waste of money and development work through regional variations in equipment, and the central functions tended to be overshadowed.

The other important provision of the 1953 Act was to free the railways from some of their onerous legal burdens. The obligations to avoid undue preference and to publish rates were abolished. Standard charges as laid down by the 1921 Act were also abolished, and replaced by maximum charges, below which complete flexibility was to be allowed. However, the Transport Tribunal retained jurisdiction over the maximum charges, and the right of appeal was also maintained. Thus although the Act permitted a general move towards bringing prices more into line with costs, some bureaucratic control was left, which made itself felt in the difficulties and delay experienced by the railways in getting their freight and passenger charges schemes accepted and implemented. Consequently, cross-subsidization continued to be the major feature of both freight and passenger operations.

Having, as they thought, resolved the problems of competition and organization, the Conservatives next turned to the railways' need for investment. It has been estimated that there was a net disinvestment in the railways of some £440 millions between 1937 and 1953, largely because of the growing average age of the capital assets.[7] The ability of the railways to offset rising costs by greater productivity had been greatly hampered by the low priority given to railway investment in the early post-war period. In 1955 the Transport Commission, encouraged by the greater availability of capital, put forward its Modernization Plan with an estimated total cost of £1,240 millions. Its aim was fourfold: Improvement of track and signalling to make possible faster speeds, replacement of steam by diesel and electric traction, modernization of passenger rolling stock and stations, and remodelling of freight services using up-to-date braked rolling stock and modernized depots. The Government accepted the plan enthusiastically without checking it in any detail and without enquiring whether the proposals, most of which had been originally put forward in the 1930s, were suitable for the changed transport conditions of the 1950s.

The plan soon ran into considerable difficulties. Successive reappraisals by the Ministry of Transport and the Commission in 1956 and 1959 revealed that the real capital cost was likely to be considerably higher than anticipated and the benefits considerably delayed. In part this was due to technical factors such as the difficulty in getting enough qualified staff to draw up and carry through the detailed plans, or lack of experience in diesel operation which led to too many types of locomotive being ordered experimentally, or difficulties in finding a suitable form of continuously braked wagon to replace the mass of unbraked stock. But it was also due to poor forecasting of traffic trends and price rises, and most of all to the arbitrary and global nature of the original estimates.[8] The Select Committee on Nationalized Industries, in its report on the railways published in 1960, had some serious criticism of the plan. It commented with acerbity: 'There is indeed some difference in tone between the Government's greeting of it at the time as "a courageous and imaginative plan" and a Treasury view of it, recollected in tranquillity, as being "... merely a hotchpotch of the things that the Commission was saying it was desirable to achieve by 1970, ill-qualified and not really readily explainable".'[9] The Committee was particularly critical of the decision to go ahead with the main-line electrification between London and Birmingham, Manchester and Liverpool, without making a comparison of net returns with those of the alternative policy of dieselization; and on the basis of an estimated net return which appeared to be unduly low even if calculated on the most favourable basis. Worst of all the Committee discovered that of the £161 million estimate for this scheme, £48 million were classified as replacement, on which the BTC did not consider it necessary to earn any rate of return at all.

As the Modernization Plan ran into trouble, the financial problems of the railways became increasingly prominent. In 1956 there was an operating deficit for the first time, although only in one year, 1952, had the railways also covered their full share of the BTC's central charges. The recession in 1958, which badly affected the heavy industries on which rail freight largely depended, caused the operating deficit to reach almost £50 million, and although the trend was temporarily broken the following year, the three years 1960–62 each added almost £20 million to the operating deficit, so that in the last of these years it topped the £100 million mark. The burden of central charges was also mounting, although fairly slowly since the interest charges on the capital for the Modernization Plan were defrayed when the Government passed the Transport (Railway Finances) Act, 1957. This Act also permitted the Minister to defray interest on the current deficit, but since it was limited to a total of £250 million it was only a temporary expedient, although one which had to be extended.

By the late 1950s it was clear that railway hopes of a return to viability would not be soon fulfilled, a judgement which was confirmed by the highly critical report of the Select Committee on Nationalized Industries in 1960. The Government therefore set up a special advisory group, the Stedeford Committee, whose outcome was a White Paper recommending a drastic reorganization of nationalized transport.[10] In turn, the White Paper led to the Transport Act of 1962.

The 1962 Act completely reversed the 1947 concept of administrative integration by breaking the BTC into five autonomous transport bodies. The British Railways Board, which inherited the railways, was given the financial task of breaking even as soon as possible. To help in this all remaining legal restrictions on the railways such as those associated with common-carrier status and those relating to maximum charges, were removed, with the exception of Transport Tribunal control over London fares and protection for coastal shipping, and there was also a considerable financial reconstruction. The liability to cover Exchequer deficit grants, already defrayed by the 1957 Act, was expunged. A further £700 million of railway capital were placed in a suspense account. Although this saved the railways around £40 million a year in interest charges, the £850 million of capital left still meant that the BRB would be liable for some £50 million annually. A last financial provision was that the Minister of Transport was empowered to make grants of up to £450 million until the railways broke even.

Just as important as the legislative changes made by the Transport Act was the appointment of Dr Richard Beeching as Chairman of the BTC from June 1961 and of the BRB from January 1963. Dr Beeching's name rapidly became synonymous with that of the railways. It is easy to exaggerate both the credit and the blame which have often been heaped upon him, since many of the ideas and actions with which he became associated had in fact been mooted before his arrival; nevertheless, he made a vital contribution by forcing the pace and impressing the railway dilemma on a suspicious public. From the first Dr Beeching made it clear that commercial principles would be paramount in the running of the railways, and that the confusion between social and commercial obligations under the previous regimes, which had been so strongly criticized by the Select Committee on Nationalized Industries, should be ended.[11] He also set in motion a comprehensive study of the various traffics in an attempt to define the railways' future role, and to discover which services paid their way and which made losses. Previous attempts at this latter task, such as that presented to the Select Committee, had been in only the most general terms.

The main results of this exercise were published in March 1963 as *The Reshaping of British Railways*, while a further document, *The Development of the Major Railway Trunk Routes*, was issued in February 1965. The fundamental analysis is best presented in the words of the Reshaping Report itself, and is worth quoting at length:

Railways are distinguished by the provision and maintenance of a specialized route system for their own exclusive use. This gives rise to high fixed costs. On the other hand, the benefits which can be derived from possession of this high-cost route system are very great.

Firstly, it permits the running of high capacity trains, which themselves have very low movement costs per unit carried. Secondly, it permits dense flows of traffic and, provided the flows are dense, the fixed costs per unit moved are also low. Thirdly, it permits safe, reliable, scheduled movements at high speed.

In a national system of transport we should, therefore, expect to find railways concentrating upon those parts of the traffic pattern which enable them to derive sufficient benefit from these three advantages to offset their unavoidable burden of high system cost. In other words, we should expect the provision of railways to be limited to routes over which it is possible to develop dense flows of traffic, of the kinds which lend themselves to movement in trainload quantities and which, in part at least, benefit from the speed and reliability which the railways are capable of achieving. Moreover, we should expect that, having been concentrated upon traffics matched to the advantageous feature of rail transport, the system would then be operated so as to develop these features to the full.[12]

There were many important aspects of the Beeching Plan, a number of which will be illustrated in other sections of this chapter, but two stood out. The first was the imaginative way in which freight was to be treated. Rather than depending on rationalizing and improving marshalling, which had been the traditional way of making the railway freight service more efficient, Dr Beeching proposed drastically to reduce marshalling, either by persuading traders to send their consignments in full trainloads, or by the novel method of setting up container bases between which liner trains would run at high speeds. The second, and much more publicized, aspect of the report was the proposal for a drastic cutback in services, particularly on the passenger side. Working from the finding that one-third of the route mileage carried only 1 per cent of the passenger traffic in terms of passenger-miles, and that one-third of the stations produced less than 1 per cent of the total passenger receipts, Dr Beeching proposed to withdraw over 400 passenger services and close over 2,000 stations and 5,000 route miles. The 'Trunk Routes' Report took the reduction in under-utilized capacity a stage further by picking out certain routes for development from the 5,000 miles of trunk routes which were duplicated.

The Reshaping Report was a radical document which attracted widespread criticism, partly of its dubious statistical basis, but mainly because it appeared to go too far, although some economists thought it did not go far enough.[13] The main criticism naturally arose from the passenger closures, and the social consequences for the fairly large parts of the country which would be left without railways. The report acknowledged the conflict of social and commercial considerations, but stuck to its basic conclusion that the country would be better served if each mode of transport carried out that role for which it was best fitted. Buses, it was pointed out, could be profitable with only about one-tenth of the passenger throughput required by a train.[14] This in no way mollified the opposition, and every threatened small town fought with all its strength to prevent its services from being taken from it. In spite of the fact that the cumbersome closure procedure was speeded up by the 1962 Transport Act, delays of three years were by no means unknown, during which a great deal of the railways' scarce managerial time and effort was spent in processing the submissions. Most closure requests succeeded, but their unpopularity grew rather than diminished. The political pressure, in fact, became too great, and the reprieve of the Central Wales, Inverness–Thurso and Inverness–Kyle of Lochalsh lines in mid-1964 signified that even the Conservatives were unwilling to implement the full logic of the report.

Difficulties over the implementation of the reshaping plan did not occur only in the area of passenger closures. There were also problems with the plans for freight, where rationalization could not be carried out as speedily as had been hoped although great improvements were made. Above all, however, the financial expectations of the report did not ensue. The report had cautiously noted that: 'If the whole plan is implemented with vigour, however, much (though not necessarily all) of the Railways' deficit should be eliminated by 1970.'[15] But this target never looked likely to be achieved. After a reduction in the losses in 1963 and 1964, resulting in large part from the provisions of the 1962 Act and the high level of business activity, the losses began to mount again, as can be seen in Table 3.1. It thus became clear that even the Beeching solution was not sufficiently radical for the railways.

(c) *The Transport Act 1968*

The Beeching philosophy was not given long in which to prove itself, since only a year after the publication of the Reshaping Report the Labour Party was returned to power, committed to a new national plan for transport which would introduce a 'new deal' for the railways. As its White Paper dealing with the railways said: 'The evolution of a new policy for the railways has been at the centre of the Government's whole transport planning.'[16] Dr Beeching himself was rather cursorily offered a post as chief advisor in the reconstruction but, lacking the executive mandate he had previously enjoyed, he declined and left the BR with a life peerage in May 1965. The plan was unfolded in a series of White Papers and then in the Transport Bill, which after much controversy finally became law late in 1968. A fuller analysis of its rationale and background will be given in chapter 6, which deals with overall transport policy, so that here it will only be necessary to detail the major changes which directly affected the railways.

In the financial sphere the Transport Act introduced a major reconstruction reducing the BRB's capital debt from £1,562 million to £365 million. This latter figure had little or nothing to do with the actual value of the railway assets, but merely provided an arbitrary figure for a capitalization which appeared realistic for achieving the primary financial objective, which was stated to be full self-sufficiency. By this was meant that the deficit grants would cease and that future shortfalls in revenue must be made up from the railways' own depreciation provisions. With two major capital reconstructions within a decade, the railways thus finally escaped from the incubus laid on them in 1947.

With respect to freight traffic, a major organizational change was made by the detachment from the railways of two major divisions, Sundries and the Freightliner service, both of which were moved to a new body, the National Freight Corporation, although the BRB retained a 49 per cent interest in the Freightliner service to encourage investment in the rail part of the operation. The railways were therefore left only with the task of selling the trunk haul of freightliner containers and sundries to NFC on a commercial basis. The detachment of the two divisions meant that the railways lost all their road vehicles, and would henceforth have to contract with the NFC or other firms for the collection and delivery of wagon-load or parcels traffics.[17] The relationship between the BRB and the

NFC was thus distinctly complex, with each Corporation being each other's customer, supplier, competitor and partner. On the other hand a major provision of the Act, although one which will not now be implemented, gave the BRB or the NFC the right to bid for certain goods consignments which would otherwise go by road, the objective being unashamedly to transfer goods to rail. This was the so-called quantity licensing procedure.

On the passenger side, a long-advocated distinction was made for the first time, between economic and social responsibilities or, put another way, between the commercial and the non-commercial sectors of the business. A proportion of the new route mileage was recognized as having little or no economic justification, but since social considerations made the continuation of services necessary, the Government would subsidize such routes directly.[18] The initial list of grant-aided lines, issued early in 1969, covered 222 services for a total cost of £61 million, and the same financial grant was also made in 1970. The services covered went well beyond the Reshaping Report, amounting to virtually the whole passenger network outside the inter-city services, and not a few of the latter were also included.

Finally, sundry other pieces of assistance were given to the Board. A grant was supplied to pay for the maintenance of surplus track and equipment or 'stand-by capacity', pending its elimination. The case for reduction was recognized in the Trunk Routes Report of 1965, but has taken a long time to implement due to the need for a concomitant rationalization of other assets. The grant, £15 million in 1969, will be progressively reduced until ended in 1974. The railways were also absolved of responsibility for road-bridge maintenance and promised compensation in respect of their subventions to bus operators for providing services after rail withdrawal.

Finally, one significant change which was not directly part of the Act, but which was very closely associated with the philosophy behind it was the decision to stabilize the route mileage, the most important single determinant of the system size, at around 11,000 miles instead of the 8,000 miles which the Reshaping Report seemed to imply. The new figure was down somewhat from the route mileage of 13,200 at the time when the stabilization was first announced in March 1967, but it was an integral part of the rejection of the Beeching philosophy.

This very brief outline does less than justice to the significance of the Act, which has radically affected every operation, cost and decision on the railways. The complete reversal of the past can perhaps best be seen in the 1969 and 1970 financial results in Table

3.1, since the railways made a profit for the first time since 1953. But to go any further at this point would anticipate the economic analysis of the forthcoming sections.

TABLE 3.1
Railway operating results selected years 1913–70
£ million

	Receipts	Expenditure	Operating results	Centrally allocated charges	Interest	Net receipts
1913	119·8	75·7	*			44·1
1920	238·9	232·0				7·0
1938	164·7	137·7				27·1
1948	346·3	322·5	23·8	31·9		−8·1
1949	335·7	325·1	10·6	34·2		−23·6
1950	351·3	326·1	25·2	36·2		−11·0
1951	348·9	351·6	33·5	33·6		−0·3
1952	416·3	377·7	38·7	35·1		3·6
1953	434·7	400·1	34·6	37·4		−2·0
1954	449·3	432·9	16·4	38·3		−21·9
1955	453·9	452·1	1·8	40·1		−38·3
1956	481·0	497·5	−16·5	41·2		−57·7
1957	501·4	528·6	−27·1	41·9		−69·0
1958	471·6	519·7	−48·1	42·6		−90·7
1959	457·4	499·4	−42·0	42·8		−84·8
1960	478·6	546·2	−67·7	45·2		−112·9
1961	474·7	561·6	−86·9	48·0		−134·9
1962	465·1	469·1	−104·0	52·1		−156·1
1963	525·2	599·0	−75·8		58·1	−133·9
1964	530·9	593·4	−62·5		58·4	−120·9
1965	530·6	602·1	−71·5		60·9	−132·4
1966	527·5	598·0	−70·5		64·2	−134·7
1967	506·5	593·0	−86·5		66·5	−153·0
1968	529·1	609·2	−80·1		67·3	−147·4
1969	611·2	555·0	56·2		41·5	14·7
1970	658·3	606·6	54·7		42·2	9·5

Notes: 1. The data are not corrected for changes in the price level.
2. Expenditure for the years 1913–38 refers to total expenditure; thereafter it relates to working expenses. Depreciation in the period 1913–38 is based on replacement cost, whereas post-nationalization a change was made to historic cost depreciation for all movable assets.
3. Central charges are estimated as 70 per cent of the BTC's total central charges for the period 1948–62, although this figure admittedly hides changes in the balance of the Commission's activities. These did not include, for the period 1957–62, interest on accumulated railway losses, nor interest on borrowing for capital expenditure for the period 1957–60.
4. The basis of calculations was changed in 1963 when the BRB was formed. It includes the ships, hotels and other activities taken over with the railways, whereas previous returns relate only to the mileage.
5. Considerable changes in the financial structure of the railways were made in the 1968 Transport Act. These are detailed in the text, and the results for 1969 and 1970 can only be seen in the context of the Act.
Sources: Railway Returns 1913–1938, BTC *Annual Reports* 1948–1962, BR *Annual Reports* 1963–1970.

III Demand

The demand for transport is almost entirely derived: transport is desired not for its own sake but to achieve some other object, that of taking people or goods from one place to another. In view of the myriads of people, places and goods, demand is highly varied but also highly specific; it is little use providing services where goods or people do not want to go. Yet the initial infrastructure costs at least of surface transport are very high indeed and not lightly undertaken, and the assets once established may exist for decades if not centuries. Moreover, there are few alternative uses for the assets once created. This relative inflexibility of transport supply, to which the railways are particularly prone, means that shifts in demand either for transport as a whole over a specific route or as between modes of transport may produce great imbalances between supply and demand. Given the long time period of gestation on the supply side and the volatility of individual demand decisions on the other, it is thus hardly surprising that transport services are rarely if ever in equilibrium.

A simple assessment of the demand for rail transport shows that far from sharing in the general expansion of the post-war period the railways have lost much of their traffic. In the last pre-nationalization year of 1947, the railways carried 1,076,667,000 passengers and 294,148,000 freight tons; in 1970 the figures were 823,867,000 passengers and 198,992,000 freight tons.[19] Moreover the relative decline of the railways as a means of transport has been very much faster than the absolute decline since the demand for inland transport as a whole has expanded at a rate of about 3 to 4 per cent per annum.

Several trends have been adverse to the demand for railway services over the decades since the expansion of motorized road transport. The first is movement from public to private transport, or more accurately from transport operated in order to provide a public service to transport operated for the owner's own purpose. This has been particularly noticeable in passenger transport where the private car now accounts for more than 70 per cent of all journeys, but it has also played a part in the transfer of freight from rail to road, particularly in the period following the Second World War, when own account transport fleets mushroomed.

A second move has been from price to service as the major factor in transport decision-making. Another way of putting this is to say that there has been a disproportionate increase in the significance of the intangible and often subjective elements in the transport decision at the expense of the overt element, namely the price. On the passenger side, there is a high income elasticity of convenience, which means that although people may have to pay a high price for ownership of a car, many are no longer content to take a walk of several minutes to the station or bus stop and then possibly have to change again before reaching their destination. On the freight side also road transport can generally be much more flexible than rail, giving a door-to-door service without transhipment. Reliability, availability and speed are other elements of service for which the railways have acquired a poor image in comparison with either private or public road haulage.

A third unfavourable factor has been the location of industry and to a lesser extent of population. Whereas at the turn of the century industry tended to be located on railway lines for the sake of the available transport service, industry now tends to favour sites for other reasons, of which trunk-road accessibility is important. Few factories are built on rail sidings today. Although this preference is more a result than a cause of the loss of rail traffic it has had an accumulative and reinforcing effect on the disadvantages of rail transport. The dispersal of population into suburbs, although it does have some favourable effects for the railways by necessitating longer journeys to work, has had an adverse effect in that the local station is likely to be less convenient and the journey itself more complex.

The fourth trend has been that those industries for which rail is particularly suited as a means of transport by virtue of their high-volume bulk transport requirements have either declined, or have grown more slowly than the rest of the economy, while industries with characteristics suitable for road transport have grown very much more quickly.[20] The rail-oriented heavy industries have also taken steps to reduce the transport component of their total costs. A factor closely associated with industrial structure is the relatively slow rate of economic growth in Britain since the war, at least by comparison with other countries, which has contributed to rail's difficulties by its disproportionately adverse effect on the heavy industries.

In addition to these broad tendencies which have in general been outside the control of the railways, other factors internal to the railways have undoubtedly contributed to the decline of demand. The technical efficiency of the railways has been poor in many respects, partly through lack of modernization, but also through misapplication of investment and an inability to rid the railways of surplus capacity. Another critical internal factor has been the costing and pricing policies of the railways whereby the pattern of demand has been distorted because the price charged has frequently borne little relation to the cost of the service. A third disadvantage, intangible but real, has been the relatively poor public image of the railways, which has sometimes magnified the faults of the railway out of their correct perspective, with consequent loss of patronage. It is obviously impossible to attribute weights to the external and internal factors causing the decline in demand, but from the similar financial plight of railway systems in almost every country in the world, it is apparent that those factors beyond the control of the railways have played a significant part.

In addition, the railways have been caused further difficulties by the almost complete inability to forecast the rate of decline. Every examination of the railways has foreseen a much more optimistic future than has actually transpired. There has thus been a high cost in capacity which has been under-utilized and investment which has brought little return. The railways, again, are not solely at fault. Transport statistics, particularly of road transport, have been notoriously bad as a tool for policy and the Ministry of Transport has until the very end of the 1960s played almost no role in coordinating demand forecasts. The Hall Report of 1963 was the first attempt to examine the future transport needs of Britain, and it had to admit wide latitude for error, largely because of the uncertainties surrounding private transport.[21] It was also conditioned by non-economic considerations. It refused to extrapolate the prevailing railway trends because this would have meant the disappearance of general goods traffic from the railways; instead, it assumed that the railways would maintain at least their 1960 level of traffics. The exercise, in other words, contained a large element of wishful thinking and is another indication of a general refusal to face the harsh reality of decline before Beeching finally did so.

In order to appreciate the problems of demand for the railways, it is necessary to look at the various separate markets in which rail competes and its advantages and disadvantages within those markets. Freight and passenger transport have very different characteristics, but even within them there are recognizable subsectors, albeit ones which shade into one another, inside which the balance of advantage for the competing modes of transport varies greatly. Moreover, the problem sectors have changed over time. Thus when the Select Committee on Nationalized Industries examined the railways in 1959/60, much of the blame for the poor financial position of the railways was placed on passenger traffic and particularly pricing methods.[22] In the last few years, however, the emphasis has shifted to the problems of freight transport, since the viability of passenger operations was improved by the Beeching reforms and more recently by the social subsidies available under the 1968 Transport Act. Our first concern, therefore, will be with the problems of railway freight.

(a) *Freight Transport*

The total market for inland freight transport as it was in 1970 is laid out in Table 3.2. The rate of increase in the market in the postwar period has been just over 3 per cent per annum in tonnage terms and just under 2½ per cent per annum in ton-mileage terms (more exact growth rates are not calculable because the data for road transport are based on small samples and are far from reliable). The disparity in these rates of growth has been detrimental to rail, since the faster rate of growth of tonnage than ton-mileage has meant a lower average length of haul.

TABLE 3.2
Inland freight transport in 1970

Mode	Tons (million)		Ton-miles (million)		Average length of haul (miles) (*1967*)
Road	1670	(85%)	50,800	(61%)	30
Rail	205	(11%)	16,400	(20%)	70
Coastal shipping	48	(2%)	14,200	(17%)	200
Pipelines	47	(2%)	1,800	(2%)	35
Inland waterways	6		100		15
Total	1,976	(100%)	83,300	(100%)	—

Source: Annual Abstract of Statistics, 1971, Table 237. The figures for average length of haul are taken from *The Transport of Freight*, Cmnd. 3470, 1967, p. 24.

As can be seen, road transport is the predominant carrier, and most of the analysis will therefore be directed at the competition between road and rail. But other modes should not be forgotten. Coastal shipping is particularly important, since it carries 17 per cent of all ton-mileage, or only slightly less than the railways, and more importantly, its average length of haul is 200 miles. Furthermore, although few statistics are available, it would be surprising if the characteristics of the loads it carries are not suitable for the trainload traffics which offer economies of scale to the railways. Yet the railways have made little challenge for these traffics, partly no doubt as a result of legislation protecting coastal shipping against 'unfair' rail competition. Section 55 of the 1962 Transport Act followed previous legislation in allowing coastal shippers to challenge the railways either on high prices for feeder routes to the ports or low prices for the trunk routes. The other mode worthy of mention is pipelines, whose rate of growth has been very rapid in the 1960s and which could be a considerable threat to the rail carriage of oil.

Two characteristics of the freight market are of major importance to the railways. The first relates to length of haul. Although the railways are most competitive over longer distances, only about 8 per cent of all freight tonnage travels more than 100 miles. By far the greatest proportion, amounting to some two-thirds, travels less than 25 miles, much of it over a distributive network which precludes rail by its requirement for great flexibility of pick-up and delivery points. Even so, almost half of rail's tonnage travels less than this distance, comprised mainly of bulk loads of heavy raw materials.

The second fact is that freight consignments are on average light in weight. A recent sample survey showed that only 9 per cent of all consignments weighed more than 5 tons.[23] Although this includes all consignments, including those by mail, and does not reflect the importance of the very heavy consignments in tonnage terms, it is apparent that there are relatively few of those several-hundred-ton trainload consignments which give the railways their economies of scale. As might be expected, it is the heavy industries, producing inputs for other industries, which provide the larger loads. Consumer-oriented industries produce very small consignments, two-thirds weighing less than a hundredweight. It is a further unfortunate fact from the railways' point of view that heavy loads are often associated with short distances. Building materials provide an obvious example. Unless the railways get large bulk loads which can be dispatched from one point directly to another, they must assemble, tranship, and marshal quantities of smaller consignments, something for which railway organization is not well fitted. The advantages of road transport in such a situation were well stated by the Director of Costing of the BTC:

Used as a provider of individual transport for relatively small quantities, a road vehicle's production costs are very low for such 'tailor-made' operations. Because it is not dependent on the large-scale operation required by rail, there is a much greater chance of conditions and circumstances in practice approaching those required for optimum costs . . . After all, it is much easier to acquire traffic totalling 16 tons at a time than it is to aggregate sufficient consignments to total 500 tons.[24]

Within the constraints of the average length of haul and the consignment weight, it might be expected that rail would carry those traffics which are both heavy and long distance. However, as Table 3.3 shows, this is far from the case. Rail's actual advantage, as opposed to its theoretical advantage, has been in the very light packages. This has reflected the widespread use of its sundries and parcels services, and is in turn partly due to the lack of enthusiasm with which road transport views the carriage of such consignments, since as the losses on rail sundries show, these are difficult services to provide.[25] At the other end of the scale it can be seen that private haulage carries a large proportion of the heavy consignments over 200 miles. For this it has been accused by both public haulage and rail of 'creaming' the traffic.

That the railways have not been carrying the traffics for which they are best suited is further emphasized by the proportion of consignments of given weights carried by each mode.[26] No less than 59 per cent of the consignments carried by rail weighed less than 112 lb, and 75 per cent weighed less than half a ton. In the higher weights, only 3 per cent of consignments weighed more than 10 tons, and only 10 per cent more than one ton. By contrast, 27 per cent of the consignments by both public and private haulage weighed more than one ton, leaving these modes a far lesser proportion in the lighter weight groups than the railways. The railways, it may therefore be concluded, are left with an unduly high proportion of those traffics which require amalgamation and transhipment, and an unduly low percentage of those traffics which amount to a full wagon.

As already noted, even within the total freight market, there are several sub-markets, within which the balance of the modes varies. Table 3.4 therefore splits rail freight into the most important sub-markets over the period 1948–70. It can be seen that, far from the decline in the heavy industries being primarily responsible for the decline in railway freight loadings, general merchandise carryings

TABLE 3.3

Mode of transport utilized by distance and weight of consignment—by percentages

Length of haulage miles	23 lb–¼ ton				¼ ton–7½ ton				Over 7½ ton			
	Private haulage	Public haulage	Rail	Other	Private haulage	Public haulage	Rail	Other	Private haulage	Public haulage	Rail	Other
0–25	83	11	2	4	84	11	0	5	63	24	4	9
25–50	35	32	31	2	83	14	1	2	48	41	1	10
50–100	20	54	24	2	64	29	5	2	51	40	3	6
100–200	12	44	42	2	42	46	10	2	13	61	24	2
200+	9	41	46	4	29	56	12	3	35	37	26	2
All	39	33	25	3	65	27	5	3	40	42	13	5

Note: The table omits packages under 22 lb, which were also included in the survey.
Source: *Transport for Industry*, HMSO, 1968, p. 35.

TABLE 3.4
Railway freight by category 1948-70

	Coal and Coke			Minerals			Merchandise						Total	
	Tons millions	Ton-mileage millions	Receipts £million	Tons millions	Ton-mileage millions	Receipts £million	Tons millions	Ton-mileage millions	Receipts £million	Tons millions	Ton-mileage millions	Receipts £million	Tons millions	Ton-mileage millions	Receipts* £million
1948	161	9,582	67·3	59	4,926	29·4	56	6,948	85·2				276	21,456	182
1950	167	10,181	77·8	60	5,029	32·5	54	6,925	88·6				281	22,135	198
1952	170	10,366	101·7	63	5,207	42·1	51	6,817	106·7				284	22,390	251
1954	173	10,488	116·0	63	5,059	46·0	47	6,542	110·8				283	22,089	273
1956	168	10,248	126·4	66	5,217	52·3	43	6,008	105·4				277	21,473	284
1958	153	8,927	122·2	53	4,268	44·9	37	5,231	92·0				243	18,426	259
1960	148	8,104	108·6	61	4,840	48·9	40	5,706	89·8				249	18,650	247
1962	145	7,304	103·2	47	3,600	37·0	36	5,200	84·2				228	16,104	224
				Iron and Steel			Other								
1963	151	7,805	107·9	39	2,617	34·3	44	4,976	93·1				234	15,398	235
1964	147	7,470	102·4	46	3,229	39·4	46	5,304	91·1				239	16,003	233
1965	138	7,005	98·6	46	3,224	40·2	44	5,200	86·6				228	15,429	225
1966	132	6,833	99·7	39	2,690	34·2	43	5,267	83·0				214	14,790	217
1967	122	5,997	87·8	36	2,427	31·0	43	5,185	76·0				201	13,609	195
1968	123	6,277	91·1	39	2,697	33·3	46	5,719	79·9				208	14,693	204
1969	119	6,307	92·6	39	2,814	35·8	42†	4,999†	68·6†				200†	14,120†	197†
1970	112	6,249	96·0	40	2,860	38·9	47†	5,905†	73·3†				199†	15,014†	208†

* This figure omits freight carried on passenger trains which has amounted in recent years to £30m–£60m annually.
† Figures for the 'other' category in 1969 and 1970 omit tonnage and ton-mileage figures for Freightliners Ltd, and National Carriers Ltd; they include the receipts from these companies, but since these only relate to the rail section of transportation, they amount to less than when the road journey receipts were also included.
Note: The change in the statistical base in 1963 involved the transference of approximately 10 million tons of traffic to the 'other' category from minerals.
Source: *Annual Reports*, BTC and BRB.

have declined at least as fast as those for heavier traffics, while the revenue from merchandise has actually declined absolutely since 1948. This has happened in spite of the change in the statistical base in 1963, which enlarged the 'other' category as compared with the old 'merchandise' category.

As can be seen from Table 3.4, the movement of solid fuels has always been the main freight business of the railways. In 1970 they accounted for 56 per cent of all freight-train tonnage and 35 per cent of all railway freight receipts. Nevertheless there has been a considerable absolute decline in rail carriage of coal from a peak of 173 million tons in 1954 to 112 million tons in 1970, a trend which will continue in the future as coal is replaced by cheaper fuels. An adverse trend in average length of haul is also likely to continue as the Electricity Board, which can site its generating stations on or close to coalfields, becomes increasingly the major user of coal. Because coal transport is generally in bulk quantities the railways have had their chief comparative advantage vis-à-vis road transport in its movement, and it has consequently been their most profitable area of operation. Even with the decline in tonnage, profitability may still be improved, since the flows of coal are likely to be more concentrated in the future. About two-thirds of all coal produced currently is transported by rail over the major part of its journey, while much of the remainder, which includes a good deal of long-distance traffic, is carried by coastal shipping. Nevertheless Dr Beeching calculated in 1964 that some 16 million tons of the 30 million tons of coal then travelling by road could suitably be carried by rail.[27]

The carriage of iron and steel is a good example of road transport's intrusion into what has traditionally been a field of railway supremacy. These traffics can be divided into two main groups: materials and finished products. Materials such as coke and iron ore, which can be carried in bulk, are still predominantly the preserve of the railways, but the amount of transport required is likely to be diminished due to further integration of production, which necessitates less movement of semi-finished products, while the expected move to coastal sites to take advantage of the large-scale movement of ores by sea will cut down traffic from ports to iron-smelting plants. At the same time, the advantages of foreign ores vis-à-vis home-produced ores are likely to grow, cutting out movement from the British ore fields. Nor is the situation better for finished iron and steel products. Already by 1962 the proportion of these carried by road had risen to two-thirds while the output of the lighter products which are more easily carried by road is increasing faster than the total. Handling and transhipping problems at either end, lack of flexibility and, perhaps surprisingly, low units of delivery are reasons given for using roads.[28] Nevertheless, taking materials and finished products together, the railways have a ton-mileage advantage over road transport, and the industry will remain a major source of suitable rail traffics, albeit one where growth prospects are limited.

The third major category, merchandise (or 'other' since 1963), is a residual covering the whole range of products outside coal and ferrous metals, and there are thus within it wide variations between the characteristics of the commodities. At one end of the scale are industries which can provide the railways with the type of bulk loads they require; examples are oil, cement and motor vehicles. The railways have made great efforts to capture new traffic in such industries in recent years, and with some success. At the other end are traffics which are sent in such small consignments or over such small distances or require such specialized treatment as to be of little interest to the railways; foods, electronics and building materials are isolated examples of this latter category.

It is in this field that the railways have the greatest opportunities for the future, since its rate of expansion of demand for transport is roughly equivalent to the rate of growth of industrial production as a whole, and certainly faster than in the heavy industries. On the other hand, it is here that road competition is at its fiercest, and the railways have lost a great deal of traffic as a result, as can be seen from Table 3.4. It has also been a highly unprofitable field for the railways in recent years, in which losses have been almost equivalent to total receipts. The railways therefore have a threefold task: to obtain new, profitable traffic; to transform most of the current merchandise carryings into financially viable traffic; and to reject such as cannot be made profitable. This is a formidable task, yet one of critical importance to the railways.

One of the disturbing aspects of the losses in merchandise traffic is that it has happened in spite of rail's price stability in money terms and consequently a considerable fall in real prices, as Table 3.5 shows. It is rather difficult to be categoric about factors contributing to demand without knowing comparative movements in road haulage prices but while the latter have benefited from constantly improving productivity, it is most unlikely that they have actually fallen over the period 1952–68.[29] Price increases in the period 1952–58 and in 1963 produced sharp falls in ton-mileage (the extent of the fall in 1963 being partially disguised by the change in the

TABLE 3.5

Merchandise ton-mileage and receipts per ton-mile

Year	Ton-miles (000m)	Receipts per ton-mile (p)
1952	6·8	1·56
1953	6·8	1·60
1954	6·5	1·70
1955	6·1	1·74
1956	6·0	1·76
1957	5·9	1·80
1958	5·2	1·76
1959	5·4	1·65
1960	5·7	1·57
1961	5·6	1·60
1962	5·2	1·62
1963	5·0*	1·87*
1964	5·3*	1·71*
1965	5·2*	1·67*
1966	5·3*	1·57*
1967	5·2*	1·46*
1968	5·7*	1·39*

* These figures relate to merchandise plus minerals other than iron and steel, and thus overstate the old category of merchandise in ton-miles but understate the receipts.

Source: *Annual Reports* of BTC and BRB.

statistical base), while the lowering of prices in the period 1958–62 and 1964–68 did little to bring back traffic. Only 1968, a year when road haulage suffered a very considerable increase in costs as a result of Government imports, is a partial exception to this argument. The conclusion must be that the railways have been on a kinked demand curve, with an elastic demand when prices are raised but an inelastic one when they are lowered. Price, in other words, while relevant within certain ranges of traffic, is far from the whole reason for a trader's transport decision.

The argument that price has only a limited significance in the transport decision is confirmed by the findings of Deakin and Seward, who compared comparative public road haulage and rail prices for 29 different commodity groups.[30] Only for five groups was the rate by road lower than that by rail on a ton-mile basis. In some instances the difference was very pronounced. It was recognized, of course, that many factors, notably average length of haul and consignment weight, would influence the results, and that the findings prove little about any one consignment. Nevertheless, it is interesting to compare those commodities where the length of haul was similar. The results are shown in Table 3.6.

The explanation of the decline in railway traffics must therefore be sought primarily in the differential aspects of service which

TABLE 3.6

Comparative prices of transport

	Total cost of transport by rail	Total cost of transport by road	Average length of haul miles
	p	p	
Flour	145	229	87
Coal, coke and patent fuels	82	127	54
Petroleum and petroleum products	66	195	92
Crude and manufactured fertilizers	97	179	92
All other chemicals and plastic materials	203	264	124
Tars from coal and natural gas	121	167	62

Source: B. M. Deakin and T. Seward, *Productivity in Transport*, p. 62.

road and rail transport give. This supposition is backed up by *Transport for Industry*, in which it was discovered that of those consignments sent by manufacturing industry for which the cost of carriage by an alternative mode of transport was known a substantial proportion was not sent by the cheapest mode. In two-fifths of these cases the charge by the preferred mode was over 25 per cent more expensive than that of the cheapest mode. The authors of the survey note that this finding about the importance of service is supported by a study of parcels traffic carried out by British Rail at Leicester, where it was found that only 2 per cent of firms could be persuaded to accept a slower service, even if quite considerable discounts were offered. The important constituents of service emerged as ready availability and speed, with freedom from damage and loss rather less significant. In the choice of transport mode, of course, it is what the shipper believes to be true of a mode which is the vital factor, not its actual performance. Image can thus be all-important, and this has undoubtedly militated against the railways. In fact, however, the authors of *Transport for Industry* make the point that after the relative length of haul is taken into account, there is not a great deal of difference in delivery times between rail and road hauliers over a wide range of traffics. They conjecture that rail's image is due to poor performance at the bottom end of its distribution of deliveries. Cook has noted that being the main provider of the sundries service, an inherently difficult service to provide efficiently, may have tarnished rail's image over the whole range of services.[31] However, while this is probably true, *Transport for Industry* noted that where there is real urgency in a particular delivery, rail does not suffer by comparison with road, due to the high-speed passenger-train parcels service. All this suggests that an improvement in service and the image of service, such as is expected from the freightliner system, will be an important factor in adding to rail's competitiveness.

In summary, the decline of the railways has been hardly surprising in view of the characteristics of the freight market, its short average distances, low average consignment weights, and its stress upon service rather than price as the most important determinant in the transport decision. In 1954 the railways performed a greater ton-mileage than road transport; at the present, road performs three times as much as the railways; and since it is thought that rail can only expect some 10 per cent of new traffics arising out of industrial growth, even the present proportion is likely to decline. The unfortunate fact from the railways' point of view is that there is not sufficient demand of a type which the railways can profitably handle. Nor, in spite of the 1968 Transport Act, are the prospects much more propitious for the future. The White Paper *The Transport of Freight* assumed that rail carryings of fuel and steel traffic would fall from 10,500 million ton-miles in 1966 to 8,000 million in 1975.[32] To offset this, the White Paper assumed that some 4,500 million ton-miles could be transferred from road to rail by the promotion of the freightliner service and company trains, together with the assistance of the new quantity licensing provisions. Even allowing for the transfer of some rail traffic to road, a net gain of 2,250 million ton-miles for rail was estimated. This looks distinctly optimistic, not only because quantity licensing will not be introduced during the life of a Conservative government, but also because the outlook for the freightliner system is not now as rosy as originally forecast. Nor does this take into account the improved conditions for road haulage that might be expected, notably better inter-urban roads and higher permitted tonnages. Furthermore, it has been assumed that much unremunerative traffic currently moving by rail will continue to do so at a price profitable to the railways, although some jettisoning of very unprofitable traffic is allowed for. A sober assessment would be that the railways will do well to maintain their 1968 ton-mileage.

(b) *Passenger Transport*

As Table 3.7 shows, the demand for rail passenger transport has held up much better than that for freight, in that there has been a continual expansion of receipts, although the numbers carried and passenger-miles both show declining trends until 1969 and 1970, in which years a heartening reversal took place. Even if much of the financial gain has been due to inflation, the passenger side of the railways has become far more important than it was before the war, when carrying passengers seemed ancillary to the railways' real business of carrying freight.

TABLE 3.7
Rail passenger statistics

	Passenger journeys millions	Passenger-miles millions	Receipts £ million
1948	996	21,259	122
1950	982	20,177	106
1952	989	20,690	112
1954	1,020	20,712	117
1956	1,029	21,133	127
1958	1,090	22,150	138
1960	1,037	21,547	151
1962	965	19,728	161
1963	938	19,230	162
1964	928	19,874	167
1965	865	18,713	173
1966	835	18,453	179
1967	837	18,089	180
1968	831	17,835	185
1969	805*	18,400*	205†
1970	824*	18,895*	228†

* The 1969 and 1970 figures for passenger journeys and passenger mileage omit some 30 million passenger journeys and 154 million passenger-miles resulting from the transfer of the Barking–Upminster line to London Transport at the end of 1968.

† This figure does not include £61 millions grant for 'social' services.
Source: BTC and BRB Reports.

As already foreshadowed, the rail share of total passenger transport has fallen rapidly over the last decade, although not as precipitously as that of the bus industry. In shares of total passenger mileage, the railways declined from 19.6 per cent in 1957 to 9.5 per cent in 1967. Much of the decline has been caused by the rapid rise in car ownership, but competition from express buses and the airlines has also been significant. Within the public passenger transport market of some £800 millions including sea and air travel as well as taxis, rail accounts for just under a quarter of the total, or about half the share held by the buses.

The rationale of the transport decision on the passenger side is even less susceptible to measurement and explanation than on the freight side, since the variables are more personal and more complex.

The parameters of what has been called the 'transportation preference function' might be listed as time, convenience, safety, comfort, and cost,[33] but we have relatively little idea of how much people value each of these. A somewhat more extended analysis for the bus–private car relationship is given in chapter 5, and this also has implications for the railways over short distances. For present purposes, however, passenger traffics, like those on the freight side, can conveniently be subdivided into three.

The express services, corresponding to the inter-city network, had a turnover of £102 millions in 1967, or well over half total passenger receipts. These are the railways commercial, non-subsidized services. The railways have their greatest comparative advantage in passenger transport in the dense flows between conurbations, since the distances involved are generally those within the 100–300-mile bracket which give the railways a chance to outperform their major competitors. Below 100 miles, the private car's door-to-door convenience tells; over that the less fatiguing nature of rail travel counts in its favour until, as the distance approaches 300 miles, the speed advantage of the aeroplane becomes a predominant factor.[34]

It is also in this area that much of the investment in the railways has been made. Consequently, there have been very considerable improvements in speed, punctuality, regularity and comfort, all of them important components of demand. There are, of course, different elasticities according to the passenger and type of route. The success of many of the Pullman services shows that price is not an important consideration for businessmen provided comfort is allied to speed. It has been calculated, indeed, that for every mile per hour extra in average speed, an extra 1 per cent of passenger traffic is generated. The results of electrification over the London–Birmingham–Liverpool–Manchester route is clear evidence of the success of better service. The rise in the number of passenger journeys between London and Manchester rose from 1·1 million passengers in 1965, the last pre-electrification year, to 1·8 million in 1969. The introduction of the Advanced Passenger Train (of which more later) in the middle or late 1970s should enable this favourable trend to be continued.[35] Moreover, the rail improvements have generated an increase in total travel, as well as taking passengers from other modes. On the other hand, although businessmen may have a relatively low price elasticity of demand, price remains an important consideration for less affluent passengers, and at this end of the market the express bus services are an important competitor, and likely to become even more competitive when motorways permit higher average speeds, since a high load factor enables them to undercut the railways by up to 50 per cent in price. Recently, however, the railways have begun to introduce more selective pricing to cater for these differing elasticities.

Over the longer distances, air competition has encroached on what is potentially some of the most profitable of all rail traffic, such as the London–Scotland routes. The London–Glasgow air route has over 700,000 passengers annually, the highest figure for a domestic route in Europe and exceeded only by ten domestic air routes in the United States.[36] For businessmen the round trip to Scotland is eminently feasible in a day by air, whereas it is impossible by rail. Moreover the frequency of the air service is now greater than that of rail, and while the full fare is much higher, there are stand-by and night fares designed to improve the load factor by attracting travellers from outside the business community.

The other two groups of services—suburban and stopping services—are subsidized as social services under the 1968 Act and their future would appear to depend entirely on the willingness of the Government to continue these subventions, since demand prospects permit no optimism that they can be self-supporting. The suburban services category, with a turnover of £53 million in 1967, primarily comprises commuter services and is mainly centred on London, for although there are eight other cities in which rail plays a significant part in the journey to work, some 86 per cent of the total revenue from suburban services in 1961 came from London.[37] Moreover whereas in London 61 per cent of workers in the central area used either British Rail or the LTB Underground for the journey to work, in no other conurbation did the percentage travelling by rail reach double figures.

London is also unique in the physical demands made upon the railway system by the peak, which is the main economic characteristic of the suburban routes. The London system must have a carrying capacity of 500,000 at the peak hour with people coming from distances ranging from one mile to 50–60 miles. Personal discomfort by overcrowding is often considerable, but is difficult to alleviate because some parts of the system are at the limits of their physical capacity, particularly junctions such as Borough Market Junction in South London. The Reshaping Report noted a peak load of about ten times the average level over the hours from 6 am to midnight, so that the route and rolling stock was only used to 10 per cent of its capacity over the hours when it might be expected to carry traffic. In spite of the heavy peak costs involved, London is also the only suburban system which has come close to being financially viable,[38] since the others must compete to a greater extent with the bus and particularly the private car. In London the buses and the underground are complementary to rather than competitive with the rail system while the distances are too long to permit private forms of commuting to be predominant. Indeed some parts of the commuter system, such as the London–Brighton line, could almost be called inter-city or holiday lines.

The third category of passenger services, with a turnover of £28 million in 1967, is the stopping services, which include the rural and some secondary inter-urban lines. Many of these have never paid their way since they were built in the nineteenth century, simply because population densities were too low. The coming of the bus and even more the private car have made them even more uneconomic. It is doubtful if a single service in this category makes a profit, while most make very large losses which can, as in the case of the Haltwhistle–Alston line, amount to 20 p per passenger mile. Yet as we have seen there is invariably bitter resistance to the withdrawal of a service, frequently by those who never themselves travel by train, but who feel that the loss of a service is a blow to the pride of the locality.

Sometimes the problems of this category of service are exacerbated by the existence of a seasonal peak, particularly in the case of lines to seaside towns. Such towns can claim that they need the railway for the holiday season, which may be true, but does not alter the fact that for nine months of the year the line is likely to be hopelessly uneconomic. However, the growth of the private car is helping to solve this particular problem by diminishing the seasonal peak. The Reshaping Report noted that the extra summer traffic in 1961 was only half what it had been a decade previously.[39]

It is clear from the foregoing that the railways are faced by strong competition in practically every sector of their operations. In such a situation, it is imperative that their costing and pricing system be sufficiently sensitive to reflect the different and often fluctuating demand elasticities and costs of operation. Unfortunately, as we shall now see, this has generally been far from the case.

IV Costing and Pricing

Costing and pricing represent the starting-point of financial management in any commercial enterprise. They measure the input and utilization of economic resources and provide a mechanism for linking the concern with the operation of the market. A generally acceptable rule would be that laid down in the 1967 White Paper: 'The aim of pricing policy should be that the consumer should pay the true costs of providing the goods and services he consumes, in every case where these can be sensibly identified.'[40] The railways, however, have found extreme difficulty in identifying 'true' costs and in reflecting them in prices. The problems lie both in principle and practice.

(a) *Costing in Principle*

In summary, the basic problem is that the units to which prices must be charged, the passengers or goods consignments, are generally very much smaller than the capacity of a train, which is the smallest unit of transportation, so that the immediate problem arises of allocating the cost of the train between the units travelling in it. But even as between trains, routes, areas or any other railway subdivisions there is a large percentage of costs which must be shared. Although this percentage becomes less the larger the unit of output, accurate allocation of all costs is only possible at very high scales of output. Yet all costs must somehow be covered in their translation into prices for the units of travel, and the problem is further complicated by the enormous heterogeneity of these units in terms of their demand characteristics and their imposition on railway resources.

The main reason for requiring a high scale of output for accurate cost determination is the technically and administratively integrated nature of the railway system, whose fixed track demands a high degree of discipline and central control, and by the consequent inflexibility of cost in the short or even the medium term. The inability to allocate costs accurately to the particular unit of travel gives rise to an incapacity to make price equivalent to cost, a lack of knowledge as to the profitability not only of the single unit of travel but also fairly large segments of railway operations, and an absence of standards for evaluating investment projects. Because of the difficulty of estimating costs, the railways have until recently attempted to maximize revenue rather than profit, the more normal commercial objective. The old railway slogan that 'all traffic is good traffic' was born of a desire to spread the indirect costs over the widest possible range of traffics; the fact that many of them might be carried at a loss and that redundant capacity might be kept in existence at a heavy cost was disregarded. When the railways had a virtual monopoly of inland transport in the nineteenth century, these difficulties did not matter very much, since profit could be guaranteed by averaging prices at a level sufficient to cover total costs. With the onset of road competition and particularly in the post-war period, the railways were faced with the urgent need to refine their cost allocation to cut out the need for averaging on a wide scale.

The best starting-point for discussion of the problem is to look at the traditional way in which the railways have analysed cost, based on a primary distinction between direct and indirect costs:

> Direct costs are those which can be assumed, in the long run, to vary with the quantity of traffic carried. They include the provision, maintenance and haulage of rolling stock, shunting and marshalling; terminal and handling facilities; documentation; and collection and delivery. Total costs include, in addition, the provision and maintenance of track and the provision, maintenance and operation of signalling, together with general administration. Appropriate allowances for renewal of assets and for interest on capital are included in each main group of costs.[41]

Indirect costs are made up of the additions to direct cost in arriving at total cost. It is easy to point out inconsistencies in this definition. The maintenance of track does vary in cost with the amount of traffic which passes over it, while the inclusion of depreciation or interest on sunk capital as a direct cost flies in the face even of normal accounting procedure. But there are two much more serious difficulties, one dealing with the fact that direct costs are a clumsy measuring rod and the other with the differentiation between direct and indirect costs.

Direct costs measure a unit of output, not a unit of charging, and even within the area designated as direct costs there are joint costs to complicate the allocation of cost to a particular unit of travel. Joint costs have been defined as 'those associated with the situation where the product enables the production of another to take place at no extra cost'.[42] A carriage is joint as between the passengers travelling in it. By contrast, specific costs are those relating to the particular output in question. Thus in so far as direct costs include joint costs, there is necessarily some degree of averaging between the products of the joint output. Clearly much depends on the unit of output; a wagonload, for instance, provides many more problems of estimation than a trainload because it involves a higher proportion of joint costs and therefore a lower proportion of costs specific to it. The smaller the unit of output, therefore, the greater the amount of judgement and/or averaging which must be incurred in cost estimation. But whatever the unit of output, in so far as costs can be broken down into joint and specific this will give a more sophisticated measuring rod than direct costs alone, and the railways are therefore now turning to the use of joint and specific rather than direct and indirect. In the past, such a division would have been academic because the railways never tried to break down direct costs to their lowest level, since the complexity of many journeys, possibly involving several transfers between trains or even regions, meant that it was not an economic proposition to do so. It is for this reason that regional accounting has never been satisfactory; to do it properly would be too expensive.

A more serious question still, which arises out of the economist's notion of cost, is whether the railways have in the past defined their direct and indirect costs accurately. The economist's approach starts from the assertion that the only economic resources which are being used in providing a particular service are those which could be saved if the service were not provided. Not all the factors utilized in providing the service will be saved, since some are indirect costs which will still have to be provided for the remaining services. But clearly much depends on the extent of the discontinuation. If a single coach is taken off a particular train, there will only be very marginal savings in fuel, assuming that the coach is needed for other trains. If a whole train is taken out of service, there will be savings of fuel, labour and rolling stock. If a whole route is closed down, there will also be savings on the permanent way and infrastructure. The idea of avoidable cost therefore involves a whole range of possible permutations, for each of which a different saving will be made. Much depends on the time period during which the saving is envisaged, and different approaches to this have led to some very different conclusions about the nature of direct and indirect cost. By examining the detailed categories of cost in the short run, Foster came to the conclusion that the proper division, using a wagonload as the unit of output, was 16 per cent direct and 84 per cent indirect rather than the 56 per cent direct and 44 per cent indirect split at that time according to the railways' definition.[43] Whilst admitting the limitations of his division, he argued that it was superior to that of the railways, since labour, maintenance and some parts of other costs should, with a wagonload unit of output, be considered as indirect costs. Foster altered the railway definition of direct costs as 'varying in the long run with the amount of traffic carried' when he defined labour as an indirect cost, since labour is variable outside the short-run, but given his short-run premises his logic is undoubtedly correct. Conversely, Joy, by taking a much longer time-span has argued that because the greater part of route-mileage has more than a single track, it should be possible to allocate the cost of any extra tracks to specific traffic flows.[44] In other words, a large part of the cost of the permanent way can be considered, albeit over large volumes of output, as a direct cost. Given his premises, he is just as right as Foster, although apparently arguing in a different direction.

The answer, of course, is that the line dividing direct and indirect costs depends on the assumptions made about the unit of output and the time period under consideration. Drawing the line in any one place has disadvantages. If the railways move too far in Foster's direction, i.e. towards a smaller proportion of direct costs, the problem of the railways in allocating the indirect costs becomes even greater. If, on the other hand, the railways were to move too far in Joy's direction, the units of charging within the vast volume of traffic covered by direct costs would not be sufficiently differentiated, which would result in a great deal of cross-subsidization and averaging.

Ideally, therefore, one would want to take into account different degrees of cost avoidability according to the size and duration of the particular contract, but this has not been possible given the rigid categories of direct and indirect cost. Recent costing developments on the railways have therefore seen the replacement of the direct/indirect system by one which uses the concepts of joint and specific costs and also that of avoidability. These developments have of course made some form of marginal costing much more feasible. Even this, however, would not escape the problem of measurement of low levels of output. Any railway costing system must lack the means to calculate cost with the same specific reference to the unit of charging which its much smaller scale road competitors can achieve. This is undoubtedly a major competitive disadvantage but it is much more a function of the organization and technology of the whole rail system than of the particular method of costing. Clearly, therefore, given the fact that no method is able to identify and allocate all costs, and that there are diminishing returns in costing down to smaller and smaller units, any costing system must be a compromise, balancing practicability, cost of operation and degrees of accuracy. We shall shortly examine how the railways have costed in the past and how they hope to do so in the future, but first we must look at the issues of principle in pricing which emerge from the problems of costing.

(b) *Pricing in Principle*

Turning now to the question of pricing, the traditional railway problem has been how to set prices which are based on direct costs and which would cover the large proportion of indirect costs. To this was added the difficulties of taking into account demand considerations which might prevent the implementation of any pricing formula, no matter how desirable its relationship to costs.

The pricing principles open to the railways are several. One which can rapidly be rejected is the 'fully distributed cost' concept of pricing, which involves an arbitrary apportionment of the unallocable costs across the traffics.[45] Although superficially attractive in the sense that it would meet the statutory duty of breaking even, it pays no attention at all to demand factors. If it were adopted, a good deal of traffic presently carried by the railways would undoubtedly move on to the roads, leaving the railways with less volume to cover almost the same costs. The result would be a Procrustean cutting of the railway system to make costs equal revenue, which would almost certainly be self-defeating.

A second possible pricing outlook is to charge what the market will bear, ignoring cost. It was a rough approximation to this system which the railways used in the nineteenth century, when price was based on the value of the goods carried, on the assumption that the more valuable traffics could afford to pay more. Charging what the market would bear also meant discrimination as between different consignors for similar traffics, and it was this which led to urgent demands for anti-discrimination statutes and the fear of monopoly. The remnants of this historical fear of monopoly can be seen in the proviso of the 1962 Transport Act which maintained control of passenger rates in the London area by the Transport Tribunal although freeing them elsewhere. But merely charging what the market would bear could be an unprofitable business when competition appeared, as the railways found in the inter-war period, since cross-subsidization was no longer such an easy way of balancing costs with revenue. It became obvious that some link between price and cost was vital to measure the profitability of services.

A further possibility, much closer to the welfare economist's ideal, would be pricing on a marginal basis, either in the short or long run. Short-run marginal cost has the attraction that it could be used to make full use of surplus capacity, of which the railways have usually had plenty. Once a train is scheduled to go from A to B, it costs virtually nothing to add extra passengers or consignments up to the capacity of the train; as has been said of passengers, the only cost is that of the ticket. But there are disadvantages, even leaving aside for the moment the old railway problem of accurate measurement. There would be considerable price discontinuities at the point where surplus capacity became fully utilized; thus the situation would arise whereby if a train held 250 persons, the 251st would have to bear the full cost of the next train, while the succeeding 249 could travel virtually free. In practice, price discrimination among customers could not be carried to this length and some averaging would have to be permitted. Moreover, given the high proportion of costs fixed in the short run, and given that the price elasticity of demand is not very great for reduced prices due to the service factor, it would be very far from covering total costs. The immense gap thus created would increase railway losses to an insupportable level. It would also create a furore among private transport operators, who would see it as most unfair competition. Furthermore, the question of the absence of investment criteria would have to be tackled at some time beyond the immediate use of existing resources.

Charging on the basis of long-run marginal cost would escape the investment problem and would also cut down the loss incurred. By making allowance only for those assets which need replacement, it would nevertheless have the advantage of not requiring the amortization of such assets as are not required. It is, in fact, accepted policy for the nationalized industries, laid down in the White Paper of 1967, that long-run marginal cost should be charged wherever possible. But the White Paper admitted that 'Not all costs can be allocated to specific services or activities, and some industries, where the area of unallocable costs is large, may find difficulty in going all the way to a pricing structure which accurately reflects the costs of particular services while at the same time covering total costs.'[46] The Prices and Incomes Board took the problem further, saying: 'To determine long-run marginal costs, since railway operations form a complex interlocking whole, costs need to be studied in terms of systems analysis.'[47] This in turn, however, involved both decisions about the size and balance of traffics and a computerized method of controlling operations and of analysing the effects of incremental traffic revenues or costs. This development, which only became possible in the late 1960s when such methods of analysis were evolved and since the railways have been given reasonable expectations of a stable system, has enabled long-run marginal cost pricing to become a practical possibility.

But even if possible, it is not necessarily desirable as an automatic system. Long-run marginal cost does not take into account demand factors, either to exploit a relative monopoly by raising charges, or to utilize surplus capacity in the short run by reducing charges. Given the competitive structure of transport and the railways' financial problems such considerations are vital. Thus no one mechanistic pricing system is satisfactory for the railways or is likely to be in the future. Judgements must be made although based of course on the best cost and market information. Indeed, it has often been said that rail pricing is more of an art than a science and while the balance has shifted radically towards the scientific side, the art will always be a necessary part.

In the period before about 1968, however, these considerations were less relevant, since the breakdown into direct and indirect costs precluded taking time horizons into account, while the absence of any overall planning for the system meant that the interaction of one operation upon another could not be evaluated. All that could be done was to use direct cost as a base, gleaning such a contribution towards indirect costs as the state of competition permitted. We shall now look at how this other system worked in practice before passing on to look at the new system which is replacing it.

(c) *Costing and Pricing in Practice*

The BTC, faced with the post-nationalization task of integrating the disparate bodies under its control, recognized from the outset the importance of the price mechanism, and immediately set up two committees to deal with freight and passenger charges. Since the considerations are different in the two sectors, we shall deal with them separately, starting with freight. The 1950 BTC Report announced that the freight-pricing system as it stood was retaining unremunerative traffic while losing remunerative; this was: '... an impossible position, and the Commission have already announced their intention to propose railway rates which will take much greater account of the actual cost of types of service on the one hand, and what the competitive market will allow on the other'.[48] The Transport Costing Service was therefore set up to bring this about, although not until 1955 was a new freight-charges scheme brought before the Transport Tribunal.

There were two basic costing procedures, particularized and generalized costing.[49] Particularized costing would be used only if the traffic were sufficiently important to warrant individual treatment, as would be the case with a long-term contract with a major firm. In this instance the costing officer might examine some or all of the following constituent operations:

(i) Haulage
    (a) trunk haul
    (b) pick-up service between small stations and local marshalling yard
(ii) Provision and maintenance of wagons
(iii) Marshalling
(iv) Terminal operations
    (a) wagon shunting
    (b) facilities for loading and unloading wagons
    (c) handling of goods and transfer to or from road vehicles
    (d) collection and/or delivery by road
    (e) documentation.

As an example of further breakdown, the cost of haulage would comprise: provision and maintenance of locomotive; wages of locomotive crew; wages of guard; fuel; lubricants; stabling and servicing of locomotive. The cost thus arrived at would then act as a basis for pricing, on top of which a subvention for indirect costs would be added.

If generalized costing were used, the coster would classify the traffic under certain categories according to type (coal, iron and steel, or general merchandise), loadability and terminal conditions, look up the relevant cost scale under the same headings, and add up. This involves a good deal more averaging than the particularized system, which itself makes no pretence of taking all the possible variations in circumstances into account. The initial scales were derived from periodic sample surveys. However, in spite of the obvious drawbacks of such a system, it would still be wrong to say that the railways used broad averages; rather they used large numbers of different averages based on particular journeys, types of load, quality of service, and so on.

The costing procedure was thus designed to impute direct costs to the particular traffic while indirect costs were to be recouped according to what the traffic would bear. However, according to a railway witness before the Select Committee on Nationalized Industries, merely to cover direct costs was not sufficient: 'We always look for a reasonable contribution towards indirect costs as well as looking at direct costs, before we take the job on.'[50]

But although this may have been the principle of pricing, it does not seem to have been followed in practice. The Reshaping Report, in providing an analysis of costs and receipts within broad categories, showed that even direct costs might not be covered for quite large groups of traffic. One of the startling revelations was that in the critical merchandise wagonload category, there was a shortfall in receipts of no less than £31·8 million on direct costs of £96·6 million.[51] This meant that receipts, at £64·8 million, covered only two-thirds of direct costs, even before considering contributions to indirects. It was no doubt findings such as this which prompted the report to declare that some traffics must be priced out of the market. However, even bringing receipts up to equality with direct costs proved far from easy. Although prices were raised in 1963 and various means of improving productivity were brought into effect as a result of the Reshaping Report, there was still a considerable shortfall for the nearest equivalent category in 1967, the last year for which figures are available. Direct costs for 'other' were £70 million, receipts £56 million, leaving a deficit of £14 million. On this basis it can scarcely be said that the railways have priced by reference to direct costs; it rather looks as if they charged whatever price would bring them traffic. Indeed, this was almost turned into a virtue. The Ministry of Transport official responsible for the railways, having expressed a preference for a pragmatic rather than a theoretical approach to pricing policy, justified this by saying: 'A pragmatic pricing policy means to me in simple terms getting what the traffic will bear and very little more than that . . . When an industry is up against it in the short term in the sense of being in very serious deficit, it is more or less forced to adopt whatever means it can to maximize its revenue.'[52]

Whether or not the railways were actually trying to maximize revenue, the trends of price volume and revenue suggest that in fact there was little leeway for the railways to increase their charges, whether or not charges were below direct costs. As we saw in the section dealing with demand, it is likely that the prices themselves were competitive, but what might be called the service gap, or an image of one, has prevented them from being raised to a profitable level. When the new Freight Charges Scheme became effective in 1957, there was a general lowering of freight rates in order to win traffic back from the roads. What appears to have happened was that the road hauliers lowered their own rates so that the railways won few traffics back, and lost a good deal of revenue. In 1957 the freight receipts for merchandise and livestock were £107 million and the net ton-miles 5,942 million, while by 1960 receipts had dropped to £89.8 million and net ton-miles to 5,706 million. The Beeching reorganization resulted in prices being raised initially, but was followed by the same cycle of price-cutting, lower receipts, and little if any gain in traffic, which seems to bear out the existence of the kinked demand curve mentioned earlier. The 1963–68 cycle, although raising ton-mileage from its historic low of 5·0 million ton-miles to 5·7 million ton-miles, nevertheless resulted in a drop in receipts of some £13 million from £93 million to just under £80 million.[53] The loss per ton on merchandise traffic was approximately £1·50 in 1967 after indirect costs had been roughly allocated, or almost equivalent to the revenue obtained.

The competitive pressure on prices in other sectors was not nearly as bad as with merchandise. This can be seen by comparing over time the receipts per ton-mile for coal and general merchandise— the one an area of comparative monopoly, the other one of fierce competition. In spite of considerable steps forward in coal handling —the use of merry-go-round trains, the greater concentration of coal customers and dispatch points and far better loading facilities, all of which must have improved productivity for the railways—the price charged per ton-mile in 1968 was 1·45 p or higher than the price for merchandise, which was 1·40 p. Yet in 1952 the receipt for coal was 0·98 p, while that for merchandise was 1·56 p per ton-mile. The difference is further emphasized by comparing the average receipt per ton forwarded. The movement for coal was slightly upwards, from 71 p to 74 p, whereas that for merchandise was considerably reduced from £2·11 to £1·74. It is very doubtful if these changes reflected movements in costs, since economies would appear to have been more easily gained in coal than merchandise. Although merchandise has a longer average haul than coal, coal moves in much denser flows, has a higher average wagonload weight, and does not involve as high transhipment or other terminal costs. It must thus be concluded that the railways exploited their relative advantage in coal vis-à-vis merchandise. Even so, although coal paid its direct costs, it was not profitable once indirects had been assigned.[54]

It was therefore clear that the method of pricing and by extension that of costing was inadequate to achieve the railways' new financial obligations to break even under the 1968 Transport Act. The end of the deficit grant meant that the railways could not depend on the Government to pay those indirect and even direct costs which price did not cover. There were also other reasons for developing a new approach. One was operational. At a time when the railways had a large amount of surplus capacity, a high degree of flexibility in train scheduling and movement was possible, but as the railways drove towards a much smaller structure and a much higher capacity utilization, much more operational discipline in the use of all resources became necessary. It was no longer feasible to send goods from A to B at the beck and call of a casual customer; the railways' resource availability had to be taken into consideration. From this an administrative issue also arose. A decentralized system for the pricing and acceptance of traffics was not compatible with the operational needs of integration and central control. In any case, the Prices and Incomes Board had commented that there seemed to be insufficient control over local salesmen, who apparently preferred throughput to profitability, and instanced this by pointing to falling average receipts at a time when road haulage rates were rising.[55] For these interconnected reasons, and others such as the increasing ability of computer technology to deal with the type of data analysis required, the railways have been moving towards system analysis as a basis for costing and pricing.

The following description is of the new method as it relates to the problematical wagon-load category of traffics, but the principle would be similar in most respects for other railway operations. The first stage in the development of a system model was to take a number of factors such as numbers of terminals and marshalling yards, length of haul, wagon utilization, quality of service, and so on, and to programme various combinations of these, producing more than a thousand alternative systems. The most advantageous solution, after allowance for the effect of the system on route and administration expenses, was then fitted with estimates of operating revenues and expenses and capital income and expenditure over a twenty-year period and the whole compared with a future without any such wagonload operations. This was a necessary preliminary stage, since there was considerable doubt about the viability of wagonload traffics.

The next stage was to prepare an operating and financial plan for BRB. Each of the main businesses, freight, passenger and parcels, works on a five-year plan each in turn built up from its own component businesses, commodity groups and finally profit centres.

Traffic flows, operating requirements, including quality of service, costs involved and potential revenues for each are worked out, pooled and computer studies made to evaluate the consequences of different possibilities, with recycling of priorities to establish operating and financial compatibility. Thus some 35,000 separate forecasts were involved in the 1971 plan. All resources including capital and manpower are allocated to specific operations to the greatest possible extent. In this way the total rail plan is arrived at, and provided the financial implications are satisfactory the first year of the plan becomes the target, and its financial features the budget.[56] At the other end of the five-year forecast, the traffic forecasts are obviously more tentative and the possibilities for alterations in the capacity of the network greater.

Returning to the individual contract, costs can be worked out with some precision in the knowledge of the other likely calls on the assets. The actual categories of cost which must be added together are naturally not dissimilar from the old system, but the new method of costing now also takes degrees of escapability into account. In the first place those costs specific to the particular traffic are estimated and also those which it shares jointly with other traffics, within a period of escapability of up to two years. Next, capital costs are estimated and finally interest and provision for replacement, although the latter two are considered as targets, not costs. These different levels of cost now give guidance to the salesman negotiating the price. As before, price is a matter of negotiation, with competitive market conditions playing a key role. Obviously the minimum price would have to cover the specific costs, but this would be used only where a short-term contract was being competed for together with some assurance of successful price discrimination, i.e. that the low rate would not be used as a lever to force down rates elsewhere. Naturally, before such a contract or indeed any contract is finalized, a check must be made to ensure that resources are available to carry it out. In most circumstances a contribution to the non-attributable costs would be essential, based on what the market would bear, with especial reference to prevailing road haulage prices and service. Larger customers may well have a two-part tariff, enabling them to pay a low price for incremental traffics over a minimum.

A somewhat special situation arises for small consignments. Under no method of costing would it be possible to cost these exactly, and the expense is in any case disproportionate. Therefore the railways have developed what are called wagonload acceptance criteria. For any weight, terminal condition and loadability there is a minimum transit distance at which carriage is likely to be profitable. Tables giving this for different traffic characteristics are therefore available to salesmen, with the minimum price being based on the road haulage charge for the journey.

It will be apparent that although day-to-day pricing and costing is not directly integrated into the planning function, it is nevertheless dependent on the computerized planning system for accuracy in budgeting for the use of assets, and perhaps just as important for providing a method of monitoring contracts once they have been made. Under the old method, the costing of the assets making up a train involved making dubious assumptions about their possible alternative or joint uses and their imposition on other railway resources. Now these can be both forecast before the event and monitored after it. The importance of the monitoring function lies not only in the possibility of better determination of the profitability of contracts, but also in providing a yardstick for cost escalator clauses. The old railway method of increasing prices used to be by general percentage increases, which took into account neither cost nor demand factors, and was severely criticized by the Prices and Incomes Board.[57] The longer term aspect of the new system also promises tighter financial control through better planning for the determination of future surplus capacity.

The costing of passenger services has always been somewhat easier than for freight since traffic operations are more regular, and passengers are more homogeneous than goods consignments. Even before the introduction of a computerized system of control, forward planning of timetables and resources was well developed. Passenger pricing on the other hand has presented its own peculiar problems. Again the BTC decided from the start that fares must be more closely related to costs, but two basic anomalies faced them in the fare structure which they inherited. In the first place there were numerous dispensations for various groups—workmen, soldiers, season-ticket holders and so on. Secondly, the standard fare was based on mileage irrespective of the cost involved. Both anomalies involved cross-subsidization and the consequent distortion of demand.

Of the two deviations from a more accurate cost–price relationship, the railways have until recently paid far more attention to concessions, and have been moderately successful in their attempts to eliminate them. Moreover, of the various reductions now available, the great majority are intended to encourage off-peak travel and hence justify lower fares in a way which the historical concessions such as workmen's tickets did not. But the problem of season-ticket holders still remains. The vast majority of the suburban lines run almost entirely for their benefit, yet in 1970 the average commuter fare per passenger mile was 0·83 p as opposed to 1·64 p for the full fare. This season-ticket fare must be contrasted with a rough calculation by the Prices and Incomes Board that the peak-time marginal cost per passenger mile in London is in excess of $12\frac{1}{2}$ p.[58] However, the issue of commuter fares has always been a delicate one in that they raise questions of the larger social advantage in preventing congestion and who should pay the costs involved.

A more important distortion than the concessions was the standard mileage charge for full fares. The level changed, but apart from a slight taper for very long distances, the fare for any one mile was until recently the same as for any other without consideration of the costs involved. Yet there were known to be immense differences in the passenger-mile costs to the railways, and somewhat smaller but still very significant differences in the seat-mile costs. As early as 1950, the Railway Executive calculated that the cost to the railways was 0·14 p per passenger mile for a non-stop express, 6 p per passenger mile for a main-line stopping train, and 10 p for rural branch lines.[59] This 75-times differential in cost, which itself measured the average of a category, was in no way reflected in the fare. Part of the cost difference could be accounted for by discrepancies in load factor; even so, the comparative costs for providing seat-mile capacity were 0·10 p, 0·42 p and 0·73 p respectively for the three categories, which still meant a seven times differential between the extremes. But although the railways were fully aware at least of the magnitude, if not the detail of the discrepancies, and in fact hinted that a change in policy was being considered when pressed on the point by the Select Committee on Nationalized Industries in 1960, they did not make changes, owing to what the Select Committee described as 'extreme sensitivity to public opinion'.[60] The railways were convinced that the public would consider anything other than mileage-based fares inequitable. The Select Committee itself admitted: 'This public reaction may be instinctive and illogical, but it exists, and is an influence on the size of the fare that the Commission is able to charge.'[61]

The railway view was strongly attacked, notably by Munby and the Prices and Incomes Board.[62] Munby challenged the theory that the public expected to pay exactly the same fare per mile, while several years later the Prices and Incomes Board pointed out the possibilities of raising much more revenue by selective fare increases according to market elasticities. The railways have since 1968 acted on these recommendations, and with very considerable success in the inter-city sector, using market research as the key to more selective pricing. Not only have considerable increases of 10 per cent per year in revenue been achieved, but the volume of traffic has also increased by 5 per cent per year as a result of faster, more comfortable services and better promotional techniques. The public reaction to the new pricing methods has disproved the railways' fears, even though some oddities have been discovered—for example, due to regional price-setting it might cost more to go from Glasgow to Birmingham than from Birmingham to Glasgow. The new pricing method is almost entirely based on what the market will bear, and there is no pretence that the fares are cost related, even though there is a much better knowledge of costs with the new system of planning. Thus inter-city fares are frequently higher than suburban and rural services even though costs are lower per passenger-mile. On the other hand, there have also been very interesting pricing developments to take up surplus capacity. Two notable examples are the Highwayman, a slow train with fares similar to long-distance buses between Newcastle and London, and a more than 40 per cent reduction on the London–Glasgow and London–Liverpool routes for booking one month ahead.

The pricing problem for the suburban and rural lines was very different. Even the most sophisticated revenue maximization could not hope to fill the gap between a cost of £70 million in 1968 for all grant-aided services excluding the London commuter lines, and a fare revenue of £20 million. Moreover, elasticities were such that the effect of fare increases on revenue might be perverse in some areas, and there was also the difficult problem of urban congestion caused by those switching to private transport. Hence the subsidies of £61 million in 1969 for 222 services. Most of these were guaranteed for a three-year period, but several for less. BRB is paid the subsidy in advance on an agreed basis, so that it can still either make a profit on the lines, by lowering costs or raising prices, or make a loss by losing more than the Ministry grant. Since the grant-in-aid include an attribution for overhead costs, it will not be in BRB's interests to close down the lines, and it must therefore try to avoid the grants becoming so large in relation to the passengers carried as to invite curtailment.[63] Except around London the railways have not yet followed the pattern of selective fare increases to maximize revenue on the grant-aided services, but this will doubtless be done in the future.

The somewhat special position in London was separately analysed by the Prices and Incomes Board.[64] The Board advocated that fares for commuters should approximate to the long-run marginal cost, following the precepts of the Government's 1967 White Paper. This meant varying fares in accordance with the costs of providing extra capacity or reliability, which in turn meant much heavier charges on the lines south of the Thames than, for instance, the routes out of Euston. After some hesitation, this suggestion was turned down by the Government, and in its place the railways raised fares on the basis of quality of service, using speed and number of stops between the particular station and its London terminal as the criterion. This decision must be seen in the context of the needs of Southern Region for capital amounting to some £350 million during the 1970s if the commuter lines are to be brought up to a desired standard and also in the context of the still outstanding obligation to make the London commuter network financially viable by 1972 in spite of the acceptance of the principle of subsidies by the 1968 Act. Another factor affecting railway pricing in the future is the trend towards devolution of financial responsibility for commuter services from the Central Government to the conurbations although London has not accepted this on a statutory basis. The Passenger Transport Authorities (PTAs) have been given the right by the 1968 Transport Act to control and 'rationalize' railway commuter fares as part of this devolution, but understandably none have grasped this particular nettle yet. The role of the BRB will merely be to tell the localities the cost of given levels of service.

(d) *Sector Profitability*

So far we have looked at the issues of costing and pricing largely in terms of the principle being applied. Now we must turn to two more practical aspects, namely sector profitability and sources of cost. Given the difficulties inherent in costing, it is not surprising to find that the railways have a very difficult task in deciding which of their operations are profitable and which are losing money. The Select Committee on Nationalized Industries in their 1960 Report noted this inability with amazement and irritation, and quoted the Permanent Secretary to the Ministry of Transport, who told them: 'We find one of the most difficult things in the Ministry is to discover where money is actually being lost. It is very difficult to get an answer to that.'[65] It is little use counting only direct costs, since this leaves a large proportion of all costs unaccounted for, and it is clearly wrong to suggest that, say, the cost of permanent way per traffic unit over a fully utilized route is the same as that over a route with two trains a day. Indirect costs must therefore be allocated even if they are not identifiably associated with specific traffics. The first comprehensive attempt to achieve this was carried out in the analysis leading to the Reshaping Report. At that time coal traffic and coaching train freight were the only categories to be making a profit after indirect expenses, and the passenger side was making a considerably larger loss than the freight side.

Table 3.8 shows the pattern as it had evolved by 1967 which was admittedly a very bad year for the railways. All categories were making a loss, and the balance of loss had now swung to the freight side, the passenger side having improved its position in all sub-categories. Particularly noticeable was the large loss made in the 'other' or general merchandise category of freight, since it will be remembered from the discussion of demand that it is here that the railways must seek future growth.

TABLE 3.8
Profitability by sector 1967
£ million

	Direct expenses	Revenue	Revenue over direct expenses	Indirect expenses	Net revenue
Passenger:					
Fast and semi-fast	76	102	26	45	−19
Stopping	45	28	−17	25	−42
Suburban	51	53	2	26	−24
Total	172	183	11	96	−85
Coaching train freight	48	55	7	13	−6
Freight:					
Coal	76	91	15	26	−11
Iron and steel	35	32	−3	12	−15
Other	70	56	−14	26	−40
Sundries	40	22	−18	8	−26
Total	221	201	−20	72	−92
Grand total	441	439	−2	181	−183

Note: The above figures relate to railway operation only; they thus omit ancillary income such as advertising and rents, or that from ships and hotels. On the other hand they also omit such expenses as redundancy payments and workshop closure costs. Interest obligations are however included, as is depreciation at replacement cost.
Source: BRB *Annual Report, 1967*, p. 51.

THE RAILWAYS 175

The figures in Table 3.8 must be treated with reserve because of the arbitrary nature of allocating indirect costs. In the 1968 Report, indeed, the BRB announced that it had decided to suspend the subdivision of profit- and loss-making areas of operation because 'the changes in traffic volume in recent years have necessitated reallocations of fixed costs which tended to be misleading rather than helpful'.[66] Whilst accepting this, it is disappointing to find no mention of the relative profitability of sectors in the latest reports now that the computerized forward-planning system has given the railways better methods of allocating costs. It may be the case of course that this has not been done for tactical reasons following the very considerable realignment in sector profitability which the 1968 Act brought about.

Profitability naturally does not only depend on sectoral characteristics. There are vast differences even within categories. Although there are obvious difficulties in cost allocation, certain types of traffic can clearly be identified as more profitable than others. On the freight side, the three critical components of reducing unit costs appear to be the type of terminal conditions, the average loading by weight, and the distance travelled. The latter two are reasonably self-explanatory,[67] but the terminal conditions may be even more important. The Beeching Report analysed different types of terminal conditions as shown in Table 3.9; the results covered wagonload

TABLE 3.9
Profitability of wagon-load freight traffic by terminal condition

Terminal conditions	Tons	%	Receipts	%	Direct costs	%	Margin
Road–road	26,800	2	145,300	7	214,100	9	−68,800
Road–station	17,600	1	64,400	3	91,700	4	−27,300
Road–dock	25,400	1	61,600	3	91,900	4	−30,300
Road–siding	111,500	7	299,900	13	376,000	17	−76,100
Station–station	30,200	2	66,300	3	91,800	4	−25,500
Station–dock	29,600	2	65,000	3	72,500	3	−7,500
Dock–dock	5,400	—	3,900	—	9,500	—	−5,600
Station–siding	246,600	14	369,500	16	379,600	17	−10,100
Siding–dock	256,300	15	190,500	8	200,900	9	−10,400
Siding–siding	946,000	56	986,500	44	746,200	33	+240,300

Source: Reshaping Report, pp. 32–3.

merchandise and mineral traffic, i.e. excluding sundries, wagonload coal and full trainloads. Even within these categories, there are variations in profitability. But nevertheless it is clear from Table 3.9 that traffic either collected or delivered by road was likely to be uneconomic. This situation is created by the uneconomic transfer frequently made by hand, from road to rail vehicles and vice versa, and by the low average load per wagon of 2·5 tons where the consignments are carried partly by road. This does not mean that all traffics which necessitated road as a terminal condition need be unprofitable, merely that those actually carried by rail generally were so. Since some 60 million tons of rail traffic starts or finishes by road (1964 figures), however, this category could not easily be discarded. What the railways needed was a better means of transshipment, and the freightliner system was a logical outcome of this requirement.

A second area shown to be of dubious economic value to the railways were those services requiring marshalling and shunting, despite the investments made in marshalling yards during the Modernization Plan. Not only did this item account for £50 million out of the total of £560 million, but the railways costing system assumed that wagons over a long haul needed marshalling every thirty miles. This was not only extremely expensive, but very time-consuming, and contributed to the poor railway image for speed of delivery, while preventing the railways from making the best of long hauls. Thus a major part of the Beeching freight strategy was to avoid the need for marshalling by using the train rather than the wagon as the unit of movement.

On the passenger side there were similar findings, although aspects such as transhipment, loadability, and terminal conditions are not relevant. We have already noted the startling cost differentials between groups of traffic as early as 1950. Much of the Beeching strategy with respect to passenger services was directed at excising loss-making lines. It is worth noting, however, that the report did not expect great savings from these cuts; the net improvement predicted was only £18 million excluding track and signalling.[68] In spite of the closure of some 3,000 route miles and the reduction of facilities on many services between the publication of the Report and the end of 1967, stopping services were still the largest single loss-making category in the railways by the end of the latter year.

(e) *Rail Categories of Expense*

A further practical way of appreciating the cost problems of the railways is by looking at the various cost categories according to activities performed and also according to factors of production. The breakdown in Table 3.10 shows the working expenses of the railways

THE RAILWAYS

TABLE 3.10

Working expenses by type of activity

	1963	%	1968	%
	£000s			
Train working	243,462	44·2	227.458	41·6
Shunting	40,455	7·4	28.728	5·2
Terminal handling	65,969	12·0	63,533	11·6
Booking and consignment of traffic	25,393	4·6	23,853	4·4
Collection and delivery by road	20,265	3·7	23,044	4·2
Miscellaneous (publicity, subsidies, compensation)	5,047	0·9	8,115	1·5
Track maintenance	54,860	9·9	57,486	10·5
Signalling	37,775	6·9	38,666	7·0
Other expenses	305	0·1	287	0·1
Administration and general expenses	56,704	10·3	75,942	13·9
Total	550,235	100·0	547,112	100·0

Note: These figures do not include interest on capital, which amounted in 1968 to £67 million. The latest figures available, those for 1969 and 1970, are not included because they are not directly comparable.
Source: BRB *Annual Reports*.

by type of activity including depreciation. The table shows a decline in expenditure between 1963 and 1968; this was achieved almost entirely by a very significant reduction in many types of assets, details of which will be seen later in Table 3.12. Of particular significance in this table is the high proportion of expenses ancillary to the actual movement of traffics. Even the train-working category is not restricted to the immediate costs of movement. Of the £227 million expended in 1968, some £59 million went on the staff expenses of drivers, firemen and guards, and some £29 million on fuel and power; the rest went on maintenance, stabling and depreciation. Thus only some £80 million or less than one-sixth of total cost went on these very short-run costs which road vehicles might regard as their lowest basis for pricing. While this is of course a considerable exaggeration since at least some terminal and shunting costs are short-run variables, the proportion does illustrate the order of magnitude of short-run avoidable costs as compared to those which are less immediately related to the individual service.

The pattern of expenditure shows that although considerable savings have been made in train-movement costs, and the costs of track and signalling have been held fairly constant, the administrative and general category has increased very considerably. While it was logical and even essential that the railways should have better management services, and some part of this category was taken up by increased deficencies in the superannuation fund due to the rundown in manpower, it is nevertheless disturbing to find that increases in control costs should take up almost all the savings in operating costs.

An alternative way of presenting the cost structure is by nature of expense as in Table 3.11.

TABLE 3.11
Working expenses by nature of expense

	1963 £ million	%	1968 £ million	%
Staff expenses	344·4	63	340·2	62
Fuel and power	47·6	8	25·4	5
of which coal	31·5		0·8	
oil	8·1		11·3	
electricity	8·0		13·3	
Materials, supplies and services	103·4	19	115·4	21
Depreciation and amortization	54·8	10	66·1	12
Total	597·8	100	572·5	100

Source: BRB *Annual Report, 1968*.

What emerges is the high proportion of labour costs, which has been only slightly diminished by the great manpower reduction of the 1960s. Even the figures in Table 3.11 understate the proportion of labour costs, since there is a certain labour cost hidden in the materials and services category. In view of the proportion of labour costs, the absolute reduction in working expenses since the Beeching Report has been a considerable achievement. All labour-intensive industries have been subjected to cost difficulties due to the faster acceleration of earnings than productivity, and the railways did better than most in stabilizing total labour costs. Moreover, although the cost reduction was relatively small in monetary terms, it was a considerably better achievement when viewed in real terms.

In spite of the cost reduction, output (measured in traffic units, a combination of passenger-miles and net ton-miles) fell faster than cost in the years 1963–68. Hence there was a rise in the expenses per unit in the years after the Beeching Report from 1·58 p in 1963 to 1·67 p in 1968. Without the Beeching reorganization the rise would undoubtedly have been much greater; nevertheless, it is a measure of the failure of Beeching that the trend was not reversed.

This rise in unit costs, in spite of a fall in total costs, points up a basic dilemma of the railway, that the various traffics are highly interdependent. This is a natural outcome of the high proportion of indirect and joint costs and the rigidity of the cost structure over long periods by normal industrial standards. No matter how efficient the railways are at carrying coal, the unit cost of carrying coal is very significantly affected by the success of the railways in the general merchandise and passenger fields. Conversely, the more coal there is to carry (or other traffics where a substantial surplus over direct costs can be charged) the more cheaply can the railways carry general merchandise because it needs to contribute less to indirects. Hence the understandable, if misleading, railway slogan: 'all traffic is good traffic', especially where there is surplus capacity.

Some comment must also be made about the unique aspect of cost which differentiates the railways from all other forms of transport, namely the provision and ownership of the permanent way and its associated signalling system. Discounting terminal facilities, which have their equivalents in other forms of transport, the costs of this provision were £96 million in 1968, or not far short of one-fifth of total railway expenses. Even this figure is somewhat lower than at the time of the Beeching analysis, mainly as a result of extensive line closures. The permanent way, because it is unique, gives rise to some interesting problems for the railways, most obviously the question of allocation of its cost between traffics. This, as we have already seen, is achieved by making the permanent way an indirect cost not directly attributable to any specific traffics, although for purposes of examining sector profitability an arbitrary designation of 0·29 p per passenger-mile and 0·21 p per ton-mile has been used. The difference is due to the higher standard of track and signalling required to cater for the greater frequency and higher speeds of passenger trains. In cases where closure is proposed, of course, the cost of the track is more specifically calculated.

The assumption that the railways have tended to make, fully accepted by the Beeching Report, has been that the provision of permanent way and signalling 'is a fixed cost, in the full sense of the term, all the while the route system remains unchanged'.[69] Joy has challenged this,[70] pointing out several possibilities: the number of tracks could be reduced; lengths of route could be put into lower maintenance categories; or the standard of maintenance itself could be reduced, especially in the lower, freight-only, categories. Costs, he argued, were therefore far from fixed even in the short term, and the realistic long-run maintenance cost, claimed in the Reshaping Report to be over £7,000 per mile of double-track passenger route, could be cut to £1,000 per route mile.

From the point of view of overall transport policy, the main issue arising out of the permanent way is that of comparative track costs.

It is of crucial importance to the economist concerned with coordinating transport, since unless costs and therefore prices are calculated on a comparable basis there can be no effective competition and resources will be misallocated. But it is also of immense practical importance to the modes of transport themselves, the scale of which can be seen in the BRB's assertion that if its view of road taxing were adopted, it could expect a market of 110 million tons of merchandise traffic by 1984; if not, and other things being equal, the market would only be 87 million tons.[71] Twenty million tons of freight represent the difference between a handsome profit and a disastrous loss. The arguments of the railways take two main forms: first, that road users do not bear the full cost of the track they use, particularly with respect to the lack of servicing of the capital involved; secondly, and more specifically, that heavy goods vehicles are not bearing their full share of road-user charges over trunk routes, where road–rail competition is greatest. This second argument was elaborated in a BRB submission to the Geddes Committee on Carriers' Licensing,[72] which purported to show that a ten-ton road goods vehicle was paying only between a third and a half of its true trunk-system costs through the licensing and taxation mechanism. Not unnaturally this was hotly disputed by the road interests, and Ministry of Transport engineers did something to demolish the railway case in arguing that, of the cost of new trunk roads, only $17\frac{1}{2}$ per cent should be attributed to heavy goods vehicles, rather than the 70 per cent which had been suggested by the BRB.[73] The railway intention was, of course, to prove that the 'true' rail costs of trunking were lower than the road costs, with a view to a redressing of the bias towards road through taxation. Unfortunately the issue has been bedevilled by conflicting statistics, and the Ministry of Transport investigation added little to the debate except to argue that a long and complex programme of research would be necessary to establish the road–rail split which would give the lowest resource costs to the country.

The problems of costing and pricing have been emphasized because of their central role in economic analysis and in the operation of the railways. But their significance should not be overestimated. It is unlikely that even a highly developed systems analysis model, giving expert guidance to costing and pricing can itself solve the railways' financial problems. As noted in the section on demand, price is in many respects less important than service. This means that better technical efficiency to overcome the actual service gap, and better marketing techniques to overcome the service image problems which the railway has, are of equal or more importance. To the first of these, covering various aspects of efficiency, we shall now turn.

V Efficiency

One of the chief characteristics of the output of transport is that it perishes with its production, so that storage is impossible. Since supply is geared to meet the highest potential demand which can be profitably dealt with, and since demand fluctuates over time, there is bound to be some waste of capacity. Efficiency in transport consists largely of minimizing that waste, whether it is of men effectively working for only half a shift, or of a half-empty train, or the infrequent use of a vehicle. For technical reasons arising from the integration and inflexibility of the railway system, there is likely to be much more surplus capacity on the railways than in road transport, where size of fleet can relatively easily be adapted to demand requirements. Efficiency is not only a function of waste capacity, of course. It is also a question of providing the correct service characteristics to traffic, of developing and introducing modern methods of operation, and of organizing human resources in the best available way.

The efficiency of the railways at the onset of the Beeching regime was unquestionably very low. Deakin and Seward, in their valuable statistical study of productivity in transport, have provided some evidence as to just how low. Measured in terms of output per total factor input (i.e. including capital and labour), they calculated that the railways actually had a negative rate of change per annum of −0·64 over the decade 1952–62.[74] By contrast, a similar measurement for road haulage showed a positive rate of change of 4·46 per annum, thus creating an annual differential change in productivity in excess of 5 per cent per annum.[75] Another way of looking at efficiency, according to the study, was in terms of absolute value of output. The authors calculated that the railway value of output per unit of combined factor input, measured in terms of pence per standardized labour unit hour equivalent was 20 p; the comparative figure for road haulage was 49·7 p, while even road passenger transport, which in many other respects performed poorly, had a figure of 49 p. A large part of the explanation for these figures can be found in the relative capital inputs: rail had a capital intensity of some £12,500 per employee, while road haulage had just over £2,000 and road passenger transport some £1,400. It goes without saying that the large amount of capital in the railways was underutilized. Indeed, perhaps the single most damning indication of low railway productivity was in its extremely low utilization of capacity. In 1962, the railways had approximately 80 per cent of total road/rail freight capacity, but carried only 17 per cent of output by value. Given that the demand for rail freight services declined over the decade 1952–62 by 28 per cent, capacity declined by only 6 per cent, resulting in a decline in capacity utilization of approximately 23 per cent. Road haulage, where capacity increased much less quickly than output, had an increase in capacity utilization over the same period of 44 per cent. Measured in terms of ton-miles achieved per capacity ton available, the discrepancy between the two modes was such that road haulage had an output 12·3 times greater than rail freight in 1962. Even more striking was the comparison in value of gross output per capacity ton in service. In 1958 the figure for the railways was £17, that for road haulage £301. Comparisons of this type inevitably involve an arbitrary definition of such concepts as capacity, and even capital intensity; nevertheless even if the figures given are taken merely as orders of magnitude they serve to illustrate the problems faced by the railways.

There were three basic areas in which the railways sought to increase their efficiency during the 1960s: (a) the productivity obtained from existing assets and methods; (b) the opportunities available from new methods of operation; (c) better procedures for investment and (d) the human resources area—the deployment of the labour force and management organization. It goes without saying that these various aspects of greater efficiency were intimately interrelated and part of a total approach. They will now be treated in order.

(a) *Asset Utilization*

The most obvious means of improving efficiency was merely to reduce the surplus capacity which existed throughout the railway system. In many instances this would of itself increase productivity almost proportionately. To take only two examples, the Reshaping Report noted that the maintenance of each freight wagon cost £30 per annum, so that its suggestion of cutting out 350,000 would save some £12 million annually; again a reduction in the stores held by the railways could reduce the capital employed by £15 million. In a few instances, however, costs were incurred by the act of reduction. In the case of marshalling yards, for instance, facilities had to be concentrated and this required investment. In other instances, of course, the extent of reduction in surplus capacity was only made possible by new working methods and investment in different parts of the system.

The name of Beeching has of course become famous for the passenger-line closures, but in fact these have been only a small part of the reduction in assets of all kinds, as Table 3.12 shows. The

TABLE 3.12
Asset reduction

	Jan. 1963	Dec. 1968	Dec. 1970*
Locomotives	12,628	4,658†	4,449
of which: diesel	3,683	4,326	4,126
electric	178	329	323
steam	8,767	3	—
Passenger carriages	33,821	19,544	18,678
Non-passenger carrying coaches	12,482	7,260	6,508
Freight vehicles	862,640	437,412	370,917
Containers	46,535	28,470	11,953
Road vehicles	14,319	9,611	—
Stations	6,801	3,235	2,868
of which: passenger and freight	2,696	314	224
passenger	1,610	2,302	2,199
freight	2,479	598	445
Marshalling yards	602	184	146
Route open for traffic (miles)	17,481	12,447	11,749
of which: passenger traffic	12,915	8,471	9,095
Total track open for traffic	47,543	33,976	31,281
Employees (rail and rail workshops only)	476,545	296,274	251,777

* Some of the figures for 1970 reflect transfers to NFC, e.g. containers, road vehicles and employees.
† This change is exaggerated by the move to diesel multiple units instead of locomotives for local passenger trains.
Source: BRB *Annual Reports*.

changes in manpower have been perhaps the most important of all. Table 3.13 gives some indices of changes in productivity, which have largely but by no means entirely been caused by the asset reductions. The table indicates a very significant improvement in all indices, but some of the improvements were not as good as they may appear since they merely recover a position which had been lost in the years before 1963. Thus the equivalent figure for the average passenger trainload in 1948 was 102, a figure that has never been achieved since. The wagon turnround time was another improvement which masks a long decline in the post-war period, since the equivalent time for 1948 was 8·8 days. This statistic was critically examined by the Select Committee in 1960, at which time the railway answer

TABLE 3.13
Indices of productivity

	1963	1968	1970*
Traffic units per employee	82,000	102,000	135,000
Traffic units per mile of track	777,000	957,000	1,084,000
Average wagon-load	12·94	16·14	17·67
coal and coke (tons)	14·39	16·30	17·24
iron and steel (tons)	15·51	18·77	19·54
other (tons)	8·44	13·91	17·30
Ton-miles per freight wagon	22,900	31,400	43,200
Traffic units per traction hour in traffic	8,590	13,390	15,100
Average wagon turnround time (days)	12·6	11·4	11·0
Average passenger trainload	90	97	103
Passengers per passenger coach	29,700	42,700	44,600

* Some of the indices for 1970 are affected by the 1968 Transport Act, e.g. transfer of employees to NFC.
Source: BRB *Annual Reports*.

was that the failure to cut the total wagon stock was the main reason.[76] But even allowing for a dramatic fall in the wagon stock and a rapid increase in average load per wagon in the 1960s, the railways cannot be satisfied with giving a wagon a different task only once every eleven days, since road haulage has in large part been successful by virtue of the extremely high vehicle utilization obtained. In 1968, moreover, the then Chairman of the BRB, Sir Henry Johnson, commented that the wagon fleet was still too old and too large: 'The existing wagon fleet, comprising more than 400,000 vehicles, restricted in speed and designed and built to Victorian standards, is the biggest and least efficient in Europe. It must be replaced by a modern fleet of say 100,000/150,000 wagons, capable of running at least at 60 mph, fitted with power brakes, and needing little maintenance.'[77] The improvement of the wagon fleet has in fact had a sad history. Its importance was recognized in the Modernization Plan, but the most important feature—the fitting of continuous brakes—was an almost total failure on mineral wagons due to design weaknesses. Even when some wagons were thus fitted, it was difficult under the marshalling system to ensure that all wagons in a train were of this kind. Thus unless the wagons were operated continuously together as trains, their value was limited. Indeed, they could be positively harmful if their coupling system did not mate with the old wagons.

Better utilization of the permanent way does not fit neatly into the tables of statistics given. We have already seen Joy's criticism of the Beeching Report's supposition that the permanent way is a fixed cost in the truest sense of the term, but in fact BR had already

THE RAILWAYS

modified the statement by the appearance early in 1965 of its further proposals *The Development of the Major Railway Trunk Routes*, which recommended some 5,000 miles of route for development as the future trunk system. The corollary of this was greater track utilization, since the study was concerned with the relationship between levels of traffic and track capacity.

The Trunk Routes Report recognized that truck utilization could be increased inter alia by better timetabling, better signalling, faster speeds, longer, heavier trains or cutting out surplus tracks or routes. One of the most important findings was that many routes were duplicated or triplicated. Without necessarily closing lines, the BRB estimated that rationalization and selective development could halve the indirect costs of movement over trunk routes. This would also help to give better utilization of locomotives, rolling stock and lineside facilities. Thus the BRB pointed out that four routes from London to the West Riding, and three to the West Country, Scotland and Manchester were all too many. It also pointed out that a good deal of extra route capacity could be created by improvement in other aspects of operation. While the capacity surplus to reasonable future expectations was not quantified, it was clearly sizeable. The object therefore became to cut down capacity at least to the level of peak demand.

For those lines not selected for development, this meant single tracking in many instances, and even then some lines would still have surplus capacity. Many lines have already been singled—some of them, such as the line between Salisbury and Exeter, on what were previously thought of as main lines. The Newcastle–Edinburgh route is another famous stretch which will probably be suitable for singling at some time in the future. Joy and Foster, continuing the logic of the Trunk Routes Report, have suggested that by 1984 there need be only fifteen routes in the whole country with double track and only two with four tracks.[78] Unfortunately, however, reduction of this surplus capacity was not necessarily or even often achieved as soon as it had been identified. Services had to be rationalized, alternative routes improved, new signalling systems installed; indeed in some circumstances it might be cheaper to leave the surplus, at least for a time, than incur expenditure to remove it.

The Trunk Routes Report also noted that better track utilization would require better train discipline. In particular it required similar speeds from all the trains on a particular section, since capacity would be wasted given a large speed differential. In fact the number of trains which can pass over a single line is greater if all

TABLE 3.14

Present and future speeds and payloads

	Average speed (mph)		Payload	
	1964	1984	1964	1984
Inter-city passenger	30–60	50 or 70	150 passengers	250 passengers
General merchandise	20–40	50	100 tons	400 tons
Oil	20–30	50	450 tons	1000 tons
Coal	15–30	35	500 tons	1000 tons
Iron and steel—raw materials	20–30	35	600 tons	1000 tons

Source: *The Development of the Major Railway Trunk Routes*, BRB, 1965, p. 36.

run at 40 mph than if alternate trains run at 80 mph and 40 mph. This meant that freight trains would have to be considerably speeded up if passenger trains were not to suffer and, as we have noted, speed is a critical element in passenger demand. Table 3.14 shows the anticipated increase in average speeds by 1984, and also that in payloads, another vital element in overall efficiency and track utilization. To achieve the required rate of improvement, replacement of the wagon fleet is vital; but, as noted, Britain still has the poorest wagon fleet in Europe. One further point is that the average speeds of freight trains shown in Table 3.14 are, of course, those of trains on the move. In the past most freight has had to undergo several marshallings, which will be progressively eliminated in the future, so that the improvement in service to the consignor will be far more than merely the improvement in average train speeds.

(b) *New Methods of Operation*

We turn now to new techniques and operating methods. The major developments in these areas, in the 1960s came mainly on the freight side. One of the most ambitious objectives of the Beeching Report was to transform the unit of traffic from the wagon-load to the train. The logic was clear; a wagon is not a means of traction. To treat it as the basic unit means that a complex organization has to be brought into play before it actually begins to move. But once the train is formed, more wagons and heavier loads require little extra organization. And if the train can remain permanently coupled, or can be made up in the consignor's own yard, the organization initially required drops sharply. To achieve this meant progressively eliminating the interminable marshalling and shunting of wagons which not only added greatly to costs, but more importantly, caused poor service through delays. Thus the railways developed three basic types of train which would each work to set patterns, preferably 'circuit' working to maximize running time, and be continuously coupled.[79] These were the merry-go-round train, the company train, and the freightliner. Each was an imaginative idea; none has quite fulfilled expectations.

Merry-go-round working was particularly applicable to carry coal from pits to power stations although it could be used for any minerals. A permanently coupled train of 28 or so wagons, each of 52 tons capacity, running between pit and power station, with automatic loading and below-track hoppers to enable unloading on the move at destination, could do five round trips a day, carrying more than 1,500 tons of coal on each trip. The expectation was that three-quarters of all coal delivered to power stations would be in block trains by 1970. But there have been difficulties from both power stations and collieries: power stations have not come on stream; collieries have had production difficulties and more collieries than estimated have been needed to satisfy the Central Electricity Generating Board.[80] The 'mix' of coal required may now necessitate carrying coal from as many as thirty separate collieries to the power station. In addition the cost of converting the loading facilities at each pit (at £300,000–£500,000) has proved much higher than anticipated so that conversion has been slow. There have also been technical difficulties in rapid loading. The upshot of these problems was that in 1969 only 9 million tons out of the possible total of 45 million tons could be rapid loaded and even for this relatively small amount the number of wagons required rose from the original 5,400 to 8,000.

The company train is a regularly scheduled train geared to the needs of a specific company. The main advantages to the railways are that it gives through working and, more importantly, the security of a long-term commitment. Somewhat less binding than the company train is the charter train, by which a customer hires a whole train capacity. The best situation for BR arises with customers' investment in their own rolling stock, for this entails a long-term commitment, on their part, and for BR a release from heavy capital costs. This approach has been successful in the oil and cement industries. Shell-Mex, for instance, has invested £20 million in rolling stock and rail-handling equipment. However, the total throughput by the variations of the company-train idea has not been all that was anticipated. Nevertheless, whereas at the end of 1963 there were 600 company trains a week, by the end of 1968 there were about 1,500.[81]

The most exciting and publicized new method of operation has been the freightliner, designed to fulfil the dual function of cutting down the high transhipment costs between road and rail and to provide a means of aggregating wagonload or smaller lots into trainload units. It is of course true that 51 per cent of the ownership of Freightliners Ltd, was transferred to the National Freight Corporation by the 1968 Transport Act, but since its primary function is to give service by rail, it is preferable to examine it in this chapter. The attractions for the customer are standards of speed, reliability, safety and freedom from vibration and pilferage far in advance of anything the railways have previously offered, and keenly competitive with road haulage. The train consists of permanently coupled flatcars capable of 60 mph on to which modular containers of varying lengths can be loaded. Under the original plan 55 special terminals were to be set up to provide links across the country for a total investment cost, including the train sets, of some £100 million. It was recognized at the time that intensive utilization—each unit to work 90,000 miles a year in place of the 3,000 by the average pre-Beeching wagon—and high load factors of around 75 per cent in both directions were vital to permit the competitive rates necessary to service the capital and compete with road haulage. Original estimates suggested a potential market of some 30 million tons, made up of some 12 million tons of existing wagonload traffics, 3 million tons of sundries and, best of all, 16 million tons of road-borne traffic which could now be carried more efficiently by rail.[82] Again, however, actual throughput has not come up to expectations. The 30 million tons by 1968 anticipated in the Reshaping Report was in fact only some 2½ million tons and the turnover £6·4 million. Against this must be set the fact that the original estimate took in all suitable traffic, and some of this is being profitably carried by the railways in other ways, as by company trains or even private freightliners. But the anticipated load factors were not being achieved except on a few routes, and in 1969 and 1970 there was a continuing, although diminishing, loss on the full costs of operation.[83] The original scheme for 55 depots has been cut to less than 30 and some established routes have been cut out. The main difficulty with the concept has been the apparent miscalculations of the mileage at which the efficiency of the rail trunk haul would overcome the door-to-door service of the road haulier and the necessity of two road–rail transfers by freightliner. The Reshaping Report suggested 100 miles; this is almost certainly an optimistic estimate for most traffics on most routes. A better break-even point would be 150 miles, with haulage able to compete under some circumstances even above 200 miles. The distance of break-even between road and rail has unquestionably been reduced, but it seems likely that it has been reduced within a distance bracket where there is not much traffic to be carried anyway. A second problem has been the high cost of collection and delivery, which has curtailed the tributary area of a terminal to about 10 miles rather than the 30 to 40 originally anticipated. Nevertheless, the freightliner is by no means a failure; some 470,000 containers were carried in 1970 as compared to some 270,000 in 1968; its use will spread and it will be profitable, even if the original estimates were too optimistic.[84]

The development of the various systems of trainload working still left major weaknesses in BR's freight operations. In 1970, out of the total freight tonnage of 199 million, 90 million still came from wagonload working. This is clearly too large an amount to be rejected easily. Moreover, even those customers who mostly provide trainload traffics also require some movement in wagonload units, and without this facility might not be as ready to maintain their private sidings. Wagonload and trainload can thus be complementary as well as alternatives to each other. The railways have thus had to accept that a viable railway network cannot do without wagonload traffics and have moved towards a systems approach for wagonload movement, in conjunction with the new methods of pricing and costing which were mentioned earlier. Instead of accepting traffics on an ad hoc basis and then sending trains to those destinations, the new concept involves a timetabled system of services like the inter-city passenger or company freight-train systems. The timetabling is of course dependent on the continuous monitoring of traffic flows and will inevitably mean more selectivity in the acceptance of consignments. However, the rationalization of this area will inevitably take a considerable time, particularly at the operating level, where the necessary faster wagon turnround, better reliability and stricter terminal discipline cannot be achieved overnight, especially in view of the outdated wagon fleet.[85]

One of the most necessary technical improvements relevant to the improvement of the freight operation was in the system of control, which was increasingly centralized with the aid of computers and electronic equipment. It was this, in fact, which made possible the overall system planning and new pricing and costing methods which we have already discussed. The slack and the tolerances which could be permitted in a system operating far below capacity were not permissible in one striving to utilize capacity to the utmost.

Electronic control was extended over the location and movement of rolling stock and locomotives, the utilization of manpower and, far from least, the whole signalling apparatus.[86] A particular example was the control of freight wagons. With the halving of the wagon fleet within six years better control was vital to maintain availability. In place of the previous existing regional and line quasi-autonomy, BR set up a Central Wagon Authority in 1963. Cutting out the regional and line staging points, the 36 districts or divisions were linked to the centre by telex. Computerized mathematical forecasting techniques were introduced to minimize empty wagon movement and cut down on stocks; thus the Cardiff division reduced its daily wagon needs by 20 per cent within a year.[87] Timetabling and forward planning became critical as the spare asset capacity was progressively reduced, since it meant that ad hoc assignments for unexpected occurrences were much more difficult to achieve.

The result of this tighter control has been a considerable improvement in the quality of the freight service. The objective in the 1971 Corporate Plan is to aim for a promise of next-day delivery for 50 per cent of consignments, and second-day delivery for at least 45 per cent of the remainder. This is a far cry from the old rule of thumb that wagons would be re-marshalled on average every thirty miles, and it should have a particularly beneficial effect on the image of railway freight service. Improvements in marketing should further enhance customer relations. By 1975 it is anticipated that 90 per cent of the traffic will originate from no more than 75 large concerns, and specific executives have been assigned to each of these key customers, thus providing that direct customer contact which has been a railway weakness vis-à-vis road haulage.

By comparison with the radical changes in freight operation, there were less marked changes in passenger operation in the 1960s, mainly because investment under the Modernization Plan had already achieved a great deal. The inter-city service was hardly new in conception, but it was given better publicity and timetabling, higher speeds, and there was greater attention to passenger comfort. The service has been particularly popular where electrification has been carried out. Aside from providing increases in revenue, the system has revived the public image of the railways. Off the main routes many rural stopping services were of course closed. In others, operating costs were cut to the bone by the introduction of diesel multiple units, track singling, unstaffed halts, simplified signalling, and the avoidance of investment. But even if the Reshaping Report's minimum 17,000 passengers per week in order to pay the full costs of operation was too high (as many claimed), few of the rural services are independently viable on any conceivable basis, and in any case, the progressive reduction of station amenities can only be a deterrent against travel. The suburban lines, apart from those which have recently been electrified, saw even less change in operating methods than the other two sectors. Around London, and especially south of the Thames, there was a considerable shortage of capacity for which there seemed to be no immediate solution.

But if the actual improvements in passenger-operating methods were of degree rather than kind, British Rail's design team at Derby was working on an entirely new conception of rail transport. This was the Advanced Passenger Train (APT), based more on aerodynamics than conventional surface-transport design, which should start operating in the middle 1970s. Its advantage is that thanks to better track-holding qualities it can travel on existing track at speeds of up to 125 mph, and on improved track at up to 150 mph. Even the former speed would permit the London–Newcastle run to be made in under three hours, or London to Glasgow or Edinburgh in under four. As such, it offers very considerable possibilities in the future battle for inter-city traffic. There is, however, likely to be a gap between the present generation of locomotives and the arrival of the APT. The intended development of a high-speed diesel train as an interim measure is unlikely to come to fruition much, if at all, before the APT. Thus for some time increased speeds will be dependent on track improvements and doubling up on locomotives.

The change in methods of traction through the phasing out of steam and its replacement by diesel and electric traction was a major cost-saver for the railways in the 1960s, as Table 3.11 showed. The Select Committee in 1960 noted that the immediate movement costs, consisting of fuel and power and footplate staff, were 25 p per engine mile for steam as compared to 17 p for electric traction and 8 p for diesel. High maintenance costs and a low power/weight ratio also counted against steam.[88] The change was, of course, a central feature of the Modernization Plan, although much of the transition was not implemented until after Dr Beeching took over and it was not until August 1968 that the last steam train ran. However, both dieselization and electrification caused difficulties which were a reflection of the faults of the Modernization Plan—rushing projects into service, and inefficient evaluation.

Mass dieselization was begun, in late 1957, without the extended trial period to evaluate different designs which had originally been envisaged. Teething troubles in operation were thus almost inevitable. Maintenance requirements were underestimated, the initial locomotives were underpowered and subject to structural fatigue.

Above all, too many different locomotive types were introduced: twenty-one types in all instead of the three to five required, creating difficulties of non-standardization over a whole range of operating issues from availability of spare parts to driver training. At least some of the blame for this must be placed on the regional autonomy of the 1950s.

The move to electric traction was also far from smooth. In this case, however, the difficulty was the high initial cost. The original cost estimate for the London–Manchester/Liverpool scheme was £118 million, the actual cost in the region of £175 million despite economies. Given the curbs on railway expenditure thereafter, electrification required special justification. Sceptics asked if diesel traction could not do the job equally well. The answer was, of course, that each could perform well in a particular situation. Indeed, the original railway intention, that electric traction should be used for densely trafficked routes and that diesel should take the rest, was perfectly justifiable.[89] However, doubts arose over the fact that the overall traffic levels were lower than expected, and also because electrification carried with it a good deal of concomitant track and signalling reconstruction. Resignalling alone cost £40 million on the London Midland electrification scheme, while a good deal of civil engineering was also required. Delays in running during the reconstruction did not help the cause of electrification. Moreover, the design problems and manufacturing faults which plagued dieselization were by no means absent from the electrified lines.

The choice between diesel and electric traction can be illustrated from the 1967 operating costs, comparing diesel with 25 kV ac electrification on the basis of yearly maintenance and total train miles.[90] Electric locomotive maintenance costs were 3·52 p per mile in main works and 2·44 p in depots; running costs were 10·12 p per mile for fuel; and there was a charge of 3·34 p per mile for fixed equipment maintenance, giving a total of 19·42 p per mile. Comparative costs for diesel were 12·0 p and 8·72 p for maintenance and 5·68 p for fuel, giving a total of 26·40 p. When the higher first cost of electrification is taken into account, there is a break-even point at which electricity becomes cheaper, which varies between 8 and 12 million traffic units per annum per mile of route, depending on the degree of locomotive utilization.

(c) *Investment*

It was for a long time axiomatic within the railways that large amounts of investment in modern operating methods could achieve a breakthrough in efficiency, competitiveness and financial solvency. This was the philosophy behind the Modernization Plan of the middle 1950s, but the hope placed in it was disproved for reasons briefly mentioned in the historical introduction. It was one of the achievements of Dr Beeching that he accepted that no amount of investment would justify the size of the network at that time. The corollary of this was to press for investment in areas of strength. Even this, however, was and remains difficult to justify in the context of continuing financial problems. There are many projects which of themselves seem desirable, but which may apparently not produce any positive return because weighed down by other sections of the enterprise. This problem of justification may be among the most severe facing the railways in the 1970s. But before looking at this issue a few general comments on the problems of railway investment may be apposite.

On the railways, the conditions for investment decision-making are far from perfect. The problems of costing provide the first difficulty, even if the formidable questions of social cost-benefit criteria for investment are ignored.[91] The railways, as we noted, find it extremely difficult to assess the present profitability of a particular piece of the system, never mind that in the future. On this basis it has been a major problem to decide which parts of the system would best repay investment and which should be discarded. Although the Modernization Plan recognized the distinction and laid down sensible general outlines, implementing these ideas produced some striking errors. Even if extra revenues could be shown to be forthcoming from an investment, it did not follow that the particular service would be making a profit. In many instances, it later transpired, a large loss was merely turned into a small loss rather than a profit.

Demand forecasting is another major difficulty. It has been very hard for the railways to accept that they are a declining industry, so that demand forecasts have in many instances proved far too optimistic. Yet because of the high proportion of fixed costs which must be borne, relatively small discrepancies in demand can result in large differences in unit costs for the traffics actually carried. Much of railway investment, moreover, tends to consist of a large number of small projects, each of which is individually difficult to relate to demand. The price system in use can also distort demand, as has been particularly true of the passenger side of the railways where the standard full fare, the unduly cheap season ticket, and the extensive cross-subsidization meant that there was little or no idea of the true elasticity of demand. On a wider scale, distortion is also caused by the absence of a market price for road usage or comparable economic criteria for road investment. But perhaps the worst problems arise from the integrated nature of the railways. There are many necessary investments which are not related to specific outputs but only to the whole system or a large part of it. The issue is further complicated by the interdependency of assets whose economic (or physical) life does not expire simultaneously. Thus the decision not to replace one asset may result in the waste of others with considerable life left. The temptation is continually to replace small assets on a piecemeal basis without asking the real economic question whether the addition of the marginal increment, however necessary, does not imply that the whole interrelated part of the system should be closed down. Lastly, rail investment is inflexible; it generally has no alternative opportunity cost at a later date. Yet rail assets typically have a very long life expectancy, and in any case cannot easily be amortized at an accelerated rate because of the industry's financial problems. Hence the need for more than ordinary care in rail investment.

The Beeching era was undoubtedly influenced by the failures of the Modernization Plan. It was clear from the start that the railways would be allowed to spend much less money.[92] After allowing for prior commitment to a number of projects, the amount necessary for implementing the Reshaping Report was judged to be £250 million.[93] However, the difficulties with investment projects were by no means over, and throughout the 1960s strained relations over investment criteria have frequently existed between the BRB, the Ministry of Transport, and the Treasury.

Soon after the Reshaping Report the Ministry of Transport sent BR a memorandum on the investment criteria which they proposed to apply.[94] This was later supplemented by certain rules laid down by the BRB itself. The Ministry asked for a five-year 'rolling' programme of investment as envisaged under the 1960 White Paper on the nationalized industries on the basis of which it would give 'as good an idea as possible' of the amounts of capital that might be available. An important change was that the case for undertaking any specific investment was to be supported by an assessment of the profitability of the existing facilities. To these the BRB rules added that estimates must be based on assumptions of changing costs, particularly wage increases, the omission of which had been a severe fault in the estimates of the 1950s. A minimum of 8 per cent return was set if the project were to be justified on financial grounds, but 12–15 per cent was to be desirable. Practicable alternatives were to be considered also. Most important of all, discounted cash flow was to be used to compare projects, with the discount rate set at 8 per cent. This approach was softened, however, by the Ministry's written recognition that investment designed merely to replace assets might worsen rather than improve the financial situation because of higher depreciation and interest charges.

Inevitably the new system has meant much closer control by the Ministry, but even so it is doubtful if it has entirely achieved its objectives, although it has been associated with a rapid cutback in the quantity of investment undertaken. In the three years 1959–61 the annual total was in excess of £160 million, but this was cut back sharply to £87 million and £69 million for 1968 and 1969 respectively. Some cutback was essential after the profligacy of the Modernization Plan, but the latter amounts do not do much more than replace necessary assets. On the other hand there has been very little back-checking of investment as a means of control, a matter about which the Select Committee on Nationalized Industries has been very critical. Moreover the BRB has shown itself far from happy with the new system, holding that its commercial judgement is being unfairly called into question, even though it recognizes that most projects have not met obstructive opposition.[95] The BRB's opinion that its investment criteria were acceptable was not held by the Ministry of Transport, which has claimed that many of the projects put forward for its approval did not show that the investment would give an adequate return.[96] It further complained that a discounted cash-flow analysis was missing from a large number of proposals. The main trouble has been with replacement projects, where the calculation is admittedly complicated because the project is already built into the system. But even more important was the comment that the Board seemed to consider 'basic operational needs' quite separately from economic factors. This amounted to saying that the BRB asked for an act of faith on the part of the Ministry: an example of this was the coaching vehicles mentioned above, where the Board argued commercial judgement as a justification.

These arguments about justification are likely to continue. Capital projects will be very difficult for the BRB to finance unless they are certain to produce a very high net return. Plans like that already mentioned of the Southern Region to spend £350 million on the London commuter network are hardly likely to meet this criteria, judged on private cost-accounting terms. But there are also three other issues related to investment which are likely to give the railways trouble in the 1970s. The first is the ceiling placed on investment by the Government as part of the overall control of public spending. In 1970 this amounted to £83 million,[97] which the BRB considers quite inadequate for its needs. The requirements of the 1971 Corporate Plan for the railways are for spending £517 million (at 1970 prices) during the years 1971–75, although this represents a very considerable fall from the early 1960s.

The second issue is that depreciation is measured on historic rather than replacement cost.[98] To make provision for replacement would cost a further £20 million or so a year, more than double the 1970 profit, although not all assets would necessarily be replaced.

The third is the source of funds. In 1970 total finance of £94·1 million was provided from depreciation and amortization (£47 million), sale of assets, largely property (£18·7 million), profit (£9·5 million), liquidation of current assets (£4·9 million), and finally bank borrowing (£14·0 million). This indicates, and the 1971 Plan admits, that it will not be practicable to finance investment from purely internal sources. Yet one of the problems of the 1960s was the rising burden of interest debt resulting from new capital found outside the business. Recapitalization under the 1968 Transport Act was designed to alleviate this problem, but as the White Paper *Railway Policy* noted '. . . there is a clear possibility and danger that the burden of interest and depreciation will again, as the years go by, mount beyond the capacity of the industry to meet it'.[99] However, by an extremely imaginative financial device, involving the formation of a company in which railway tax losses can be offset against the profits of partners, the BRB hopes to obtain its new equipment at one-third below the normal net price. But while this will certainly help, funds will remain in short supply.

(d) *Labour and Management*

The last means of improving efficiency was by a better organization and utilization of people, which in the early 1960s primarily meant a radical reduction in labour force. Despite a 25 per cent drop in total employment since 1948, labour costs at the onset of the Beeching regime still accounted for well over 60 per cent of direct working expenses, so that unless substantial savings could be achieved here, other improvements would count for little. In practice, a rapid speed of rundown was attained, from 476,000 at the beginning of 1963 to 296,000 at the end of 1968. Such a reduction was bound to create human relations difficulties, especially in an industry with strong unions and an almost civil service tradition of security. In view of this, it is not surprising to find that labour relations in the years following the Reshaping Report were far from good.

Yet in spite of the inevitability of difficulties it is arguable that the problems of decline were not handled as diplomatically by the railway management in this period as, for instance, in the coal industry. The Reshaping Report itself, although offering general provision for redundancy, created a good deal of alarm by pointing to the need for large cuts in the labour force without specifying the areas or occupations involved. Perhaps the lack of detail was deliberate, since the report followed soon after a considerable furore over the railway workshops, but if so it was hardly successful. The workshops had provided a particularly difficult situation, since they contained large concentrations of skilled men who could not easily be redeployed. To keep open all the twenty-nine main workshops was clearly wrong in view of their need for modernization and the diminishing demand for their services. It was therefore decided in mid-1962 that the number would be reduced to sixteen. This meant considerable hardship for some communities; even a large town like Darlington was to lose employment which accounted for 15 per cent of its insured male population. As a result of the decision, 18,000 men in the workshops were given notice that they would become redundant over a five-year period. The joint consultation which had previously been a feature of rail industrial relations was ignored. There was an immediate outcry at the announcement, followed by a one-day protest strike on 3 October 1962, the first national rail stoppage since 1926. It is easy to say that better consultation with the unions should have produced a more friendly reception for the whole railway reorganization. In practice there would probably still have been hostility. The main point, however, is that the employees and unions deserved more chances for negotiation, if not on the principle of the cuts, on the way they affected particular groups, on retraining opportunities, on redundancy payments, and on results of the cuts.

The implementation of the Reshaping Report itself also caused labour difficulties. There was a particularly fierce public battle over the refusal of the cartage staff to allow private enterprise road vehicles into freightliner terminals which delayed the introduction of the service and caused difficulties thereafter. There were also several battles over manning, some of the major ones being between the two major operating unions, the National Union of Railwaymen and the Amalgamated Society of Locomotive Engineers and Firemen, as much as between management and employees. Two courts of inquiry and several threats of national strikes have been the outward signs of unrest, together with localized, small-scale strike or go-slow action by groups such as drivers or signalmen. Sometimes the results of the cross-pressures had an air of tragi-comedy. Thus at the end of 1966 some 1,600 firemen were left with nothing at all to do while awaiting absorption as drivers after the no-redundancy agreement on manning in 1965. Although the extent of unrest should not be exaggerated in view of the rapid reductions the railways were able to achieve, the unsettled labour situation was undoubtedly exploited by road hauliers who emphasized it as part of the lack of reliability of the railways.

Redundancy may have dominated the railways' labour problems in the 1960s, but other issues were also important. Paradoxically, recruitment was a problem in some areas, stemming from the nation-wide pay scale of the railways, which meant that levels of pay were inadequate to attract staff in areas of high employment and earnings. The unions, however, fought strongly against district differentials. In fact the whole question of pay, never easy at the best of times, caused great difficulties after the financial deficit mounted rapidly in the late 1950s.[100] To look into the problem, a committee of inquiry under Mr C. W. Guillebaud was set up to establish standards of comparability with jobs outside the railways. Thus when it reported in 1960 the committee created a precedent which was subsequently used by the unions to their advantage. Management naturally saw this principle as taking no account of the railways' ability to pay. Nor was management prepared to use increased productivity as a basic criterion, since much of the increase came not from the employees but from the diminution of surplus capacity and the high level of investment. The problem of criteria thus constantly troubled the industry's negotiations, whose machinery culminated in a three-man arbitration board of persons from outside the industry, the Railway National Staff Tribunal. In 1965 the newly formed Prices and Incomes Board was given the problem to examine.[101] The Board strongly criticized comparability because of its inflationary leap-frogging effects. Instead it recommended productivity bargaining to achieve this and it suggested that the prior separation of pay and productivity discussions under different bodies should be ended. It further suggested that there was room for both a cutting down of the amount of overtime worked, and for much greater flexibility as between grades. The Board also backed some of the complaints of the unions about poor management communications and inadequate measurement of the savings to be expected from proposed changes.

Not unexpectedly, the suggestions of the PIB took some time to be developed, but in August 1968 a major productivity agreement was signed. It cost the railways £13 million annually or about 7 per cent on basic rates, payable in advance of the productivity gains, which themselves were to amount to only £13·3 million. In spite of this apparently dubious bargain, the railways have gained far more than from any previous agreements. The most interesting and potentially valuable proposal was a move from the conventional 40-hour week split into five eight-hour shifts to four ten-hour shifts. This permitted a move from three eight-hour shifts in the working day to two ten-hour shifts, leaving a four-hour dead period at the least useful time of day. In particular the ten-hour shift would with the help of overlapping shifts enable the commuter peak to be bridged by a single shift rather than two. The railways also obtained much greater flexibility, most notably from the previously intransigent footplatemen–guards rivalry. Under the old system 170 jobs were grouped into only 35 categories with only ten pay rates. Moreover, a second productivity agreement, this time costing £15 million annually, was signed in 1969. Given the fears, the rivalries and the demarcation lines, and the encrusted tradition of the railways, those agreements were a very considerable feat. Nevertheless, bearing in mind the labour-intensive nature of the railways in an era when wage increases will probably continue to outstrip productivity in the economy as a whole, and also the fact that such an integrated system is vulnerable to pressure from small groups of workers, industrial relations is always likely to be a potential Achilles heel of railway operation.

If industrial relations until recently received too little attention, the same can hardly be said of the other main area concerning human resource, the structure and organization of management. There are considerable problems in finding the best format, since there is a basic conflict between the needs of technology which point towards a centralized, integrated management structure, and the needs of marketing in which a high degree of local flexibility is desirable in order to compete with the railways' smaller-scale rivals. As was noted in the historical section, after nationalizaton there was a sharp move towards centralization, which was followed by an equally sharp move back towards regional autonomy when the Conservatives came to power. In the early 1960s there was an attempt to go in both directions at once. The 1962 Transport Act gave the six regional boards more power than the area boards which they replaced, but at much the same time Dr Beeching initiated a move back towards centralization by increasing the importance of the central functions. These changes were of course important, not least for their disruptive effects, but it is arguable that their real importance was symbolic, that successive governments, by depending on them, were seeking internal solutions to what were in large part external problems.

The 1968 Transport Act did not itself make major changes in management structure, although it did make provision for the repeal of the statutory obligation for the regional boards to have operating responsibility for the railway system. But the review of the Joint Steering Committee, which preceded and was a mainspring for the Act, and an examination by the management consultants, McKinseys, immediately after the Act, did lead to radical changes. Perhaps the main recommendation was that the Board itself should concentrate on policy questions and on long-term planning; the members, of whom fewer would be needed, would therefore be freed from day-to-day executive responsibilities. Below the Board there came into existence a thirteen-man Railway Management Group, of which only two members were also members of the main Board. The composition of the group was the second main recommendation. For the first time the chairman of the five regions sat at the same table as the chief executives of the main central functions—freight, passenger, finance, systems and operations, and personnel. The thirteenth man was head of BR Workshops, which was given a separate and almost autonomous status by the 1968 Act. Further down the management hierarchy there is the introduction of profit centres at all points where resources used for particular traffic flows can be identified. This means that managers can be much more fully accountable for the results they achieve, and is yet another desirable by-product of the forward planning and budgeting system.

VI Conclusions

Given the situation of the railways, it is natural to look for the causes of their decline. Was it an inexorable function of technology, was it the fault of management, was the public or were successive governments to blame? Some decline was inevitable, and for this the main reason has been technological. The railways are insufficiently flexible to give the convenience of the point-to-point service of the road-based industries, while railway infrastructure requires a far greater degree of organization and discipline than the virtually self-regulating road system with the freedom it affords for thousands of concurrent movements. Following this and given the need for the retrenchment of an over-extended system, it has been the problems of organizational adjustment which have caused most trouble. As Deakin and Seward have pointed out 'The organizational problem of matching capacity to demand is enormously different in the expanding case from what it is in the contracting case.'[102] Some aspects of the problem have been the integrated and high fixed cost nature of the railway system; the social obligations imposed by law and custom, both externally to the public and internally to the employees; the great difficulty of recognizing long-term trends in demand; and the loss of many of the economies of scale on which the railways have depended to offset the flexibility of their road competitors. It is perhaps not surprising that neither British railway management nor any other in the world has found any easy solution.

Even if decline was inevitable and difficult to achieve smoothly, the railways have still cost Britain dearly. Well over £2,000 million in written-off capital (which still has to be paid to the stock holders) and deficit grants, and a good deal more in investment which has never produced any return has been expended since the war on a service which now accounts for only a minimal proportion of Britain's transport. To try to attribute blame for this situation is perhaps not very edifying, but the faults were great. Management, governments and the public must all take a share of the blame.

Railway management must be indicted because it failed to search for a new role for the railways in the changed conditions of the post-war world. It is an even greater criticism that the recognition of this fact when it did come had to be imposed from the outside by Beeching rather than coming from within. Yet it is only fair to add that once the lead had been given, management reacted rapidly and favourably. The 1960s were a decade of revolution unparalleled in railway history. In almost every respect vast strides were made, in the reduction of the system size and particularly manpower, with commensurate gains in productivity, in introducing new methods of operating, and perhaps most important of all, in developing better methods of financial planning and control. Indeed, its ingenious scheme for exploiting tax losses has set the pace for the whole of British industry. It is true that much of this has yet to bear fruit, that it was not until it was told to do so by the Prices and Incomes Board that standard price increases were abandoned, and that investment evaluation still does not please the Ministry. Nevertheless if railway management deserves a major share of the blame for the railways' performance, it is more for its lack of foresight in the 1950s than its lack of change in the 1960s or its preparedness for the 1970s.

The role of governments of both parties has not been a happy one. They positively encouraged the railways in their non-commercial attitudes, partly because they too hoped that something would turn up, but also because they feared public disapproval. The theory of ministerial control over the nationalized industries is perhaps seen at its worst in the history of the railways. On the one hand there was no attempt until the 1960s to evaluate the function of the railways and to set a clear policy to ensure public value for money. Policy guidance was virtually non-existent, especially with respect to the inherent contradictions in the obligations of the railways. On the other hand, the so-called 'rules' of the Nationalization Acts and the 1961 and 1967 White Papers were not very applicable to the railways. The financial deficit precluded either breaking even under the 1947 Act or being set any target under the 1961 White Paper, while difficulties of measurement in both the costing/pricing and investment fields meant that long-run marginal cost pricing and the test rate of discount, the two main guidelines of the 1967 White Paper, could not easily be made relevant. But if governments neither gave policy leads nor applied rules, they did interfere a great deal to the detriment of the professional management. Two comments can serve to illustrate this. As the Permanent Secretary to the Ministry of Transport rather bewilderedly told the Select Committee: 'The relationship is different [from that with other industries], because over the years in relation to the railway industry something has gone terribly wrong.'[103] The Select Committee translated this in their conclusion: 'The Committee . . . believe that the continuance of the detailed Ministerial intervention that has been experienced by British Railways would seriously call in question the position of the Board as a partly autonomous public corporation. If Ministers are to concern themselves in detail and in depth with commercial management, then direct Ministerial operation might be preferable.'[104]

A final paragraph must be reserved for the public's share of blame. Essentially governments did little more than reflect the undoubted public desires for incompatible objectives. A unique love–hate relationship always existed between the railways and the public, which made rational decisions even more difficult than would otherwise have been the case. Letters to *The Times* about the latest railway outrage against commuters could be sure of a sympathetic response; a rise in the price of railway tea could become a headline. On another level, transport, and particularly British Rail, regularly provoked more questions in Parliament than any other topic. Admittedly, however, there was little attempt to educate the public to what could reasonably be expected of the railways.

However blame should be apportioned, by the second half of the 1960s it was already apparent that the railway policies laid down in the first part of the decade were not going to be successful in the terms laid down by their creators in spite of very considerable improvements in many spheres. The Conservative Government had staked the future of the railways on competitive freedom and the drastic reconstruction envisaged by Dr Beeching. The failure of this policy could not reasonably be blamed on non-implementation of the reshaping proposals even though the network size of 8,000 miles that Beeching had prescribed never looked like being achieved. There was a failure of nerve on the part of the Conservatives, some reversal of policy by the Labour Party on passenger closures, and numerous delays with other proposals, but the major recommendations of the report were broadly carried out. Yet the end of the 1960s saw the financial position of the railways no better and in some respects worse than at the start of the decade, primarily because the freight situation did not improve as expected by the Reshaping Report. True, the losses had been stabilized, but the easily available short-term economies had been exhausted, and costs were still rising. In other words, the financial deficit had to be accepted as inescapable given the railways' obligations; no conceivable changes in marketing or technical efficiency were going to eradicate it. It was clear that yet another policy was needed. The choice seemed to lie among three options: even more savage cutting of the system without any guarantee that any viable commercial base could be found short of complete shutdown; a drastic change in the financial rules under which the railways operated, or a reconsideration of the railways' place in the whole transport system, involving the recognition that viability could not be achieved by dealing with the railways in isolation. The answer was of course the 1968 Act, which took up the two latter possibilities.

Looking now to the future rather than the past, one of the main objectives of the 1968 Act was to make the BRB financially viable. This aspect was summed up by Stephen Swingler, the Minister of State for Transport: 'The Bill has been widely represented in some quarters as featherbedding for the railways. This is just not so. The new financial remit given to the Railways Board will, in fact, be a very tough one indeed. But it will not be unfair.'[105] Mr Swingler was right to call the result a very tough one. In 1969 and 1970 the margin of profit came from the ancillary activities (hotels, shipping and property) and the grant-aided lines, and there was a small loss on the commercial network proper. No wonder, therefore, that the railways are anxious about the possible 'hiving off' of the ancillary activities and the possible end of the grants. Moreover, wage increases, in contrast to the virtually self-financing agreements of 1968 and 1969, have in 1970 and 1971 had only minimal arrangements for productivity. It will also be recalled that full provision for replacement and depreciation would necessitate a profit of £35–£40 million, and that many of the financial advantages of the 1968 Act taper off over time. Finally, the severe recession in 1971 has severely affected traffics, especially on the freight side, and a loss of up to £20 million is expected for the year as a result. For all these reasons, the financial position looks distinctly fragile, a situation which was emphasized by the BRB's unwillingness to sign the CBI's price initiative in the summer of 1971 promising to hold down price increases to 5 per cent in the ensuing year in spite of the Government's strong support for the scheme. In order to overcome this reluctance, the Government has offered a grant of £27 million for 1972 to enable price increases to be kept within these bounds. But whatever its short-term justification, such a move must cast doubt on the already narrow dividing line between commercial and subsidized activities.

Yet the basic economic conditions of operating the railways have not changed. The freight side in particular looks weak, and almost certainly continues to make a net loss, since the inter-city passenger services, the only commercial part of the passenger network, are very profitable. Indeed, the BRB's then Chairman, Sir Henry Johnson, actually suggested in 1969 that in certain circumstances social subsidies should be paid for freight services similar to those for passenger services, but got an unsympathetic response from the Ministry of Transport. The freight side, moreover, will have to manage without quantity licensing, which the Labour Government's White Papers had seen as a means of transferring 4,500 million ton-miles of freight from road to rail. Nor has the rate of national economic growth, to which railway freight is sensitive, adhered to the rate expected in the White Paper. A third area of doubt about the validity of the White Paper expectations is in the performance of the National Freight Corporation, which has made it quite clear that it will interpret narrowly its obligation to transport goods by rail where it is economic to do so, and has even suggested that it will be just as frequently economic to transfer goods from rail to road.[106] All this is not to say that the Act and its associated policy has not been helpful to the railways. It undoubtedly has, not least in the way the capital reconstruction has influenced all categories of cost, but the net effect on the freight side has been considerably less than intended. One important issue for the future will be the availability of investment funds to replace the wagon fleet, without which the drive to improve the quality of service, the most critical marketing need of rail freight, will be made very difficult. Yet it has been made very clear that rail investment will not be lightly undertaken.

At the same time as the railways have to face the future without their expected assistance and in doubt about investment, their road rivals should become considerably stronger. The development of the motorway system is bound to make hauliers more competitive with rail over longer distances, while at some time in the future increase in the maximum weight regulations would be a further aid. Furthermore, the new freedom from licensing restrictions should permit a stronger organizational structure to emerge. It is true that the Road Safety Act of 1967 and the Transport Act of 1968 added considerably to road costs, and that the haulage labour force looks like becoming more militant, but the railways are more labour intensive than haulage and also must face rising costs.

Passenger transport does not present such immediate problems as freight. In 1969 and 1970, in fact, with passenger journeys showing an increase for the first time in many years, their receipts were greater than freight receipts for the first time ever, although admittedly the annual £61 million for grants played a large part in the financial reversal of the two sides of the business. The grants-in-aid include an attribution for overhead cost, but this has been carefully designed to prevent any use of the grants as a means of paying the indirect costs more properly attributable to other services. Nevertheless the contribution in indirect costs is most welcome, especially where routes are shared with commercial services. Thus far from wanting to close down loss-making lines, the BRB can be expected to argue strongly for their retention. The intention is that they should be reviewed at least every three years, and the case for the social subsidy re-examined.[107] The uncertainty thus created does of course create difficulties for future railway planning and investment. Indeed the railways would do well not to count too much on the social grants; the withdrawal of the £15 million a year revenue grant from the London commuter lines in October 1970 indicates that the Conservative Government may well not be as generous as its predecessor, even though the Labour Government was technically committed to making the London routes break even.[108] More ominous still, many of the original grants come to an end in 1971; a review body is examining their future, and further substantial cuts are expected. Two contrary tendencies are likely to be seen. In the PTAs, where the local areas will soon have to assume the high cost of subsidizing commuter services, there will be local pressure to eliminate the services if the Central Government refuses to continue subsidies after the statutory period, as seems likely on the basis of the London decision. In the rural areas, on the other hand, since the localities bear no part of the cost of the subsidy (but must do so in the case of bus subsidies), there will be heavy political pressure to retain services, especially in Scotland and Wales.[109] These tendencies, of course, are the wrong way round from the economist's point of view. Urban commuter lines, in spite of their low proportion of total commuting, may nevertheless pay their full social even if not their full private costs by their contribution to the easing of urban congestion, while rural railways have little justification as compared to buses except where roads are totally inadequate.

On the non-subsidized inter-city routes, the greater flexibility in charging according to demand elasticities should permit the Railways Board to continue to increase total revenue, and although it is probably unrealistic to expect long-term increases in numbers of passengers, the boom caused by improved services must encourage optimism. Further into the future the Advanced Passenger Train will unquestionably be a major technical breakthrough in the middle or late 1970s, but against it must be set the probability of competition from motorway-based express buses capable of averaging close to 70 mph and vertical takeoff and landing aircraft travelling from city centre to city centre. There will also be the operational difficulty that the faster passenger trains go, the more difficult it will be to schedule freight trains without a complete renewal of the wagon fleet.

The Act does not mean that the last difficult decisions have been taken about the future of the railways. Doubts about financial viability must remain until disproved by experience, and although the White Paper on *Railway Policy* said that the railways were being set a target they could realistically be expected to achieve, this has been confidently asserted several times previously. It has been made clear that the 11,000 mile route mileage is far from sacrosanct, and that social subsidies will not automatically continue for ever, while on balance changes in technology are likely to be adverse to the railways. Any decisions, moreover, will inevitably have a high political content in view of the delicate balance of communication and public service. On the other hand, the last few years have seen a considerable improvement in the methods, organization and, perhaps most important of all, the morale of the railways. They may therefore yet confound the prophets of obsolescence.

NOTES TO CHAPTER 3

1. This figure includes a contribution from the railways to the central charges of the British Transport Commission, which was not official practice in the presentation of financial reports.
2. The history of the railways is more fully covered in C. I. Savage, *An Economic History of Transport*, (Hutchinson, rev. ed. 1966) and for the post-1914 period, D. N. Aldcroft, *British Railways in Transition*, (Macmillan, 1968).
3. Savage, op. cit., p. 112.
4. The Departmental Committee on Railway Agreements and Amalgamations reported in 1911 that competition between companies had come to play only a small part in promoting efficiency, and that more formal and complete unions between companies were likely to involve less danger to the public than informal combinations.
5. Sir Eric Geddes, the Minister of Transport, estimated that the savings would amount to £20 million annually, which proved in practice a gross over-estimate. Savage, op. cit., p. 101.
6. See D. H. Aldcroft, 'Innovation on the Railways', *Journal of Transport Economics and Policy*, January 1969, for the reasons why diesel and electric traction were not introduced in the inter-war period except on the Southern Railway's commuter lines.
7. K. M. Gwilliam, *Transport and Public Policy* (Allen and Unwin, 1964), p. 170, quoted from R. Redfern, 'Net Investment in Fixed Assets in the United Kingdom', *Journal of the Royal Statistical Society*, *1955*.
8. Some traffic forecasts, especially those resulting from the electrification of commuter lines, underestimated the results, but this was not generally true, particularly on the freight side.
9. Select Committee on Nationalized Industries, *British Railways*, (HC 254—I: HMSO, 1960), p. xi.
10. *Reorganization of the Nationalized Transport Undertakings* (Cmnd. 1248: HMSO, 1960).
11. SCNI, *British Railways*, p. xcii.

12. British Railways Board, *The Reshaping of British Railways* (HMSO, 1963), pp. 4–5.
13. See D. L. Munby, 'The Reshaping of British Railways', *Journal of Industrial Economics*, July 1963.
14. Reshaping Report, p. 17. This assumes passenger traffic only on the route. But even if profitable freight were assumed, the proportion only rose to one-seventh.
15. ibid., p. 60.
16. *Railway Policy* (Cmnd. 3439: HMSO, November 1967), p. 1.
17. This amounted to the considerable sum of £16 million per annum.
18. The actual method of determining the size of grant was taken from the recommendation of the Joint Steering Group (*Railway Policy*, Section 3). It is designed to cover all the costs incurred for the service, including proportions of joint and indirect costs, which are not recoverable from receipts. The grants are payable in advance rather than retrospectively, which means that the railways stand to gain from a better performance than anticipated but conversely will be responsible for any losses above the estimate.
19. Taking the somewhat more sophisticated measure of traffic units—the amalgam of freight ton-miles and passenger-miles—the picture is similar. In 1947, 43,878 million traffic units were carried; in 1970 only 33,909 million.
20. This is the reason for the decline in rail freight stressed by the White Paper *The Transport of Freight* (Cmnd. 3470: HMSO, 1967), Appendix 1.
21. *The Transport Needs of Great Britain in the Next Twenty Years* (The Hall Report), HMSO, 1963.
22. SCNI, *British Railways*, pp. xxxiii–xxxiv.
23. *Transport for Industry* (HMSO, 1968), p. 32. This survey is extremely useful as the first major study of demand characteristics in freight transport and is therefore quoted at some length in the ensuing discussion, but it has inevitable limitations, particularly that transport services, costs and demands are so heterogeneous that almost any findings are averages covering such a wide spread of individual instances that the average may not be representative of the sub-markets, cost variations, quality considerations and other factors.
24. D. M. Dear, 'Some Thoughts on the Comparative Costs of Road and Rail Transport', *Bulletin of the Oxford University Institute of Statistics*, February 1962, pp. 63, 71.
25. The rail sundries division has of course been taken over since 1969 by the NFC as National Carriers Ltd, but the use of rail as the trunk carrier for sundries traffics has probably not diminished.
26. The following figures are derived from *Transport for Industry*, p. 31.
27. Dr R. Beeching, 'The Nationalization of Transport', *British Transport Review*, January 1964, p. 217.
28. For a critical examination of rail transport in the steel industry, see W. F. Cartwright, 'Transport and Steel', *Institute of Transport Journal*, January 1962. However, more recent moves by the steel industry to

offer bigger discounts for higher tonnages have been favourable for the railways.

29. One calculation is that the exponential rate of increase of haulage prices over the period 1954–63 was 0·3 per cent per annum, suggesting that some price stability was achieved, although not a decrease. (B. M. Deakin and T. Seward, *Productivity in Transport*, Cambridge University Press, 1969.)
30. ibid., pp. 60–3. Road prices were based on a sample survey; rail prices are the average rate per ton-mile, including collection and delivery, as supplied by British Rail; the figures are for 1966. The same qualification should be given to these findings as to those from *Transport for Industry*, namely that they are averages covering very wide variations.
31. W. R. Cook, 'Transport Decisions of Black Country Firms', *Journal of Transport Economics and Policy*, September 1967, p. 338.
32. *The Transport of Freight*, p. 26.
33. See J. Campbell, 'Transportation Quality', *Traffic Quarterly*, July 1963.
34. Thus while the railways claim to carry 50 per cent of total passengers from London to Manchester, and 48 per cent to Newcastle they carry only 29 per cent to Glasgow, as against 41 per cent travelling this route by air. (*The Times*, 14 September 1970.)
35. See p. 191.
36. On the other hand, the BEA London–Glasgow service lost £566,000 in 1968. (*The Times*, 4 September 1969.)
37. Reshaping Report, p. 20.
38. While the Reshaping Report found that the London system almost covered its full costs, by 1969 the deficit had grown to some £15 million.
39. Reshaping Report, p. 14.
40. *Nationalized Industries: A Review of Economic and Financial Objectives* (Cmnd. 3437: HMSO, 1967), p. 8.
41. British Railways Board, *Annual Report 1967*, p. 51.
42. *Railway Policy*, p. 60. Some economists would make another category, that of common costs, but the term is not used by the railways and its use here would further complicate the argument.
43. C. D. Foster, *The Transport Problem* (Blackie & Son, 1963), p. 88.
44. S. C. Joy, 'The Variability of Railway Track Costs and Their Implications for Policy, with Special Reference to Great Britain', unpublished Ph.D. thesis, London University, 1964.
45. This concept is further explained in W. J. Baumol et al., 'Costs and Rail Charges', in D. L. Munby (Ed.), *Transport* (Modern Economics Series, Penguin, 1968).
46. *Nationalized Industries: a Review of Economic and Financial Objectives*, p. 10.
47. National Board for Prices and Incomes, Report No. 72, *Proposed Increases by British Railways Board in Certain Country-Wide Fares and Charges* (Cmnd. 3656: HMSO, May 1968), p. 17.
48. BTC, *Annual Report*, 1950, p. 57.

49. This account is taken from C. D. Foster, 'Some Notes on Railway Costs and Costing', *Bulletin of Oxford University Institute of Statistics*, February 1962, and from SCNI, *British Railways*, Appendix 39.
50. SCNI, *British Railways*, p. 223. The idea of a two-part tariff was mentioned in evidence to the committee, but appears not to have been taken any further at that time.
51. See Table 3.8, p. 174, for the data mentioned in this paragraph.
52. SCNI, *Ministerial Control of the Nationalized Industries* (HC 371—II: HMSO, 1968), p. 401. Such an argument, without reference to costs or profitability is merely a repetition of the railways' nineteenth-century approach to pricing. As the railways then found, such a short-term view can lead to longer term trouble.
53. There was a statistical break at 1963, so that the two cycles do not deal with comparable categories. The point might be made that lower prices would be acceptable if accompanied by lower unit costs. However, this was not the case. See p. 178.
54. See Table 3.8, p. 174.
55. NBPI, Report No. 72, p. 16.
56. For a fuller description of BRB's computerized planning, see N. J. B. Alexander, 'Computers Aid BR's Freight Planning', *Railway Gazette*, 3 April 1970. The account given here greatly oversimplifies the procedures.
57. NBPI, Report No. 72, p. 14.
58. National Board for Prices and Incomes, Report No. 112, *Proposals by the London Transport Board for Fares Increases* (Cmnd. 4036: HMSO, 1969), p. 10.
59. National Board for Prices and Incomes, Report No. 137, *Proposals by the British Railways Board for Fare Increases in the London Commuter Area* (Cmnd. 4250: HMSO, 1969).
60. SCNI, *British Railways*, p. xxvi.
61. ibid.
62. D. L. Munby, 'Economic Problems of British Railways', *Bulletin of Oxford University Institute of Statistics*, February 1962, esp. p. 22; and NBPI, Report No. 72, p. 20.
63. It is hoped to keep the subsidy down to a maximum of $2\frac{1}{2}$ p per passenger-mile on any one route, but this may not be realistic.
64. NBPI, Report No. 137.
65. SCNI, *British Railways*, p. xxxiii.
66. BRB, *Annual Report, 1968*, pp. 31–2.
67. To illustrate, in its analysis of wagonload traffic the Reshaping Report noted that there was a very strong correlation between increasing weight of consignment and increasing distance and profitability. The break-even between direct costs and receipts was a consignment weight per wagon of around 8 tons, while with respect to distance by far the greatest losses were for that category of wagons travelling less than 25 miles (pp. 82–3).
68. Reshaping Report, p. 19.
69. ibid., p. 9.

THE RAILWAYS 211

70. S. C. Joy, 'British Railways' Track Costs', *Journal of Industrial Economics*, November 1964.
71. Quoted in G. F. Allen, *British Rail After Beeching* (Ian Allan, 1966), p. 80.
72. *Report of the Committee on Carriers' Licensing*, HMSO, 1965.
73. *Road Track Costs*, HMSO, 1968, pp. 30–1.
74. Deakin and Seward, op. cit., p. 115. The other statistics given in this paragraph come from chapters 4–6 of the study.
75. It is only fair to point out that the authors' provisional calculations for the 1962–65 period show rail output per total factor input as +4·03, while that of road haulage fell to 2·62. Rail's gain was entirely due to the reduction of inputs rather than any increase in output.
76. SCNI, *British Railways*, p. lxxv.
77. Sir Henry Johnson, 'Twenty Years of Nationalized Railways', *National Provincial Bank Review*, August 1968, p. 5.
78. Quoted in *The Economist*, 29 July 1967.
79. Continuous coupling also had the major advantage that compatibility with other wagons was no longer important.
80. These details are taken from *Modern Railways*, February 1969.
81. BRB, *Annual Report, 1968*, p. 11. It is hoped that by 1975 about a quarter of all railway freight will be moving in privately owned vehicles.
82. Reshaping Report, Appendix 4.
83. It is perhaps unfair, however, to take the expected progress anticipated in the Reshaping Report too literally in view of the delays which have occurred.
84. For a fuller analysis of the freightliner, see H. C. Garnett and K. M. Johnson, *The Economics of Containerization* (Allen and Unwin, 1971). The 1971 Corporate Plan assumes a throughput of 14 million tons by 1975.
85. The 1971 Corporate Plan assumes that the proportion of trainload operation should have risen to three-quarters by 1975, leaving only one-quarter to be operated by wagonload.
86. As an example, the Southern Region claimed that it could reduce its 1965 total of 500 manned signal-boxes to 30; again, the new signal-box at Rugby saves 70 signalmen every shift. New signalling by itself adds about 10–15 per cent extra track capacity. However, the first costs of electronic power signalling are very considerable and will probably rule out extension to remote single-track lines.
87. Allen, op. cit., p. 308.
88. SCNI, *British Railways*, p. xxxiii.
89. Britain has fewer route miles electrified than most comparable countries: UK 1,977, France 5,475, West Germany 5,028, Japan 3,331 (1969 figures).
90. The details in this paragraph are taken from *Modern Railways*, December 1968.
91. The classic use of this technique as an investment criterion is detailed in C. D. Foster and M. E. Beesley, 'Estimating the Social Benefit of

Constructing an Underground Railway in London', *Journal of the Royal Statistical Society*, 1963, pp. 46–58.
92. In 1960 the railways were instructed not to spend more than £250,000 on any one project without permission from the Ministry of Transport.
93. Reshaping Report, p. 55. In practice railway investment declined from its high point of over £160 million per annum in the years 1959–61 to £87 million in 1968.
94. 'Criteria for Capital Investment in Railways', 18.9.1963. (Reproduced as Annex A, Appendix 34, SCNI, *Ministerial Control*, Vol. III. The BRB document is reproduced as Annex C.)
95. ibid., Appendix 34.
96. ibid., Appendix 27, Memoranda by the Ministry of Transport, 'Relations with British Railways Board on Capital Investment'.
97. The very existence of a ceiling inevitably casts doubts on the use of the test rate of discount as the primary criterion for investment. However, at least one major project, the Crewe–Glasgow electrification, will be partly financed from outside the ceiling. Moreover, a relaxation of the ceiling seems probable, given the Government's expressed intention late in 1971 to bring forward capital projects in the nationalized industries to boost the economy.
98. The grant-aided services have their depreciation paid at replacement cost, which makes a useful addition to cash flows.
99. op. cit., p. 5. The BRB would like to have equity capital substituted for some or all of its interest-bearing debt, but in view of its past performance it is perhaps not surprising that this desire has not been met.
100. It was a railway pay issue which led to the famous dictum by the Cameron Court of Inquiry: 'Having willed the end, the Nation must will the means'. (Cmnd. 9352; HMSO, 1955.)
101. National Board for Prices and Incomes, Report No. 8, *Pay and Conditions of Service of British Railways Staff* (Cmnd. 2873: HMSO, 1966). To give the wage issue some perspective, the railway workers performed reasonably well in terms of wage rates. On an index of 1948 = 100, male railway rates had reached 234·8 by the end of 1965, against a national average of 220·9. (Figures are taken from Devons, Crossley and Maunder, 'Wage Rate Indexes by Industry, 1948–1965', *Economica*, November 1968.) However, whereas wage rates on the railways were close to actual earnings, this was not true of much of British industry. Even so, the PIB found that rail earnings had kept pace with industrial earnings over the period 1960–65.
102. Deakin and Seward, op. cit., p. 167.
103. SCNI, *Ministerial Control*, Vol. II, p. 400.
104. ibid., p. 106.
105. 'The Implications of the Transport Bill', *Institute of Transport Journal*, November 1968, p. 14.
106. National Freight Corporation, *Annual Report, 1969*, p. 20. The Freight Integration Council, the body whose task it is to advise on integration within the public sector, has not exercised much influence, as will be further discussed in chapter 6.

107. Outside London and the South East, where the commuter situation is rather special, the total cost of running the grant-aided services was some £70 million in 1969, while fare revenue was only some £20 million.
108. On the other hand, the Government has widened its definition of infrastructure grants in urban areas to include the refurbishing and improvement of current structures as well as building new ones. This should be worth some £10 million to the railways.
109. An example of what might happen is given by the Machynlleth–Pwllheli line. The Ministry of Transport, seeking methods of developing cost–benefit analysis, chose this line for a pilot study, which was published as *The Cambrian Coast Line* (HMSO, 1969). The results showed that the total benefits came nowhere near the cost of retention under any of the three possible sets of conditions postulated. Yet the Ministry even after its publication late in 1969 decided on an annual grant of £241,000 for the line for 1970 and 1971. Clearly, therefore, the decision to close or subsidize a line is in the last analysis political rather than economic. Nevertheless, the onus of a speech by Mr Eldon Griffiths, Under-Secretary at the Department of the Environment, addressing the Rural District Councils Association in October 1971, was that the bus must replace the train in rural areas. Pointing out that rural rail services were being subsidized to the extent of £30 million annually, he said: 'No Government can afford to shell out this sort of money indefinitely.'

4 ROAD HAULAGE

I Introduction

The transport of goods accounts for some 9 per cent of the total costs of all production industries in Britain, and of this around 90 per cent is spent on road transport. To look at the transport picture another way, the roads carry more than 80 per cent of the tons and almost 60 per cent of the ton-mileage of all the goods carried in Great Britain. These are shares, moreover, which have increased rapidly in the past and will increase further in the future. It is clear, therefore, that road transport is of great importance to the economy. The advantages of road transport are obvious—ubiquity, flexibility, service in its many guises, frequently price. But conversely, its disadvantages are also obvious—problems of safety, noise and congestion would all be alleviated if goods vehicles were taken off the roads, and road transport has therefore become a focus of concern about the environment.

Within road transport a distinction must be made between those firms primarily carrying their own goods and those carrying 'for hire or reward' for others. The latter is commonly referred to as the road haulage industry, and although the distinction between the two groups was destroyed by the 1968 Transport Act, it remains useful, and the road haulage sector will be the primary focus of this chapter, even though for some purposes it will be helpful to talk about the whole of road goods transport. Haulage, as an industry, remains in most essentials what it was when it first started after the First World War, predominantly comprised of small, not to say minute, operators between whom competition is fierce, carrying large quantities a relatively short distance in fairly small units. The small-scale nature of the industry has been responsible for considerable obscurity in its operations, and even today many elementary statistics are not accurately known.[1]

The state-owned sector of road haulage is small by comparison to state holdings in other industries, controlling 29,000 vehicles out of the 230,000 used primarily for 'hire or reward'. The proportion becomes smaller still if the whole of road goods transport is included, for this increases the number of commercial vehicles to some 1,500,000. Indeed, the state group has constantly emphasized that its position is very far from being a monopoly; it has even gone so far as to decry the validity of the title 'nationalized industry'. It is certainly true that it can be viewed only in the context of the larger road haulage industry, and it is in that context that we shall examine it. Yet the forty-odd companies which collectively comprise the National Freight Corporation (and will henceforth be designated the NFC) are by far the largest single group in road goods transport. By virtue of its size and its dominant position in certain sectors within the industry, notably long-distance haulage, parcels and heavy haulage, in which it exercises a degree of price leadership, the NFC is a major influence in the industry.

Any account of the road haulage industry is as much a study of the institutions with which successive governments have sought to regulate and de-regulate it as it is of purely economic factors. As Mr G. W. Quick-Smith, the chief executive of the Transport Holding Company and later the National Freight Corporation, has pointed out: 'There never has been one clear five year period when drastic changes on the freight side were not either threatened or being implemented'.[2] Indeed, it is arguable that the constant changes have done much to suppress economic tendencies. Of the various policies since the 1930s the striking aspect is that their rationale has resulted less from events within the industry than from external, if closely related, developments. The first of these has been the decline of the railways. Because the two industries are in competition with each other, or at least are thought to be so, concern for the railways has spilled over into intervention in the road haulage industry. Indeed, the most recent piece of legislation, the 1968 Transport Act, purported to look not at the two industries, but rather at the single function of transporting freight. Second, the tremendous growth of road traffic of all kinds, resulting in a growth of the demand for road space far faster than its supply, has led to suggestions that goods vehicles be penalized or even have their traffic removed from them in order to solve the environmental problems concerned with road usage. These two issues, and to a lesser extent internal ones such as competition and labour relations, have been the main factors in road haulage policy.

II Development of the Industry

The spread of the internal combustion engine for both private and public transport in Britain was not as rapid as in some other relatively developed countries, and it was not until after the First World War that road goods transport seriously began to challenge the hegemony of the railways.[3] In 1919 there were only some 62,000 goods vehicles of all kinds in Britain, but expansion at this time was given an impetus by a large number of ex-servicemen, attracted by the possibilities of self-employment in a growing field, buying ex-military vehicles and setting up as hauliers. By 1928 there were over 300,000 vehicles in use. This rapid growth of the new industry saw a good deal of 'cut-throat' competition for the best traffic, and rate-cutting was extensively practised. Little heed was paid to safety, there were no minimum labour conditions, and fraudulent practices were far from unknown. Moreover, the flexibility of the new form of transport, both in its operation and its pricing policy, shocked the railways with their system of rate classifications according to the value of the goods rather than the cost of the transport.

For these reasons of 'wasteful competition' on the roads and unfair competition to the railways, the Royal Commission on Transport was set up in 1928.[4] The Commission endorsed the view of the larger hauliers and the railways that there was 'bitter and uneconomic strife' in road transport, and recommended licensing for both the goods and passenger sides of the industry. On the other part of its brief, the co-ordination of transport, it had little to offer. Passenger licensing was soon implemented, but such was the opposition to licensing on the goods side, that nothing was done until, in 1932, the Salter Conference was convened. This consisted of four rail and four road representatives under an independent chairman. Since the road representatives came from the established long-distance sector of the industry, there was a definite bias towards regulation in the make-up of the conference. Thus it is not surprising that it emphasized

> '... what the Road Haulage Association rightly term the evils of overcrowding and unbridled competition in the transport industry. It is clear that these evils exist ... Any individual at present has an unlimited right to enter the haulage industry, without any regard to the pressure on the roads or the existing excess of transport facilities ... This unrestricted liberty is fatal

to the organization of the industry in a form suitable to a carrier service purporting to serve the public.'[5]

These premises of licensing have been attacked by advocates of a non-regulatory system,[6] following the argument that while there was instability, it was much exaggerated, and was in any case to be expected with an infant industry. Even at that time patterns of traffic were already emerging, and some moderately large firms were running regular services.

The government of the day nevertheless accepted the Salter Conference Report and passed the Road and Rail Traffic Act of 1933. The Act introduced three types of licence: the 'A' licence, for those carrying exclusively for hire or reward; the 'B' licence for those who wished to carry partly for themselves and partly for others; and the 'C' licence for traders carrying only their own goods. The 'C' licence was to be issued as a matter of right, but the other two were to be issued according to the existing capacity in the industry and its ability to meet demand. A licence was to be granted only if a physical need for an additional service was shown, as opposed to an offer of lower charges or better service. Moreover, the onus of proof was to be on the proposer. The licensing system was to be applied by the chairman of the area Passenger Traffic Commissioners, sitting as Licensing Authorities. Appeals from the decisions of the Authorities were to be heard by a Transport Tribunal. To pacify the railways, licence fees for goods vehicles were to be introduced as a means of forcing hauliers to assume some responsibility for road-track costs. The Act also tried to enforce certain minimum wage and employment conditions in the industry.

The effect of the Act was to give preference to existing operators, and to discourage new entrants to the industry. These inherent tendencies were increased by the interpretation of the Act by the Licensing Authorities, whose decisions were not based on statistics of traffic flows or even on an analysis of proposed prices, but merely on existing capacity as viewed by hauliers, their customers and those opposing the application.[7] The rapid growth of business in the 1920s was succeeded by near stagnation in the 1930s, although the general economic situation was as responsible for this as was licensing. One significant development of the period was that the railways, still finding that they could not compete adequately in many sectors, developed their own holdings of road transport until they were among the largest operators in the country by the start of the Second World War.

The war produced the first use of direct control over road haulage when the Road Haulage Organization was set up in 1943. This body controlled outright many of the larger undertakings, and hired all vehicles engaged in long-distance haulage, i.e. those doing hauls of more than 60 miles for more than 75 per cent of the time. Some 34,000 vehicles came under the Organization's control, all of which were handed back in 1946.[8]

Soon after the Labour Party came into power in 1945, it was announced that nationalization of most inland transport was intended. Some two years later, under the Transport Act of 1947, the ownership of the various transport properties to be nationalized was vested in the British Transport Commission, while their operation was placed in the hands of subordinate Executives, of which the Road Transport Executive controlled the road holdings. As far as haulage was concerned, a division was made between long- and short-distance operators, such that only the former were to be nationalized. This meant that all companies the preponderance of whose business was the carriage of goods over 40 miles were to be acquired by the State, while the vehicles left in private hands were not to carry goods more than 25 miles from their operating base without a special permit from the Road Transport Executive. Licensing was to continue within the private sector, but all State-owned vehicles were to be exempt. An exception to these rules was made in the case of certain specialist vehicles for carrying livestock, liquids in tanks, furniture removals, and heavy indivisible loads.

As stated in the 1947 Act, the objective of transport nationalization was 'to secure the provision of an efficient, adequate, economical and properly integrated system of public inland transport and port facilities', and it was in order to achieve this that long-distance haulage was nationalized. However, the means of implementing integration, which was the key term in the statement of objective, were left to the Commission without any real guidance as to policy.

As we shall discuss further in chapter 6, this was a great deal to expect of the Commission, and two aspects of the Act as passed made its task even more difficult. First, the Act provided that 'any person desiring transport for his goods must be allowed freedom to choose such of the services as provided as he considers most suitable for his needs'. This free choice between modes of transport within the nationalized sector, while doubtless good for the trader, helped infuse a sense of rivalry rather than integration as between the various modes. Secondly, in the Committee stage the Government was prevailed upon to withdraw its inclusion of 'C' licence vehicles in the distance limitations of the Bill. This left 'C' fleets to grow at the expense of both public haulage and the railways. Another practical difficulty facing integration was that the introduction date for the 25-mile permit did not come into effect until the beginning of 1950, only eighteen months before the Labour Party lost power. Thus integration had little chance to work effectively.[9]

To complicate matters further, the consummation of nationalization presented difficulties in welding into a single organization the thousands of small operating units which constituted long-distance haulage. In no other industry did nationalization face such problems of organization, for in all the others large-scale operation was already a fact. Apart from the railway fleets, no single operator owned even 1 per cent of the total number of vehicles. Nevertheless, in three years, the Road Haulage Executive (the Road Transport Executive having been split into Haulage and Passenger Executives) managed to acquire 3,500 undertakings and 42,000 vehicles, together with some 80,000 employees, and integrated them into an operating company, British Road Services. Many vehicles were acquired without the corresponding traffic; some were abandoned in the street by their owners for BRS to take. Not least were the human problems of adjusting to the new structure, for many of the previously individualistic operators who accepted management or other jobs within BRS now had to conform to the needs of a large organization.[10] Initially, the Road Haulage Executive made the mistake of over-centralizing and providing too many layers of management, a result of the railway-dominated viewpoint prevalent within the BTC. Thus under the headquarters there were 9 divisions, 30 districts, 227 groups and some 1,000 depots. However, the lesson was soon learned: in 1951, BRS started a move towards decentralization by announcing that 'the operational groups comprised in each District would be small enough to ensure the personal service which had always been so valuable a feature of road haulage'.[11]

All in all the Road Haulage Executive did its work well in its creation of BRS—ironically perhaps too well, since many supporters of nationalization had expected that it would lead to a flow of goods back from road to rail. Instead BRS as it emerged was in many respects even better able to compete with the railways than the thousands of small businesses it replaced. The BTC, moreover, could not be too repressive with its road haulage side, since its profit contribution was vital to the shaky finances of the Commission.

The return of the Conservatives in 1951 heralded a reversal of the nationalization of road haulage and this was duly embodied in the Transport Act of 1953, which purported to embody the principles of competition and decentralization. A board was set up to dispose of BRS vehicles other than those obtained from the railway companies, with instructions that small buyers were to be encouraged by refusing to sell vehicles in lots of more than fifty without ministerial permission. In addition, the 25-mile radius was abolished, and certain changes were made in the licensing rules to enhance freedom of entry to the industry.

But if nationalization had not worked out as planned, neither did denationalization, since resale of the vehicles proved less easy than anticipated. Because of the recognized value of interconnected services, the regular trunk operations were to be sold in larger lots, as were the specialist services such as parcels. However, few buyers emerged, due partly to the comparatively large amounts of purchase capital required, and partly to threats of renationalization but also to 'fears of the formidable competitive ability that BRS will still have'.[12] The great majority of vehicles sold were in very small lots. Out of 18,000 vehicles sold by February 1956, 11,800 were in lots of four or less, including 3,000 sold as single vehicles. Many of the present small operators in haulage date from the opportunities given to them by these sales. Furthermore, some large companies which had contracts with BRS, such as Lyons, Crosse and Blackwell, Cadbury and GEC, refused to allow their contract to be transferred to a purchaser; nor would they buy the vehicles themselves. At last, in 1956, the Conservative Government recognized that there was no satisfactory alternative to leaving the trunk services with BRS.[13] In total, BRS was left with some 16,000 vehicles by the end of 1956, and was still incomparably the largest single firm in the road haulage industry.

During the rest of the 1950s, the nationalized transport scene became increasingly dominated by the railway losses which worsened rapidly even though the railways had been substantially freed from their onerous legal obligations by the Transport Act of 1953. In a White Paper in 1960,[14] the Government argued that the problem was at least partly due to the diverse commitments of the BTC over a wide range of undertakings, and that the solution was to separate out the railways into a more manageable entity. The Transport Act of 1962 therefore split up the various transport holdings. The state road transport interests were put together with the bus, shipping, tourist and manufacturing interests to form the

Transport Holding Company. In all some ninety companies were involved. The most important innovation came on the financial side, where the THC was instructed to manage the securities vested in it as though it were engaged in a commercial enterprise. This meant that it would be 'the duty of the Holding Company to secure the best possible results for the public purse'. This was a significant change from the existing policy towards the nationalized industries, since the other industries had been set specific targets in terms of rates of return.[15] In practice, moreover, the THC was given a degree of latitude to pursue its policies in other directions which no other state undertaking enjoyed. There was also an important change in the organizational structure. The individual companies were to have full operational responsibility, while the Holding Company, as its name implies, was to exercise overall supervision. This further movement towards decentralization completed the full cycle away from the monolithic structure envisaged in 1947.

Hardly was the 1962 Act on the Statute Book, however, than the whole structure and system of regulation in the road haulage industry were challenged from two different directions. In 1963 Mr Marples, the then Minister of Transport, set up the Geddes Committee to enquire into the workings of the licensing system. The following year came the election of the Labour Government, pledged to provide a national plan for transport, which was duly presented in a series of White Papers and culminated in the Transport Act of 1968. Both the Geddes Committee and the Transport Act will be given further examination,[16] but the Act in particular was so revolutionary in its effects that it is necessary here to give in outline its provisions as they affected the industry in order to provide an institutional framework for the rest of the chapter. Even if the Conservative Government elected in 1970 did not agree with many of the Act's provisions, and promised to repeal some, they nevertheless provide a necessary starting-point for discussion.

The chief organizational change in nationalized freight transport was the creation of a new holding company, the National Freight Corporation, which was established to look after the state-owned road haulage interests, the railway Sundries Division, henceforth known as National Carriers Ltd, and the Freightliner service.[17] In other words it was given control of all traffics which start or finish by road within the nationalized system, whether or not the trunk part of the journey is made by rail. With respect to this latter point, the new body has the obligation 'to secure that . . . goods are carried by rail whenever such carriage is efficient and economic.'[18]

Financially, the NFC's obligation reverted to the pre-Transport Holding Company system of balancing the books, 'taking one year with another', and to assist in this a subsidy was announced to the extent of £60 million paid over five years on a tapering basis to compensate for the expected losses of the old Sundries Division. In addition to the NFC, another organization, the Freight Integration Council, was established by the Act to give advice to the Minister of Transport on the arrangements for freight integration as between the various state enterprises.

In the wider sphere of road goods transport, dramatic and controversial changes were made in the system of control over road goods transport. Licensing of vehicles by proof of need was abolished and the attendant licence categories under the 1933 Act were replaced by two new forms, quality and quantity licensing, respectively designed to achieve the objectives of higher standards of safety and operation,[19] and the better co-ordination of freight transport by road and rail.

A third important item for which powers were taken and were ultimately made effective in 1970 related to drivers' hours, serving to cut down the long hours traditionally worked in the industry. The maximum working hours were reduced from 14 to 11 hours, with a maximum of 10 hours actual driving.[20] Moreover, a maximum of 60 hours could be worked in any one week, and drivers were to be given at least one full rest day per week.

III Regulation of the Industry

The categories of goods transport set up by the licensing system under the 1933 Act still remain the basic divisions for describing the industry, for although no longer applicable they provide the only source of many statistics. Even more important, the effects of the 1933 Act have been the main formative force in the structure of the industry, and they will continue to influence it for many years to come.

Table 4.1 shows the growth of the various licence groups since 1938. The slow growth of the 'A' licence is particularly noticeable, and to a lesser extent that of the public sector, as compared with the 'C' licence fleet. But as will be seen later, mere numbers of vehicles do not necessarily correspond with the amount of work done. The category of contract 'A' licences is one which was created in the 1930s to take account of those operators who leased vehicles to the same trader for a period of at least a year, such that the vehicles were largely under the control of the trader. There has been argument whether these should be counted as public or private haulage, but for the most part they are placed in the former. There is also some difficulty with the 'B' licence, since it was designed to cover those who carried both for themselves and for others. But since about 80 per cent of the tonnage carried by vehicles in the class is for hire and reward, it seems fair to include this group also in the public haulage category.

TABLE 4.1
The growth of goods vehicle licenses

	'A' Licence	Contract 'A' Licence	'B' Licence	'C' Licence	Total
1938	83,700	9,500	54,900	365,000	513,100
1948	73,600	14,900	63,800	591,400	743,700
1958	88,500	20,400	64,700	1,049,000	1,222,600
1968	104,000	38,000	96,000	1,236,000	1,474,000

Source: *Highway Statistics* 1968 and *Basic Road Statistics* 1968.

Whatever the justification for licensing in the 1930s—itself a matter of dispute—its relevance to the 1960s was decisively challenged, first by a Conservative-appointed committee, and then by Labour's 1968 Transport Act. In 1963, Mr Marples, the Conservative Minister of Transport, appointed a committee under Lord Geddes to evaluate the licensing system 'in the light of present day conditions'. Its findings were that licensing was not achieving the possible objectives of government policy, that it had some unfortunate side effects, and that restrictions on the capacity of and entry to the industry, the distinction between public and private haulage, and the type of work a vehicle might do, should be removed.[21] It also found that conditions had indeed changed since the 1930s, and that the law as applied had diverged in some respects from the apparent intention of Parliament in 1933.

The potential objectives of policy which licensing might be said to further and which the committee examined were: the promotion of safety for the public, efficiency in road transport operations, the reduction of harmful effects of road transport upon amenity, the promotion of greater use of rail facilities, and the reduction of road congestion. On four of these licensing had had no discernible effect, and picked out for particularly critical comment were the industry's poor safety record and the apparent inability of licensing to instil discipline. On the fifth, efficiency, the committee found that licensing had had positively detrimental effects by lessening competition, inhibiting the efficient use of vehicles, and reducing the adaptability of the industry.[22] One objective deliberately not considered was that of co-ordination, since the term was felt to refer to 'a policy embracing in various degrees . . . the policy aims we have considered.'

The committee found that in the implementation of the 1933 Act increasing constraints had been placed on licence-holders, through the application of what came to be called the 'normal user' conditions, particularly to the 'A' licence. While the 'A' licence had originally been intended to give permission to carry any goods anywhere in the country, the Licensing Authorities, in examining the need for new facilities, had to ask what work the applicant intended to do, and the tendency to make applicants stick largely to this type of work was increased by a provision in the 1953 Transport Act empowering Licensing Authorities to revoke a licence if the statement of intention was not fulfilled. Thus the outcome was that the freedom of operation even of the 'A' licence holder was curtailed. 'A' licences were in any case extremely difficult to obtain. In the other main category of public haulage, the practice had grown of granting a 'B' licence to hauliers who had no other business of their own, but who were willing to accept strict conditions of operation in order to obtain a licence at all. Thus the distinction between the types of licence had become blurred, and related primarily to the severity of the conditions of operation imposed. To add to the problems of entry and operation, an intricate body of case law had developed out of the legalistic use of precedent by the Transport Tribunal. Because of this complexity, hauliers usually had to secure legal advice, which tended to give an advantage to the established operators.

Of particular interest was the finding that licensing had had little or no effect on the declared intention of the Salter Conference to secure a 'better' division of goods traffic between road and rail. Because road haulage could generally offer a superior service, because road and rail were in any case serving essentially different demands, and because the advantage to the public of diversion of traffic to rail could not be argued before Licensing Authorities, the system had done little to help the railways. Effective objections to licences were in practice confined to other road hauliers. The committee looked at other means of diverting traffic to rail, but could find no answer except to increase the attractiveness of the railways.

The conclusion that haulage should be freed from licensing except for more stringent safety standards was not popular with the Road Haulage Association, which forecast increased bankruptcies, and might have been expected not to be popular with the new Labour Government, which was committed to co-ordinating road and rail.

Nevertheless, it seems likely that the Geddes Report had a significant effect on the Labour Government's thinking in the 1968 Transport Act, and therefore deserves to be considered as the first step in the creation of a new policy. The 1966 White Paper on Transport Policy stated:

> The Government accepted the Committee's view that the present carriers' licensing system is wasteful, ineffective and unduly complicated; it agrees that it is ill-designed to achieve the objectives for which it was set up, even where those objectives are still relevant. But it does not agree that the system should be scrapped. On the contrary it believes it will be necessary to devise a licensing system which is an effective instrument of a modern national freight policy.[23]

The policy which emerged in the 1968 Transport Act had two main prongs, known as quality and quantity licensing. The former was primarily designed to meet the Geddes recommendations on safety, the latter as an instrument of road–rail co-ordination in spite of the scepticism expressed by Geddes at the possibility of this being successful. Quality licensing covers all vehicles above $3\frac{1}{2}$ tons plated weight, or where this is not applicable, 30 cwt unladen weight. The 900,000 vehicles below this mark which were previously registered under commercial licences were thus freed from any licensing or recording requirements, except those imposed on private cars, a move which was immediately unpopular with established operators fearful of competition from lightweight vehicles. For the 600,000 vehicles above the $3\frac{1}{2}$ tons mark there are requirements essentially based on considerations of safety. The operator of goods vehicles over this weight must satisfy the Licensing Authority that he has adequate facilities for maintenance, adequate control over the loading of his vehicles, adequate financial resources, and lastly that he or some senior employee holds a manager's licence. This latter is designed to ensure professional competence, and it is envisaged that there will be at least one person holding such a licence in every depot of any one firm. Coming immediately after the Road Traffic Act, 1967, which laid down much more stringent standards of testing for goods vehicles, quality licensing promised to improve considerably the safety and operating standards which the Geddes Committee on Carriers' Licensing had found so low.

Of all the component parts of the Act, the most controversial was quantity licensing, since it represented an open attempt to transfer goods from road to rail. Operationally, a quantity licence was required for vehicles carrying more than 16 tons gross weight a distance of more than 100 miles, or carrying a specified list of goods for any distance. These latter included bulk products such as coal, iron ore and some steel products. All traffics were to be covered by quantity licensing, including those carried on own account; there was thus to be no repetition of the convenient loophole of the 1947 Act. We shall examine this concept of licensing more closely in its role as a potential mechanism of co-ordination in chapter 6, but further discussion here is rendered irrelevant by the statement of the incoming Conservative Government that it would be repealed at the earliest possible opportunity.

It is much too early yet to forecast how successful even the 'quality' clauses of the new licensing system will be. It is by no means impossible that the Conservative Government could change or decline to activate some of them.[24] On the face of it, both the operator's and manager's licence do no more than set some much-needed standards for the industry, but legislation in the industry never seems to work exactly as it was intended. Licensing Authorities will require to be much harsher in the future when examining applications for operators' licences if the notorious law-breaking in the industry is to be curbed. In the year ending 30 September 1968 there were only seventeen cases where licences were revoked in the whole of road goods transport, even though the total number of convictions was 35,849, mainly for offences concerned with hours, record-keeping, overloading and vehicle safety. The sheer number of convictions also suggests that there was probably a great deal of successful avoidance of the regulations. One hopeful sign is that previous convictions and MOT vehicle tests can be taken into the examination. On the other hand, objections are now more difficult to make, since it was much easier to object on the grounds of surplus capacity than it is to obtain documented proof of the undesirability of a particular operator. For that reason alone there will probably be a short-term increase in the number of hauliers. The manager's licence presents rather more difficulties, since the qualifications required can vary enormously according to the size of fleet. It may even be necessary to have several categories of licence. The leaders of the industry rightly desire more professionalism in haulage management, but the example of other professions suggests that this can be used as an excuse for unduly restricting entry.

IV The Structure of the Industry

One dimension of the structure of the industry was given by Table 4.1, which showed numbers in the now out-of-date licence categories. This breakdown is clearly artificial, and much more important subdivisions can be made by ownership, specialization of function, and length of haul, which we shall now go on to examine.

(a) *Ownership*

(i) THE STATE

The holdings of the NFC, as briefly noted earlier, contain the old Transport Holding Company haulage interests, consisting of BRS companies and Pickfords, Tayforth and Harold Wood and various smaller subsidiaries; the ex-British Rail Sundries Division, now renamed National Carriers Ltd; and Freightliners Ltd, also previously owned by the railways. In view of this dual background and of the NFC's ownership of rail terminals, cranes, containers and so on, it is obvious that the group is not a road haulage company in the traditional sense of the word; rather it is a company for the transport of freight. This fact, which was repeatedly stressed by the White Papers and the company itself, must be borne in mind when considering it as part of the road haulage industry. The fifty or so operating companies are joined into three groups: general haulage and container traffics, with some 12,900 powered vehicle units; parcels, with 13,900 such vehicles; and special traffics with 2,200.[25] Other important statistics are that the NFC has a capital of some £99 million, an annual turnover of some £170 million, and a labour force of 66,000. The turnover figure amounts to some 5 per cent of the total freight market, including own account transport, and compares by no means unfavourably with the rail freight turnover of £255 million in 1969.

Organizationally, the NFC has continued the THC's policy of giving operating companies the maximum autonomy. Effectively, this means that the main groupings are run as separate businesses, and the operating companies within these groups come together only for accounting purposes. In its first report the NFC quoted the White Paper's conception of the organization required:

> The role of the NFC Board will be to set the framework within which its various subsidiaries will operate rather than to manage them. Freight transport is not a single, indivisible industry; its numerous parts vary enormously. Flexibility is therefore essential, and the new Board will be given the task of devising the structure most appropriate to its many-sided activities.[26]

The NFC has tried to adhere to this precept by maintaining short lines of communication to the operating units, which are themselves of a size designed for effective management and easy accountability. There are some central services such as staff relations, purchasing and legal, provided by the National Freight Corporation (NFC) Ltd.

(ii) PUBLIC HAULAGE OUTSIDE THE STATE SECTOR

The exact number of public hauliers at the present is not known and never will be known exactly, since there will always be an unknown number of operators who use their vehicles mainly on their own account who may also ply for hire under the 1968 Act. The term 'public haulage' is still relevant however in describing the industry within which competition takes place. Even before the 1968 Transport Act there was no certain way of taking an annual count since the data from the Licensing Authorities merely reflected numbers of licences, which might not be the same as numbers of operators. Since the 1968 Act the position has become even more difficult as the old licensing categories have been withdrawn and such new statistical classifications as might be devised have not been published. Table 4.2 shows an approximate breakdown in 1963.

TABLE 4.2
Size of fleet in the public sector of road haulage, 1963

Size of fleet	No. of operators	% Operators	No. of vehicles	% of vehicles
1–5 vehicles	39,130	84.5	69,100	34
6–50 vehicles	6,940	15.0	90,900	44
51–100 vehicles	160	0.4	10,100	5
101–200 vehicles	33 }		6,600	3
Over 200 vehicles	17 }	0.1	28,900	14
Total	46,280	100	205,600	100

Source: Ministry of Transport, *Public Haulage Operators, Analysis by Size of Fleet*, 1963, Table 2.

The average size of fleet is very small indeed; in fact of those operators with 1–5 vehicles, no less than 23,130 had only one vehicle, while of those operators with more than 200 vehicles, by far the lion's share was accounted for by the state companies, BRS and British Railways. Very few hauliers are publicly quoted companies: Transport Development Group and United Transport are examples, but they also have interests outside haulage. The road haulier is, moreover, highly individualistic. Only 17,600, well under half the total, have thought it worth while joining the Road Haulage Association, the industry's association.

(iii) OWN ACCOUNT OPERATORS
The term 'own account operators' is now outdated, since there are no licensing restrictions to prevent those who need to hold a 'C' licence from carrying other people's goods.[27] Nevertheless, the distinction between public and private haulage is still useful. Own account operators vary greatly, from the butcher's delivery van to the transport fleets of giant companies. Again, there are no accurate up-to-date statistics, in particular on size of fleet. Own account operators control by far the greater proportion of all vehicles, some 80 per cent, although in terms of work achieved their importance is far less. This is partly because this sector contains a disproportionate number of small vehicles—just over one million weigh less than three tons unladen weight, leaving only the 226,000 over three tons as effective competition for public haulage. Nevertheless, this is still more than the number of public haulage vehicles over this size. But the own account sector has frequently been accused of inefficiency by the public road hauliers, who argue that in general 'own account' firms do not know the real costs of their own transport fleet,[28] and are less efficiently operated than public haulage. It is sometimes also argued that own account operation received its major boost from the licensing system on the one hand—since 'C' licences were easily obtained—and the nationalization of long-distance haulage on the other, since only own account vehicles could carry goods more than 25 miles as of right. In fact there are many reasons why traders should want to run their own fleet. Reliability, availability, secrecy, greater control and other aspects of service may seem sufficient reasons to the trader, while different patterns of vehicle usage may account for apparent differences in efficiency. Nevertheless there has been a movement from private to public haulage; in 1952 public haulage carried 46 per cent of total ton-mileage, while in 1968 the proportion was 60 per cent.

(b) *Specialization*

Some degree of specialization is almost inevitable in road haulage. For one thing, vehicle requirements vary a good deal according to the type of goods being carried. Livestock, bulk liquids, furniture, and frozen food involve very different vehicle specifications. The Road Haulage Association deals with twelve main categories, as shown in Table 4.3.

TABLE 4.3

RHA breakdown of membership by specialization

Speciality	*Number with one speciality* Members	Vehicles	Drivers	Total staff
Agriculture	789	3,945	3,550	4,733
Bulk liquids	115	379	417	531
Car transport	24	146	190	263
Express carriers	298	3,904	4,204	8,108
General haulage	3,997	31,976	31,976	43,766
Heavy haulage	189	1,512	1,512	2,570
International	12	74	81	155
Livestock	362	1,520	1,368	1,672
Long distance	1,271	11,820	13,002	17,730
Meat	181	1,267	1,267	1,774
Milk	146	922	1,014	1,198
Tipping	4,414	30,898	30,898	40,167
Total, one speciality	11,798	88,363	89,479	121,667
Total, mixed specialities	5,802	91,637	93,321	130,333
RHA Total	17,600	180,000	182,800	252,000

Source: *Roadway*, September 1969, p. 34.

The table, which covers RHA members only, under-represents the strength of general haulage but otherwise is probably a fair reflection of the industry. It would clearly need a very large firm to specialize in every category, and even BRS does not participate in several of the above groupings, such as tippers, livestock and agricultural haulage.

BRS was created to be a long-distance haulage group, and this is still its main activity, as can be seen from Table 4.4.

It is worth noting, however, that the proportions for general and parcels haulage were tending to diminish before being reinforced by the addition of National Carriers and Freightliners Ltd to make up the NFC in 1969. The increase came in the more specialized sectors—heavy haulage, bulk liquids and powders, household removals, motor car delivery and particularly contract hire. These changes reflected changing patterns of profitability within the

TABLE 4.4
BRS activities by vehicle mileage, 1968

	%
General haulage tramp	34.5
General haulage trunk	12.7
General haulage collection and delivery	3.7
General contract hire	17.1
Parcels trunk	9.3
Parcels collection and delivery	11.1
Heavy haulage	1.1
Bulk liquids and powders	6.1
Household removals	3.2
Motor car delivery	1.2
	100.0

Source: THC, *Annual Report*, 1968, p. 27.

industry away from general and towards specialized haulage. On the other hand, commodities carried remain widely spread although omitting important areas such as building materials and agricultural products. An analysis by commodity reveals that iron and steel products with 22 per cent, food, drink and tobacco with 13 per cent and building materials with 12 per cent are the only groupings representing more than 10 per cent of total BRS tonnage.[29]

(c) *Length of Haul*

Journeys by road goods transport are overwhelmingly over short distances, with only 2 per cent of all journeys being over 100 miles.[30] Similarly, 83.8 per cent of all tons carried by road go less than 50 miles, and 92.7 per cent go less than 100 miles. The picture changes quite dramatically, however, with respect to ton-mileage, as would be expected from a figure which multiples for every mile travelled. No less than 39 per cent of all ton-mileage carried on the roads was found to be on journeys over 100 miles in the 1962 Road Goods Survey. These figures relate to all road transport, including own account vehicles. If only public haulage is taken, 11 per cent of tonnage, 7 per cent of journeys, and 53 per cent of ton-mileage are over the 100 miles mark. Long-distance haulage is therefore small in terms of vehicles involved, journeys completed and tonnage carried, but very important in terms of the total work performed.

BRS, as one would expect from a group with long-distance origins, carries its tonnage much further than the average for public haulage.

Table 4.5 shows this by comparing BRS with all commercial vehicles, and the 'A' licence category to which most BRS vehicles belong.

TABLE 4.5
Road goods vehicles by length of haul

% of tons by mileage	All vehicles (1962)	'A' Licence (1962)	BRS 1968
0–50	83·8	62·5	30·5
51–100	8·9	15·5	21·8
101–150	3·8	10·2	18·6
151–200	1·7	5·2	15·3
201–300	1·6	5·8	10·7
300 plus	0·2	0·8	3·0

Source: The figures for BRS were taken from the THC, *Annual Report*, 1968, p. 10; the other figures were obtained from the *Survey of Road Goods Transport*, 1962, Table iv.

Looking at the interaction of these categories it seems reasonable to assume that specialization and to a lesser extent a longer average length of haul are correlated with greater economies of scale and thus larger firms. Capital costs, knowledge, regularity and wide coverage would seem to give advantages to the largest operator, but these arguments are mostly speculative, since the requisite data is not available.

The fact that most journeys are over short distances, in the public as well as the private sector, means that markets are for the most part only local. This adds to the importance of individual contacts and goodwill, and moreover, since most contacts are personal, there is less need for market institutions performing a brokerage function. A few clearing houses do exist, but the Geddes Committee noted that they are few in relation to the traffic, and that there are few links between them.[31] Instead, subcontracting on an individual basis fills the gaps in temporary over- or under-capacity. Indeed, it is this individual basis of much of the bargaining in the industry which makes its operations so obscure.

In the long-distance sector the situation is somewhat different, since backloads are more important, and individual contacts are less so. It may well be that BRS performs the role of a clearing house in this sector, since it offers a full range of services between most points in the country, such that prospective consignors know that BRS can handle any given load, or will subcontract if necessary. Thus while a consignor will be aware of the competitors to BRS over routes he uses regularly, he may well turn to BRS for loads to somewhat unusual destinations. We have already noted the competitive advantage of BRS's size in providing a distribution network for large companies.

The extent of competition in road haulage is difficult to evaluate. The industry prides itself on being highly competitive, and this opinion was endorsed by the Geddes Committee.[32] The Prices and Incomes Board was rather more sceptical when it commented, '... we are convinced that continued, and possibly more intense competition is necessary if the pace of change in this industry's attitudes, working practices and institutional framework is to be accelerated'.[33] Competition is certainly widespread, but is probably stronger in some sectors than others, and there are also variations between users. Some firms use several hauliers, and are prepared to change them if given unsatisfactory service. Other firms, with less interest in, or awareness of, transport costs, keep the same haulier without checking other charges. As between sectors, general haulage, in which most hauliers participate and to which entry is easiest, is more competitive than those which require specialized vehicles, although earth removal with tippers is a notoriously competitive and unprofitable area. Perhaps the best measure of competition, however, is the unwillingness of hauliers to pass on increases in cost to their customers. Even when the Road Haulage Association recommended specific increases in charges, many hauliers maintained their old rates rather than risk losing traffic.

(d) *Economies of Scale*

The structure of the industry, and particularly the small average size of company, has led to interest in the existence of economies of scale in the industry.[34] This question is also very relevant to arguments for and against nationalization, since the case for nationalization would clearly be much stronger if it could be shown that there were extensive economies of scale or even a natural monopoly in at least some sectors of the industry. It is significant, however, that road–rail integration rather than available economies of scale has always been the primary argument for haulage nationalization. As with many service industries, the basic unit of production does not change with differences in the scale of operation—the vehicle plus driver is the only indivisible factor of output. Economies of scale it would therefore seem must come from better organization and utilization of the various factors. The continued success of

BRS and the development of a few large privately owned haulage fleets such as that of the Transport Development Group, with 4,663 vehicles and a turnover of some £25 million, suggest that such possibilities do exist. Moreover an analysis of its membership by the RHA, published early in 1969, showed some interesting developments since the survey in Table 4.2 was carried out. Although based on a sample, and covering only RHA members, it showed 234 operators with fleets of between 51 and 100 vehicles, 76 with between 101 and 200, and 19 with more than 200. This means there has been a substantial increase in the numbers of medium-sized firms since 1963.[35] However, the entry of small firms into the industry could have resulted in much the same size distribution being maintained.

Those who argue against the existence of economies of scale point to the continued preponderance of small operators and explain this by lower overheads. The small man does not need to employ specialists for maintenance or administration,[36] nor does he need a sophisticated depot. Moreover, because he has lower fixed costs to spread and because he is closely involved in each individual task, it is likely that he can price more closely to the true cost of each operation. Beyond these economic arguments there is also widespread agreement about the goodwill deriving from personal contact with customers, as contrasted with the impersonality of the large firm. It has also been argued on behalf of the small operator that the licensing system has had a bias in favour of the larger and established firm because it has proved its respectability and can afford expensive legal advice.

The arguments in favour of economies of scale are largely technical. The larger operator should be able to achieve more precise vehicle choice for each load, higher loading factors by accumulating small volumes into large, more intensive use of labour, regularity of service, mechanization of depots and cheaper access to capital. Because he has larger vehicles, which give substantially lower costs on a per ton basis, he will be able to obtain scale economies if he can fully utilize his capacity. But while these advantages can be theoretically deduced, they have never been satisfactorily translated into either cost of service advantages even if the RHA statistics above lend some credence to them. BRS may be something of an exception here. It does enjoy certain advantages as the only supplier of a comprehensive network of service, but these seem to come on the demand rather than the supply side. Such a network is useful to companies which require widespread patterns of distribution, because it saves using dozens of different hauliers. Fish distribution across the country from Grimsby, for example, is handled by BRS. In the same vein, when Walters was evaluating the performance of BRS, he found it to be most successful among the larger firms, which presumably had more widespread distribution requirements.[37] Such advantages come only from large size; building them up may be a difficult and perhaps even impossible task, since no other company has been able to achieve them. It might therefore be argued that there are discontinuities in the cost curve such that an organization like BRS has to be created by external action if it is to exist at all, since it cannot grow naturally.

There is also a middle line of argument on economies of scale, espoused by Harrison, and Edwards and Bayliss, that costs are constant irrespective of scale, but with Harrison arguing that the larger firm has a somewhat better survival capacity in times of recession and Edwards and Bayliss that larger firms will gain because they tend to use larger vehicles. Thus over time some growth in average size could be expected. At the moment the evidence is inconclusive. The industry is too heterogeneous, with too many different sub-markets and too many variations from any theoretical average, to permit of any clear advantage one way or another. Licensing, furthermore, has been instrumental in freezing the structure of the industry much as it was in the 1930s, except for the emergence of BRS. At all events, the end of licensing by proof of need will provide an opportunity for the argument to be proved, although there may be contrary trends in the first few years as inefficient firms, protected by licensing, leave the industry, while new firms, which could not have gained admission under licensing, will enter, and the efficient firms will have a chance to grow. Even so, Bayliss has argued that the small haulier is at no disadvantage vis-à-vis the large, as far as either demand or supply factors are concerned, and will continue to play an important role in the industry.[38]

Part of the difficulty about economies of scale may arise from a confusion between ownership and operational integration. The larger privately owned firms are financial amalgamations, with operating control left as before in the constituent companies.[39] BRS has itself completely accepted operational decentralization. We noted a move in this direction as early as 1951. After the parcels operation had been split off in 1953 to prepare it for a separate sale, the virtues of separate accounting and operating units were recognized, and, following the Transport Act of 1962, a federal company structure with intermediate functional groupings was introduced.[40]

As further companies were acquired after 1964 when the Labour Government permitted this type of growth, they were added to the basic groupings without any attempt to integrate operations. The present philosophy and its logic was strikingly stated in the 1965 Annual Report:

> As regards road transport it is part of its very nature that the smaller unit at least tends to hold its own as far as efficiency is concerned ... Moreover, road transport services need a supervision that is local and immediate, and capable of taking decisions. The services must be fitted in with the particular and fluctuating demands of customers, especially on the freight side, and above all there must be a matching of costs and earnings over quite small units of services, which themselves are not capable of being standardized. In such circumstances the net advantage of the relatively small unit may well exceed the benefits offered by an advanced technological direction which is placed, inevitably, remote from the actual scenes of action. What is needed is direct, fully responsible management, on the job, and a strong but short chain of managerial command.[41]

V Demand

The demand for road goods transport is a derived demand, and is primarily dependent upon industrial production. Fluctuations, therefore, are greatest in those sectors which serve industries susceptible to the trade cycle. Steel and heavy engineering are obvious examples of such industries, together with the carriage of cars and other durable consumer goods whose demand is frequently constrained by government policy. At the other end of the scale, haulage trends in food distribution or other repeat purchase consumer goods industries for which road transport is well suited, are little affected by overall industrial performance. The construction industry is an exception to this general observation, since although it does suffer from considerable fluctuations it is largely dependent on road transport.

Two other aspects of the demand for road haulage are also favourable to the stability of the industry. One is that goods transport is free from the bane of passenger transport, the peaks at the beginning and end of the working day. Vehicle utilization can therefore be much closer to capacity; for the long-distance sector, if not the distributive sector, this means round the clock operation.

Secondly, seasonal variations are much lower than might be expected. The 1962 Roads Goods Survey found that differences between seasons amounted to only 4–6 per cent of ton-mileage.[42] This statistic might, however, hide balancing fluctuations between industries. In winter, for example, increased distribution of coal may balance reduced demand for haulage in construction. A further possible source of instability is that although there are no statistics sufficiently detailed to differentiate between the various types of road transport during the trade cycle, public haulage may fluctuate rather more than private haulage, since a proportion of the work of public haulage comes from traders who use their own fleet for regular work and contract out for less regular requirements. A further expectation would be that small public hauliers would suffer more than large, since the sub-contracting from large operators on which they depend for much of their work would not be available.

Table 4.6 shows the index of road haulage compared to that for rail and industrial production. The growth in haulage has not only been due to considerable gains from rail, but also because the industries for which road transport is well suited have grown faster than production as a whole. Within the various sub-markets of haulage there has been a trend towards specialization of function, but this has not prevented the general haulage market from growing. The one area where a secular decline has set in is parcels, with a drop of about 4 per cent per year by volume in the late 1960s. It is thus unfortunate for the NFC that it is so heavily committed to parcels through NCL and BRS Parcels and, as we shall see later, their concentration on a declining market will pose considerable organizational problems for the Corporation.

TABLE 4.6

Growth of demand for transport
(1958 = 100)

	Road	Rail	Industrial production
1938	(39)	88	63
1953	78	124	94
1958	100	100	100
1963	139	91	120
1966	165	87	133
1969	177	84	145

Source: *British Economy—Key Statistics*, Table C.

Measurement of the demand as reflected by turnover figures can do little more than estimate orders of magnitude. One estimate put the total market for goods transport by road in 1967 at £2,485 million,[43] subdivided into a turnover for own account transport of £1,900 million and for public haulage of £585 million; of this second sum BRS accounted for £85 million or just under 15 per cent.

Some aspects of modal choice between road and rail have already been examined in chapter 3, particularly the findings of Deakin and Seward and the Ministry of Transport's study *Transport for Industry*.[44] It is not proposed to re-examine the data here, but it is relevant to repeat that by and large road has been successful in carrying the lion's share of the heavier and potentially more profitable traffics while leaving rail with a disproportionate share of what are prima facie unprofitable traffics. Road has also won traffics even where it has a price disadvantage because of its superior service characteristics.

In an examination of competition between the public haulier and the own account fleet, *Transport for Industry* found the most significant factor to be length of haul, with the former mode being favoured as distance increased; the reason was connected by the ability of the public haulier to achieve higher vehicle utilization by means of load amalgamation and the availability of return loads. An interesting secondary aspect of the analysis was that there were no great subjective quality differentials in the minds of shippers as between public and private haulage; it might therefore be expected that price differentials would play a more important role than where subjective quality differentials did exist, as between road and rail. This might help to explain the growth of public vis-à-vis private haulage and the better performance of public haulage over longer distances, as well as the tendency to use private haulage for the heavier consignments.

VI Costs

The heterogeneity of the industry has constantly been emphasized, but nowhere does this make conclusions more difficult to draw than in the area of costs and pricing. The most significant fact about the cost structure in road haulage is that there are no high capital costs of entry into the industry, which helps to explain the preponderance of small operators. It is quite possible to operate on an initial capital of a few hundred pounds, although obviously existence at this level is precarious. The one-man operator also has no fixed labour costs if he pays himself out of profit and does his own administration. In such instances, marginal cost can obviously be extremely low in the short run. As firms become larger, they must pay increasingly more administrative and fixed asset costs (offices, depots, etc.), and the costs of these must of course be recouped through greater efficiency, such as ensuring a high annual mileage and high load factor for their vehicles. Such considerations raise once more the question of economics of scale, but there is no inherent reason why only large organizations should be able to achieve any higher operating efficiencies than the one-vehicle operator, since the single vehicle is the unit by which efficiency must be calculated.

Fortunately the NFC has published a breakdown of its costs, which are given in Table 4.7.

TABLE 4.7
NFC cost breakdown by group 1970

	General haulage %	Parcels %	Special traffics %	Total %
Salaries, wages, National Insurance	40	56	44	48
Fuel duty, licence charges	12	6	9	9
Subcontractors charges and charges for hire of vehicles	20	16	10	17
Stores and services	20	17	30	20
Depreciation	8	5	7	6

Source: NFC, *Annual Report*, 1970.

As can be seen there are very considerable variations between the operating groups and the figures undoubtedly hide further variations between companies within the groups. There are probably two main differences between the NFC groups and other hauliers. In the first place fixed costs are likely to be lower for other hauliers, which lack the NFC's extensive depot and administrative structure. The smaller the haulier, the smaller these fixed costs are likely to be. The other difference is that subcontractors' charges are likely to be lower. This is not to say that there is not a great deal of subcontracting outside the state sector, but the NFC has a particularly close link with the railways through the freightliners and National Carriers.

A further notable aspect of these costs is the relatively low labour component compared to other surface transport industries. Where the railways have over 60 per cent of costs taken up by labour cost, and the buses around 70 per cent, even when all wages and salaries and ancillary costs are taken into account in the NFC, the labour cost is only 48 per cent. For the parcels companies, with a good deal of manual handling, labour cost is over half the total, but for general haulage the figure is only 40 per cent. This lower proportion may be a key factor in future road–rail competition in view of the rapid escalation of labour costs in recent years.

For the rest of the industry, hauliers jealously guard their costs, if they know what they are. The difficulties of gathering accurate information in the industry are shown by the experience of the Prices and Incomes Board. Out of the 330 requests for cost information which it sent out, only 38 firms sent sufficient information for close analysis, making definitive results impossible.[45] On the same reference, the Road Haulage Association, in seeking information to put before the Board, plaintively recorded that of its 17,000 members, less than a dozen opened their books to give information.[46] However, several estimates of cost are made as a guide to the individual haulier in pricing his services. The best known of these is probably that provided by the *Commercial Motor*, which breaks down costs per mile for a wide range of different vehicles.[47] But even the sets of figures provided by *Commercial Motor* cover only average and therefore theoretical situations. They say little about the true cost of carrying particular goods over particular routes. Factors such as the probable availability of a return load, the time spent in turning round, the extent of congestion on the route, and the division between weight and bulk of loads are all factors concerning the cost of the individual journey which by the nature of the task cannot be accurately costed. This is essentially a practical difficulty, not a technical one. The long-term contract, of course, allows for more accurate costing than the individual load, but even this will vary considerably from the *Commercial Motor* figures. The inherent difficulties of costing, together with the fierce competition in some sectors, have led larger hauliers to charge smaller operators with pricing below long-run costs. The non-existence or very rudimentary nature of accounting techniques in the industry naturally exacerbates the problem. Indeed the RHA claimed before the Prices and Incomes Board in 1965 that it was the ignorance of the small haulier of his costs which justified their recommendations of increases in charges. Yet road haulage has not had a notably high rate of bankruptcies as compared with other small-scale businesses.

For the decade prior to 1961, haulage costs were remarkably stable, permitting the claim that charges per ton and per ton-mile had been falling in real terms.[48] Operators were able to use the better performance and higher capacity vehicles being produced by the manufacturers to offset increases in items like wages. However, in that year a duty was introduced on fuel oil, and since that time costs have begun to escalate rapidly. The *Commercial Motor* reported an operating cost increase of 32 per cent for a seven-ton lorry over the five years 1963–67.[49] Much of the increase has come from government imposts in the form of higher licence fees, the Selective Employment Tax and higher fuel duty. The Road Safety Act of 1967, the Industrial Training Act of 1964 and many aspects of the Transport Act of 1968 have all added further cost burdens, while wage increases have, as in most industries, added significantly to labour costs. Finally, congestion in city centres, port approaches and similar bottlenecks has decreased efficiency. In the period 1967–70 cost increases reached an annual rate of 15 per cent over the whole industry.[50] As an offset to these increases in cost, better inter-urban roads, a higher speed limit, and concessions in construction and use regulations to permit a gross weight of up to 32 tons have tended to reduce costs. However, the net effect has undoubtedly been a considerable increase, and such gains as there have been are mainly of value to long-distance haulage.

VII Pricing

The price structure of the industry is an almost complete mystery and no better account of it has been written since Gilbert Walker tried to describe it thirty years ago.[51] Haulage is the only industry in which the State has an important stake where there is no control, direct or indirect, over prices. The reason is simple; the industry is too competitive, and insufficiently sophisticated, to brook any regulation. Some large firms, including those owned by the State, publish a scale of charges, but these are usually regarded as a basis on which to bargain, and the true rates given to any particular customer are generally jealously guarded secrets. This goes for BRS as much as any other firm. An exception to this rule might be made in the case of parcels or 'smalls' traffic, where bargaining over every small consignment is obviously impossible and a tariff is therefore adhered to. What can be said is that there is no one rate for the job, and that estimates are likely to vary considerably for the same task as between any two hauliers, not only because their costs are different, but also because they calculate the job in different ways or are prepared to give differing degrees of service.

Prices are probably set by a combination of considerations. The *Commercial Motor* costing or something equivalent devised by the haulier himself gives some idea of variable and fixed costs which need to be covered. Knowledge of competitive rates is then imperfectly obtained by examining the published rates of BRS and the larger operators. Some allowance is made for various aspects of the particular job, such as the 'loadability' of the cargo, the weight/size ratio, the probable turnround time, and the possibility of a back load. As already noted, in the nature of things these latter aspects cannot be accurately estimated for the odd job, although more accurate costing is possible for the longer-term contract.

A considerable difficulty in pricing is that there is no standard unit of output in the industry. The use of ton-miles to express work done is no more than an official convention; it has very limited practical use. A ton of steel takes up far less space than a ton of mattresses; furniture or glassware requires special handling; thirty miles on the motorway has a very different cost to thirty miles across London; and so on. Other possible ways of measurement are on a time basis or a cubic capacity basis, but both of these have similar drawbacks. Thus to the extent that some rule of thumb estimation is inevitable, there is bound to be a divergence between price and cost. This divergence, however, need not be large for an experienced haulier who knows what the individual job entails, and it is precisely because so many different considerations need to be taken into account in price-setting that decision-taking needs to be pushed as close to the customer as possible.

Apart from these problems, there is also the familiar economic issue of allocating joint costs and overheads. However, the joint-cost problem is not nearly as great as on the railways. In essence it is exemplified by the haulier's decision whether to charge the full cost of a round trip on the outward journey, or whether to assume that he will be able to obtain a return load and thus spread the charge. Overhead costs are probably most conveniently allocated according to ton-mileage, or revenue, but the possibility is that a small job may cost as much in overheads as a large one. The traditional arguments about pricing in the nationalized industries have revolved round the applicability of marginal cost pricing. The importance of this argument, however, is not as great for road haulage, since in the absence of high capital costs there is not the same divergence between average and marginal cost. Particularly for the small or medium haulier, there are few if any fixed assets which would not have to be replaced or could be treated as bygones over more than a very few years. Indeed the fact that marginal cost beyond the very short run is likely to be high relative to average costs, in contrast to the situation on the railways, is an argument against the accusation that hauliers charge uneconomic rates in competition with rail. But while hauliers are sometimes accused even by their fellows of short-run marginal cost pricing (the low cost of a return journey is well known to every haulier who has never heard of the economic concept) in practice the difficulty arises of isolating such prices. In spite of the secrecy with which negotiations are conducted, price discrimination cannot easily be achieved, and the RHA frowns on marginal pricing of this type for fear of a downwards rate spiral.

In the absence of a going price, the RHA for many years recommended rate increases based on cost increases. This had the dual objective of giving a lever for use in bargaining with customers and making hauliers aware of cost increases. In the ten years preceding 1965, the price-rise recommendations of the RHA were largely based on increased wage costs. Nevertheless, despite the recommendations, it is well established that rates frequently did not go up as much as recommended, or even at all. The major reason for this seems to have been that the RHA took little notice of potential productivity increases which hauliers could use to offset rising costs. In some cases it may have been true that there was ignorance of costs, or that there was resistance from customers, who in some instances have been given a virtually monopolistic position by the licensing system, but profitability does not seem to have been unduly low in the period, so that the first explanation seems the most likely. In 1965 the Prices and Incomes Board was given haulage rates as its first reference, but due to the lack of information with which to do a full analysis, it could only suggest that the RHA should stop recommending increases in view of the wide differences within the industry.[52] Two years later, the RHA itself requested that the Board examine the industry to judge whether higher rates were justified. The Board agreed that the claim was generally upheld, but refused to recommend any specific figure because cost increases had not been uniform.[53] Since then, the RHA has neatly evaded the issue of recommended rates by merely advising members to re-examine their costs, thereby giving a lead which has been substantially followed. Nevertheless, the fear of the RHA that there would be a downwards spiral in rates, or stagnant rates in a period of rising costs, does not seem to have been justified over the last few years.[54]

Now that there is no longer the same degree of central leadership on the question of rates, it seems likely that price leadership will become more important. BRS charges have been used as an important reference point for charging in the past; this function may well become even more important in the future. Just how competitive BRS prices are, how far service wins or loses contracts for it and how far its actual rates differ from its published rates must be matters for conjecture. But its published rates, at least, would seem to provide an upper maximum for competitive quotations in that traders frequently use BRS quotations to check the charges of their regular haulier, while hauliers try to establish BRS rates as a benchmark for themselves. Indeed, private hauliers have often praised the state company for its role in helping to stabilize rates.

Part of BRS's pricing policy came under examination when the Prices and Incomes Board was referred a request for a rate increase by BRS Parcels in 1967.[55] The parcels operation is somewhat different from the rest of BRS since with its regular runs, relatively high percentage of fixed costs and genuine published tariffs, BRS Parcels has some of the characteristics of a bus service rather than a haulage concern. This element of predictability should, of course, make its pricing task easier rather than harder. Yet the Board had great difficulty in establishing any price criteria. It found that the company had not been able to ascertain its long-run marginal costs, yet at the same time there was no financial objective in the shape of a target rate of return set for the company by the Transport Holding Company or the Minister of Transport, nor any test rate of discount to evaluate investment. Moreover, the Board felt that the capital valuation of the company did not sufficiently reflect the current value of its assets to use this as a price criterion. As a last possible criterion, it suggested comparability with rates of return in the private sector, but was unable to discover what these were. The Board thus had to declare itself baffled as to a basis for evaluating the company's request, although it admitted a rise in rates was needed.

The other area of pricing policy which is of interest concerns cross-subsidization. In the industry as a whole, and unlike other areas of transport, cross-subsidization is not a live issue. This is partly because road hauliers have no common carrier or public service obligations, but even more because the industry is small scale. The larger the firm, the more likely it is that there will be some averaging of costs in its pricing policy because managerial decentralization cannot be carried far enough to ensure that each rate takes into account all the factors relevant to the particular journey. This, in turn, is one of the factors accounting for the survival of the small man, since once the larger operator begins to average, he leaves the way open for the smaller to undercut him on those journeys where he is charging more than the true cost. It was this, of course, which was responsible for much of the loss of rail traffic to road in the inter-war and post-war period.

BRS, as the largest firm in the industry, is in some danger of cross-subsidizing if price decisions are centrally made on the basis of averages. The early period of its existence saw some moves in that direction. Walters, who studied the BRS rates structure in 1955/56, found that one group, the West Midlands group, which tried to integrate its pricing policy into a single tariff structure, had a much higher degree of averaging than another group in Scotland which had essentially accepted the rate structure which it had inherited from private enterprise.[56] His findings in the Midlands, although admittedly not based on a comprehensive sample due to lack of information, are nevertheless interesting. An increase in the average length of haul of one mile resulted in an increase in cost per ton of 1·25 p, but an increase in revenue of 1·46 p. Over a long distance, revenue therefore exceeded cost by a very large margin. Again, an increase in load factor of 1 per cent decreased cost per ton by 2·39 p, but revenue per ton by only 0·83 p, which meant unduly high revenue for higher weights. The taper for both weight and distance was therefore not nearly great enough, but could easily be exploited by a competitor pricing closer to cost. BRS's answer has been to decentralize pricing to the depot level, except for the parcels operation and a few large national contracts negotiated in London.

VIII Technical Efficiency

Changes in technology of the road haulage industry were for a considerable time limited to larger and better designed vehicles which could take a larger payload at a cheaper price per ton, and more recently better roads on which to run them.[57] More permissive regulations as to vehicle size, weight and payload have also played a large part in this progress.[58] These factors, all external to the industry itself, helped to keep down the cost per ton-mile, which according to one estimate rose from 2·70 p in 1952 to 3·16 p in 1965,[59] or considerably slower than the rise in the general price index.

The sizes of goods vehicles have changed radically in the post-war period, as can be seen from Table 4.8 below.

TABLE 4.8
Commercial vehicles by unladen weight

Unladen weight	1952	1958	1969	1970
Under 1 ton	359	507	527	548
1–2 tons	219	243	419	452
2–3 tons	330	292	135	130
3–5 tons	67	135	245	234
5–8 tons	21	32	121	132
Over 8 tons		8	46	55
Total	996	1,217	1,493	1,551

Source: The data for 1952 are from Glover and Miller, *Journal of the Royal Statistical Society*, 1954, Part 3, and that for the later years from *Annual Abstract of Statistics*, 1971, Table 245.

The reason for the rapid growth of the larger vehicles, apart from changes in the Construction and Use regulations, is simply that larger vehicles can carry an increase in payload which amounts to two or three times the increase in unladen weight. Table 4.9 graphically illustrates this advantage of the larger vehicle for the 'A' licence category.

TABLE 4.9
Work done by 'A' licence vehicles, 1962

Unladen weight	Million miles	Million tons	Million ton-miles
Under 1 ton	12,400	360	3,700
1–2 tons	11,100	920	8,200
2–2½ tons	9,500	1,220	16,300
2½–3 tons	13,600	1,520	36,700
3–5 tons	26,100	2,640	124,700
Over 5 tons	34,200	3,630	293,000

Source: *Road Goods Survey*, 1962, Part I, Table 28.

The cost advantages of the large vehicle are clear, since costs increase less than in proportion to payload. Thus Edwards and Bayliss note that while the cost per mile for 'A' licence vehicles of less than one ton unladen weight was 10 p, that for large vehicles of more than 8 tons unladen weight was only 16·3 p.[60] Again, there are very considerable gains to be made by running a vehicle for larger annual mileages, a function of the proportion of fixed to variable costs. Thus an estimate showed that whereas a 20-ton capacity vehicle cost an index of 100 per mile if it ran 30,000 miles, the same vehicle cost 86 per mile for 40,000 miles and 72 for 50,000 miles. To keep pace with vehicle size, engine design has also been improved, giving better power to weight ratios and practically all long-distance vehicles are now diesel.

It is also evident, however, that larger vehicles, to be profitable, need to run at high load factors, since if a smaller vehicle could carry the particular consignment, the extra size would be wasted. Here, unfortunately, there is very little hard information, although the fact that only a very small proportion of consignments weigh anything like the maximum payload of the larger vehicles means that loads must be amalgamated in many instances.[61] The concept of maximum payload is itself somewhat indeterminate, since factors such as bulk density, loadability and consignment compatibility play a part as well as weight. For these reasons it would be surprising to find many vehicles operating consistently with a maximum weight load.

Capacity utilization is also an important relative term in comparing the efficiency of different modes of transport, and here public hauliers appear to have performed far better than either rail or private haulage. A simple comparison based on 1962 figures of ton-mileage performed per capacity ton available showed a figure of 14,417 for public haulage, 7,219 for private haulage, and 1,169 for rail freight. Moreover, the rate of increase for public haulage was far faster, since similar figures for 1952 had been: public haulage 9,988, private haulage 6,961 and rail 1,523.[62] Some part of these favourable figures for public haulage may have been due to the constraints of the licensing system, while the unfavourable rail figures incorporate redundant capacity which should have been written off, but the comparison is still revealing.

Changes in the size of vehicle, although probably the most important, are by no means the only technical changes currently facing road goods transport. The 'container revolution' has been much heralded, and is clearly going to have a considerable impact on transport. Indeed, both sea and rail transport are to a considerable extent pinning their future to it. In road transport, however, the effect is likely to be less, although still significant. In the first place, the vast bulk of road traffics travel such short distances as to make the container irrelevant. Second, not all the goods which travel by road are suitable for containers. Third, the container is most useful as an easy means of transferring goods from one mode of transport to another; road transport, on the other hand, can offer door-to-door transport which obviates the need for transhipment between modes. Nevertheless, there are likely to be considerable repercussions for the long-distance sector of road haulage, including the state-owned companies. If goods can be transhipped more easily, this will make rail much more competitive, especially over long distances, and the role of road transport may be confined to pick-up-and-delivery services at either end. The critical question then becomes at what distance it becomes profitable to incur the double transhipment at the terminals which rail usually involves in order to take advantage of the cheap, trainload transport which rail can offer. The present presumption is that early estimates were much too favourable for the freightliner system, and that road transport will be much more competitive.[63]

Another sphere of development has been in techniques of fleet organization. This has been necessary in the face of lengthening delivery and turnround times as congestion becomes worse and the periods available for delivery grow shorter. The extreme example of this type of problem comes at the docks, where delays of two or three days are not uncommon.[64] Shift work and night services are ways of increasing vehicle utilization, but the one important answer has been the growing use of articulated vehicles. By using one tractor in conjunction with two or possibly more trailers, the motive power unit at least can be kept on the road. Articulated units cost more to buy and run and fortunate is the firm which has no design incompatibilities between its tractors and its trailers, but the flexibility gained is vital in saved time. A further very important improvement has been the use of the teleprinter and the computer to speed communications and co-ordinate vehicle movements, although the computer is clearly only for the largest firms, and BRS may well be the only company in the industry to boast one to itself. The BRS computer is deliberately not used for pricing purposes. In the future its main use may be in applying operations research techniques to journey patterns. The Prices and Incomes Board has strongly advised the use of the 'serpent' technique for minimizing journey distances, which it notes has already enabled NCL to reduce its fleet by some 300 vehicles, and which it estimated could enable a reduction of some 10 per cent in the BRS Parcels fleet.[65] The use of such techniques may prove to be a considerable advantage for the more sophisticated, and usually larger, firms.

IX Labour

The optimum use of the industry's 250,000 employed workers has been and continues to be a leading problem in road haulage. Even though almost half of this number work for the 78 firms with more than 250 employees (including the state companies), the average number of employees per depot is small. Moreover, the main occupation, driving, precludes direct supervision.[66] The competitive nature of the industry and the individualistic spirit of most of those engaged in it at all levels further add to the difficulties of control which are experienced by government, industrial association, management and unions alike.

There is a long record of government intervention through legislation in labour matters, but legislation has never been completely successful. The Road Traffic Act of 1930 introduced a fair wages clause and also regulated hours. The 1933 Act made the issue of public hauliers' licences dependent on compliance with these regulations. But in a period of depression the system did not work very well with regard to wages, and in 1938 it was replaced by the Road Haulage Wages Act, which established statutory wage regulation by means of joint boards, later brought together into a single Wages Council. Since the war, the enforcement of wages has been less of a problem, but the regulation of hours and drivers' records has become more difficult. In the year ended September 1968 there were no less than 19,058 convictions for hours and records offences.[67]

The problems of the unions and the Road Haulage Association are similar and arise from their inability to organize the whole industry. The 17,600 operators who belong to the RHA are for the most part the larger ones, but even they by no means always follow RHA policy, while those outside are difficult even to reach. The unions have the same problem of organizing in very small establishments, and they also face the difficulty that the close relationship between the small operator and his employees often precludes interest in a union.[68] Attempts by the RHA and the unions to set up a national Negotiating Committee in 1965 foundered because neither side was fully representative and the enforcement of decisions was so difficult.

These problems are further exacerbated by the wage structure, since the low basic wage rates set by the Wages Council has resulted in both sides, if for different reasons, looking for excuses to achieve higher earnings. Consequently, the relationship between work done, time spent on the job and earnings is extremely elastic. This situation is best illustrated by regard to the amount of overtime worked, or at least paid for. The average weekly hours in 1967 were 58·6 with almost four-fifths working more than fifty hours a week.[69] It was to deal with the obvious safety implications of some drivers being on the road for up to seventy hours per week that the drivers' hours provisions of the 1968 Transport Act were passed. With a standard week of 41 hours, it is not surprising to find that overtime pay in 1967 made up to 37·7 per cent of average total earnings, which amounted to £22·39 p.[70]

The Prices and Incomes Board in its first reference strongly castigated the amount of overtime worked, saying that it had 'serious economic and social implications',[71] deplored the inability of the Wages Council to do any more than set minimum conditions, and made several recommendations for increasing productivity. Two years later, the Board again examined the industry, but was forced to conclude that 'little, if any, progress has been made by the two sides of the industry towards the objectives set out in our Final Report'.[72] Following this some local productivity bargains were negotiated, and the Board was referred some of these in August 1968. On reporting, the Board criticized the agreements for having an unclear connection between the wage increase and the changes expected of the drivers.[73] It is also noted that most of the agreements had been made on the initiative of the unions involved. The conclusion must be that in an industry as small scale and competitive as road haulage, it is almost impossible to effectuate national decisions and policies, if only because the management structure is too weak.[74] As *The Times* put it: 'Basically in too many respects the industry does not have the instruments for putting into effect the techniques which the Board tries to encourage.'[75] All in all it seems likely that industrial relations issues will become increasingly difficult in road haulage. Although it has not been notably strike-prone, there has been increasing wage militancy among groups such as car-transporter and tanker drivers and more general militancy over issues such as tachographs and possible financial loss resulting from the drivers' hours legislation, while the Industrial Relations Act of 1971 may well expose the inadequacy of dismissal and other procedures in the industry.

The state groups have a somewhat different set of industrial relations problems, which may be even more intractable. On the one hand the negotiating structure and procedures are superior to those in the rest of the industry. BRS always had its own negotiating machinery separate from the Wages Council, and, of course, did not have the RHA's problem of enforcing terms. The BRS companies were also among the first haulage firms to negotiate productivity agreements.[76] Thus the labour problems of the state group lie elsewhere, and in fact are an inevitable consequence of the acquisition by the NFC of NCL. The NFC finds itself with surplus capacity in a diminishing parcels market, such that the Prices and Incomes Board has bluntly said that BRS Parcels and NCL together could well need to reduce their resources, including their 35,000 staff, by half by 1974.[77] Even if the figure of one half is too pessimistic, substantial redundancy seems inevitable and will be made the more difficult by the fact that the two main companies deal with separate and rival unions resulting from their heritage and have maintained the separate bargaining arrangements of the pre-NFC period. To co-ordinate the bargaining machinery and reconcile the unions to the hard choices of the next few years will be no easy task. Nevertheless, an encouraging sign was the inclusion in the 1971 NFC Report of a joint statement by the union leaders concerned that clear progress in industrial relations had been made.[78]

X Profitability and Investment

Like many other measurements in road haulage, that of profitability is extremely difficult. It is apparent that the rapid post-war increase in demand, together with the limitation on entry and therefore curb on surplus capacity provided by the licensing system, produced an acceptable overall level of profits. This can be deduced from the great competition to obtain new licences, such that the Geddes Report noted that 'A' licences were sold for up to £300 a licensed ton.[79] As the report went on to note, one interpretation of this would be that a price represents the capitalized value of the profits available from possession of the licence.

On the other hand, profitability certainly varies between sectors. Tipping, which is notoriously competitive, is unlikely for that reason to be very profitable although there may be some lucrative contracts to encourage entrants. General haulage has also been a less profitable sector, probably because entry is easier than in the specialist sectors. The Transport Development Group noted in its 1967 Annual Report that 'developments in the haulage field continue to underline the wisdom of the group companies in concentrating on specialist traffics and on contract hire'. BRS has similarly noted the relative unprofitability of general haulage, which can be seen in Table 4.10 below, and has moved its business towards the specialized sectors.

A profit comparison between the state companies and their privately owned competitors would obviously be a good test of the relative efficiency of the state interests. One of the few glimpses of profitability in the privately owned part of the industry, since there are almost no public companies with published profits, is provided by the Road Haulage Association's evidence to the Prices and Incomes Board in August 1967, in connection with the request for higher rates. The firms belonging to various sectors of the industry were taken and their profit averaged out over the previous five years, corresponding roughly to the period 1963–67. The RHA considered these firms, which were medium sized, with total assets of just over £1 million, and fleets ranging from 7 to 70 vehicles, to be a reasonable cross-section of the industry, although in fact they disregard the large number of small operators. Table 4.10 gives profit as a percentage of turnover for these firms and compares them with the BRS groupings.[80]

TABLE 4.10
Profit comparison of BRS and ten private companies as percentage of turnover

	1963	1964	1965	1966	1967	1968
Private companies	9.8	9.8	10.5	9.0	4.2	—
BRS General	3.5	7.4	6.0	2.9	1.2	2.2
BRS Parcels	12.1	12.2	12.8	5.4	3.8	3.1
Pickfords	11.7	12.2	11.3	11.1	9.3	9.0
All BRS	7.5	10.3	8.8	5.5	3.3	3.7

Source: The figures for BRS come from THC, *Annual Report*, 1968; those for the private companies from *Roadway*, December 1967.

BRS therefore did not perform quite as well as this sample from the industry. The performance was nevertheless respectable by the industry norms, especially if it is remembered that the sort of firm which is willing to divulge its profits to the RHA is likely to be a progressive and relatively efficient firm.[81] BRS's performance was also respectable by comparison with other nationalized industries.

For various reasons the results shown in Table 4.11 are not comparable with the equivalent companies in 1968, but in broad terms

TABLE 4.11
NFC financial results 1969/70

	Receipts £m 1969	Receipts £m 1970	Profit £m 1969	Profit £m 1970
General haulage				
BRS group	54·3	60·2	1·4	1·4
Freightliners	10·7	14·6	(2·2)	(0·8)
Tayforth and others	13·5	14·4	0·5	0·5
Parcels companies				
BRS Parcels group	22·5	25·9	0·2	0·8
National Carriers*	47·4	53·2	1·9	1·9
Others	6·1	7·1	0·3	0·6
Special traffics—Pickfords	12·8	14·6	0·7	0·3
Others	5·5	6·6	0·2	0·4
Total † ‡ §	172·8	196·6	4·7	6·7
Short-term interest and				
Headquarters expenses			0·8	1·1
Interest on capital			5·8	6·8
Overall loss			1·9	1·2

* Including Government grant for National Carriers of £17·0 million in 1969, £13·4 million in 1970.
† Gross Receipts include £5 million in 1969, £7 million in 1970, of traffics carried by one subsidiary for another.
‡ Profit is after payment of minority interests, of which BRB is the largest.
§ Profit includes results for shipping subsidiaries of £0·1 million loss in 1969 and £0·5 million profit in 1970.
Source: NFC, *Annual Report*, 1970.

the loss on National Carriers has been reduced from some £20 million to under £13 million, while the Freightliners operation has almost become viable. However, for reasons common to the rest of the industry, the old road companies have suffered a decline in profits and in April 1971 BRS Ltd announced a cash crisis caused by a slump in key industries such as paper, steel and food. It is clear, therefore, that the overall profitability of the NFC is far from firmly established yet.

The most important aspect of investment in road transport is the very low amount of capital required to begin operations. As little as £200 deposit for a vehicle bought from a hire purchase company can set up an operator in business, although of course licensing has presented a much bigger barrier. Another consequence of the small units of capital is that firms can build up their fleets slowly and replace them piece by piece.

Depreciation can be fairly accurately gauged to permit refinancing, and there should thus be no need for large capital outlays after the initial commitment to set of vehicles. The possibility of accumulating small units naturally differentiates haulage from most manufacturing industry, where indivisibilities in plant investment are the source of economies of scale, and also from most of the other industries in which state ownership is important.

The low capital requirement is not as true of some sectors of haulage, however, as for general haulage, and this is no doubt one of the factors accounting for the low profitability of general haulage. Thus heavy haulage, bulk tanker, refrigerated and other specialized vehicles require a much greater initial outlay than the typical flat or box vehicle. Nevertheless, a general haulage firm such as BRS Ltd, can typically be self-financing out of depreciation and retained profits. This BRS has generally been successful in achieving, although the acquisition of other companies has required Ministry of Transport and Treasury permission.

BRS growth policy in the period up to 1964 was largely by means of larger capacity vehicles, since the Conservative Governments would not permit purchase of outside companies, and new licences were difficult to obtain. After 1964, the Labour Government encouraged the purchase of other fleets. The frustration under which BRS had worked in the pre-1954 period emerges strongly from the 1964 Report:

> In general the THC does not advocate expansion for its own sake. But road transport itself is expanding, and even to maintain the Holding Company's relative position a certain growth in its activities is required. More important, perhaps is the consideration that an organization that stands still is doomed to wither; lively development and a natural expansion are essential to the health of a sound undertaking. It is also necessary to expand where the expansion will result in a sounder strategic position, and, above all, where it will introduce new men of the right calibre.[82]

Perhaps a little surprisingly there was a steady stream of enquiries from private hauliers about the possibility of being acquired by BRS, amounting to over a hundred in 1965.[83] BRS therefore had numerous opportunities of expanding and as a result a major stake in the bulk-tanker sector by purchasing Harold Wood Ltd, with 541 vehicles, and also in the car-carrying sector through Mortons of Coventry. The Tayforth group, with 1,594 vehicles, itself a conglomerate of smaller companies, was the largest single purchase. Possibly an important factor in the willingness to be purchased was the promise from BRS of considerable autonomy:

It will often be sound policy, in such circumstances, to preserve and encourage the entity to grow, nourished by its own roots. Certainly it would be sheer folly, especially in the case of large and efficient concerns, to begin by breaking them up forthwith, for piecemeal absorption in other parts of the older structure.[84]

If this means that in some instances one BRS company is competing against another, this is presumably seen as an inevitable concomitant of decentralization.

XI Conclusions

One obvious area where concluding remarks are needed is the role of the nationalized sector within road haulage generally. Perhaps the most apposite comment about BRS as an entity within the road haulage industry was made by a commentator in *Commercial Motor*. 'The Company shows a desire, almost an anxiety, to be treated like any other haulier, with neither extra privileges nor extra responsibilities.'[85] This has certainly been the case since the 1962 Act and it was strongly reinforced by the 1968 Act and the formation of the NFC. Indeed the NFC has adopted a belligerently self-sufficient slogan as its objective: 'Non-monolithic, Non-bureaucratic, and Non-subsidized: A Commercial Public Corporation.' In the early stages of its existence, BRS was dominated by a British Transport Commission which was drawn almost entirely from railwaymen, and was largely concerned with railway problems. This was inevitable. Road policy scarcely existed because there were no statistics on which to base it, nor was there anyone with the stature or experience to know what was required, while railway problems were obvious and urgent. But as has been noted, BRS gradually moved away from the centralizing policy of that time and towards greater independence and self-confidence. The most symbolic act by the BRS was its joining as an associate member of the Road Haulage Association, for that body has traditionally been hostile to government interference of any sort and especially to nationalization. Indeed BRS became a valuable part of the lobby for road interests. Obviously there were times when BRS could not take the RHA viewpoint on political matters, while for its part the RHA was not at all pleased by the company's expansion after 1964, but BRS made a notable intervention on behalf of the road industry in its strong rebuttal of the argument on road-track costs put forward by British Railways to the Geddes Committee.[86]

Within the industry itself it might be argued that the impact of a large nationalized haulage company has really been fairly small. Rather than BRS 'rationalizing' the industry by its presence and competition, as has sometimes happened after the formation of a large company in a small-scale industry, the reverse tended to happen. BRS reverted to the customs and practices of the industry, and did relatively little to change them. In the eyes of bodies such as the Prices and Incomes Board, which equate 'rationalization' with greater efficiency,[87] the lack of change brought about by BRS must be something of a disappointment. Certainly, BRS has introduced better management techniques to many private hauliers by employing them for a period in their careers, and it has been useful to the whole industry in such diverse matters as vehicle design and price stability. But the industry is essentially the same as it was when BRS was formed. The tens of thousands of small operators remain, while the stronger companies have grown only slowly or through amalgamation. This lack of impact might be blamed on the licensing system, the political control over BRS in the period of Conservative rule, or even to the inherent disadvantages of public ownership. But more likely it is due to the economics of the industry and to BRS policy. If BRS has taken advantage of some of the potential economies of large scale such as those given by the intricate network of regular service and the use of the computer to co-ordinate traffics, for the most part it has moved determinedly in the other direction. Geographical and functional decentralization, the practice of not engorging acquired companies, the slimming down of the management structure, and the refusal to expand into all the various sectors of the industry, all help to show an acceptance of the economies of small-scale operation. In this view the NFC certainly concurs, as witness its slogan and the fact that it inherited its chairman and much of its management structure from the Transport Holding Company.

By comparison with most other nationalized bodies, the NFC starts with considerable advantages. In the first place, it is not a monopoly, and therefore has its commercial standards forced upon it by external competition. Even when it did legally possess a monopoly between 1947 and 1953, rail and particularly 'C' licence competition prevented complacency. Secondly, it does not come into touch with the public except in peripheral areas, which has prevented too much publicity being attached to its activities and particularly its shortcomings. By the same token, it does not have the disadvantages of any public service obligations, which have resulted in cross-subsidization in many State-owned sectors. It does not even have the obligations amounting to the status of a common carrier, so that its operations can be carried out on purely commercial criteria. A further advantage has been profitability, although this relates more to the period before the formation of NFC. This, of course, is an internal rather than an external factor, but it clearly has been useful that the industry as a whole has been enjoying an expansion of demand and at least reasonable profits since the Second World War. This has certainly meant far less political interference than would have been the case had state haulage continually run up losses. The fact that it has needed little external capital has also been important in keeping it out of the political limelight.

These advantages have been in commercial operations. In another sense, state haulage has been more of a political football than any other nationalized sector with the exception of steel. Changes in the first ten post-war years were based more on political ideology than on economic rationale. Road haulage is neither a natural monopoly nor a declining but essential industry, and its part nationalization owed more to its relationship with the railways than its suitability for centralized control. Similarly, its denationalization ignored the virtues of the nation-wide structure that had been created. Unfortunately the issue continues to fester. The 1966 THC report pointed out that political objections were being levelled at the THC for two widely differing reasons, the one criticizing its state ownership and the other its commercial organization.[88] The 1968 Act brought fresh changes which again created controversy over the structure of state haulage. Sir Reginald Wilson, then chairman-designate of the NFC, made a strong plea for a period of stability just after the Act was passed, saying that public transport, whether privately or publicly owned, should have a chance 'to get on with it'.[89] Unfortunately, in spite of Sir Reginald's commercial philosophies, the structure of the state-owned part of the industry is far from settled. The Conservative policy of 'disengagement' from 'unnecessary' state ownership has not yet been so explicitly stated as to mention road haulage, although questions asked in Parliament about the Government's intentions have received a negative reply. Nevertheless, one Conservative MP grouped the state haulage interests together with the state-owned public houses, Penarth Docks and Thomas Cook as 'peripheral State interests' which 'should be sold off'.[90]

This political uncertainty, together with the commercial uncertainty mentioned in the last section and the report of the Prices and Incomes Board early in 1971, led in May 1971 to an organizational re-examination and new operating structure which seemed to have had the dual intention of financial co-ordination and helping to withstand any possible government attempts to sell off profitable parts of the combine. The Board report centred on the problems of the parcels group, and it suggested four alternatives ranging from the virtual disbandment of NCL to differentiating the functions of BRS Parcels and NCL, either geographically, by quality of service or by size of parcel.[91] However, the reorganization has gone well beyond parcels. Six groups in all have been created, each with a co-ordinator to ensure the achievement of financial objectives. The six are: BRS Ltd Group; Parcels Group; Freightliner and Irish Traffics Group; Tayforth and Tank Haulage Group; Special Group; and Overseas Group. The Special Group will have two sections, one basically made up of the Pickfords companies except that for overseas forwarding, and the other containing Tartan Arrow, Airlink and Northern Ireland Carriers. One of the consequences of these changes will be greater central control, a reversal of previous policy. In the difficult area of parcels, the proposals would mean that BRS Parcels would concentrate on high-speed services over dense routes, while NCL would be the national parcels distributor. However, the BRS Parcels unions, fearing substantial redundancies, have at the time of writing refused to accept this scheme. A solution to the parcels problem is clearly imperative for the financial health of the whole concern. One final organizational change has been the removal of the shipping companies from NFC control, Atlantic Steam Navigation being sold to a private company and Humber Lines being wound up.

    The NFC's relationship with the railways will be further discussed in chapter 6 under an examination of the problems of co-ordination, but a few comments may also be relevant here. It is difficult to say what practical effect the NFC's statutory obligation 'to secure that goods are carried by rail whenever such carriage is efficient and economic' has had and indeed, since this obligation merely reinforces what would on the face of it appear to be the sensible commercial policy, it might seem to be superfluous. The fact that it was included may therefore be taken as expressing concern about the new Corporation's attitude to the railways, given the long history of rivalry between road and rail under the BTC. Certainly the relations between the NFC and the BRB have not been as cordial as they might in view of their very close links. For that matter the NFC has, of course, a competitive road–rail split within itself. Every traffic must be examined to see which mode is the most suitable; indeed, something not unlike a quantity licensing procedure must be followed, with powerful groups within the Corporation having an interest in the outcome. It would thus be unrealistic to assume that internal strains do not exist, however much the NFC might claim that its objective is 'to build up new loyalties based on "Freight Business" rather than on the old conflicts of "Road versus Rail".'[92]

Looking now briefly beyond the state group to the larger haulage industry, the future pattern is likely to be different from that under the pre-1968 licensing system, and the changes may well be in apparently opposite directions. On the one hand the more progressive and efficient companies will be enabled to grow faster than when proof of consumer need had to be shown. At the other end there will be good opportunities for small operators using vehicles below the minimum weight for licensing requirements. Some traffics may also be taken away from public haulage by own account operators into surplus capacity, and although the number of these actually entering the market may be small, they could have a disproportionate effect on rates. Again, the much more stringent requirements with respect to financial stability, safety and maintenance imposed by the quality licensing regulations will put a premium on good organization. In the middle, therefore, some of those firms previously protected by the old licensing system and the difficulties it created in changing haulier may go out of existence. Haulage will certainly be much closer to a free and competitive economic market in spite of the likelihood of some concentration in the number of operators and continuing specialization into subsectors, and in spite of being associated in the Common Market with what are generally more restrictive policies. In total, the hauliers can well afford to be confident about the future, at least in so far as the economy can provide industrial growth on which the industry can feed. Even though the rapid rise in costs must represent a continuing source of concern, there is no practical alternative to haulage for most goods traffics.

NOTES TO CHAPTER 4

1. See D. L. Munby, 'Road Transport—A Gap in the National Statistics', *Bulletin of Oxford University Institute of Statistics*, November 1960, although the picture has improved since then. Even so, many operating statistics are only available from surveys, of which the most important are: *Survey of Road Goods Transport*, Parts I–IV (HMSO, 1964–66); B. T. Bayliss and S. L. Edwards, *Transport for Industry* (HMSO, 1969) and

S. L. Edwards and B. T. Bayliss, *Operating Costs in Road Freight Transport* (HMSO, 1971). Another road goods survey was carried out in 1967/68, and when its results become available in 1972 it should be the most comprehensive source of operating statistics in the industry. However, the nature of the industry is such that no statistics are likely to be completely reliable, and some inconsistencies are to be expected.
2. G. W. Quick-Smith, 'Contrasting Concepts in Transport Organization', *Institute of Transport Journal*, May 1967.
3. A much fuller account of the history of road goods transport is to be found in C. I. Savage, *An Economic History of Transport* (Hutchinson, rev. ed. 1966).
4. The Commission's terms of reference were: '... to take into consideration the problems arising out of growth of road traffic and, with a view to securing the employment of the available means of transport in Gt. Britain to the greatest public advantage, to consider and report what measures if any should be adopted for their better regulation and control, to promote their co-ordinated working and development.' Royal Commission on Transport, *Final Report* (Cmnd. 3751, HMSO; 1930), p. vii.
5. *Report of Conference on Road and Rail Transport* (Salter Report) (HMSO, 1932), para. 100.
6. See W. M. MacLeod and A. A. Walters, 'A Note on Bankruptcy in Road Haulage', *Journal of Industrial Economics*, November 1956; and P. E. Hart, 'The Restriction of Road Haulage', *Scottish Journal of Political Economy*, June 1959.
7. The Act provided for the Authorities to require the keeping of operating records, but this section was never enforced. This missed opportunity has been in large part responsible for the poor quality of road haulage data.
8. Sir Cyril Hurcomb, the Director-General at the Ministry of Transport during the war, and afterwards the first Chairman of the British Transport Commission, was sceptical about the results obtained from the RHO; 'Detailed allocation of traffic has not been practicable, nor, indeed, has it been easy to find any fixed principles on which to allocate at all ... It must be confessed that wartime allocation of traffic has not been based on principles or methods likely to be applicable to ordinary conditions.' (Quoted at Parl. Deb. 5th. Ser. Vol. 431, Col. 1639, 1947.)
9. The British Transport Commission did issue a document intended to be the basis of integration, entitled *Integration of Services by Road and Rail: A Statement of Policy*, in July 1950. In the last few months of the Labour Government common commercial services between road and rail were introduced in East Anglia, only to be dropped as soon as the Conservatives regained power. As for the 'C' licence gap, in the four years from December 1946 to December 1950, the 'C' vehicle fleet grew from 383,000 to 734,000. Not all of these, of course, were long-distance vehicles, but the effect of such growth on the nationalized holdings must nevertheless have been considerable.

10. These difficulties are graphically described in J. H. Smith, 'The Rise of a Bureaucracy', *Transactions of the Third World Congress of Sociology*, Vol. II.
11. British Transport Commission, *Annual Report*, 1951, p. 123.
12. *The Economist*, 9 July 1956, p. 144.
13. Mr Hugh Molson, for the Ministry of Transport, said that the Government recognized the need for trunk services running on fixed schedules which could be provided only by a large organization. He added: 'We felt that it would be entirely wrong to destroy an organization of that kind. To have done so, we felt, would have been to sacrifice a valuable national asset to an ideological prejudice.' (Parl. Deb. 5th Ser. Vol. 548, Col. 1818, 1956.)
14. *Reorganization of the Nationalized Transport Undertakings* (Cmnd. 1248: HMSO, 1960).
15. *The Financial and Economic Obligations of the Nationalized Industries* (Cmnd. 1337: HMSO, 1961).
16. For a fuller discussion of the origins and implications of the Act, see chapter 6.
17. The BRB retained 49 per cent of Freightliners Ltd. The shipping companies previously under the control of the THC were also given to the NFC, but it is likely that a majority interest in them will be acquired by the BRB.
18. Transport Act 1968, Section I (1)(a)(ii).
19. The Road Safety Act 1967 is also important in this connection. Its major provisions introduced a new annual inspection system for goods vehicles and a new system of 'plated' weights to indicate maximum loads for vehicles.
20. The Act provides for the hours to be reduced to nine, but the Conservative Minister of Transport has indicated that he will not activate this section.
21. *Report of the Committee on Carriers' Licensing* (Geddes Report) (HMSO, 1965).
22. This finding is not incompatible with the suggestion that licensing had increased certain productivity indices by promoting a higher degree of capacity utilization through the curtailment of entry. See B. M. Deakin and T. Seward, *Productivity in Transport* (Cambridge University Press, 1969).
23. *Transport Policy* (Cmnd. 3057: HMSO, 1966), p. 23.
24. The operator's licence was introduced as from March 1970, with a period of transition; discussions are proceeding on the manager's licence at the time of writing and no date for introduction has been announced.
25. The groupings were changed as from May 1971, but since no data are available on the new basis, the chapter will retain these traditional groupings, which are similar to those under the THC. For the new structure, see p. 258.
26. NFC, *Annual Report*, 1969, p. 3.
27. Some large fleets, such as Unilever's SPD, always carried for other

people whilst being preponderantly own account operators. Most 'B' licence operators, however, carried preponderantly for other people, and the 'B' licence category has generally been classified as public haulage.
28. This is borne out by Sharp, who found that half of all 'C' licence operators had only the most general idea of their costs. C. Sharp, *The Allocation of Freight Traffic—A Survey* (Ministry of Transport, 1970), p. 27.
29. THC, *Annual Report*, 1968, p. 10.
30. The figures in this paragraph were obtained from the *Survey of Road Goods Transport*, 1962, tables 21–6. Although they are now out of date, the pattern is unlikely to have changed very much.
31. Geddes Report, p. 25.
32. ibid., p. 26.
33. National Board for Prices and Incomes, Report No. 48, *Charges, Costs and Wages in the Road Haulage Industry* (Cmnd. 3482: HMSO, 1967), p. 9.
34. See Edwards and Bayliss, op. cit: B. T. Bayliss, *The Small Firm in the Road Haulage Industry* (HMSO, 1971); G. Walker, *Road and Rail* (Allen & Unwin, rev. ed. 1947), ch. VIII; M. Chisholm, 'Economies of Scale in Road Goods Transport? Off-farm Milk Collection in England and Wales', *Oxford Economic Papers*, October 1959; A. Walters, 'Economies of Scale in Road Haulage. A Comment', *Oxford Economic Papers*, February 1961; A. J. Harrison, 'Economies of Scale and the Structure of the Road Haulage Industry', *Oxford Economic Papers*, November 1963.
35. *Roadway*, May 1969, pp. 28–9.
36. Briggs gives it as his opinion that the good small operator can deal with the day-to-day problems of up to six vehicles, but thereafter he must engage specialized staff in addition to his drivers. G. W. Briggs, *Road Haulage Management* (Butterworth, 1965), p. 129.
37. A. A. Walters, *The Integration in Freight Transport* (Institute of Economic Affairs, 1968), p. 40.
38. Bayliss, op.cit., p. 31.
39. See P. S. Herman, 'TDG: Operating a Transport Group', *Modern Transport*, November 1966.
40. See G. W. Quick-Smith, 'Contrasting Concepts in Transport Organization', *Institute of Transport Journal*, May 1967.
41. THC, *Annual Report*, 1965, p. 13.
42. *Survey of Road Goods Transport*, 1962, Table xi.
43. Sir Reginald Wilson, 'Transport and Common-Sense', *Institute of Transport Journal*, March 1969, p. 103.
44. See pp. 144–53.
45. NBPI, Report No. 14, *Road Haulage Charges* (Cmnd. 2968: HMSO, 1966), p. 4.
46. *Roadway*, December 1967, p. 17.
47. *Commercial Motor Tables of Operating Costs*, Published annually.
48. H. E. Osborn, 'Road Haulage and Roads', *Institute of Transport Journal*,

July 1966. Deakin and Seward give credence to the claim by their calculation of a price increase of only 0·3 per cent per annum, op. cit., p. 180.
49. *Commercial Motor*, 12 July 1968.
50. The Centre for Interfirm Comparisons, in a study for the RHA, estimated that on a base of 1967/68, the index number for all operating and financial costs per mile in long-distance haulage had risen to 147·0 by 1970/71. (*Roadway*, February 1971.) Wages, contrary to common conception, had risen slightly less than the index as a whole.
51. *Road and Rail*, Chapter 3.
52. NBPI, Report No. 1, *Road Haulage Rates* (Cmnd. 2695: HMSO, 1965).
53. NBPI, Report No. 48.
54. The licensing authorities have occasionally refused to issue licences if they consider that the rate quoted in a contract is too low. The Northwestern Authority insisted in one instance on the rate for a four-mile haul being raised from $12\frac{1}{2}$ p to $17\frac{1}{2}$ p a ton before granting licences (*Roadway*, December 1967, p. 17). Nevertheless, it is noteworthy that one of the main concerns of the RHA's prize essayist of 1969 was how to deal with the rate-breaker. Suspension or expulsion from the RHA was the favoured method.
55. NBPI, Report No. 48.
56. Walters, op. cit., p. 23.
57. BRS have performed a useful function for the industry as a whole by offering testing facilities for new designs, especially those for specialized tasks.
58. The Construction and Use regulations currently specify 32 tons as the maximum permissible load. The road transport organizations have campaigned to have this increased to 36, 40 or even more tons, but in December 1970 the Minister decided, largely on the grounds of environmental preservation, that the current limit should be retained. A higher limit would of course considerably increase the potential efficiency of the largest road vehicles, and manufacturers have for some time had suitable vehicles available in anticipation of the change.
59. The figures are calculated from market estimates in H. E. Osborn, op. cit. As they represent a division of ton-mileage estimates into turnover estimates, and both of these sources are far from exact, the figures are only very rough approximations.
60. Edwards and Bayliss, op. cit., p. 98.
61. See *Transport for Industry*, p. 32.
62. Deakin and Seward, op. cit., p. 187.
63. See H. C. Garnett and K. M. Johnson, *The Economics of Containerization* (Allen and Unwin, 1971).
64. NBPI, Report No. 1, p. 13.
65. NBPI, Report No. 162, *Costs, Charges and Productivity of the National Freight Corporation* (Cmnd. 4569: HMSO, January 1971), p. 14.
66. It was the intention under the 1968 Transport Act that tachographs which measure speed and driving time, should be introduced as a means of monitoring the driver's performance. But partly due to

intense driver reaction against 'the spy in the cab' and partly due to a shortage of the instruments, the clause was not implemented, and the incoming Conservative Minister has said that he has no plans to implement it.
67. Quoted in *Roadway*, August 1969, p. 36.
68. About half of employees are organized in four unions, of which the Transport and General Workers is by far the most important.
69. NBPI, Report No. 48, Appendix C.
70. ibid.
71. Report No. 1, p. 11.
72. Report No. 48, p. 2. The 'Final Report' referred to was Report No. 14.
73. NBPI, Report No. 94, *Productivity Agreements in the Road Haulage Industry* (Cmnd. 3847: HMSO, 1968), p. 12.
74. The NBPI has argued strongly in favour of amalgamations which it considers would strengthen the management structure.
75. 7 December 1968.
76. Although the first of these, signed in August 1968, was favourably commented on by the NBPI (Report No. 94, p. 13) a later one signed in December 1969 received implied criticism when the Board noted: 'Experience shows that the workers covered have in fact obtained large increases in income and indeed that these much exceed the savings obtained.' Report No. 162, p. 15.
77. Report No. 162, p. 18.
78. NFC, *Annual Report*, 1971, pp. 32–3.
79. Geddes Report, p. 60.
80. Profit as a percentage of turnover rather than capital assets is compared because the BRS capital structure is not comparable to those of private firms and because BRS only gives turnover and not capital asset figures for its groups.
81. The Prices and Incomes Board has suggested that BRS should earn commensurate profits with the private sector if it is to justify its existence (Report No. 162, p. 11). Unfortunately in suggesting that BRS does not currently do this, the Board took an incorrect rate of return on capital for the private sector (15 per cent), thus vitiating its implications that BRS's performance is poor. The report referred to, which was prepared for the RHA by the Centre for Interfirm Comparisons, argued that profits in haulage were still inadequate despite increased productivity.
82. THC, *Annual Report*, 1964, p. 18.
83. ibid., 1965, p. 20.
84. ibid., p. 21.
85. *Commercial Motor*, 25 June 1965.
86. THC, *Road Costs and Revenue*, memorandum to the Committee on Carriers Licensing, 1964. This interchange proved conclusively, if proof were needed, that there was very little common interest between the two nationalized bodies.
87. In its first report, the Board commented: 'First, we accept the view that some strengthening of the structure of the industry is needed and that this can best be brought about by some enlargement of units so that

better use can be made of modern management techniques.' NBPI, Report No. 1, p. 4.
88. THC, *Annual Report*, 1966, p. 10.
89. Sir R. Wilson, 'Transport and Common-Sense', *Institute of Transport Journal*, March 1969, p. 100.
90. C. Tugendhat, 'Defining a Role for the State', *Financial Times*, 22 December 1970.
91. NBPI, Report No. 162, p. 19.
92. NFC, *Annual Report*, 1969, p. 5.

5 ROAD PASSENGER TRANSPORT

I Introduction

The bus industry in Britain, after a long period of relative stability, not to say stagnancy, is now in the early 1970s going through the most severe crisis in its history. After being taken for granted for decades by the public as a natural and proper social convenience, the industry and its operations are now becoming an important public issue. The magnitude of the crisis is not unlike that of the railways in the early 1960s; as in that case the problem is financial, resulting from declining demand and rising costs. Again, the whole philosophy and structure under which the industry is operated are being called into question, and again the immediate short-term answer is a mixture of subsidies and retrenchment of services. In many respects, however, the social implications of the crisis on the buses are even more serious than was true of the railways, since the buses have no realistic substitute in the provision of the dense network of public transport which is vital for mobility over short distances. It is especially in rural areas that the present network is most immediately threatened, yet the Royal Commission on Local Government noted that 42 per cent of rural households, or some 10 million people in all, have no private transport apart from bicycles. But the problem is not only a rural one. Financial pressures are also being felt in the urban areas, and here the situation is compounded by congestion and the cost and environmental effects of road construction which are forcing a reassessment of the roles of the private car and public transport.

At the heart of the crisis in the bus industry lies the question of responsibility. The industry has hitherto been self-sufficient and has maintained its wide range of services by cross-subsidizing between the profitable and the unprofitable. Even if this was not altogether to the liking of economists, who detected a misallocation of resources, it was eminently satisfactory to the vast majority of operators and the public, not to mention governments. Indeed, the whole regulatory system in the industry is built on this tacit assumption. Now, however, complete self-sufficiency is proving impossible. The 1968 Transport Act provides for the possibility of central and local government subsidies, but the necessity for and extent of these subsidies can vary enormously from company to company and service to service according to how the public welfare is defined and how costs are measured. These are matters which are only at the first stages of resolution, and the full extent of change in the industry is not yet apparent.

By far the greatest part of the industry is now publicly owned, part by the State, and part by municipalities. The State-owned companies are mostly concerned with inter-urban and rural routes, although they are also responsible for some urban services, and the municipal undertakings are almost entirely concerned with urban routes. But while everybody knows who owns the municipal buses, it is doubtful if more than a few are aware of the extent of state ownership. In contrast to other areas of nationalization, the old bus companies have kept their separate identities after takeover. Moreover, acquisitions by the State have been piecemeal and through voluntary negotiation rather than compulsion and, apart from a brief period in the late 1940s, there has never been much ideological discussion of public ownership. Nor has state ownership played an important role in the economics or structure of the industry, which remain essentially what they were in the 1930s. For instance, in spite of the recent creation of the National Bus Company as a national holding company, there has been nothing equivalent to the creation of BRS in the goods sector, with its wide-ranging but integrated network of services. But if the State as owner has played a relatively passive role, the State as regulator has dominated through the licensing system, giving a degree of control greater than that exercised over several industries with more obvious claims, from the extent of ownership, to be called nationalized industries.

II History and Development of the Industry

The road passenger industry had its antecedents in the stage-coach of the pre-Industrial Revolution era. In the nineteenth century this developed into the horse bus, the horse tram and then the electric tram. Even at this stage the scale of operation was quite large; thus in the late 1850s the London General owned some 500 to 600 vehicles and 6,000 horses, and ran 63 distinct services.[1] The turn of the century saw the municipalization of many tramway systems at the same time as the petrol-engined bus was making its début, so that there was a natural development of the municipal bus system which exists today. Moreover, the petrol bus did not become important until after the First World War, when, as with goods haulage, the industry expanded rapidly with the sale of war surplus equipment and its purchase by ex-servicemen. In this period of rapid growth and adjustment in the 1920s, there was inevitably a good deal of cut-throat competition while the passenger services were highly irregular and unreliable. Thus of some 1,888 passenger operators in 1922, there were less than 200 regular service undertakings working to a timetable.[2]

Throughout these various developments there was a form of licensing by local authorities under an Act of 1847, originally designed for hackney cabs but also covering other modes of road transport as they came into operation. This system hardly amounted to supervision, however, since in practice the authorities did not fully exercise their powers, and licence definitions and enforcement were very loose. Vehicles and not services were licensed, and to make matters worse, there were 1,097 different authorities, so that a co-ordinated system of control was almost impossible.

It was in the light of these confusing conditions for all concerned that in 1928 a Royal Commission on Transport was appointed 'to take into consideration the problems arising out of the growth of road traffic'. Its findings that a new system of licensing was required for road passenger transport won almost unanimous agreement from the established operators and the political parties, and its recommendations were put into effect by Parts IV and V of the Road Traffic Act of 1930. To administer the Act thirteen sets of Area Traffic Commissioners were created, each consisting of one permanent Commissioner appointed by the Minister and two part-time colleagues representing local authorities.[3] The new system was based on three types of licence: one granted a public service vehicle licence to the vehicle: a second was granted to the driver or conductor of the bus; the third, and much the most significant from an economic point of view, was the licence for a particular road service or route. This last gave the Commissioners complete control over entry to the industry, with the exception of contract hire work.

The effects of the 1930 Act were to force some of the less reputable operators out of business and to create a structure for the industry which in all essentials still remains. The Act did not itself initiate the consolidation of undertakings into larger groups which was a feature of the 1930s; this had begun in the 1920s, but the Act in stifling competition helped to encourage the trend. This was still further emphasized in that the railways, recognizing the threat of the bus to their traffic, bought into the three major groups which emerged, Thomas Tilling, British Electric Traction and the Scottish Bus Group, which between them controlled some two-fifths of the buses in the country by the end of the 1930s.

The arrangements made for the nationalization of road passenger services in the Transport Act of 1947 were much vaguer than for other sectors of transport. The Minister merely noted that they were 'not immediately provided for'.[4] The shares previously held in the large bus groups by the railways passed naturally to the British Transport Commission, so that the State acquired a substantial stake in the industry. Other than this, the BTC was given powers to acquire undertakings, which were used to negotiate for the outstanding shares in Thomas Tilling and the Scottish Bus Group, together with some smaller companies. The British Electric Traction group rejected all overtures and remained under independent control but with a large minority of shares owned by the State. In contrast to the situation in road haulage, both the larger groups acquired already had a large-scale financial and organizational structure, so that the immediate problems of co-ordinating management were eased. The Road Passenger Executive was nevertheless set up in 1949 to remove some work from the overloaded Road Transport Executive.

Of much greater potential importance was the concept of area schemes outlined in Part IV of the 1947 Act. These schemes would have created regional bodies to decide questions of ownership, the provision of services, and the relationship between road and rail undertakings. If put into operation the schemes would have been the biggest move towards transport integration under the 1947 Act. However, although plans were fairly far advanced for the Northern area, and work was begun on the Eastern and South-Western areas, the end of the Labour Government prevented any of the schemes from coming to fruition. But a further obstacle appears to have been opposition from some municipal undertakings which were reluctant to lose their own services. Newcastle, even with a Labour-controlled council, was an especially vehement opponent. The Conservatives later accused the Labour Government of itself abandoning the area schemes, and certainly Labour prior to the 1951 election had announced the demise of the Road Passenger

Executive, the body entrusted with the detailed planning of the scheme.

In any case, the 1952 Conservative White Paper on Transport[5] brought the end of further work on the schemes. The Thesiger Committee[6] was set up to enquire into the working of the 1930 licensing system, and pending its report the Minister merely took powers under the 1953 Transport Act to order the divestiture of state holdings in road passenger transport. As Gilbert Walker suspected, this power was never used, and denationalization gained little support.[7] The Thesiger Committee found no fault with the existing system, and specifically rejected the easier entry into the industry which the 1953 Act had tried to create in goods haulage. In other words, the committee found, and the Minister apparently concurred, that freer competition would not be in the public interest. Thus the two sides of road transport, hitherto treated with the same philosophy if not identically, were in 1953 put on divergent paths of competition and continued protective control.

Given the report of the Thesiger Committee, there was no impetus to change the structure or method of control of the industry during the period of Conservative Government between 1951 and 1964, although one important event occurred when the State-owned groups were affected by the break-up of the British Transport Commission under the Transport Act of 1962. The bus interests became part of the new Transport Holding Company with its new financial objectives to act as a 'commercial enterprise', but in spite of a promising start the new body was not to be given much time to prove itself. The Labour Party was returned to power in 1964 with its promise to draw up a national plan for transport. Particularly relevant to the bus industry were statements in the Labour manifesto that public transport must play the dominant part in the journey to work and that public transport should provide a 'reasonable' service for those living in rural areas.

As noted in earlier chapters, the Labour plans were brought to fruition in the Transport Act of 1968 after the framework had been laid down in a series of White Papers.[8] One significant event which was precipitated jointly by the imminence of legislation and the declining financial climate in the industry was the sale of the remaining BET interests to the Transport Holding Company early in 1968, giving the State overwhelming control of inter-urban routes. We shall examine the provisions of the Act in greater detail later in the chapter, as well as looking at the extent and rationale of the Act in chapter 6, so that here only a brief description is necessary.

A new holding company for the state bus interests was formed, called the National Bus Company; an exception was made for Scotland, where the Scottish Bus Group was amalgamated with various shipping and ferry services to form the Scottish Transport Group. On the other hand, the NBC was to be given the London Transport Executive's 'country' buses once the Greater London Council accepted responsibility for the LTE at the beginning of 1970. Much more radical than this change was the creation of four Passenger Transport Authorities to control public transport in the conurbations centred on Birmingham, Manchester, Liverpool and Newcastle. Their duties were 'to provide a properly integrated and efficient system of public transport to meet the needs of that area'.[9] Other than the institutional changes the industry was also given financial assistance by the Act, the first time, apart from some fuel duty rebate, that the Government had recognized the financial difficulties of the industry. The assistance came under four categories: a grant of 25 per cent for new buses of standard design; an increase in the fuel duty rebate so as to cover all but 10 p of the duty per gallon; a 75 per cent capital grant for fixed investment in public transport, including items such as bus stations and depots; and finally a possible subsidy of 50 per cent of the deficit from running unremunerative rural services, the rest to be borne by the local authority. This assistance was to be available to all operators, not merely the nationalized or municipal undertakings. A third very important area in which the Act affected the industry was in respect of drivers' hours, serving to cut down the extremely long hours frequently worked.

III The Structure of the Industry

The industry's structure can be examined according to several different dimensions: ownership, type of service and size.

(a) *Ownership*

There are three major ownership groups. In the first place there is a state-owned sector, consisting until January 1969 of the Transport Holding Company bus companies and thereafter of the National Bus Company and the bus interests of the Scottish Transport Group. These companies consist of the three major pre-war groups, Tilling, BET in England, and Scottish Motor Transport in Scotland, together with various independents and a few municipal undertakings which have been taken over and integrated into the groups or their subsidiary companies.[10] At the end of 1970 the NBC owned 53 main operating companies, and the Scottish Transport Group will have 7 operating bus companies after David McBrayne Ltd is integrated into the other existing companies. In 1969, before the acquisition of the London 'country' buses, the state-owned companies between them operated some 42 per cent of all passenger service mileage, carried 32 per cent of all bus passengers, and took 39 per cent of total revenue.[11] Organizationally, the guiding principle of the NBC is decentralization, that each subsidiary should have the maximum operating autonomy with central control being restricted to financial aspects such as budgets and profit forecasts. The NBC has however an intermediate grouping of companies into ten regional associations each headed by a chairman, and these are also used as units of financial accountability, with the stronger companies in any region being expected to help the weaker. At the top, the NBC itself as a holding company is composed of part-time members with a single full-time chief executive, another reflection of dispersed control, although there is also an executive board, called the NBC Federation Ltd, composed of the Chief Executive, the chairmen of the regions, and the chief central officers.

The second ownership group is also publicly owned, but locally rather than nationally. Before the Transport Act of 1968 there were 93 municipally owned undertakings, controlled through the transport committees of local councils.[12] The 1968 Act added a considerably more complex form of local ownership in the Passenger Transport Authorities. (The authorities themselves are supervisory agencies, while the professional day-to-day management is carried out by the Passenger Transport Executives.) There are several factors differentiating the PTA from other municipal, or indeed any other, bus companies. For one thing they also control the railway commuter lines within their conurbation. Secondly, they will be withdrawn from the jurisdiction of the Traffic Commissioners after a period yet to be specified. Thirdly, their boundaries are different from any other local function, since they are basically formed out of several municipal undertakings. Also in the category of local control must be put the London Transport Executive, which reverted from national ownership to ownership by the Greater London Council at the beginning of 1970. The range of size in this form of ownership is enormous, ranging from the 7,700 buses of London, through the PTAs with over a thousand buses each, right down to two authorities with less than five buses.

The last grouping is the independently owned sector, which includes some large companies such as Lancashire United and Barton, but which for the most part comprises small, frequently minute, operators often owning only a single bus. The larger independents have more affinity with the state-owned groups than with their smaller fellows, often having operating and boundary agreements with the nationalized companies. Even so, only four private stage service companies have more than sixty vehicles and independents carry only 4 per cent of stage service passengers. The small operators are in fact largely concerned with other activities than the provision of stage services, particularly contract hire where the licensing requirements are less constraining. Nevertheless some small operators do provide most valuable stage services in rural areas, where their lower overheads enable them to run services that would be uneconomic for larger companies and their significance in such areas is likely to grow as the state companies retreat.

(b) *Types of service*

A second way of analysing the structure of the bus industry is according to the type of service it affords, which can be split into the four categories seen in Table 5.1. By far the largest category is that of the stage services, which are run on specific routes at given times for a controlled fare. They are the main short-distance means of public transport in the country; almost half (44.6 per cent) of all bus journeys fall within the distance bracket of over 1 but under $2\frac{1}{2}$ miles.[13] It is with this category that most of the discussion in this chapter will be concerned. The second category encompasses the express services, which are similar to but over longer routes than stage services; they are defined as having a minimum fare of 5 p but also offer services between places as far apart as London and Glasgow. Third, there are excursions and tours, which are irregular in timing and routing, but are nevertheless controlled by the Traffic Commissioners because they receive their payment directly from individual members of the public. The Traffic Commissioners keep a watchful eye on such services in order to ensure that there is no competition with any regular stage or express service. Finally, there is the contract hire sector, covering those situations where the public does not directly and individually pay fares, whether this takes the form of a school or works bus or a club outing. Because this sector does not come under the jurisdiction of the Traffic Commissioners with their strict controls, a highly complex traffic law has had to be developed in the courts to delineate its boundaries and to ensure that there is no encroaching on the jurisdiction of the Commissioners.

TABLE 5.1
The bus industry by type of service, 1959–69

	Passenger journeys (million)		Bus mileage (million)		Receipts (£ million)	
	1959	1969	1959	1969	1959	1969
Stage service	13,552	9,323	1,956	1,672	262	341
Express	65	71	102	119	11	19
Excursions and tours	38	32	68	62	8	12
Contract hire	282	397	241	358	24	46
Total	13,937	9,823	2,367	2,211	305	418

Source: *Passenger Transport in Great Britain*, 1969, Tables 37, 39, 41.

The decline in the stage service sector is evident from the table, although the smaller sectors have not shared in the decline of the stage services; indeed the contract hire sector has had an annual rate of increase in passenger journeys of some 5 per cent. Also interesting has been the performance of the express sector, since prima facie evidence from the increase in car ownership and the decline of the rail passenger services would have suggested a decline. Instead, it may be the case that rising rail fares have induced a shift to the buses on price grounds. Better roads may also have helped the express buses by diminishing the speed gap between the two modes.

(c) *Size of Fleet and Economies of Scale*

As can be seen in Table 5.2, there has been some increase in concentration in the bus industry since the Road Traffic Act of 1930, but there is still a very large number of small operators owning only one or two vehicles. The pattern of size of fleet is in fact not unlike that in road haulage, except that the scale of operation is distinctly greater, since just over 1 per cent of the operators run more than half the total buses. The degree of concentration becomes more obvious if the criterion used is ownership rather than operating units, since while the State owns one-third of all buses, the state companies are counted separately in Table 5.2. Nevertheless the very fact that it has been found advantageous to allow the state companies to operate virtually autonomously, combined with the

TABLE 5.2
Size of bus operators

No. of Buses	1932 Operators	Buses	1952 Operators	Buses	1968 Operators	Buses
1–9	5,949	13,566	4,443	13,639	4,430	12,704
10–99	423	10,735	696	15,069	647	14,934
100–199	29	4,177	38	5,283	36	4,976
200+	31	17,752	62	32,805	67	42,653
Total	6,432	46,230	5,239	66,796	5,180	75,267

Source: Annual Reports of the Traffic Commissioners.

continued existence of the small operator, has raised, as in road haulage, a considerable discussion about the existence of economies of scale. An immediate differentiation is between the types of task performed. It is interesting to find that as in haulage the small men are the specialists in ad hoc tasks; where the service performed is heterogeneous or irregular, it pays to have all decisions made on the spot.[14] On the other hand since stage services, which represent the bulk of bus services, are valued for their regularity and reliability, and give an opportunity for planning and centralized control, it is not surprising to find that the main stage service operators are large. The average size of fleet for the state companies is 950, and that for municipal undertakings, which have geographical limitations, 190. The considerations that the passenger is a relatively homogeneous unit easily adapted to a standardized system of pricing and that there is a demand for a network of services with interchange facilities within any one area may also give opportunities for economies of scale vis-à-vis road haulage.

Even so the average size is large only in relation to haulage; the largest unit in the bus industry outside London Transport is the Midland Red with under two thousand buses. This represents a relatively small unit by comparison with much of manufacturing industry or even the railways or major airlines. The THC fused some small acquired companies into its subsidiaries, but there has been no real attempt to increase the average size of unit. On the contrary, one of the largest companies in the Scottish Bus Group, W. Alexander & Son, was split into three in the interests of efficiency in 1961. Thus if economies of scale do exist, they would seem to be exhausted fairly quickly.

One obvious reason for a lack of economies is that because of limitations on bus size there is not the same possibility as in manufacturing industry of increasing the amount of plant relative to other factors of production. Nor are there the problems of control which force technical integration upon the railways. Another reason is that problems of effective management mount with size, although better communications aided by the telex and the computer may help in countering this. The White Paper, *Public Transport and Traffic*, in 1967 suggested that a thousand buses are the maximum for efficiency for this reason.[15] Moreover, some apparent evidence of diseconomies came from a survey of municipal concerns in 1967, which showed that operating expenses in pence per mile rose steadily with the size of fleet, from 18·17 p for fleets with less than fifty buses to 22·24 p for fleets of over a thousand buses,[16] although this can be explained at least partially by the less favourable operating conditions usually found in the larger cities. Lee and Steedman suggest that the weight of evidence favours constant returns to scale,[17] since they found the variations in cost between undertakings of the same size to be of far greater significance than variations between size groups of undertakings. However, it is arguable that a more important factor pertaining to economies of scale than any of those so far mentioned has been the industry's system of licensing, and it is to it and its effects that we now turn.

IV The Licensing System and Its Effects

The linchpin of the bus industry's organization since 1930 has been the licensing system, which has been able to exercise a far stricter control over the industry than its counterpart in road haulage, and has thus been more successful in fulfilling the objectives of the framers of the Act. Moreover, as briefly noted in connection with the Thesiger Committee, until recently relatively few voices were raised against the system, even though there were some trenchant criticisms in the name of greater competition.[18] But in 1968 the Transport Act obliquely undermined the system, and in July 1971 the Minister for Transport Industries announced some major modifications for rural areas. Even so, licensing is far from dead.

The 1930 Act gave very wide powers to the Traffic Commissioners, mostly through their jurisdiction over the road service licence. It listed four considerations which the Commissioners might at their discretion take into account before granting a licence. The desirability of the service, the suitability of the route, and the current provisions for the public cover the first three considerations, but the last is the most significant: 'the needs of the area as a whole in relation to traffic (including the provision of adequate, suitable and efficient services, the elimination of unnecessary services and the provision of unremunerative services) and the co-ordination of all forms of passenger transport, including transport by rail'.[19] This sub-section is the basis of the Commissioners' interest in promoting cross-subsidization to provide unremunerative services and also the basis of their power to offer route monopolies as a quid pro quo. There is nothing in the Act by which the Commissioners can *require* the provision of unremunerative services but as the Thesiger Committee blandly noted some twenty years later, 'in practice operators have recognized an obligation to provide as full as possible a network of services for the area they cover'.[20]

It is clear, however, that the section quoted is full of difficult provisions. 'Efficient' services are at odds with the provision of unremunerative services; there are no standards of 'adequacy';[21] nor are there any indications of how 'co-ordination' might take place. In the event the Commissioners have exercised their power according to what D. N. Chester called the principles of Priority, Protection and Public Need.[22] Priority refers to the established operator, who was in 1930 almost invariably given a right of tenure on the route he ran. Protection is designed to shield the established operator where there is a possible overlap. Thus regular operators must be protected against too many excursions over their routes, 'country' buses must not be allowed to poach customers from urban services within town limits, and the railways must be given a measure of protection against seasonal bus express services. Public Need is more difficult to define. Clearly there is a public need for a service which is capable of producing a profit. When the service is unremunerative the issue is less clear and the operator may want it only because he hopes to develop the route later. In this case the Commissioners may permit only a skeleton service at first. But public need may also work in the opposite sense, as when existing loss-making services are continued in operation to retain the goodwill of the Commissioners.

Once they have granted the service licence, the Commissioners may also attach restrictions under the Act. The relevant sub-section says: that the fares shall not be unreasonable; that where desirable in the public interest the fares shall be fixed so as to prevent wasteful competition; and that passengers shall be set down or picked up at specified stops.[23] Since these powers have been exercised to the full, the Commissioners control most facets of the bus company's operations. Control over fares we shall return to later.

The objectives of introducing licensing under the 1930 Act were, as well as safety, to eliminate wasteful competition within the road industry and between road and rail, and to facilitate the provision of unremunerative services. Although by no means everyone would accept that these are desirable objectives in themselves, it is in their context that licensing must be judged. Within the road industry, the elimination of 'wasteful competition' is undoubted although many would argue that some measure of competition is highly desirable. The road–rail situation, however, is more complex. On the one hand, there is no doubt that rail has gained by the restrictive and protective aspects of bus licensing. On the other hand, as the Thesiger Committee noted: 'It must be admitted that, if co-ordination is used in the broader sense of referring to a planned division of functions between the two forms of transport based on the economic possibilities of each, then there has been little or no co-ordination between road and rail.'[24] Nor, the committee went on to say, did it see anything further being achieved in this direction in view of the great disparity between road and rail fares, 'without some form of common ownership'. Although it may seem odd that the committee did not consider the extensive bus holdings and the monopoly of rail of the BTC to be common ownership, this was not an unreasonable position to take in view of the relative autonomy of the BTC's constituent parts, in spite of the Commission's 1952 policy instruction that railway officers and bus managers were to regard road and rail passenger services as two sections of a single service. With respect to the last objective of the 1930 Act, the provision of unremunerative services, the Thesiger Committee noted that the licensing system had been 'remarkably successful'.[25] The provision of such services goes to the heart of the licensing system, namely acceptance of the principle of cross-subsidization, or using the routes on which a profit is made to pay for those on which a loss is accepted. But operators, like the framers of the 1930 Act and the Thesiger Committee, generally accepted this principle until the end of the 1960s. Thus in its 1965 Report, the Transport Holding Company asked for 'a wider acceptance of the principle of averaging between areas that are rich, trafficwise, and those that are poorer; this principle needs care in application, however, and in the main it should be used only where there is at least some community of interest, and where the mutual support entailed does not involve an undue amount of cross-subsidy'.[26]

Some of the justifications of cross-subsidization that have been given are that bus transport is a public utility and at least to some extent a social service; that differential tariffs according to cost would be difficult to administer; that the bus companies are not so large as to make grossly unfair demands upon some consumers; that they do already make some differentiation as between types of route; and least tangibly but perhaps most importantly, that the public would not accept pricing according to cost. It is said that the man in the street is not willing to accept that a five-mile journey in one direction should cost several times that of what seems to him to be an identical journey in another direction. Against cross-subsidization there are the traditional economic arguments that it results in a misallocation of resources both within the industry and within the whole transport sector, and that any redistributive effects which are sought would be better achieved by other means. Closely related is the argument that costs should be fully borne by users, most cogently expressed by Hibbs: 'If people are prepared to pay for it, public transport will be provided. If they are not prepared to pay for it, then there is at least a prima facie case for saying it is not required.'[27] It is also argued that bus services are not a public utility in the sense of there being strong technological reasons for having a single supplier as in the cases of gas or electricity. Finally, and perhaps most pertinently, there is the undeniable fact that however feasible cross-subsidization may have been in the past, the number of routes on which profits are available are becoming too few to pay for those on which losses are made. But one of the chief difficulties in these arguments is that there are no hard facts except for the last point made; the extent of cross-subsidization has never been accurately determined, and clearly much depends on this.

The inevitable and deliberate concomitant of a regulatory system based on cross-subsidization has been the demise of competition. The main competition faced by bus companies is external, from other forms of transport, most notably the private car, rather than internal. Within the industry even on those few routes where more than one operator has running rights, price competition is not permitted. Newcomers have found it almost impossible to break into established routes; indeed, the fact that it is rarely even attempted removes one of the few potential competitive spurs to efficiency under the system. Route licences are normally granted for three years at a time, but in the absence of challenges from other operators, and in view of the Commissioners' obligations to allow incumbents to keep their profitable routes to subsidize the unremunerative ones, renewal is normally a formality. But it is not altogether fair to blame the licensing system alone for the lack of competition, since 'area agreements' had already begun to grow up between the larger operators before the 1930 Act. The later takeover of the groups by the State naturally further retarded the possibility of competition.[28] Since then 'rationalization' of services between the State companies has largely bypassed the licensing system.

A further example of anti-competitive tendencies within the industry is the pooling arrangements which have grown up between state and municipal undertakings in many cities where there is a joint route shared between a 'country' bus on its way out of the city and a 'town' bus on its way to the municipal boundary. Such arrangements have generally been acceptable to the Commissioners and have been considerably reinforced by the 1968 Transport Act. Section 36 states that the Minister of Transport must be satisfied with the degree of co-ordination of bus services within the area of any municipal undertaking as a prerequisite to the operation of the undertaking.

One area of the industry where competition does thrive, however, is in the contract hire sector, over which the Commissioners have no jurisdiction. Because the service being performed is tailored to the needs of a group rather than separate individuals, there is a good chance of a high load factor. Moreover, revenue is guaranteed in advance by the contract. It is therefore not surprising to find fierce competition in the tenders for school or works contracts, and even plenty of operators content with irregular group outings. Frequently such an operator will run another business, such as a garage, in addition to whatever contract business he can get. This field is generally the preserve of the small man, although the larger companies have tried to make inroads into it, arguing that they should be given educational or other local authority work in view of their need to cross-subsidize unremunerative stage services.

To return to the licensing system itself, there are clear signs that the system as it has operated may be nearing its end, primarily because the economic environment which the Commissioners were set up to regulate no longer prevails. As the underlying economic situation changed, the method of regulation was not capable of inducing changed methods in response. There was for instance, very little movement towards one-man operation of buses until the Prices and Incomes Board strongly recommended it,[29] since the Commissioners are not capable of examining such factors in any detail. But beyond efficiency audits of this kind, the licensing system has proved unable to sustain the cross-subsidization which has been its trademark. The 1968 Transport Act, by creating the possibility of subsidies for unremunerative services, undermined the justification for cross-subsidization by providing an alternative means of achieving the same objective. In creating the PTAs, the Act also created areas which would ultimately take over control from the Commissioners. The blunt threat of the NBC that it could no longer support cross-subsidization was another blow to the system.[30] Finally, there has been a statement by the Minister of Transport Industries in July 1971 that the system will be substantially modified.

The proposals by the Minister will exempt from road service licensing small vehicles, excursions and tours, works and school-contract services, services provided by a rural bus grant and those provided in lieu of a rail service closure. Whole rural areas will be specified for exemption from licensing, and the procedure for fare changes and road service licenses will be simplified. The term 'small vehicles' will have two divisions. Those carrying less than eight passengers will not require PSV licences, but those carrying between eight and fifteen passengers, while exempted road service licences, will require PSV licences. The objective of these provisions, which will be further discussed in the section on rural services, is to encourage greater flexibility by encouraging the use of mini-buses and even private cars for public transport.

The proposals have met with a mixed reception, but it is perhaps noteworthy that the operators have not been particularly vociferous against them. Most of the criticism has come from unions fearing a loss of jobs. Nevertheless, the effects of the proposals will not by any means destroy the current system throughout most of the country, bearing in mind that urban, suburban and inter-urban stage services constitute the vast majority of the industry's operations.

V Demand

Factors affecting patterns of demand in the road passenger industry fall into three main categories, each of which has a major impact on the industry. The first group relates to the long-term decline in total demand, the second to fluctuations in demand, and the third to the special problems of rural buses.

(a) *Long-term Decline of Demand*

The largest volume of passengers carried on buses was in 1953, and the longest mileage was run the following year. Since then there

TABLE 5.3

Passenger transport by modes
(thousand million passenger miles)

	Bus and coach	Private transport	Rail	Air	Total
1954	50·0	47·2	24·2	0·20	121·6
1956	48·6	59·5	24·5	0·27	132·9
1958	43·4	72·9	25·5	0·30	142·1
1960	43·9	89·1	24·8	0·48	158·3
1962	42·4	107·1	22·8	0·70	173·0
1964	40·3	132·1	23·0	0·94	196·3
1966	37·5	155·9	21·5	1·15	216·0
1968	36·3	177·7	20·8	1·2	236·0
1969	35·7	184·0	21·6	1·2	242·5

Source: *Passenger Transport in Great Britain*, 1969, Table 1.

has been a continuous decline in carryings, although total revenue, as Table 5.1 showed, has roughly kept pace with inflation by dint of rapid increases in fares. Table 5.3 shows the passenger mileage by the principal forms of transport since 1954, while Table 5.4 expresses the same figures in percentages. What is noticeable is the drastic rise of the private car and the fall in surface public transport, especially buses, although this is more marked in terms of the percentage share of the total market than in absolute passenger mileage. Nevertheless, the rate of loss of passenger mileage by the bus industry has been over 3 per cent annually since the middle 1950s and the rate has been accelerating. Although the full industry figures are not available on the basis of Table 5.3, 1970 was a particularly bad year for the industry, which carried 7 per cent less passengers, and particularly for the NBC, which carried 10 per cent less.

TABLE 5.4

Shares of passenger mileage as a percentage

	Bus and coach	Private transport	Rail	Air	Total
1954	41·1	38·8	19·9	0·2	100
1956	36·6	44·8	18·4	0·2	100
1958	30·5	51·3	17·9	0·2	100
1960	27·7	56·4	15·6	0·3	100
1962	24·5	61·9	13·2	0·4	100
1964	20·5	67·3	11·7	0·5	100
1966	16·6	72·9	10·0	0·5	100
1968	15·5	75·2	8·8	0·5	100
1969	14·7	75·9	8·9	0·5	100

Source: *Passenger Transport in Great Britain*, 1969, Table 2.

The decline of the bus is clearly related to the rising ownership of private cars. The car has clear and obvious advantages in terms of speed, convenience and flexibility, and in an affluent society it is one of the chief means of increasing the individual's freedom of choice. Yet the issue is not as simple as the rapid demise of an industry with an outdated technology. The mobility and enjoyment made available by the car cease to exist if road facilities become overcrowded. The Buchanan Report[31] and many others have emphasized the urgent need to reconcile the freedom to enjoy affluence through the private car with the apparent physical and financial impossibility of providing enough facilities to do so. It has also been frequently pointed out that there will always be millions who will still have no access or only intermittent access to a car. Public transport, and particularly the bus, has been seen as the main hope of solving these dilemmas. Yet an examination of the relationship between the bus and the car destroys any illusion that matters will improve without a drastic reconstruction of transport priorities.

The problems relate to accelerating trends in both price and quality. With respect to price, the disadvantage of the bus (or, for that matter, the train) results largely from the different costing principles on which bus operators and private motorists work. The decision to own a car and the decision to use the car for any specific journey may involve different reasons, although obviously the two are interdependent. A car may be bought for occasional trips, at weekends or on vacations, which public transport would find it very difficult to cater for. But once the car is bought, the owner naturally becomes predisposed to make the maximum economic use of an expensive asset. This means costing on short-run principles, which is something the bus cannot do. The bus must charge a price sufficient to cover total costs or, if some capital is accepted as irretrievably sunk, long-run marginal costs. Clearly, depreciation, labour, fuel and administrative costs must be paid for in the bus fare. The motorist, however, once he has invested money, forgone the potential interest on capital, and taxed and insured his car, can at least temporarily forget these sunk costs and compare the price of alternative forms of transport by costing his car on its immediate variable costs only, petrol, oil, and sometimes tyres and repairs. He also invariably neglects to cost his own labour, which is the major cost item of public transport. The result is that the costs which are actually compared are very unfavourable to the bus. Assuming a petrol price of 35 p per gallon and a small car, the cost for petrol and oil alone is only about 1 p per mile. There are no overall statistics on mileage fares for the bus industry, but for the Scottish Bus Group, which is a very sizeable unit within the industry, the estimated receipt per passenger-mile in 1971 was 1·53 p.[32] Assuming this not to be wildly unrepresentative of the industry, it can be appreciated why, even on cost grounds, the bus is not seen as being competitive.[33]

Quality is compounded of numerous facets. As noted in chapter 3, the 'transportation preference function' has been said to be composed of time, convenience, safety, comfort and cost factors, but the interaction of these for any one person's journey is impossible to assess. One thing which seems fairly certain is that as society becomes more affluent, the non-cost factors in the transport decision will become more important vis-à-vis cost. This in itself explains much of the change to private transport. But there are also other, more objective factors.

A major reason for preferring to travel by car is that both homes and places of work are increasingly breaking out of the old siting patterns. When the bus (or tram) could run through densely populated residential areas, picking up people for work in or near the city centre, it could work efficiently and give a good service. Nobody had to walk far at either end. Now people live further from their work, and because they live in much less densely populated suburbs, neither bus stops nor the time intervals between buses are likely to be as convenient. The location of work itself is also changing to the periphery of cities, so that people want to go from one suburb to another rather than in radial directions. Journeys are thus now vastly more complex and in smaller point-to-point flows. An individual may have to make more interchanges than previously at the same time as his dislike of walking and waiting is increasing with growing affluence. Meanwhile for the public transport operator a sparse population, small flows, and complex journeys mean lower profitability. A second reason is that once a number of people have made up their minds to travel by private car, there is a feedback effect on the buses which must share the roads with them. The more people use cars, the greater is the effect of congestion on the buses, which are much less manoeuvrable than cars, and hence suffer a disproportionate worsening of trip times. Services are disrupted, timetables become impossible to follow and the public grows steadily more dissatisfied. A survey of bus-users in Manchester showed that of twenty possible priorities, ranging from more courteous staff to season tickets at reduced rates to guaranteed space on the bus, three times as many passengers voted for 'strict timekeeping' and 'reliability' as for any of the other possibilities.[34] There is thus a tendency for the rate of substitution between bus and car to be increased as services become more uncertain. At some point before traffic paralysis sets in, solutions are naturally sought. One much in evidence is to say that because people prefer to use cars, more road space is necessary. This, however, is a conclusion based on false premises, because the car-users are not being made to pay the full social costs of their journeys, only the private costs. It has been the lack of concern for social costs which has almost destroyed surface public transport in the United States, and a new awareness of such costs which promises to lead to its revival.

Quality is obviously a difficult concept to measure, but Quarmby, in an interesting study in Leeds,[35] asked car-owners how sensitive they were to certain changes in the relative attractiveness of the bus and the car as a means of travelling to work. 69·1 per cent of the car-owners normally used their cars to go to work. If the bus were made 15 minutes faster, 54.6 per cent said they would still use their cars to go to work; if 10 minutes faster, 59·6 per cent would still do so; if 5 minutes faster, 64·4 per cent. If bus fares went down 1d (0·416 p), 67.6 per cent would use the car; if 2d (0·832 p), 66.1 per cent; if 3d (1·248 p), 64·5 per cent; even if buses were free, 52·8 per cent would still go by car. If bus frequencies were doubled, 66·0 per cent still preferred the car. If parking charges were to be raised by 5, 10, or 15 p, the percentages would be 59·8, 50·0 and 40·5. These statistics reinforce the view that it is very difficult and may even be impossible for bus companies to win back passengers—even the offer of free buses won back only a quarter of car-users, while improved frequencies made even less impact. And as convenience becomes more important, it seems likely that many of those not yet using their car for the journey to work will wish to do so. Of the 6,309,000 people found to go to work by bus in the 1966 Sample Census, 2,102,000 had a car at home, and it seems likely that the main reason for this was a lack of parking facilities rather than any preference for public transport as a form of travel.[36]

(b) *The Problem of the Peak*

The second main aspect of demand in the industry is its peaked nature centred at the beginning and end of the working day although a seasonal peak also exists. The problem has been exacerbated by the overall decline in demand, since the sharpest drops have come at off-peak times, especially weekends and evenings, and to a lesser extent during the non-peak day. The 1965 National Travel Survey showed that over half the journeys by stage service bus were for the purpose of going to work or school,[37] and the proportion seems to be increasing. Although not all journeys to work or school are in the peak periods, those which are not are counterbalanced by buses being used for other purposes during the peak period. Changing patterns of leisure activity, most notably those resulting from television, new modes of shopping, such as the mobile shop and the postal catalogue, and the availability of private transport for non-work activities even when it is not feasible or available for going to work, have all contributed to the growth of the peak. It has always been considered that the off-peak services cross-subsidize the peak, but if the level of demand falls below paying for the immediate running costs of the off-peak service, this will cease to be true. For some routes at certain times it may already have happened.

Peaks mean that a large proportion of the vehicles in a fleet must pay for themselves and their overheads in a very short space of time. Worse still, although large traffic flows are normally in one direction only, two-way services must nevertheless be provided as an operating imperative. The THC Report for 1967 showed the nature of the peak for Tilling buses on a winter weekday.[38] Some 7,800 buses were required in the half-hour from 8.30 to 9.00 am and 4.30 to 5.00 pm. So short is the period that some buses are needed for only two runs a day. In the lowest midday period, the half-hour from 11.00 to 11.30, only some 4,500 were required. In addition to the 7,800 a further 900 were required as spares for stand-by duty, overhaul and maintenance, and, during the summer, approximately another 400 to take care of seasonal services. Thus less than half the total fleet is being used in the middle of a normal winter day; this creates obvious problems for the deployment of the labour force. Even the THC situation is more fortunate than some municipal bus services. Manchester, in 1966, needed 1,090 buses at peak times and 400 at the midday off-peak; Birmingham with 1,356 at the peak, had only 350 at the off-peak.[39] In most municipal services the ratio of peak to off-peak is at least two to one and it is sometimes much worse.

The industry therefore lurches in a very short space of time between periods of extreme strain and surplus capacity. No other industry, even the electricity industry with its notorious peaks and troughs, undergoes quite the vicissitudes of the buses. The only fortunate aspect is that they are predictable. Many of the possible arrangements to ease their impact, however, involve difficult problems of labour relations, which we shall examine later.

(c) *The Rural Bus Problem*

The problems of the rural areas have come into increasingly sharp focus in recent years. It was largely for the benefit of these areas that the system of regulation and cross-subsidization was set up, yet in the post-war period the challenge of the private car has been even greater than in the urban areas. Not only are car-ownership levels higher, but the congestion and parking problems which plague the urban motorist are not so common in rural areas. Falling traffics from the middle 1950s onwards led to the abandonment of a few routes, and this, as the Jack Committee noted, led to hardship for a few and inconvenience for rather more.[40] Until recently, however, the balance of traffics was sufficient to support most of the existing services, but now falling demand and rapidly accelerating costs have forced a reappraisal of the situation. The National Bus Company issued a major policy statement in September 1970, which stated in part:

> The practice of cross-subsidization has been a reasonable means of providing unprofitable rural services in the past. It was not inequitable when a large part of the population used the buses, since the fares paid on the better services were then not significantly increased as a result. The growth in ownership of cars and the change in the way of life which car ownership brings with it has greatly reduced the number of bus users who support the rural services by cross-subsidization ... The burden on fares outside the rural areas is thus becoming too high ... The National Bus Company finds itself compelled, therefore, to instruct its subsidiaries to reduce the burden of loss-making rural services by announcing their withdrawal after reasonable notice ... They will, however, be willing to continue these services, if the local authorities are prepared to provide rural bus grants at an adequate level.[41]

This statement is of course a rejection of the philosophy of the 1930 Act, and carries important implications. Section 34 of the 1968 Act permits a subsidy to be paid to rural bus operators by local authorities, and within certain criteria the Central Government has agreed to repay half this cost.[42] However, the first approach by the operators is to local authorities, and it is to them that the NBC companies have put wide-ranging demands, in many areas covering a high proportion of existing services. Whole counties have been threatened with a complete withdrawal of services, as was the case with Wigtonshire and Kirkcudbright in Scotland. In making their demands, the state companies have tried to argue value for money, and have contrasted the cost of maintaining bus services with that of the rail subsidies. In the 1970 Report, for instance, a map showed a wide range of routes in Cumberland which would be saved by a subsidy of £13,600, in comparison with the £365,000 subsidy for the Carlisle–Barrow railway line. Up to November 1971 the amount of subsidy requested has been only £1 million. This figure will undoubtedly increase very rapidly since the Central Government circular giving criteria was not issued for more than two years after the Act was passed and, given the threat expressed by the National Bus Company, the total may well amount to considerably more than £4 million estimated as the eventual figures. Some local authorities have refused to pay, partly as a matter of principle that transport should not be subsidized from the rates, and partly through fear that the initial demands are only the thin end of the wedge. Indeed, the concept of subsidy may well spread far beyond what were termed 'the deep rural services' to which the provision was meant to apply. Two important issues are the question of deciding what is an unremunerative service, and whether the NBC is the lowest cost operator to subsidize. The former question we shall leave to the next section, but the latter may result in the taking over of a number of NBC subsidiaries' routes by local private operators, who might well be able to operate more effectively. It has never been the policy of the state groups to squeeze out local operators. As a THC *Annual Report* said: 'By and large it is desired to keep these operators in existence. They have a special function to fulfil, and in remote areas they can fulfil this function better than a large company can hope to do. They are more economical. They are more flexible. They have a local understanding and a local interest.'[43] Many such operators can combine a morning and evening commuters' and school bus with running a garage, or some other activity. It is apparent, however, that even small operators will not always be able to provide a regular stage service, and it was with this in mind that the Minister for Transport Industries proposed changes in the licensing regulations. It is hoped that experimentation will produce different solutions for different circumstances. The postal bus, the community minibus, the group taxi service and paid lifts in private cars are seen as some alternatives to the traditional bus. It could even be that in some cases better services will result from communities being forced to re-evaluate their transport needs.

VI Costing and Pricing

(a) *Costs*

Given the industry's diminishing demand but almost static mileage, it might be expected that great efforts would have been made to reduce costs. But the industry does not lend itself to major technical changes, and it consequently faces severe cost problems. The most detailed breakdown of costs available is that given in the annual survey of passenger transport in Great Britain and is shown in Table 5.5. This covers all operators of more than 24 buses; it thus misses the smallest operators but gives a good picture of most of the industry. Two features of this table stand out. One is the small proportion of fuel costs, amounting to less than 10 per cent, which indicates the nature of the comparison private motorists make when they compare their petrol costs with bus fares. The other notable feature is that the proportion of labour cost is extremely high with more than 70 per cent of total costs currently accounted for by wages. Moreover this proportion has been a constantly rising one. Unlike the railways, the bus industry has not been able to achieve a rapid rundown in its labour force. The result has been that because labour costs have escalated more rapidly than other types of cost, labour

TABLE 5.5
Total expenditure. Financial year ended 31 March 1969

	£000s	%
Wages of drivers and conductors	173,393	48.6
Petrol or other fuel	34,039	9.6
Wages for all other staff	80,123	22.5
Local authority rates	3,825	1.1
Repair and maintenance	18,661	5.2
Vehicle insurance	2,257	0.6
Other, including interest, capital expenditure and profits tax	23,953	6.7
Depreciation for vehicles	14,802	4.1
Other depreciation	2,513	0.7
Redemption of debt	3,133	0.9
	356,699	100.0

Source: *Passenger Transport in Great Britain*, 1969, Table 29.

has represented an increasing share of total cost, with important implications for productivity which we shall examine later. In 1949, for instance, the proportion of total expenditure spent on drivers and conductors was only 41 per cent.

The rise in costs faced by the industry can be best expressed in terms of working expenses per vehicle mile in service. In 1950, the first full year in which the Tilling and Scottish bus groups were both state owned, their average cost per mile was 6·6 p. By 1957 this had risen to 10·2 p, and by 1967 to 14·7 p. In 1970 the cost for the NBC was 20·5 p, or three times as much as in 1948, while at the same time average bus loadings have declined.[44] Even so, costs in the company sector are considerably lower than in the municipal sector, partly because wage rates are on the whole lower, partly because the company sector uses smaller buses on average, but mainly because of the more difficult operating conditions in urban areas. In London Transport the vehicle mile costs rose from 8·8 p in 1948 to 27·0 p in 1969, the last year for which suitable comparisons can be made.

The rise in operating costs has meant that fares have also had to rise; indeed, because passenger demand is declining faster than the decline in the provision of services, it has been necessary to raise fares even faster than the rise in costs in order to maintain profitability.

The other aspect of cost, which causes such difficulty on the railways, relates to the distribution of costs between traffics. But although the industry shares with the railways the difficulty that the unit which must be charged, the passenger, is much smaller than the minimum effective unit of output, the bus, the problems of cost allocation have never been given as much attention as is true of the railways. There are three main reasons for this, none of which is entirely justifiable economically, but which have nevertheless served to prevent cost analyses from being carried out. The first and most important is that the industry is fairly small scale, is not internally competitive, and has been moderately profitable, such that discrepancies between price and cost have not had serious financial consequences. It is further argued that the breakdown of costs into smaller units of output would be unduly expensive for the economic benefits derived. The second reason is that passengers, unlike freight, are homogeneous so that averaging has provided an easy and publicly popular, if not altogether economically acceptable, method of allocating costs. The third is that the proportion of indirect costs is lower than is true of the railways, since relatively little capital is employed and there is a far lower proportion of ancillary staff to direct operating staff. But in connection with this last point the time period and the treatment of labour are of course critical. If a sufficiently short period is taken, almost all costs become fixed and marginal cost varies enormously according to whether any surplus capacity exists. Thus taking the daily peak period, even on a long-run marginal cost basis, the marginal cost of an extra bus becomes very high, due largely to the indivisibility of labour inputs over periods less than a shift. In its examination of London Transport, the Prices and Incomes Board calculated this cost to be some £6,300 per annum, or approximately 13 p per peak hour passenger-mile in London.[45]

Given the degree of volatility of costs within short time periods, and bearing in mind the social necessity of the journey to work as well as the other considerations mentioned above, it has not been thought worth while to base costing on an exact allocation between traffics. The result is that the industry typically uses as its unit of cost measurement total operating expenses divided by miles in service, giving a figure expressed in pence per mile. This has obvious disadvantages, notably that the miles driven are by no means homogeneous, some being urban, some rural, some on motorways, and all with different cost characteristics. With an average cost figure for a whole company, it is impossible to determine with any accuracy the profitability of particular routes. This costing principle of course rules out any use of marginal analysis in the industry; indeed it even precludes the division of costs into simple direct and indirect categories such as the railways have used.

Nevertheless, there will be considerable pressure in the future for a more sophisticated cost breakdown as the viability of individual routes comes into question. The instruction of the NBC to its subsidiaries to withdraw loss-making rural services unless a direct subsidy is granted obviously raises the general issue of what is a loss-making service. At the present such a service appears to be one whose revenues per mile are less than the average operating cost of the company in question, which is clearly unsatisfactory for the reasons given. The Ministry circular to local authorities setting out the terms under which the Central Government would contribute to the subsidy payable under Section 34 of the Transport Act gave no assistance on this question, merely stating that the operator should be asked to explain the basis of his calculations. Even a rather more detailed circular from the Rural and Urban Councils Associations to their members went no further than to suggest that costs would vary and that items such as administration and depreciation should not automatically be included in the grant, since spare capacity might be available. This makes it likely that very different cost criteria will be used in different parts of the country until a uniform set of costing principles are involved. An associated problem of cost allocation, not directly the concern of bus companies but of great indirect importance to them is the question of splitting the cost of the subsidy between different local authorities if, as will frequently be the case, a service runs across several boundaries. Again no specific criteria appear to have been devised.

(b) *Pricing*

The key aspect of pricing in the bus industry in the early 1970s is the exceptionally fast rate of increase in fares, which has been accelerating in the period since 1968. In turn, this has cast doubt on both the philosophy and the machinery of pricing under the 1930 Act.

TABLE 5.6
Index of stage service fares. 31 December 1961 = 100

	Total	London Transport	Local Authorities	Other operators
31 December 1961	100	100	100	100
31 December 1962	105.9	106.2	106.1	104.6
31 December 1963	109.9	109.0	111.8	109.1
31 December 1964	118.3	127.4	116.9	114.6
31 December 1965	126.4	127.4	130.8	122.8
31 December 1966	133.3	139.9	133.8	129.4
31 December 1967	141.3	141.1	148.0	136.8
31 December 1968	148.5	154.2	151.9	142.8
31 December 1969	160.1	180.3	160.0	150.0
30 September 1970	183.9	212.2	177.8	174.4

Source: *Passenger Transport in Great Britain*, 1969, Table 31.

As can be seen in Table 5.6, fare increases have accelerated dramatically since 1968, but even before that increases were considerably faster than the rise in the general retail price index, which stood at 141.5 at the end of September 1970, on a similar base to Table 5.6. Since there is some, albeit low, price elasticity of demand, the result has inevitably been a further loss of passengers and a virtual breakdown of the whole principle of cross-subsidization.

Prior to this recent surge in fares, pricing had played a remarkably passive role in the bus industry as compared with most other industries. As already noted, fares are subject to the strict control of the Traffic Commissioners under the licensing system. As a result of their policy of granting route monopolies and because of the relatively low price elasticity of demand for bus services, the Commissioners have been able to insist on cross-subsidization as a basic pricing principle. This has generally involved equalizing the rate per mile as between some or all the routes operated by a particular undertaking.[46] Such a mileage basis for fare calculation is relatively simple and appears equitable, but it does mean that operators have been pushed well away from equating price with cost for individual routes. This is not to say that fare structures are not sometimes quite complex. Cross-subsidization has been decreased by some operators having three or four levels of rate, such as rural, urban and suburban, especially where population densities may vary considerably within the one territory. On the other hand cross-subsidization is increased by various types of concessionary fares, most notably for children and old age pensioners. Special concessions for workers, which were anomalously granted at peak periods when costs were at their highest, are now much less common. Another common type of cross-subsidization is the charging of special fares to and from new housing on the outskirts of cities so as to prevent a large increase in the transport costs of people who had previously lived in city centres. The typical fare structure therefore consists of one or more mileage scales, with various concessions built in. Changes in it are made by dividing total cost by expected passenger mileage to create a new scale, although of course on occasions one end of the scale might for a variety of reasons be disproportionately favoured or burdened.

Fare scales vary quite widely between companies, even where operating conditions would not appear to be very different or where undertakings overlap or intermingle. The company sector's fares are typically higher for similar journeys than those for municipal undertakings, owing to the need for a greater amount of cross-subsidization of unremunerative routes. But even within the company sector there are considerable differences. Table 5.7 compares the maximum mileage available for given prices from six large company operators. Although the figures are now well out of date, the pattern is still fairly representative.

Unfortunately no detailed study has yet been made of the pricing decisions of the Traffic Commissioners, and without this, analysis is difficult. The fact that hearings are held in public, with local authorities as the main statutory objectors, should act as a curb on

TABLE 5.7

Maximum mileage scales—selected companies, 1960

Fare value pence	Western National	Thames Valley	Yorkshire Woollen District	Cumberland	Midland Red	Bristol Omnibus
0·83 (2d)	0·5	0·7	0·7	0·6	—	0·8
1·25 (3d)	0·8	1·2	1·3	1·1	1·0	1·3
1·66 (4d)	1·1	1·5	2·0	1·7	1·4	1·8
2·50 (6d)	1·7	2·4	3·7	2·9	2·6	2·9
3·75 (9d)	2·8	3·9	6·7	4·9	4·4	4·7
5·00 (1/–)	4·2	5·5	9·5	7·0	6·2	6·8
7·25 (1/6d)	8·0	8·7	15·8	10·6	10·4	11·4

Source: *Bus and Coach*, August 1960.

too close and easy a relationship between the Commissioners and the operators, but the objectors are too constrained by lack of detailed information to act as efficient public watchdogs. This also applies to the Commissioners themselves who, in evaluating requests for changes in fares, are not well placed to make a detailed assessment of the economics of the individual operator.[47] Basically, all they can do is to measure the proposed fare increases against cost increases. Because they are performing a role which was intended to be legal, social and political as much as, if not more than, economic, they tend to prefer simplicity of fare structures for institutional as well as social reasons. Except for pressure towards a mileage basis for fare structures, they have tended to accept the fare structures they found in 1930 and to concentrate on the level of fares. No criterion was laid down in the 1930 Act to help them do this other than that fares should be 'reasonable'. By the same token, the operator clearly had to be allowed a 'normal' rate of return on capital. But what this might mean in any particular instance is dependent on the views of the particular Commissioners, and especially those of the chairman.[48] It is certainly arguable that pricing according to cost, with its consequent wide variations between fares, would not be regarded by the Commissioners as reasonable within the terms of the Act. Certainly there seems to have been little or no inclination by the state-owned part of the industry to move towards long-run marginal cost as a basis for pricing as instructed in the Government's 1967 White Paper.

Although it was noted in the discussion of costing that financial pressures will force the operators to determine more accurately the profitability of individual routes, it does not follow that cost-related pricing would necessarily accompany such developments. For many people, including the Commissioners, the equity argument remains strong, but there are also more persuasive arguments, notably the need for administrative simplicity. The introduction of one-man operation has put a further premium on ease of fare collection. The flat fare is common in systems abroad and, while it has not yet become popular in this country, municipal systems in particular are moving towards more coarsely graded fare structures containing only three or four fare levels. The peak surcharge would be feasible because it would merely raise the level of fares, but more sophisticated attempts to relate price to cost between or even within routes seem unlikely. So, for that matter, does any attempt to charge what the market will bear, based on differential elasticities of demand such as is being done on the railways, since individual routes except perhaps for some express ones are not long enough to make it worth while carrying out market-research exercises into demand.

However, one interesting development is the extent to which social costs should be considered in the price structure. There is of course the alternative that they may be taken into account through subsidies or by control of private transport rather than by changing the bus price structure. The effect of social costs upon private cost-accounting procedures is still debatable, but there is likely to be increasing discussion of the issues involved which were taken up by the Prices and Incomes Board during its investigations into fare increases in London.[49] Although agreeing that long-run marginal costs would bring about the best allocation of resources, the Board noted that difficulties arose when some of the costs incurred were external, particularly with respect to added road congestion from an increase in bus fares. The extent to which this is true is naturally dependent on the degree of price elasticity. This varies between areas; in London a fare increase of 14 per cent was expected to generate an increase in total revenue of rather less than 9 per cent, commensurate with a fall in passenger journeys of 6 per cent; a greater degree of elasticity could probably be expected in other areas, where the private car is a more flexible alternative under most circumstances. As far as London alone was concerned the Board calculated that on the very conservative assumption that 10 per cent of the lost public transport journeys reappeared as private transport journeys, the loss in time alone due to increased congestion would approximate to some £7 million annually. Admitting that this rough approximation represented only one area of increased social costs resultant on fare increases, the Board suggested that the

Ministry of Transport should provide guidance for methods of computing social costs. However, no such developments have yet appeared.

The Board was particularly interested in social costs in the context of a proposal for a peak-hour fare surcharge on the London buses. In its first investigation the Board found the administrative objections to a peak-hour surcharge had been exaggerated and recommended that the LTB should consider it. However, in its later investigation the Board argued that the increase in social costs resultant from a peak pricing differential was very considerable, and hence that the case for peak pricing was not proved. The mathematics of the calculation were somewhat involved, but the net result was that each passenger who shifted from peak-hour travelling by bus to travelling by car:

(1) saved London Transport 12 pence per mile
(2) saved bus congestion costs of 23 pence per mile
(3) incurred car costs (net of petrol tax) of 1·5 pence per mile
(4) imposed car congestion costs of 37 pence per mile

giving a net addition to costs from the point of view of the community as a whole of 24·6 pence per mile.[50] As can readily be seen the most significant factor in the equation is the extra congestion cost of the private car. This again will vary considerably between areas, but the same general conclusions may be valid for most urban areas. At least until road pricing is introduced and/or new road space made liberally available, the logical outcome of this sort of calculation is that it is cheaper to subsidize public transport than to try to make it pay its way and hence persuade people to use private transport.[51]

VII Profitability and Investment

In an industry without internal competition, profit does not act as a satisfactory criterion of efficiency, and this is certainly true of the bus industry. Many factors outside the control of the bus company, such as the decisions of the Traffic Commissioners, which may vary as between areas, the density of population, the level of car-ownership, and the traffic conditions, are probably more important than operating efficiency in determining profitability. Thus rural companies, like the Highland Company in Scotland, could not be profitable by themselves, since there are no urban routes to cross-subsidize the loss-making services in the very sparsely populated areas. It is because companies whose territories include many rural routes cannot expect to be very profitable that the regional associations of the THC were formed and continued by the NBC. Other factors also detract from profitability as a useful economic indicator. Many municipalities subsidize their bus services as a matter of policy or else aim to break even without making provision for capital requirements. It has not been uncommon in recent years for more than half the municipal undertakings to report a deficit. In London the London Transport Board was refused permission to raise its fares in 1966; instead, under the Transport Finances Act of the same year, it was directly funded from the Exchequer to the extent of some £8 million annually. Finally, the remit of the Passenger Transport Authorities, in permitting a levy on the rates, seems to expect financial deficits.

Nevertheless profitability naturally has some significance as a source of funds and as a means of preventing the intensity of public scrutiny which British Railways has had to undergo for the last fifteen years. And while it has been a recurrent theme of this chapter so far that the industry is facing increasingly difficult financial problems, most operators managed to remain independently viable throughout the 1960s, but with the notable exception of London Transport's bus division. In fact the state companies performed very creditably from a financial point of view until the 1969 and 1970 results.

The state bus companies under the THC regime had no specified target rate of return, although the direction in the 1962 Act to act as 'a commercial enterprise' clearly meant that profit was an important objective. In the event, their profit record approximated to the 8 per cent which was for a long time the target figure in the nationalized industries for rates of return on new investment. Between 1963 and 1968 the variation was only between 7.6 per cent and 9.1 per cent, based on return on net assets after depreciation but before tax.[52] In fact the passenger transport side was the primary profit producer for the Transport Holding Company with net receipts of around £7 million annually over the years mentioned, and because of its own relatively modest capital requirements, was able to help finance some of the THC's other activities. It is arguable that the real rate was considerably higher than the 8 per cent quoted, since the figure for the net assets has included over £30 million of goodwill mostly inherited at the time of nationalization, which has nothing to do with the current value of the physical assets involved.

On the other hand, it is possible that the retention of this accounting convention may have induced the Traffic Commissioners to be more generous to THC companies than others when determining the level of fares which will produce a 'normal' profit.

In 1969 and 1970, owing to numerous changes in the basis of the accounts, the financial results are not directly comparable with earlier years, but there is no doubt of a disastrous deterioration, as Table 5.8 indicates.

TABLE 5.8
NBC financial results 1969–70
£ million

	1969	1970
Revenue	148.7	163.7
Expenses including depreciation at historic cost	141.7	158.8
Operating surplus/deficit	7.0	(5.1)
Other net income	0.5	0.4
Consolidated profit/loss	7.5	(4.7)
Interest payable on commencing capital debt	4.8	4.8
	2.7	(9.5)
Taxation (recoverable in 1970)	1.9	1.5
	0.8	(8.0)
Profits to other shareholders in manufacturing companies	—	0.1
Revenue surplus/deficit	0.8	(8.1)

Note. The 1969 and 1970 results are not directly comparable for the following reasons: the acquisition of several new companies, notably London Country Bus Services; a change in the status of the manufacturing companies from subsidiary to associated companies; and changes in other items of accounting such as holiday pay, training grants and insurance.
Source: NBC, *Annual Report*, 1970.

Matters would be made worse to the extent of £4.0 million in 1970 and £3.2 million in 1969 if depreciation were assessed on replacement rather than historic cost.[53] No target was set by the Government for the NBC in its first year, but for 1970 and 1971 an annual operating surplus of £8 million was set. The Minister noted at the time that it would have been desirable to set a higher target, but the NBC itself commented that many of the factors affecting the achievement of the target would be outside the company's control. In the event the shortfall from target was more than £12 million in 1970. Some of the relevant factors in this were a rapid increase in wage costs, the introduction of drivers' hours regulations, widespread industrial action, and delays in the introduction of new fares. This last item alone was estimated by the NBC to have cost some £3 million in 1970. No forecast has been given for the results in 1971, but they are likely to be bad. Indeed, the Government has offered a grant of £7 million for 1972 to enable the NBC to adhere to the CBI's initiative of asking companies to keep within a 5 per cent price rise from mid-1971, without going into deficit. A general subsidy of this sort, as opposed to subsidies for specific routes, clearly vitiates not only the Bus Company's financial responsibility under the 1968 Transport Act of breaking even taking one year with another, but also the whole concept of financial targets as part of a system of economic control over the nationalized industries. Even before this occurred, the NBC in its 1970 Report had indicated some retreat from commercialism to merely being a contractor for public authorities: 'Given these physical measures and the essential financial support, the operators can concentrate on the efficient and economical provision of the public transport services that the community decides it needs.'[54] A question mark must therefore hang over the precise nature of the financial responsibility which the NBC can uphold in future.

Since profitability is not very meaningful for municipal undertakings, the other area of the industry where profitability is of interest is for the independents. Although specific figures are not available, Beesley and Politi[55] found that there was a higher rate of return in the controlled sectors than in the uncontrolled, i.e. contract, sector. Since the small independents derive most of their revenue from contract hire, this suggests that they are on average not as profitable as the other ownership group.

Investment in the bus industry is, like pricing, an area to which relatively little attention has been paid. The unit cost of buses is relatively low, such that they can be acquired or replaced over a period of time without the requirements of large amounts of capital. Similarly, technological advances have not been of major significance, and have been phased into fleets during the replacement cycle. Again, the declining demand in the industry as a whole meant that there has been no incentive to invest for future growth. For all these reasons capital needs have generally been paid for out of depreciation provisions or the sale of old buses, and this was the case during the lifetime of the THC with the important exception of the purchase of the outstanding shares in the BET companies. However, 1971 may see a new trend; after the bad results of 1970, the Government has had to lend the company up to £6 million towards capital expenditure. The actual rate of investment has not been high.

The THC's capital expenditure on buses amounted to some 8 per cent of its net assets over the period 1963–68, which was a very much lower figure than for the haulage side. While there are no recent figures for capitalization in the whole industry, the industry's expenditure of some £28 million annually on new buses and coaches[56] does not suggest that the rate in the industry as a whole has been much higher than that for the THC.

However, at the present time the investment situation is somewhat unusual. The opportunity to obtain a 25 per cent government grant for standardized buses should be an incentive for operators to replace their fleets during the seven-year period for which the grants will operate. In view of the age composition of many fleets,[57] an increase in the rate of ordering new buses may be expected. The grant should also be important in increasing the speed of introduction of one-man buses, since many older buses are not capable of conversion. The NBC is setting up at Workington in Cumberland a company to be jointly owned with Leyland Motors for the production of new buses. Already the demand for new buses has had effects on the availability of spares, and many undertakings have had buses off the road for extended periods of time as a result.

VIII Productivity and Industrial Relations

Falling demand, without commensurate cutbacks in service would suggest a fall in productivity unless there were some important technical or organizational savings available. These have not been forthcoming, and productivity trends in the industry throughout most of the post-war period have been negative as a result. Crude measures of productivity show that the number of passengers carried per employee per annum fell from just under 50,000 to just under 40,000 between 1958 and 1968, and that there was also a fall in miles driven per employee. Although the brunt of the loss of productivity has been borne by the urban services, the nationalized part of the industry has not escaped. Taking the state companies alone, comparable figures show that while 50,000 passengers were carried and 9,620 miles were driven per employee in 1956, ten years later the figures were 33,800 passengers and 9,450 miles.[58] (There is no imputation of relative efficiency involved in comparing the absolute figures of the THC and the industry as a whole; differences merely reflect different operating conditions.) This decline, of course, does not mean that there has been any lessening of the physical efforts of the bus crews. Indeed, growing congestion has probably made the physical effort greater now than ever before, especially for drivers. Even so, the tendency for average speeds and the total annual mileage per bus to decrease has contributed to the decrease in productivity.

A more sophisticated measure of productivity has been made by Deakin and Seward,[59] who divided net output by total factor input, thus including both capital and labour, and derived an exponential rate of change per annum. The result can be seen in Table 5.9.

TABLE 5.9
Movements in output, total factor input and output per unit of total

	1952–62	1952–58	1958–62	1962–65
Output (value at 1958 prices)	−2·30	−2·84	−1·49	−3·74
Total factor inputs	−1·02	−0·41	−1·93	0·90
Output per total factor input	−1·25	−2·42	0·50	−4·63

Source: Deakin and Seward, op. cit., p. 115.

This performance is significantly worse than any other form of transport, even the railways. The crucial point is that output fell much more rapidly than factor inputs. However, in defence of the industry, it should be noted that the absolute level of productivity, as opposed to the alarming trends, remains good. For 1963 Deakin and Seward calculated that after adjusting for labour quality differences, road passenger transport had an output of 49·0 p per standardized labour unit hour equivalent, very little beneath the growth sectors of road haulage and air transport and very much better than the railways. In large part, however, this is a function of the relatively small amounts of capital employed in the industry (less than £1,500 per employee), and the relatively rapid increases in the industry's prices (7·8 per cent per annum exponentially 1954–63).

Technical opportunities in the bus industry are unfortunately fairly limited. The development of the gas turbine engine will be valuable for express routes, especially over motorways, and it is possible that the electric bus can contribute to cutting costs as well as pollution in urban areas. There is also a continuing need for buses with a better power-weight-fuel consumption ratio. Unfortunately technology, at least in the short run, is bounded by the fact that the unit of production is a single bus, whose maximum size is limited by the need for manoeuvrability in crowded streets and its minimum size by the requirements of a capacity geared to the peak. Outside these constraints, better system planning provides another area of possible improvement. Changes in the organization of services, with the aid of operations research techniques to examine route structures and timetabling, are being adopted by many undertakings. An imaginative idea in this area is that of dial-a-bus, whereby buses on the instructions of a computer could weave a path through housing estates to pick up passengers, thus cutting out their walk to the bus stop. Such a scheme is, of course, some distance into the future, and other devices depending on remote control or involving moving belts or the like are further away still. The most desirable immediate changes for the industry, except those in the labour area, which we shall discuss shortly, are outside its control. These would consist of giving buses more favourable traffic conditions by means of special bus lanes, running against traffic flows in one-way streeets, special turning lights, and so on, or staggering times to reduce the peak load. It was partially for this purpose that the 1968 Act gave local authorities much greater freedom to control traffic, while outside the Act the White Paper, *Public Transport and Traffic*, noted that the Minister would require authorities to prepare and submit plans for handling traffic in their area. These plans would be required to strike a balance between the claims of traffic, safety, accessibility, environmental amenity and not least between private and public transport and between pedestrians and vehicles. But progress in these areas has been slight in spite of a good deal of discussion of the possibilities.

With labour costs representing some 70 per cent of total costs it might have been expected that the first source of cost savings as demand fell would have been to cut the size of the labour force. Until a rapid reduction in the late 1960s, however, this hardly happened at all; throughout the late 1950s and early 1960s, with passengers ebbing away, there was little or no effort by the industry to cut the labour force, never mind use what was left more efficiently. Thus a labour force of 282,000 in 1958 had fallen only to 263,000 ten years later, in spite of a drop of one-third in passenger journeys. Part of the reason was that the bus is an indivisible unit, and that there has always been a much higher proportion of operative to ancillary staff than, say, on the railways. Thus if the industry wanted to maintain its level of services, as it did, it appeared that the labour force was a constant, tied to this level. But such a view was the source of many of the industry's present financial problems. Its recognition since the mid 1960s of the need to improve labour efficiency and reduce labour-intensiveness has coincided with a general increase in labour militancy and labour costs so that the net effect of changes on total cost has been small. What the industry needs is a highly flexible labour force, capable of being adjusted to both long-term and short-term patterns of demand. But this has proved very elusive.

The labour situation is so important that it is worth extended examination. Union resistance to change is part of the story, but this is only one manifestation of deeper problems relating to the nature of the job. Hours are long and irregular, the amount of responsibility assumed is quite high, and the hourly rate of pay is frequently not competitive with the manufacturing sector. A busman may be required to work separate four-hour shifts covering the two peak times, with a spread-over period in between; or he may be put on to cleaning or maintenance work to keep him occupied in the off-peak period; or he may be required to take the place of an absentee, or called upon to do some extra overtime. All these are irritating, if necessary, obligations. It is not therefore surprising that morale in the industry is frequently poor.

Restrictive practices have also become a problem. There has been resistance to one-man operation, but this is not the only, and perhaps not the most serious, labour problem faced by bus operators. A whole range of restrictive practices exist throughout the industry, the great majority of which hamper flexibility in labour deployment. One difficult issue is created by the 'spread-over' period between peak requirements; there is reluctance to accept alternative work such as cleaning in the interim, and an increasing insistence that spread-over periods should be paid at full rates. Duty scheduling has also caused problems and there is widespread objection to the use of part-time labour to alleviate difficulties at the peak periods, both daily and seasonally. However, productivity bargaining at the local level has often been able to alleviate some, if not all, of these areas of dispute.

Although earnings in the industry have come up to the national average,[60] they have done so only by reason of long hours of overtime, with average weekly hours worked of 55·7 in 1966. This make-up factor has now been reduced in significance as a result of the 1968 Act. As with other conditions, there are considerable variations in earnings in different situations; Lee and Steedman in their examination of the municipal sector found a range of labour cost per hour from 38 p to 67 p.[61]

Labour shortage problems have also been unevenly spread throughout the country, and these have often been exacerbated by high turnover and absenteeism rates. In general the companies operating in the more prosperous industrial areas fare worst, since they are faced with labour markets in which competition is keener and higher pay in other jobs more common. In some areas rural bus driving or conducting is still a respectable job with adequate status; in the cities, where road conditions are much more tiring, it has become a job which is frequently left to immigrant labour. The state companies as a whole fare better than the municipal operators, but even so many face considerable difficulties. Thus shortfalls from the establishment figure for platform crews range up to 20 per cent, necessitating a great deal of overtime to maintain services, while turnover rates in some companies are as high as 50 per cent per annum. Furthermore, the Transport Act of 1968 introduced restrictions on drivers' hours which, whatever their desirable effects on safety, threaten to make even worse the labour shortages in the industry. The restrictions were essentially the same as those already described for road haulage, namely a maximum 60 hour week, at least one full rest day per week and a daily maximum of $12\frac{1}{2}$ hours of which only 11 could be actual driving. However, on the strong representation of the industry, some temporary concessions were obtained, and a further examination of the situation has been promised.

Collective bargaining in the bus industry takes place in three main groupings, although again with local variations, especially in productivity bargaining. London Transport does its own bargaining. The municipal sector, with a few cities excepted, bargains through the National Joint Industrial Council for the Road Passenger Transport Industry. The company sector, i.e. the state interests plus the larger independents, bargains through the National Council for the Omnibus Industry. The smaller independents follow the pattern set in this last grouping. On the union side the largest union by far is the Transport and General Workers Union, but the National and Municipal Workers and the Railwaymen also have some members, the last-named being a historical curiosity dating from the period when the pre-war railway companies had large holdings in the industry. Not unnaturally negotiations have tended to be based on comparisons between sectors, with London playing the role of pacemaker in wage rates and earnings. The Prices and Incomes Board has suggested that the municipal and company sectors should link together for bargaining purposes, largely to prevent the various claims for parity of treatment which had grown up between the two sectors. It also suggested that such a body should set a framework for local productivity bargaining. No such body, however, has yet been developed.

In the late 1960s the bargaining relationships were strained as the busmen sought to alleviate their problems of status and morale. This resulted in a major clash with the Government's prices and incomes policy in 1967/68, springing from the issuance of the 'Busmen's Charter' in the middle of 1967. In addition to a substantial increase in basic rates, it requested more favourable working conditions, which would have had the effect of intensifying the very working practices which the operators had hoped to make more flexible. The municipal sector took the brunt of the pressure, but when the NJIC negotiated a 7 per cent wage increase in December 1967, the Government refused to permit it because there were no corresponding productivity provisions, especially the one-man operation which the Prices and Incomes Board had seen as the best means of improving efficiency. The Prices and Incomes Board was asked to make another investigation of the industry, and in the interim the increase was 'frozen'. When the Board found that the increases were not justified, local bargaining again started, only for many of the agreements subsequently arrived at to be 'frozen' again for offering back pay without productivity provisions. A national strike was narrowly averted, the Board had to be called in to make still further investigations, there was a strike at Dundee which almost resulted in Frank Cousins, General Secretary of the Transport Workers, being charged with violation of the Prices and Incomes Act, and finally at the end of 1968 the 'freeze' powers expired, leaving the busmen free to collect the backdated pay from their original agreement without making any productivity concessions. The whole long episode did nothing to improve either industrial relations or to forward the incomes policy, while the Prices and Incomes Board had to produce no less than nine reports on this single industry within three years.

The most obvious gain in labour utilization is through dispensing with the conductor and using the driver to collect fares. One-man operation is not a new idea, and is almost universal abroad, even in such difficult conditions as New York. It may in fact be one of the most pertinent criticisms of the British industry that its introduction was so long delayed. At all events, in the late 1960s it emerged as the obvious way of solving the labour shortage, cutting costs and yet increasing the individual's pay. The actual savings through the system have been estimated at some 14 per cent of the cost of operating a bus, but the Prices and Incomes Board, which refused to give a specific figures for savings, noted that they varied considerably according to offsetting cost increases, such as slower average speeds, added capital costs and higher pay for the driver.[62] Its introduction has been slow, partly because a change to rear-engined buses must be made, partly because of difficulties in large buses in dense traffic conditions, and also because of resistance by the unions. At the end of 1969 a rough estimate put its extent as rather under 15 per cent in the municipal sector, while the proportion rose from 25 per cent at the same time to 34 per cent at the end of 1970 in the company sector. The higher figure is largely because the state companies are better placed than most to make use of one-man operation by virtue of their largely rural and suburban routes. Consultants to the Board have suggested that the maximum passenger loading is in the range 100–150 passengers per hour; above this delays in boarding grow, the task of the driver becomes increasingly burdensome, and average speeds fall rapidly.[63] Flat fare schemes would help by enabling automatic fare collection, but it has proved impossible for most operators to set a fare which will not lose a disproportionate amount of revenue at either the short- or long-distance ends of their routes. Some gradation of fares is therefore desirable. The availability of more sophisticated fare-collecting machinery will thus be an important factor in the extent to which one-man operation spreads.

A last point in this section relates to management. Successive reports by the Prices and Incomes Board found many suggestions to make about operating efficiency, and criticized management's foresight and control. With respect to the municipal sector, in fact, the Board commented that: 'Inadequate management in some parts of the municipal bus industry has led to an accelerating loss of control over actual operation and above all over industrial relations.'[64] Part of the difficulty in this sector, the Board pointed out, was due in some instances to too close control, verging on interference, by local authority transport committees. The state companies do not have this problem, and would not deserve such criticism. Nevertheless, many of the problems which good management could aid are not restricted to the municipal sector.

IX The Role of State Ownership in the Bus Industry

We have seen that those parts of the bus industry now under state ownership became so in some measure by an accident of history, that the comprehensive road passenger planning scheme envisaged in the 1947 Act came to nothing and that policy since then has largely been one of letting well alone. Thus the state's bus interests might be considered a classic example of passive nationalization. It has been symptomatic of their apparent lack of cohesive structure that until the formation of the NBC there has not even been a composite name by which to call them.

It is difficult to see what effects, if any, nationalization has had upon the 'company' sector of the bus industry. There was no discernible pattern of behaviour differentiating the Tilling or Scottish groups from the BET group during the long period when the latter was operating independently. For that matter there is nothing to differentiate the present independent companies from the state-owned ones. The individual state companies appear to have had almost complete latitude of operation within the constraints of the licensing system. Ministerial intervention has been virtually non-existent, but even within both the THC and the NBC operating decentralization has meant that the influence of the holding company has been minimal. There has been no attempt to develop economies of scale, or to exercise price leadership, in the way in which the haulage companies tried to operate in the period before 1953. Even such possibilities as the standardization of bus designs for all the companies were hardly pursued at all until imposed by the offer of a 25 per cent Government grant under the 1968 Act. It is of course true that management has been moved from one state company to another, and that there have been some central financial requirements including a degree of cross-subsidization between companies in the same region, but the extent of this has, at least until the NBC itself was set a specific target, been geared to what the companies think they can achieve rather than having specific requirements imposed upon them. It is possible that nationalization has had certain intangible effects—a somewhat greater reluctance to close unremunerative routes, a greater acceptance of the area agreements, a reinforcement of the axiom of cross-subsidization because there are no shareholders for whom profits must be maximized, but these principles were already enshrined in the Act of 1930 and would certainly have continued without nationalization. It may be suggested that common ownership might have brought a close liaison between road and rail, but the links between BET and the railways before 1968 seem to have been as close as those of the state groups. There has been little attempt to make employees feel part of a state concern, while the ideological arguments which have so bedevilled road haulage have, with the exception of a brief flurry in 1949 when the area schemes were being mooted, largely passed over the heads of the bus companies. The buses have in fact operated in a quiet backwater in contrast to the controversies over other sectors of nationalized industry for which the financial self-sufficiency of the companies, on both the current and capital accounts, has been largely responsible. Any inflow of public funds or cutback in services will result in more public discussion of the bus situation, and there are already many instances of this happening up and down the country. Even so, because of the localized scale on which this is likely to happen, it seems improbable that the extent of surveillance will be as great as on the railways.

X The Future of the Industry

It was probably inevitable that there would be a re-evaluation of the bus industry's licensing system, given the return of a Conservative Government committed to enhancing competition, an accelerating collapse of the rationale behind the 1930 Act, and a rising tide of public resentment about the increasing cost and declining reliability of services. Indeed, some of the proposals made by the Minister for Transport Industries do much the same in freeing the bus industry from restriction as the Labour Government did for road haulage in the 1968 Act. Equally importantly, the main aspects of licensing have been retained at least for the present. But it would be premature to suppose that the transformation of the industry, which is currently taking place so rapidly, can continue without even more important issues presenting themselves.

Two major and interrelated questions are germane to the future of the industry. The first is one of organization, the second one of the wider role of public transport. Organizationally, three main suggestions present themselves. One is that the concept of the Passenger Transport Authorities should be widened so that the localities would look after their own transport problems. This would be most appropriate when the expected reorganization of local government takes place in 1974/75. However, the new local boundaries were not drawn with transport in mind, and such a suggestion must remain purely speculative. If it is true that there would be a closer affinity between the operating body and the body making financial provisions, this has not always proved an advantage in the municipal sector. A more likely version of this possibility is that the number of PTAs will be expanded, at least to the conurbations centred on Glasgow,[65] Leeds and Sheffield, and that the reform of local government will lead to a reconstitution of the remaining municipal services, probably through integration into the state system.

A second alternative is a more thoroughgoing reconstitution of the licensing system so as to permit freedom of entry and pricing in the stage service sector. This case has been most forcefully stated by

Hibbs in the two editions of his Pamphlet *Transport for Passengers*.[66] His argument is that road service licensing has been responsible for the inability of the industry to respond to its changing environment, and that only competition could ensure that price and quality would be matched to effective consumer demand. Present operators, including the state companies, would be encouraged to remain in business, and might well be assisted by having some peak traffic taken from them. The concept is attractive, but suffers from two disadvantages. The first of these is that competition would be detrimental to reliability, which is one of the most important consumer demands from a bus service. The second, more serious, is his recognition that: 'There is room for subsidy in specific cases, where there is a real need left uncatered for by the working of the market . . .'.[67] It was, of course, precisely this recognition that 'real' needs would be uncatered for that led to the setting up of the system of cross-subsidization in the first place, to avoid the difficulties in measuring need by some public machinery. This is still the key problem in the industry, and it is increasing in scope. As the NBC said in its 1970 Report: 'The question as to who should pay for socially necessary services *outside** the rural areas is becoming a major issue.'[68] Moreover, it is arguable that the demise of the rationale for cross-subsidization and the desire for organizational survival will push existing operators into pricing initiatives.

The third organizational possibility is a continuation of the present structure, and this seems the most probable in spite of the various problems. The National Bus Company has decentralized control and strong historical local connections, but its responsibility is primarily a national one, and the setting of an operating surplus target has increased the significance of the national level. Yet if it is to be able to meet local needs, it must have ways of gauging them and sounding out opinions. Enlightened negotiations with local authorities over subsidies will not achieve all of this objective; nor have the Transport Users' Consultative Committees been sufficiently successful on the railways to warrant their extension. This is the problem the state companies must solve if they are to remain the dominant form of organization in the country. If so, the fact of state ownership will become even less relevant than it has been to date. But in any case, some considerable retrenchment in both the quantity and quality of services seems probable in the state-controlled areas, together with some growth of local private operators where the companies retreat, and some extension of control in the present municipal sector.

* Author's italics.

The other major issue is the wider role of public transport than that of providing a commercial service. In the rural areas the decision has already been taken to make the bus in part a welfare service. This question will also become relevant in urban areas, but in a slightly different context, namely how far public transport is seen as the only way of preventing cities from physically swamping themselves. As we saw with respect to London and the proposal for the peak surcharge, bus services geared to private accounting costs are likely to result in a further transfer to the private car. This transfer will accelerate with increasing car-ownership and more diffused locations for living and working, such that no increased road-building will be able to solve the problems of congestion.

The social service and anti-congestion views of public transport lead to three potential levels of solution. All three could and in some places probably will be invoked simultaneously, but they nevertheless represent distinct stages of commitment to public transport. The first stage is more effective planning, to maximize the operating efficiency of public transport while still maintaining the present freedom of choice of mode for users. Leeds offers a good current example of this approach, using parking policies to maintain a balance between traffic volumes and road capacity by excluding much traffic from key central city areas by ring roads or pedestrianization, and also maximizing the scope for traffic management.[69] Traffic control is a key element, since without it congestion is likely to prevent attractive bus services. Unfortunately, it is true that buses by their constant stopping and starting, frequently close to intersections where people want to alight, themselves cause a good deal of congestion.

A second level means accepting that decisions should take into account social costs. The building of the Victoria Line in London was premised on a path-breaking cost-benefit analysis which showed that although the line would not make a profit taking all costs into account, it would benefit motorists whose congestion problems would be eased. Rapid transit systems in Manchester and Newcastle are being considered on the same basis. It is, moreover, relatively attractive to evaluate projects on a cost–benefit basis in so far as capital costs are concerned, since the Government grant will amount to at least 75 per cent, while the rest can be financed by long-term loans.

The third solution is to subsidize operating costs. Although some municipal authorities have traditionally subsidized their buses, this has not been an operating subsidy and its extent has not been very great. An open-ended commitment would be very different, since it creates one more public service at a time when the whole of local government finance is under considerable strain. The ultimate subsidy would involve the provision of free public transport, and it is significant that this solution is now being seriously discussed and costed. Indeed, it has already been tried experimentally in a city as large as Rome. The cost might be less than some would fear—20 p in the £ has been given as an estimated increase on London rates, but on the other hand the increase in the quality of environment might be less than others hope, since no public transport system could cope with the complexities of many journeys.

Beyond these measures lie yet other possibilities such as road pricing and new forms of transport, but these lie outside the range of this chapter. Nevertheless if one thing is clear it is that the bus industry is not going to be able to perform the tasks required of it in a purely commercial manner, taking into account only private accounting costs. Public decisions involving factors far outside the bus industry will be required, for the equation is a complex one, especially as it affects the private car. In the last analysis, the balance between public and private transport and thus the future of the bus industry is likely to be decided on political as much as economic grounds.

NOTES TO CHAPTER 5

1. C. I. Savage, *An Economic History of Transport* (Hutchinson, rev. ed. 1966), p. 88.
2. ibid., p. 119.
3. There are now only eleven sets of Traffic Commissioners.
4. Parl. Deb. 5th Ser. Vol. 431, Col. 1631, 1947.
5. Cmnd. 8538: HMSO, 1952.
6. *Report of the Committee on the Licensing of Road Passenger Services* (Thesiger Report), HMSO, 1953.
7. G. Walker, 'Transport Policy Before and After 1953', *Oxford Economic Papers*, March 1953.
8. The White Paper most relevant to the industry was *Public Transport and Traffic* (Cmnd. 3481: HMSO, December 1967).
9. Section 9(3).
10. The NBC also took over the bus manufacturing companies of the THC.
11. *Passenger Transport in Great Britain* (HMSO, 1969), Tables 36, 38, 40.
12. After the 1968 Act, the number of municipal undertakings fell sharply to 68, largely as a result of the amalgamation of many of them into the four Passenger Transport Authorities, but also because the NBC took over the Luton, Exeter, and Gosport and Fareham undertakings in 1969/70.

13. *Passenger Transport in Great Britain, 1967* (HMSO, 1969), Table 13.
14. Hibbs has pointed out that various parts of the market have their peaks at different times of the week and year, and this permits the small operators to sub-contract to the larger ones to their mutual benefit. (J. Hibbs, 'Sub-Contracting in Road Transport; a Note on Some Seasonal Aspects of the Problem of the Peak', *Journal of Transport Economics and Policy*, January 1971, pp. 91–5.)
15. *Public Transport and Traffic* (Cmnd. 3481: HMSO, 1967), p. 6.
16. *Bus and Coach*, December 1967, p. 419.
17. N. Lee and I. Steedman, 'Economies of Scale in Bus Transport: Britain', *Journal of Transport Economics and Policy*, January 1970.
18. See J. Hibbs, *Transport for Passengers* (Institute of Economic Affairs, 1963 and second edition 1971), and G. J. Ponsonby, *Transport Policy: Coordination through Competition* (Institute of Economic Affairs, 1969).
19. Section 72(3).
20. Thesiger Report, p. 39.
21. Some bus systems in the United States have obligations to maintain a given number of seats as a ratio of the number of passengers offering. No such approach to defining adequacy exists in Britain.
22. D. N. Chester, *Public Control of Road Passenger Transport* (Manchester University Press, 1936), chapter XI.
23. Section 72(4).
24. Thesiger Report, p. 38.
25. ibid., p. 39.
26. THC, *Annual Report*, 1965, p. 30.
27. Hibbs, *Transport for Passengers*, p. 24.
28. It was strongly argued before the Thesiger Committee that the extent of bus company ownership by the BTC had been responsible for a less effective operation of the licensing system by curtailing objections to applications, but the Committee had little difficulty in showing that the same conditions operated where non-BTC companies operated. Some concern was implied, however, that the common ownership of road and rail services might curtail competition between the two modes. (Thesiger Report, chapter IX.)
29. NBPI, Report No. 16, *Pay and Conditions of Busmen* (Cmnd. 3012: HMSO, May 1966).
30. To make matters still more complex, the PTAs themselves were enjoined not to permit cross-subsidization. *Public Transport and Traffic* stated (p. 7): 'If costs in a particular part of the area are low, it would seem right for the travelling public in that area to enjoy the benefits.'
31. *Traffic in Towns* (Buchanan Report), HMSO, 1963.
32. Information from STG.
33. It must also be remembered that a large number of motorists are to some extent subsidized in their driving, from occasional trips where expenses are paid by the firm to situations where virtually all costs are paid by other than the user, and that the cost per person is reduced for each extra person carried by car.
34. Quoted in *The Guardian*, 21 January 1970.

35. The data are taken from a paper on the choice of mode for the journey to work read at Wadham College, Oxford, in 1966, and partly reported in D. A. Quarmby, 'Travel Mode for Journey to Work', *Journal of Transport Economics and Policy*, September 1967. His findings receive backing from a similar study in Chicago, where it was found that in order to induce 50 per cent of private-car commuters to use public transport, those changing mode would have to be *paid* 50 d (21 p) per trip. (L. W. Moses and H. F. Williamson, 'Value of Time, Choice of Mode, and the Subsidy Issue in Urban Transportation', *Journal of Political Economy*, June 1963.)
36. One of the difficulties faced by some bus companies is the provision of parking space for their bus crews, even though they have free transport to and from work.
37. *Passenger Transport in Great Britain* (HMSO, 1967), Table 9.
38. THC, *Annual Report*, p. 25.
39. *Bus and Coach*, November 1967.
40. *Report of Committee on Rural Bus Services* (Jack Committee), HMSO, 1961.
41. Press statement 15 September 1970. It should be noted that the THC had previously argued strongly against direct subsidies, saying that 'a transfer of responsibility to "bottomless purses" would lead to an inability to resist higher standards of service and lower fares than are justified'. (THC, *Annual Report*, 1965, p. 30.)
42. The most important limitation, issued in a separate circular, was that the service must pay at least half of its operating cost with fare revenues. There has been some pressure from Labour MPs for the Central Government to pay more than 50 per cent of the subsidy.
43. THC, *Annual Report*, 1964, p. 36.
44. The comparative figures in this paragraph are taken from the Annual Reports of the British Transport Commission, the Transport Holding Company, and the London Transport Board. The comparison of the Scottish and Tilling groups with the NBC is not of course exact, but gives an indication of the magnitudes involved.
45. NBPI, Report No. 112, *Proposals for Fare Increases by London Transport Board* (Cmnd. 4036: HMSO, 1969), Appendix 3.
46. In Scotland there is a pronounced distance taper. The Scottish companies also have a much greater similarity of fare structures than those in England.
47. As cost inflation and declining demand have hit the industry, so the role of the Commissioners in 'rubber-stamping' fare rules has increasingly become a target for criticism. (See comment by Leslie Huckfield, MP at Parl. Deb. 5th. Ser. Vol. 812, Col. 271, 1971.)
48. An interesting position seems to be developing since the NBC was set an operating surplus target by the Minister of Transport early in 1970. The NBC broke the target down between its companies, and they in turn have quoted this figure when applying for fare increases. However, various sets of Commissioners have seen fit not to regard this as a relevant consideration in deciding what are 'reasonable' fares.

49. NBPI, Report No. 56, *Proposals by the London Transport Board and British Railways Board for Fare Increases in the London Area* (Cmnd. 3561: HMSO, 1968), and Report No. 112.
50. NBPI, Report No. 112, Appendix 3. The new Passenger Transport Executive for South East Lancashire and North East Cheshire became the first undertaking to introduce a peak surcharge in 1970. This was an across-the-board surcharge of 1·67 p (3d) for all fares in the Central Division. However, no attempt was made to calculate the balance of social costs involved. See also W. J. Tyson, 'A Study of Peak Cost and Pricing in Road Passenger Transport', *Institute of Transport Journal*, November 1970.
51. In practice the NBPI did not recommend a subsidy for public transport in London, in spite of the logic of its conclusions, since it had to accept the need for the LTB to be profitable before being handed over to the Greater London Council.
52. The figure of 9·1 per cent, which relates to 1968, is slightly too high, since it includes the results of the BET companies from March of that year, but not January or February, which are often loss-making months.
53. Prior to 1968 the companies had made up the difference between historic and replacement costs by using cash reserves, but under the 1968 Act the accumulated reserves of £23 million, also covering other facets of operation such as pension funds, were not transferred to the NBC. The company therefore began life without any cash reserves, and although the capital indebtedness (currently £97·6 million) was reduced by the extent of the withheld reserves, this was no substitute for a lack of liquidity.
54. NBC, *Annual Report*, 1970, p. 23.
55. M. E. Beesley and J. Politi, 'A Study of the Profits of Bus Companies, 1960–66', *Economica*, May 1969.
56. *Passenger Transport in Great Britain* (HMSO, 1968), Table 52.
57. At the end of 1969, almost 10 per cent of the Scottish Transport Group's buses were over 15 years old and almost 40 per cent over 10 years old.
58. In 1970 the not directly comparable figures for the NBC were 9,560 miles and 30,500 passengers per employee.
59. B. M. Deakin and T. Seward, *Productivity in Transport* (Cambridge University Press, 1969). The data in the following paragraph are taken from chapter 4.
60. Contrary to most impressions of the industry, busmen's earnings in the post-war period have in fact moved up marginally faster than the national average. Using 1948 as a base year, Devons, Crossley and Maunder calculated that whereas national average weekly earnings for men had moved to 220·9 by 1965, similar calculations for bus workers showed London Transport crews at 223·0, the municipal sector at 233·8, and the company sector at 226·7. (E. Devons, J. R. Crossley and W. F. Maunder, 'Wage Rate Indexes by Industry, 1948–65', *Economica*, November 1968.)
61. Lee and Steedman, op. cit.

62. NBPI, Report No. 50, *Productivity Agreements in the Bus Industry* (Cmnd. 3498: HMSO, 1967), chapter 2.
63. One-man operation with double-decker buses has nevertheless been tried and is spreading. For the experience of Manchester, the pace-setter in the use of one-man operation in city centres, see J. Hall, 'Problems of One-Man Bus Operation', *Institute of Transport Journal*, May 1969. Hall noted that lack of passenger co-operation was perhaps the worst problem.
64. NBPI, Report No. 63, *Pay of Municipal Busmen* (Cmnd. 3605: HMSO, April 1968), p. 19.
65. The setting up of a Glasgow-based PTA was announced late in 1971.
66. See note 18.
67. *Transport for Passengers*, p. 80.
68. NBC, *Annual Report*, 1970, p. 11.
69. Leeds City Council, *Planning and Transport, the Leeds Approach*, HMSO, 1969.

6 TRANSPORT POLICY

I The Concept of Co-ordination

It will have been evident from the foregoing chapters that many aspects of policy determination in the nationalized sectors of the transport industries cannot easily be disentangled from transport policy as a whole. There are two main reasons for this: one is the large proportion of private ownership in transport, and the other relates to the ease of substitution both between private and public ownership and also between the different modes. Transport and the means and extent of its control have long presented difficult problems of policy, which are still far from resolution. It is arguable, indeed, that we have not even decided the most basic question of all, namely the role and function of transport in the economy. Is it to be regarded as a public utility, as a welfare service, or as an industry subject to the 'normal' constraints of the self-regulating market? Or, if it is to be regarded as a little of each, where are the boundaries to be drawn, since the categories are at least to some extent mutually exclusive? Decisions such as these, of course, are not entirely economic and to this extent the whole transport sector is not susceptible to assessment on purely economic criteria. Nevertheless this chapter proposes to examine the problem of transport policy in an economic context, considering first the difficulties involved in an economic solution, then briefly examining the rationale of the policies undertaken, and finishing with a look at the 1968 Transport Act, by far the most comprehensive and ambitious piece of legislation in British transport history.

The problem of the interaction of the transport modes is seen by the economist as a problem of resource allocation with the objective of meeting the demand for transport at the lowest cost in real resources. This is commonly called the problem of co-ordination, or sometimes integration, although it is as well to note that co-ordination is a highly ambiguous term. The man in the street, for instance, may think of co-ordination as primarily technical, as for instance to facilitate the interchange of goods between modes, or to provide a common timetable for buses and railways. But even economic co-ordination as an end objective can be confused with co-ordination as the means used to achieve that objective, such as administrative directives or institutions on the one hand or fostering a self-regulating market based on the price mechanism on the other. Moreover, neither the means nor the ends of economic co-ordination in transport should be examined without reference to resource allocation between the transport and other sectors of the economy, but to do this would be beyond the scope of this book.[1]

Even within the transport sector, however, it has never been very clear just what co-ordination means in practice, and we must therefore distinguish between the ideal conception of co-ordination, that of meeting demand with real resource minimization, and the co-ordination which we shall examine in the next few pages, which is an amalgamation of many different considerations and bears little resemblance to the ideal version. It is nevertheless the case that governments have paid sufficient lip-service to the ideal version for it to be accepted as a desirable end objective in transport policy, even if, as already noted, the place of transport in the overall economic and social framework remains unsettled.

It would be a neat solution if co-ordination could be achieved through a self-operating economic system, but in fact, for reasons which may have emerged throughout the preceding chapters, and which will be further discussed below, transport is very far from being such a system.[2] As was noted in chapter 1, while successive governments have tried to improve the economic rules under which the nationalized industries operate, not only do these rules fall short of providing a self-regulating system, but they have not been implemented even in their limited form. There are two main groups of reasons why this sort of co-ordination has not been feasible.

The first group of factors complicating a self-regulating solution is the difficulty of defining and measuring the economic concepts involved. Especially in view of the long life expectancy of transport infrastructure, it is important that policy should be based on sound estimates of trends in demand, but the nature of the demand in this sector gives rise to serious measurement problems and in practice forecasts have been extremely inaccurate. Demand in transport is almost infinitely heterogeneous in its geographical, time and qualitative dimensions. With respect to the first two, it is also highly specific, with no short-term substitutes. Services must be provided where they are required and at the time they are wanted. Even the qualitative characteristics of demand are constantly changing to respond to the increasing affluence of individuals and industry's need for more efficient service. Moreover the problem is not only that of the single mode, because the very high cross-elasticities in transport mean that forecasting must take into account potential changes in all other modes. In order to achieve co-ordination, such forecasting would need not so much to take account of demand as it stands, but demand as it would be were it not distorted by different pricing mechanisms in the different modes. Furthermore, the rapid growth of the private sector, composed as it is of such small units on both the passenger and freight sides, has added very considerably to the difficulties and expense of measuring and predicting demand. The result has been that some agencies, especially the railways, have continually been over-optimistic about the future, such that a good deal of wasteful surplus capacity has remained in existence, while for others, notably the roads, demand has constantly been under-estimated.

Costing presents both conceptual and practical difficulties. The problems of measuring and allocating costs to individual customers have already been mentioned in the chapters on each industry. These arise primarily because the smallest unit of movement, the train, bus, aeroplane, or lorry, is usually much larger than the separate units which are transported. The more centralized the agency, the more difficult this issue becomes. Secondly, co-ordination would necessitate that the same basis for costing be used for each mode. It is this aspect of co-ordination to which much thought has been given by economists, with particular reference to the vexed issue of road and rail costs. Suggested solutions have been to turn the responsibility for rail track over to the Government, or to make the railways adopt a standard charge per mile run to pay for the track, or in some way to make road users pay for track use in an equivalent way to the railways.[3] However, even if a satisfactory solution to this issue were found for the public agencies, and those mentioned have been subjected to considerable criticism, there would still be the difficulty that private transport, both passenger and freight, but especially the former, would not use similar costing conventions. Private-car owners, in so far as they evaluate costs at all once they have made the initial decision to buy, do so on a very short-run basis which cannot rationally be adopted by public agencies with financial responsibilities and a high proportion of labour costs. The measurement of social costs presents a third problem area in costing. It is easy to talk of measuring social costs and having agencies charge long-run (or short-run) social costs, but the practical problems of measuring this are immense. There have been numerous arguments over the valuation of time in cost–benefit studies, but this is probably the easiest of the components of social costs to measure. How are we to measure the cost of noise, pollution of the environment, accident liability and similar factors? Crude averages could be attempted, but measurements would need to be specific to time and place to achieve correct resource allocation. Finally, with particular reference to the road system, there has never been any agreement on just what costs should be included in the total. Should interest be charged on the capital invested on roads, for instance, and should the police be charged for? Should there be a rent for the use of land? Even if the costs to be included were agreed, the problem of allocating these among road users would still exist and would be even less tractable than on the railways.

Pricing problems are naturally the mirror-image of costing problems if price is taken to be a reflection of marginal or any other type of cost. However, if there is a different ratio of fixed to variable costs between modes, and if one mode has areas of residual monopoly, the question will arise as to the extent to which short-run marginal cost should be charged in areas of competition, and all the fixed costs recouped in the areas of monopoly. With the amount of surplus capacity which has traditionally been endemic in most areas of transport, price discrimination is an attractive approach for operators. In so far as internal cross-subsidization is pursued in this context, either for social service reasons or because costs are not accurately known, co-ordination will suffer. Certainly the ratio of price to marginal cost is likely to be vastly different in competitive and non-competitive situations. There is a further argument between long-run and short-run marginal pricing. In an equilibrium situation, of course, the two should be equal, but because of the length of life of the infrastructure, the indivisibilities in many fields of transport, and the nature of demand, it is in practice virtually impossible to plan for such an equilibrium, so that surplus capacity is the almost inevitable outcome, creating the long-run/short-run pricing problem. The resolution of this issue is also crucially dependent upon the investment tests proposed and the question of covering total costs if short-run marginal pricing is advocated. Whether total costs should be covered is particularly relevant where public agencies are competing directly with privately owned ones. It has been argued that the railways have been able to charge unrealistically low prices, amounting very roughly to short-run marginal cost, because it was accepted in practice that they need not cover total costs, and that this was unfair competition in comparison with road-based competitors who had to pay full costs. The major problem in pricing, however, might prove to be an inability to introduce the price mechanism on the roads. Some element of pricing is provided by the taxation system, and a certain amount can also be introduced by measures such as parking charges, but the state of cities everywhere in the world is evidence that the net price is nowhere near sufficient to offset the social costs incurred. Nowhere in the world has road pricing in this sense been introduced, a clear indication of the severe technical and political difficulties of doing so.[4]

The problems of investment co-ordination follow largely from the difficulties of demand forecasting and pricing. Some investments in transport give no cash return, for some there are social as well as financial returns, and others are judged purely on a financial basis. Clearly this creates difficulties in comparability. Yet investment is the activity where policy has perhaps the best opportunity of promoting the ends of a rational economic policy, since measurement according to marginal principles should be most applicable here. Capacity would be increased or reduced according to whether expected revenue is greater or less than cost, and if this were done for all modes together, there would be a tendency towards a long-run equilibrium and thus co-ordination. However, although the road system is by far the largest user of public investment,[5] in the absence of any direct financial yardstick, criteria must be based almost entirely on time and accident criteria. This is not to say that road investment decisions are made on easier criteria than the railways—all the signs are that the rates of return on new roads are very high by normal investment standards—but rather that there is no easy way of comparing investments in different modes.

This comparison again raises a point introduced in the discussion of demand. To take the example of transport between London and Manchester, considerable investment has been laid down by road, rail and air in the last decade as a result of motorway building, rail electrification and the introduction of new generation aircraft. As far as is known no consideration was given to the cross-elasticities between these forms of transport in making investment decisions. Not only should this have been done as a matter of course, but the evaluation should have been on common and compatible costing and pricing principles. Yet at the time BEA was cross-subsidizing its internal services by external ones, while the railways were in all probability using profits on the London–Manchester route to subsidize losses everywhere, and the motorway of course had no pricing system at all. Any demand forecast of cross-elasticities should thus have first allowed for these differences. The test rate of discount on new investment is designed to provide a mechanism for choice, but if it is to be used efficiently it requires far more accurate demand forecasting on a common base than is now available. Social costs and their measurement add another dimension to investment decisions. It is well known that the Victoria Line was justified on this basis, but only by accepting and compensating for a situation which was not following economic rules in the first place. All decisions involving urban areas must be made under this constraint. Nevertheless, in spite of these problems, investment is an area where better techniques can produce a more rational solution.

The economic factors just mentioned are obviously severe constraints on achieving an ideal resource allocation, but the problems created by conflicting policy considerations are at least equally important. We talk of transport policy, but in fact the practical goals of long-term transport policy, as opposed to paying lip-service to real resource minimization, have never really been examined, much less defined. This has been the more reprehensible in view of the long-term nature of transport investment. What has happened is that there have been a number of wider considerations, each of which has had some influence on transport policy, and which taken together have prevented the operation of a self-sufficient market mechanism, but have not themselves added up to a positive policy. They also create difficulties in that an individual measure of policy may be directed at only one aspect of transport, so that different facets are treated by different criteria. This problem of inconsistency has in fact been among the most difficult for economists to solve; if all branches of transport were treated equally, economic rules would be much more easily applicable.

Governments have always had an interest in the provision of transport services for reasons other than resource distribution. Ever since the Romans built roads for military and administrative purposes, communications have always been central to political cohesion and commercial and industrial development. The latter are still very important in transport policy. More recently the interest has widened. One of the most important aspects is now public safety through the imposition of discipline on joint users of limited facilities, as on the roads. An even more recent concern is the preservation of the environment and its amenities from the noise and congestion which seems endemic to modern transport. Another aspect is that the capacity for personal mobility is an increasingly important dimension of individual freedom, and in this capacity the availability of transport has come close to the status of a welfare service such as education or health. However, the extent of this conception has never been defined, since much of transport is undeniably commercial. The social service approach can also be interpreted as encouraging cross-subsidization, such that in so far as the service must be paid for, the change should as far as possible be the same as for similar services, even if they cost different amounts to supply.[6] By contrast, governments may require transport undertakings to achieve certain financial obligations, such as breaking even, which may be considered more important than any pricing desiderata. Again, in terms of scarce land and capital, particularly the latter, transport must be seen as only one among many priorities in what the Government sees as its overall social and economic policy. A further complication is that governments have seen transport as a source of tax revenue irrespective of the implications for resource allocation of the incidence of the tax. Finally, political ideology, irrespective of the objective facts of the situation, has been evident in transport policy. Co-ordination has meant different things to the different parties, even if both have accepted it as an objective. The Conservatives have preferred co-ordination 'by the natural interplay of economic forces', while Labour has preferred a planned solution. Not a few fluctuations in policy have been derived from this difference in the desired degree of intervention. Nevertheless, as in so much of British public policy, the difference is far from absolute. The Conservatives have maintained the regulatory licensing systems and have accepted the necessity of paying subsidies, while the Labour Party has for its part placed its administrative planning approach in the context of maintaining user choice.

In view of the problems of measurement, the lack of long-term goals within the sector, the potentially conflicting objectives which might impinge upon it from the outside, and the ideological division about means, it is far from surprising that a self-regulating system has not been feasible. Nor is it surprising that the actual policies formulated by successive governments have been shortsighted, political as much as economic in nature, and based on the structure of the industries rather than the economic forces to which they must respond. As Munby has pointed out: 'Politicians and civil servants are biased in favour of . . . "institutionism", the belief that economic problems can be solved by altering institutions rather than laying down the policies required to achieve given ends.'[7] 'Institutionism' has inevitably meant that attempts at co-ordination have been at a fairly crude level, with no clear end in sight and no real means of measuring success. This last point, of finding it difficult to evaluate the extent of co-ordination, has been a real problem, and has perhaps led to an over-hastiness in seeking new policies every few years.

There have been major pieces of transport legislation every seven or eight years on average for the last forty years: 1930, 1933, 1947, 1953, 1962, 1968 are the most significant Acts, each seeking a fresh solution to the problems of control and co-ordination. They have almost entirely dealt with road and rail transport; other modes, such as water, both inland and coastal pipelines, and air, have not really been considered in the context of co-ordination, which is yet another indictment of policy as it has emerged. Such an amount of legislation at such frequent intervals raises obvious questions about the success of the various policies and the mechanisms which have been used to effectuate them. Almost every device that could be thought of has been used at one time or another in the pursuit of co-ordination: administrative tribunals, joint ownership, selective fiscal measures, capital write-offs, management reorganizations, financial objectives, centralization, decentralization, pricing instructions, and operational controls. Together, they represent a continuing intervention by governments in transport affairs. Even so, the extent of intervention should not be overestimated or overemphasized, since one of the salient reasons why recurrent new legislation has been needed is that market forces have continued to operate and have vitiated many of the instruments of control which have been set up. Indeed Britain has on the whole had less restrictive controls on transport than many other countries.

Before looking at the various phases of policy, one more general factor affecting policy must be mentioned. This has been the desire to protect the railways. In the days of rail monopoly, a vast network of regulation was imposed in the name of protection for the consumer. In the inter-war period, as the national mood swung from fear of monopoly to fear of 'wasteful' competition, governments assumed that the best balance would come from compensating controls over the competing industries, not from freeing the railways from their obligations. This attitude of protecting the railways, which has tended to persist throughout successive pieces of regulatory legislation, is based on two premises, of which the first is that the railways can be lower-cost suppliers than their rivals provided there is a sufficiently high throughput, and the second that it is better to utilize the surplus capacity of the railways than make new investments in other modes. Although respectable in themselves, these arguments are misconceived, since they ignore the tremendously diverse demand for transport services, particularly in their qualitative characteristics. As a result other modes have developed anyway and the railways' potential economies of intensive operation of large-scale enterprise have not been achieved. In fact it has been a characteristic of transport policy generally that demand considerations have been subordinated to considerations of supply.

II Co-ordination in Practice

There have been four main approaches to transport policy since the rise of the road industries, and the first three of these will now be briefly examined prior to a more extended look at the fourth, which is embodied in the Transport Act of 1968.

(a) *Pre-Nationalization: Anti-Competitive Regulation*

The first examination of co-ordination was made by the Royal Commission on Transport of 1928–30, which was requested to consider, as well as the possible regulation of the burgeoning road industries, 'the coordinated working and development' of 'the available means of transport in Great Britain'. The demand for such an enquiry arose not only from the need to consider public road safety, but also from the railways, which had fallen far short of the standard revenues that had been set for them by the Act of 1921. The commission found little difficulty or disagreement in dealing with traffic control or the regulation of public service vehicles; its problem was how to deal with the co-ordination of freight transport. Admitting it could see no positive solution it summed up the issue as follows:

> Broadly speaking, we have on the one hand organized undertakings [railways, waterways, shipping] bound by their statutes, agreements, rules, practices, and all other adjuncts which are associated with a highly organized business; while on the other hand we find that the goods branch of the road transport industry is in a condition which lacks all unity and is operated by a number of independent firms and individuals who, while endeavouring to

compete with other forms of transport, are at the same time engaged in bitter and uneconomic strife with each other in their own particular branch ... In our opinion the organization of the industry is an essential precedent to any attempt at general co-ordination with other forms of transport.[8]

Organization, to the commission, meant licensing, and preferably larger units. However, since the method could not be agreed to, the Salter Conference was set up with similar terms of reference, although it was also specifically instructed to safeguard the interests of trade and industry. The most influential evidence was from the long-distance hauliers formed in the newly organized RHA, and the result was the 1933 Act, creating a licensing system based on proof of need. Like the Commission, the Salter Conference made few recommendations on co-ordination, except to hope that there would be collaboration between road and rail;[9] ironically, one of their main areas of interest in this direction was in the use of containers. The Act did not do much to 'organize' the industry into the larger units which the Commission had clearly thought desirable, nor did it help the railways to compete more effectively. Admittedly a vehicle taxation system was created to help allocate the costs of highway building and maintenance, and some modification of the railways pricing system was permitted but, although the railways vigorously opposed many applications, the net result was to freeze the structure of the haulage industry rather than transfer traffics to the railways.

The Act did, however, as the Royal Commission had suggested, set up a Transport Advisory Council to assist in co-ordination. The Council made its first report in 1937, in which it suggested that while it would be impractical to allocate services, all forms of transport should be rate-controlled, with rate publication and non-discrimination; if stable rates could be established it thought co-ordination would be achieved. The proposal included having a Statutory Area Rates Committee in each area, but the problem of creating a set of road rates was not further examined, although the road and rail representatives agreed to set up joint conferences for rate-making purposes. The following year this concept was apparently reversed by the Square Deal Campaign of the railway companies, in which they sought to free themselves from some of their more onerous legal restrictions. However, the railways professed themselves no less willing to enter into voluntary rate agreements than previously. Trading interests, fearing higher prices, protested vociferously, and the railways were forced to modify their proposals. All proposals were, however, overtaken by the war, during which a good deal of experience of central control (if not co-ordination) was gained.

The arguments and activities of the decade of the 1930s show that co-ordination was equated with legal regulation, cartelization, and an antipathy to competition. This arose because the transition from the rail monopoly to road–rail competition happened very rapidly and its implications were not fully grasped. In the nineteenth century the law had been required to control monopoly in the public interest; it was by no means self-evident that transport should lose its public utility characteristics when competition arrived. At the same time there was no clear idea of what co-ordination meant, and certainly no recognition of the central role of costs. In so far as the price mechanism was thought to be a desirable means of allocation, it was within the context of continued cross-subsidization.

(b) *Nationalization—Integration by Common Ownership 1947–51*

The second major phase of co-ordination brings us more into the mainstream of the book, namely that which sought to use common ownership as the means of integrating the transport modes. Nationalization of transport had always been high on the Labour Party's list of priorities, and the apparent success of the London Passenger Transport Board gave some credence to the argument that integration through nationalization would mean greater efficiency. Just before nationalization overtook them the hauliers unavailingly offered to accept almost the full public service obligations of the railways—no discrimination, public carrier national rate structures, standard conditions—and also opened up various possibilities of technical co-ordination such as co-operative road and rail delivery services. This would have made the British situation akin to that in the United States. The main outlines of the 1947 Transport Act have already been described in earlier chapters: the obligation to provide an efficient, adequate and properly integrated system of public transport; the nationalization of rail and long-distance haulage; but the acceptance of user choice [10] and the omission of own account haulage from control, and of any rules of economic behaviour as guidelines for the Commission. Although it was recognized that a much closer price–cost relationship was a sine qua non if the railways were to compete effectively, it was not possible to present a new set of freight charges before 1955. Given this and free user choice, it was little use for the BTC to detail those traffics which were especially suitable for each form of transport in a statement of policy on the integration of freight services. To do this implied a knowledge about the economics of different types of traffic which did not really exist.

Integration had no real opportunity to work because most of the time was taken up in administrative reorganization and because virtually no money was available for investment; nevertheless, its beginnings were not auspicious. The BTC itself could not become involved in the allocation of traffics because its financial position did not permit it to do without the profits which the Road Haulage Executive was making. Indeed the cross-subsidization of rail by road seems to have been intended in the Act. In spite of attempts such as the provision of joint road and rail commercial services in East Anglia, the road and rail managements remained fiercely competitive with respect to each other, to say nothing of the unions, which were strongly against any handover of jobs, however much they might favour integration in principle. Moreover, the vast expansion of own account transport, and for that matter of private cars, took the BTC by surprise, since it had been thought that the Commission would dominate the whole transport scene.

Nationalization was in many respects a logical extension of the policy of the 1930s with respect to co-ordination. There was the same antipathy to competition, an uncritical acceptance of the regulations of that period, a loading on the agencies of even more obligations and a belief that 'organization' could solve economic problems. Co-ordination remained as elusive as ever, even if a start was made on trying to bring prices more into line with costs.

(c) *Co-ordination Through Competition 1951–64*

The return of a Conservative Government in 1951 heralded the third basic approach to transport policy, namely that competition, even if modified, will produce the best approximation to co-ordination. A White Paper in 1952 argued that there had been little progress towards a co-ordinated whole under the BTC, and that 'even if integration in the fullest sense were practicable, it would result in a huge unwieldy machine, ill-adapted to meet with promptitude the varying and instant demands of industry'.[11] Decentralization thus became the order of the day, not only of road haulage by denationalization, but also of the railways into semi-autonomous areas, such that 'the existence of these separate areas should encourage a healthy rivalry between them'.[12] However, the

White Paper also ruled out the possible results of competition by arguing: 'The railways are a national asset. They must remain an essential element in transport and cannot be allowed to fall into decay.'[13] The 1953 Transport Act also promoted competition by withdrawing most of the railways' statutory obligations, but on the other hand maintained the existing detailed controls over the road industries.

As we have noted, the promise of a safety-net was taken up by the railways to the point where they were losing over £100 million a year. The resultant deficit grant almost certainly outweighed the gains to the country of increased competition. BRS by this time was competing with the railways as enthusiastically as any private haulier, and the BTC had become much more a holding company than a co-ordinating agency.

Although the Stedeford Committee and the Select Committee on Nationalized Industries looked only at the railways, the implications of their reports were wider than this, since the 1962 Transport Act which followed them created a new structure for the nationalized transport sector, dismantling the BTC and splitting the railways away from the road industries. This was a further degree of decentralization, which was paralleled within the railways by the creation of regional railway boards with even more autonomy than the previous areas. At the same time almost all[14] the remaining legal obligations were removed from the railways so as to enable them to compete on equal terms, but it was recognized that this would necessitate a smaller system, and in place of the open-ended commitment, the White Paper mentioned a system 'of the right size'.[15] However, although a large amount of the accumulated financial deficit was either written off or suspended, the Government still left the railways with the obligation of maintaining their social service passenger lines as before, whilst admitting that in practice they would be paid for out of continuing deficit grants. The road industries, now in the THC, were given an injunction to perform as though a private enterprise, the most free-ranging terms of reference ever given to any of the nationalized industries. Co-ordination was not entirely forgotten. The Minister of Transport remained charged with overall co-ordination, including the co-ordination of investment, and to help him he was given a new advisory body, the Nationalized Transport Advisory Council, consisting basically of the various industry chairmen. No more specific remit was given to the NTAC.

During the Conservative era the move towards competition and freedom grew more pronounced as time went on. If the Geddes Committee on Carriers' Licensing and the Railway Reshaping Report had been carried out according to the intentions of their authors, competition would have been still further enhanced. Even so, the Conservatives did not manage to produce a more commercial attitude from the railways until the very end of their period of office. This was largely due to their own poor handling of investment, since the almost complete lack of criteria or planning in transport investment gave no incentive to the railways to improve their performance. The Conservatives also permitted increasing deficit grants, insisted on the maintenance of social obligations and by extension cross-subsidization, and interfered in railway operations far more than a policy of commercial freedom should have warranted.

(d) *The 1968 Transport Act—Selective Solutions*

On the return to power of the Labour Party in 1964, the situation in transport was clearly unsatisfactory. Since the 1968 Act to a much greater extent than preceding measures tried to tailor the solutions to fit the situation, albeit within an overall philosophy, it may be as well to recapitulate the essential issues which faced the new government:

(i) The 1962 Transport Act was clearly failing in its attempt to make the railways break even under a competitive formula; the financial deficit was not being appreciably reduced in spite of the drastic cutbacks recommended by the Reshaping Report, and to a considerable extent carried out. Nor was it clear that even more extensive reductions in services would necessarily achieve viability in conventional financial accounting terms.

(ii) In any case, despite the financial losses, the solution of retrenchment had been badly received by the public, industry and the unions. Although, as noted, a good deal of pruning has taken place, it has been only at the cost of considerable resistance by the various interested parties, and in practice even the Conservatives recoiled from the full logic of the Reshaping Report. Opposition intensified as clearly unremunerative operations were eliminated, leaving those for whose retention a good case could be made on social, regional or other grounds. There was therefore increasing pressure not to permit massive cutbacks in the size of the railways, but rather to guarantee a stable framework for the future and to find some new method of financing it.

M

(iii) In spite of the bleak general outlook for the railways, two exciting technical possibilities held out a promise that rail viability might ultimately be achieved. One was integrated freight transport by means of the container and the freightliner system, which promised greatly to reduce the transhipment costs of carriage by rail. The other, further into the future, was the development of the Advanced Passenger Train, which might enable rail to compete more effectively with air services and the private car over long distances. It therefore seemed premature for technological as well as social reasons to talk of closing down the railways.

(iv) Road passenger transport, although still viable overall, faced increasingly difficult physical operating conditions and continually declining demand. And as with the railways, social pressures prevented cutbacks in the services at a rate commensurate with the increases in cost and the fall in demand. The difficulties were worst in the cities where operating hardships exacerbated the financial problems, and in the deep rural areas where the sparse population also had a high level of car-ownership. In the worst position of all, London Transport, with losses of over £8 million annually on the buses, was directly funded from the Exchequer as a result of the Transport Finances Act of 1966.

(v) In road goods transport also a fluid situation was created by the findings of the Geddes Committee in 1965 that the licensing system was not fulfilling any of its original objectives, especially that of a 'better' balance between road and rail, and that it should be replaced. Although the Labour Government was unlikely to agree with its laissez faire conclusions, the Committee provided an excellent rationale for restructuring the controls over the industry.

(vi) In spite of these very significant issues in the public sector of transport, by far the most powerful force in transport was the explosion in private motoring, causing social problems which went beyond the limits of transport. The mileage driven by private cars almost trebled between 1957 and 1967, while forecasts of an increase in private-car ownership between 1967 and 1974 from 10 million to 16 million promised no respite for the future.[16] The worst impact of the problem came in the urban areas. In fact, there was a growing recognition, crystallized in the Buchanan Report, that the very nature of urban life would be changed if the demands for road space resulting from the vast growth of private motoring were to be met. These doubts about the desirability of providing unlimited road space were accompanied by a physical and financial inability to meet all the growing demands so that attention turned to mechanisms for allocating the available space. Priority, furthermore, was given to the building of the inter-city motorway system. Here, although the situation was not as bad as in the urban areas, it was calculated that in spite of increased spending the mileage of heavily overloaded trunk roads would rise by 50 per cent between 1966 and 1970.

(vii) All these points were given urgency by an increasing awareness of the importance of the transport infrastructure in producing a faster rate of economic growth. Although Britain had at last begun to invest in transport in the late 1950s after decades of stagnation, her efforts were still less than those of many comparable countries. Better communications became the sine qua non for faster growth, although this argument frequently degenerated into unthinking demands for more roads without regard to the rest of transport.

In *Transport Policy*, the first of its six White Papers on transport, the new Government laid down what it considered to be the basic themes of the new legislation:[17]

(i) the transport infrastructure and services (rail, road, ports, etc.) must be modernized. Since total resources are limited, this means planning investment as a whole, increasing productivity and developing better criteria to assist choice;

(ii) the problem of traffic conditions in towns must be given greater priority. Here again the solution lies in integrated planning. New machinery is needed for the conurbations, where the problem is most acute:

(iii) the transport system must take account of the social as well as the economic needs of the country;

(iv) public transport must play a key role in solving our transport problems. Publicly owned road and rail services must be integrated on a functional basis.

These themes covered at least four new approaches to the issue of transport policy. The first of these dealt with the role of planning, which in many respects represented a synonym for co-ordination.

The Labour Government had already promised in its election manifesto to draw up a national plan for transport. This was only one part of an overall commitment to central planning as a means of fostering economic growth. It had, in fact, taken the place of widespread nationalization as a means of controlling the economy; the threats to renationalize road haulage made in the middle 1950s were quickly forgotten. Planning is clearly a more flexible instrument than public ownership per se, and it does not imply that control is necessarily less complete. The commitment to planning and thereby to co-ordination in the context of transport and of the role of transport in the wider economy was strongly emphasized by Mrs Castle, the then Minister of Transport, in introducing the Second Reading of the Transport Bill in 1967:[18]

> As a socialist I believe that transport is a vital service to industry and to our people, and that, if economic planning or the physical planning of our environment is to mean anything at all, transport planning must form part of it. In the same way, transport services must be planned in relation to each other—not allowed to go their own sweet way regardless of consequences.

The second major premise was a recognition that the nature of the transport problem had itself changed. Previously the main issue had been to ensure correct resource allocation within public (i.e. for hire) freight transport; passenger services had been seen as essentially complementary rather than competitive, although of course this should not have prevented analysis to discover the optimum supply. Now, however, the main problem was posed by the motor car in the private passenger sector of transport. This had become by far the largest sector in transport and provided a challenge of which the implications went well beyond transport. The third premise followed largely from the second and from the argument that social as well as economic considerations must be taken into account. It was that private accounting costs might not be a suitable measuring rod for evaluating the efficiency of and need for transport. Social costs must be taken into account, if necessary through the device of direct subsidies. The fourth premise involved a new approach to transport policy. As opposed to assuming the modes to be separate industries, it took a functional approach, examining the end, namely the transportation of goods or passengers rather than the means by which this was done.

Of the many provisions of the Act, several were specifically designed to co-ordinate or integrate different modes of transport and hence are of particular interest here. The quantity licensing system in road haulage, the Passenger Transport Authorities to integrate conurbation public transport and the Freight Integration Council to give advice on the problems of the publicly owned freight agencies are perhaps the most obvious, and we shall examine their purpose and possibilities in more detail shortly. But there were also other measures designed to achieve co-ordination. Municipal bus operators were instructed to co-operate with any 'company' bus operators coming within their territory. On the freight side, changes were proposed for abnormal loads and heavy vehicles which were designed to make these traffics pay the true cost of road maintenance applicable to them. Although these last were dropped before becoming law, they did represent a move in the direction of making the user pay the true cost of his service, which is the essence of the efficient use of resources. The very idea of the National Freight Corporation was to co-ordinate those public agencies concerned with moving freight at least partly by road which had previously operated within individual industry limits. On a wider basis, the Act contained an important section decentralizing powers to deal with traffic, part of the purpose of this being, as the White Paper noted, that the Minister would require local authorities to prepare plans for handling the traffic problem in their locality, and that particular attention should be paid to balancing the competing needs of private and public transport, safety, accessibility, environmental amenity and pedestrians. Finally, the White Paper, if not the Act itself, noted the need to integrate transport planning with land use and general planning. Even outside these overtly co-ordinating intentions, almost all the policy expressed in the Act dealt with compensatory mechanisms, especially those designed to ensure the viability of rail and bus undertakings.

In spite of the wide-ranging statements of policy and the numerous mechanisms set up to balance various aspects of transport, the Government's approach was by no means all-embracing. It is clear that no single Act could have achieved everything involving transport in the objectives. Indeed, there were many complaints that this immensely long Act, the longest passed in modern British history, dealt with far too many topics for a single piece of legislation. This very fact is an indication that in spite of the inter-connection between its constituent parts, transport is too widely spread an activity to be susceptible to anything other than very complex solutions. As it was, a considerable part of the legislation consisted of skeletal enabling powers to be fleshed in with more detailed policy at a later date. Nevertheless if the Act was to be the basis for transport policy as a whole, there were several notable omissions. The Act did nothing to bring domestic air transport into the inland transport equation, in spite of the considerable interaction between surface and air transport, which will certainly increase with developments in technology such as the Advanced Passenger Train. Similarly, port and coastal shipping policy was not given the same close attention as that given to land-based transport modes. But more important were the problems left in relating surface transport modes, particularly those of investment criteria and social costs. For all the talk in the White Papers of developing better criteria for investment, there is still no means of relating the amounts of capital going to the different modes, especially road and rail. The crude criteria at present in use point to very high returns on road construction, rising as high as 50 per cent and certainly far higher than the railways can aspire to. But since they are based on savings in travelling time, vehicle operating costs and the cost of accidents, these criteria do not provide a real test of commercial viability such as is demanded of the railways. Moreover road construction and maintenance is undertaken by many different authorities. To overcome these problems some have suggested a National Roads Corporation to operate as a nationalized industry and use equivalent financial standards and methods of measurement. But to do this would imply some capacity for road pricing, which brings us to the second problem, namely that roads are still not treated as economic resources. Until this problem is solved, and it is intimately related to the investment issue in that demand patterns and hence apparent rates of return would be radically changed by a road-pricing mechanism, it is arguable that the whole of passenger transport demand will be distorted. Subsidies to public transport can act as a partial substitute for road pricing, but they will do little to curb congestion and will in any case become increasingly onerous given an almost inevitable cost escalation in the labour-intensive public transport sector. Thus although the Act (or rather the White Papers preceding it) recognized the main problems of transport as being those of integrating the private car and the road system into the total transport network, the solutions proposed fell far short of dealing with them. Indeed, in its proposals for action, the Government went so far as to say that 'The evolution of a new policy for the railways has been at the centre of the Government's whole transport planning.'[19] Since the railways supply only just over 10 per cent of the country's transport needs, this was over-emphasizing a relatively small part of the total.

But within its areas of activity the Act was probably the best economic policy yet devised. It steered clear of the two simplistic extremes of integration merely by the act of nationalization on the one hand and undirected competition based solely on private accounting costs on the other hand and thereby promised to quieten, if by no means to still, some of the arid arguments which have bedevilled the transport scene since the war. These in any case have lost some of their relevance by the blurring of the lines between industries, the emphasis on function rather than mode and the recognition in the Act that co-ordinating mechanisms must be differentiated according to purpose. As a result a range of different mechanisms—administrative, organizational, licensing, and fiscal—was constructed, but both the level and the incidence of these was selective. Thus the bureaucratic direction of traffic by special authorization was put side by side with greatly increased competitive opportunities; indeed competition and choice were generally accepted as desirable. Mr Marples' experiment with the holding company concept was cheerfully accepted and extended. Decentralization of accountability was similarly adopted as providing a more accurate means of financial control. As a result cross-subsidization was in general discouraged. It was realized that co-ordination must take place at the local as well as the national level, and that some powers must be developed from the national to the local level for this purpose. Financial viability was accepted as a desirable objective for public corporations whilst providing, through subsidies, a means for reconciling this with necessary social obligations. Altogether the result was much the most pragmatic piece of transport legislation yet devised, and provided a policy which blended the commercial and social facets of transport better than in almost any other country.

Whether the mechanisms which were set up will be successful is quite another matter. In spite of the Act's attempts to provide means of integration, the whole concept is still far from clear.[20] The mechanisms certainly will not operate automatically, as can be illustrated by taking a closer look at three, namely quantity licensing, the Passenger Transport Authorities, and the Freight Integration Council.

(i) QUANTITY LICENSING

Of all the provisions of the Act, undoubtedly the most controversial was that concerning quantity licensing, by which the Licensing Authorities would be given the right to issue special authorizations for certain types of road goods traffics, notably all those being transported more than 100 miles on vehicles of more than 16 tons plated weight, and for certain bulk commodities over shorter hauls, only if there were no appeal from either British Rail or the NFC that the haul could be done more efficiently by rail. In the latter instance the Authority would have the task of deciding on the merits of the cases put forward.

The proposal raised important questions both of principle and criteria for operation. The White Paper explaining quantity licensing disavowed any undue bias to rail, saying 'it is not the Government's intention that the licensing system should be capable of being used as a means of diverting traffic to rail uneconomically'.[21] This invited the immediate response that 'the normal forces of competition are sufficient to ensure that all traffic which is suitable for rail will go there without any need for any additional pressures from licensing'.[22] The Government had to admit that this would be the case in the long run, but felt that 'there will often be a natural reluctance by consignors to alter their habitual arrangements for the transport of their goods ... Inertia and habit will play their part and some consignors may not even be aware of the advantage to them of the new rail services, nor of the true economic cost of their present arrangements.'[23] This suggested that consignors did not know what was good for them, and even if this might in some cases be true,[24] it meant abandoning the old-established practice of user freedom of choice.

But if the principle was controversial, the practice threatened to be even worse. An extremely cumbersome bureaucracy would be necessary to administer the system, with economic assessors to assist in the evaluation of the evidence. The criteria laid down in Section 74(2) were to be 'speed, reliability, cost and such other matters relevant to the needs of the person for whom the goods in question are to be carried as may be prescribed', together with other regulations as might be made by the Minister. Numerous problems emerged from this definition. Ostensibly, cost to the consumer was whatever price the transport undertaking cared to charge, but this raised issues about the costs on which the price would be based. Should the railways be permitted to charge on a short-run basis, effectively ignoring their fixed costs beyond the period of the contract, or should they be made to adhere to some 'fully distributed cost' system of charging, which would be far from economic due to differing elasticities in the sub-sectors of the market? On the other side, should hauliers be permitted to price on a marginal basis, since many would have been left with surplus capacity if quantity licensing had been introduced? But perhaps the key problem in costing would have been that of determining a proper rate for own account haulage to compare with the rail rate. Even costing, however, would have been easy compared with measuring the quality variables of speed, reliability and so on, and we have seen that these are generally more important than price. At the very least a highly complex set of legal case-laws would have emerged to provide general standards for determining cases. Outside the licensing system itself, there were suggestions that the response of hauliers might be to avoid having to apply for authorizations by devices such as using smaller vehicles or transhipping en route to avoid going more than 100 miles. This sort of activity would clearly have lowered net efficiency in the transport market as a whole.

Such were the difficult questions involved that it is perhaps as well that the quantity licensing system will in all probability not now go ahead. The new Conservative Government has promised not to implement it, but even before this the Labour Government had shown no undue haste to introduce it, since it had been recognized to be dependent on a development of the Freightliner network far beyond what has been achieved in practice. Thus the introduction of quantity licensing would have meant a clumsy system with only small returns for the railways. Nevertheless the railways would still like the selective introduction of some aspects of quantity licensing, for instance for bulk aggregates,[25] even though their partners, the NFC, have made clear their dislike of the whole idea.[26] This latter attitude may partly be because BRS would have been one of the worst hit companies; the Reshaping Report noted that 7·4 million tons, or 45 per cent of the total tonnage carried by BRS at that time, was suitable for carriage by rail.[27]

(ii) THE FREIGHT INTEGRATION COUNCIL

The Freight Integration Council was set up to advise on the integration of freight within the state sector including the airlines, waterways and the Post Office, as well as its main preoccupations, the NFC and the BRB. Bodies such as the FIC have not been notably successful in the past—the Nationalized Transport Advisory Council met only twice—and it is difficult to foresee a much better fate in this instance. The reason is simple. Even in the state sector the managerial drive towards a high throughput and revenue operates so that none will easily relinquish a market share already obtained. This was evident as between BRS and BR under the British Transport Commission, and it has been no less true since the companies were separated in 1962. It was perhaps symptomatic of the relationship that when the railways wrote strong recommendations to the Geddes Committee on Road Haulage Licensing, it was the Transport Holding Company which made a sharp response on behalf of the haulage industry. Since the 1964 Act a similar division of view has already arisen between the BRB and the NFC over a number of issues.

The BRB made it clear in its 1969 Report that it resents having to hire road vehicles from the NFC or elsewhere for wagonload traffics requiring cartage to destination with the implication being that it would prefer its own, and also made clear its feeling that since the essence of the Freightliner service is the trunk haul, 'the present basis of ownership reverses what would normally be the commercial relationship between the two partners'.[28] The NFC, not unexpectedly, did not support these suggestions, which 'in its view were not only contrary to the remit under the Act about integration, but also destructive of any real possibility of getting rid of the heavy loss on public freight services generally'.[29] But one of the main areas where the two clash is parcels and this was the first task given to the FIC to tackle, as an area where the problem is too much, not too little, competition. The parcels business amounted to some £150 million in 1969; of this £130 million was in the public sector, split 40 per cent to the NFC subsidies, National Carriers Limited and the old BRS Parcels group, 38 per cent to the Post Office, and 22 per cent to the railways. There was a considerable net loss by NCL, the Post Office and the rail express parcels, with only the BRS-Tayforth group making a profit, and that only of some £500,000. The total loss of all taken together could well be in the region of £30 million, with a considerable degree of excess capacity, and it is hardly surprising that some degree of co-ordination was thought desirable. The FIC pointed out in its annual report that 'there is considerable overlap, and a risk, which is increasing, of duplicated investment and marketing effort.'[30] The Council pointed out the need for closer co-ordination, which would enable the undertakings to make the best use of their collection and delivery fleets, and aggregate the traffic into concentrated flows for the trunk haul between the main centres. It therefore suggested that the Post Office, BRB and NFC 'should endeavour to negotiate a commercially satisfactory solution to the problem, in which the marketing, investment and operational aspects of the four parcels businesses are re-organized to the benefit of the national economy and business.'[31] The logic of the situation, as *The Times* pointed out,[32] was that the NFC should be the single entity providing the bulk of the public sector service, while small parcels could stay with the Post Office. However, this could hardly be acceptable to the railways, so long as the service pays more than its short-run marginal costs, irrespective of any fully distributed cost accounting losses.[33] Such a suggestion is hardly likely, moreover, to emerge from the FIC itself, since the Council includes among its nine members the chairmen of the BRB and the NFC and also representatives of the unions concerned: unanimity would seem almost impossible, except in the most general terms. The bland statement noted above illustrates the weakness of the FIC; it can be little more than a forum for discussion instead of a genuinely advisory body. No report was issued during 1971, and at the time of writing it is uncertain whether any further reports will be issued. Certainly there has been no move into fresh areas of investigation. Thus if solutions are to be found, they would seem to require imposition on the Minister's initiative rather than merely hoping that the parties will achieve agreement themselves.

(iii) THE PASSENGER TRANSPORT AUTHORITIES

The Passenger Transport Authorities originated from three propositions: that the growth of conurbations necessitated a more up-to-date public transport structure than the frozen boundaries of the 1930 Act permitted; that unless public transport gets more recognition from and integration into the other aspects of local authority planning the private car would swamp the cities; and that the scale of operations and thus of financial responsibility in public transport should be the choice of the people using the services. The concept is not new; the London Passenger Transport Board of 1933 provided a successful precedent, while other conurbations, including those based on Liverpool and Manchester which now have such authorities, considered them in the 1930s. The duties of the PTAs are to provide 'a properly integrated and efficient system of public transport to meet the needs of the area'.[34] By a narrow definition this meant being responsible for public transport as such, the railway commuter lines, municipal companies, and any 'company' bus operators, and ferries, but the Labour Government recognized that this was not in itself sufficient: 'The basic defects of the present situation are that the main elements in the transport system—public transport, road building and maintenance, and traffic control—are separately planned and financed; that transport as a whole is not being integrated into the general planning of conurbations . . .'.[35] Going further, the Government admitted: 'In the long-term the right solution seems likely to be found in the establishment in these areas of single authorities with responsibilities covering land use, highways, traffic and public transport.'[36] Thus the first problem of the PTAs arises from the fact that they do not meet this need; not only are the PTAs far from constituting such authorities in that they only cover public transport, but they do not even have similar boundaries with other authorities with complementary powers.[37]

Admittedly, it was recognized that fundamental change must await local government reform, but even the Royal Commission on Local Government did not directly address itself to this problem.[38]

Even as public transport undertakings, however, the PTAs seem likely to face difficulties, largely arising from financial issues and from the fact that they must co-operate with the BRB and NBC. Since all the bus services when taken over were losing money and since the PTAs will eventually have to take over full responsibility for rail commuter lines, which are also losing money, there has been a need for a precept on the rates, the power for which is granted in the Act. The Authorities were most unfortunate in being inaugurated at a time of rapidly rising costs; the ensuing financial problems may not have been their fault, but this has not saved them from being accused of profligacy. Moreover, although the precept on the rates will naturally cover the whole area, the bus services of the Executive do not serve all the people; on Tyneside, for instance, they serve less than half at the time of writing, so that many people will be paying for services they do not receive.

Two other important financial issues will also arise. One is that the railways are likely to be viewed with disfavour because of the costs they will impose,[39] even though on a social cost–benefit analysis their value would be enhanced by their effect in helping to reduce congestion. Admittedly, because of the different fixed to variable cost ratios between bus and rail and their different contributions to congestion, there is a case for making maximum use of the rail services if it is decided to retain them, but retention may well be too expensive for many of the lines. The Tyneside PTA has looked at an all-bus service, with the possibility of taking over rail tracks for fast buses. The decision of the Conservative Government to end the £15 million subsidy to the London commuter services makes it very unlikely that an appeal to Central Government for a continued subsidy in the PTAs will be successful. With less favourable demand elasticities than in London, the future of the PTA rail services looks bleak. The balance against rail will be further tipped by the continued availability of 75 per cent Central Government grants for most urban road construction.

The second issue is likely to come in relations with the NBC. The 1967 White Paper, *Public Transport and Traffic*, specifically noted that:

> The agreements between the Executives and the NBC companies must not destroy the basis on which the NBC companies

can operate profitably. The NBC companies will be maintaining a wide range of services outside the main towns: on many of these the level of profits is inevitably low, and they will need a proportion of more profitable urban routes if the "mix" of their services is to enable them to be viable undertakings.[40]

This appeal to permit the NBC companies to continue cross-subsidization may not be favourably regarded,[41] especially since the fares per mile of the NBC companies are already higher than those of most municipal or PTA undertakings. PTAs already claim that they are subject to double taxation, having to meet local and national taxes to subsidize transport, and would claim that a further element of subsidy is excessive. In any case, as the Merseyside Statement of Policy has indicated, so long as it is necessary to issue a rate precept to cover an operating deficit, it must be expected that ratepayers will look to the Authority to provide them with broadly comparable standards of service at similar prices.[42] Since they rather than the Traffic Commissioners will have power to control fares in their areas the Authorities can insist on a rationalization of fares or the granting of concessions, even if some difficulties are caused for the NBC companies and their financial targets. What is effective co-ordination inside the Authority may cause the reverse outside. Because of this, the agreements which must be negotiated between the PTAs and their NBC counterparts may be difficult to achieve. The different criteria for financial success will be only one problem. Another may be the desire of the PTA or rather its Executive to operate all the services within its area.[43]

A last point about the PTAs is whether they may not be too large to be efficient. This relates to the argument put forward in the White Paper, *Transport Policy*, that the efficiency of bus operation in many areas is hampered by the small size of the undertakings.[44] However, elsewhere it is admitted that there is a finite limit to any economies of scale in bus operation, probably at around a thousand buses.[45] Since the PTAs have far more than this number, subsidiary undertakings or divisions have been set up, but this seems to vitiate the original argument in favour of integration.

In summary, although they do represent an undoubted step forward as a co-ordinating mechanism, the PTAs face many different problems, and cannot as they stand be the only answer to the undoubtedly difficult problems of urban transport co-ordination and efficiency. These three examples have not been taken merely to criticize the 1968 Act. As has already been said, it is considerably the best reasoned and most constructive piece of legislation in the transport field yet. The three co-ordinating mechanisms mentioned are probably as good as anything that could be devised for the purposes intended, but their very imperfections point up the very great difficulties of co-ordination as a concept.

III Conclusion

The inclusion of transport as part of an 'umbrella' Ministry of the Environment in the governmental reshuffle by the incoming Conservative administration in 1970 is an acceptance of a role for transport far wider than its own traditional sector, and certainly far wider than the ambit of nationalization. How this role can be stated in economic terms by the interaction of political, social and geographical terms it is fortunately beyond the task of this chapter to attempt, but it is clear that wider considerations such as Common Market transport policy, the needs of the development areas or the desire to maintain a British airframe industry will continue to be as important as narrower economic factors. Perhaps more important still, environmental considerations will need to be taken into account. Thus while the Conservatives came into power in 1970 with the intention of introducing tighter commercial standards, in practice there has been a retreat from these towards subsidies for various parts of public transport as an attempt to achieve a better balance between public and private transport. Part of this change has resulted from a notable swing away from urban motorways on both environmental and increasingly on cost grounds, and part from a recognition that public transport would be reduced to an unacceptable degree without help.[46]

At the same time, economic methodology holds out little hope of determinate solutions even to the problems of measurement over such a different range of interlinked activities as transport presents. Thus although some aspects of a 'total sum' approach to transport co-ordination may become easier with the development of computerization and systems analysis, the 'true' co-ordination of the self-regulating market will remain a chimera over transport as a whole, even if an approximation to it is achieved in some areas. Policy and institutions will be needed to make choices which the market cannot make, although the function of nationalization as a centralized co-ordinating mechanism seems likely to continue to diminish and be replaced by local responsibility for co-ordination.

Within the nationalized industries themselves, however, progress towards a degree of conformity with the 1967 rules may be expected, especially in so far as specific direct subsidies take the place of deficit grants and cross-subsidization to maintain social services, since this means that the nationalized sector will have to price and cost in line with its private substitutes.

One continuing development within transport worth emphasizing is the disparity between passenger and freight transport which has emerged in recent years. Since the 1953 Transport Act there has been a trend towards less regulation in freight transport, a trend which was continued by the abolition of licensing by proof of need in the 1968 Act but partly reversed by quantity licensing. Now that quantity licensing is not to be introduced, however, the freight market has become almost completely free and competitive except in certain corners, such as the remaining subsidies to the BTC and the protection for coastal shipping against unfair rail competition. This is an almost unique situation anywhere in the world, and even if it does not represent co-ordination in the narrow sense in which we have defined it, since many issues such as that of track costs remain to be resolved, economic market forces are without question the primary influence on performance.

Passenger transport, however, presents many greater problems. If a private accounting cost system can be made to work in freight, this seems very dubious on the passenger side. It is passenger transport which occasions most of the high social costs of congestion and pollution (although heavy lorries must not be forgotten in this respect), it is the passenger sector which gives rise to a social welfare demand for services (although there is also a demand for subsidized freight shipping to the islands), it is primarily the private car which creates an almost inexhaustible call on capital investment, and, of course, there are the major problems of introducing a price mechanism. Even within the public sector of passenger transport, the extent of co-ordination is highly unsatisfactory. There are currently differential obligations between the various operators, with the NBC and BEA being expected over wide areas to cross-subsidize some services from the profits of others, the BRB being in part purely competitive, in part subsidized by the national government, while the PTAs are expected to use public transport as a tool of conurbation planning and to pay any consequent costs. The fact that passenger services are on the whole complementary rather than competitive does not justify unequal burdens in the areas where they are competitive. Above all, the twin problems remain of controlling the private car and how (or whether) to provide for those without cars, and these are more political than economic decisions. Even free public transport, although it would alleviate some urban problems at a considerable cost, would not be suitable for those with increasingly complex concentric rather than radial journeys to make. There is also an organizational problem on the passenger side in that transport responsibility is both becoming increasingly localized and also analogous to such welfare services as education, public health and housing. The more such developments continue, the more difficult it will become to operate in the manner of other nationalized industries, for even though there is no inherent reason why a nationalized industry should not act as a contractor for local authorities, in practice the implications for pricing policy and managerial control in dealing with such bodies are likely to be very different from those dealing direct with the consumer.

In spite of the divergence of freight and passenger policies, the two must inevitably interact, since it would be facile to pretend that there is no economic connection between them; especially on the railways and in road investment decision, the interdependence of the two is very high. The operation of a free market in the one, but the growth of a highly protective interventionist market in the other are not ultimately compatible. Thus road haulage would gain greatly from new urban motorways even if these were built to assuage the private car, while the railways' grant-aided services are of some assistance in paying the fixed costs of rail freight. The goal of co-ordination must not only be to co-ordinate functional sub-sectors, but also to relate them to each other.

A final point to be made about policy is that the 1968 Transport Act is unlikely to be the final word in transport organization, even though if there is one thing that all forms of transport would like, it is a period of respite from changes in government policy, and an opportunity to consolidate policies of their own. Even if party politics do not dictate organizational or financial restructuring, changes in the environmental, technological and economic situations are likely to do so. There have been predictions of a transport revolution in the next few decades as significant as that which accompanied the Industrial Revolution. The Advanced Passenger train, the jumbo jet for both freight and passengers, nuclear ships, the vertical takeoff and landing aircraft for city centre flights and the dial-a-bus system for suburban public transport are extensions of current technology. Tracked hovercraft, urban monorails, personal autogyros, nuclear airships, computer control of motorway

TRANSPORT POLICY 345

traffic, electric cars and autotaxis are more or less futuristic projects which involve considerable advances in technology. As realistic possibilities, however, they will have a considerable impact on the future of transport, and particularly on the relationship between the different modes of transport. Economics will be a critical factor; much of the future of transport will depend on how much society is willing to pay for mobility. But other considerations must also be taken into account; the quality of the environment, as affected by transport-generated pollution, congestion and demands on space, is perhaps the most important. All in all, transport in the future will have to change its organization at a rapid rate to keep pace with new demands and new technology, and this will make the task of policy in co-ordinating such developments as difficult as it has always been.

NOTES TO CHAPTER 6

1. Nor is it proposed to enter into the 'second-best' argument with regard to the overall distribution of resources between those who said that following welfare rules in one sector only might not improve overall welfare and those who think that working towards a welfare solution within a single sector will be advantageous.
2. This is not the place to deal with the various ideas that have been put forward in this context. There is a fairly extensive literature, and the reader is in particular referred to: J. R. Sargent, *British Transport Policy* (Oxford University Press, 1957); C. Foster, *The Transport Problem* (Blackie, 1963); and H. M. Kolsen, *The Economics and Control of Road–Rail Competition* (Sydney University Press, 1968, Sydney).
3. See H. O. Mance, 'The Perennial Question of Coordination', *Journal of the Institute of Transport*, January 1951; and Sargent, op. cit.
4. There has of course been a great deal of discussion of the practicability of road pricing, including investigations by the Road Research Laboratory. The Prices and Incomes Board has argued that the time has now come for practical trials lasting several years (NBPI, Report No. 159, *London Transport Fares*, Cmnd. 4540: HMSO, November 1970); and the Government announced in February 1971 that practical experiments involving 5,000 invited motorists will soon begin. The method will be electronic: a black box will be fitted beneath vehicles, and on entering a taxed zone an impulse will be transmitted to a central computer from a strip in the road, thus providing a metering device not unlike the telephone system. Many problems still remain, however, and road pricing is still many years from general introduction, if indeed it is ever possible.
5. £609 million for both maintenance and new construction in 1969; £391 million of this was on trunk road construction.
6. This is not to deny that transport operators can put forward an economic

case for cross-subsidization based upon problems of cost allocation and administrative simplicity.
7. D. L. Munby, 'Mrs Castle's Transport Policy', *Journal of Transport Economics and Policy*, May 1968, p. 136.
8. Royal Commission on Transport, *The Coordination and Development of Transport* (Cmnd. 3751: HMSO, 1931), p. 92.
9. The conference did recommend that 'the Minister of Transport should obtain powers to prohibit by regulation classes of traffic which are borne by rail and which having regard to the character of the commodity and the distance together, are unsuitable for road haulage, from being transferred in future to the road'. No attempt was made to define what 'unsuitable' meant, and the idea was not taken any further, at least until the 1968 Act.
10. This acceptance was not, however, absolute. Section 3 (2) of the Act stated 'Where the Commission are for the time being providing regular goods transport services of different kinds available between the same points, it shall be their duty to allow any person . . . freedom to choose such of the services so provided as he considers most suitable for his needs.' 'For the time being' could be read to mean that a planned solution would ultimately eliminate the less efficient service.
11. *Transport Policy* (Cmnd. 8538: HMSO, 1952), p. 2.
12. ibid., p. 3.
13. ibid.
14. Those remaining were the Transport Tribunal in the London area and protection for coastal shipping.
15. *Reorganization of the Nationalized Transport Undertakings* (Cmnd. 1248: HMSO, December 1960), p. 3.
16. These are the estimates used for preparing the White Papers. See *Railway Policy* (Cmnd. 3439: HMSO, 1967), Appendix G.1. Another way of measuring the increase is by a breakdown of private consumption expenditure. Private spending on motoring was 9 p of every pound in 1968 as against 5 p ten years earlier.
17. *Transport Policy* (Cmnd. 3027: HMSO, 1966), p. 31.
18. Parl. Deb. 5th Ser. Vol. 756, Col. 1281–2, 1967.
19. *Railway Policy*, p. 1.
20. Mr S. C. Robbins, the BRB Executive Director for freight, blamed the imprecise wording of the Act for what he called the 'virtual unworkability in practice' of the integration provisions. He commented 'After nearly two years we have not progressed beyond the stage of debating what the words mean' (*Financial Times*, 10 November 1970). On the other hand it could be argued that the concept is not susceptible to clear definition. This is the position taken by the first report of the National Freight Corporation, 1970, esp. ch. IV.
21. *The Transport of Freight* (Cmnd. 3470: HMSO, 1967), p. 15.
22. ibid., p. 16.
23. ibid.
24. See Sharp, C., *The Allocation of Freight Traffic—A Survey* (Ministry of Transport: HMSO, 1970).

TRANSPORT POLICY

25. BRB, *Annual Report*, 1969. p. 10.
26. NFC, *Annual Report*, 1969, pp. 16–17. The NFC stated 'Certainly it would be wrong to attempt to "integrate" by the arbitrary and often unnatural "allocation" or "direction" of traffics in detail, regardless of economics.'
27. Reshaping Report, p. 90.
28. BRB, *Annual Report*, 1969, p. 2.
29. NFC, *Annual Report*, 1969, p. 20.
30. Freight Integration Council, *Annual Report*, 1970, p. 7.
31. ibid.
32. 24 September 1970.
33. Or for that matter to the Post Office, which is investing in mechanized handling of parcels in the expectation of a high throughput.
34. Section 9 (3).
35. *Transport Policy*, p. 13.
36. ibid., p. 14.
37. Even if there were such similar bodies, co-ordination would be far from easy. An attempt was made in London to solve the problem by the creation of a co-ordinating council headed by the Minister of Transport himself, but it could not overcome the basic defects of divided responsibility and lack of executive power. See *Evidence of London Transport Board to the Select Committee on Nationalized Industries—Ministerial Control*, 10 May 1967. On the other hand, some authorities have commissioned studies, e.g. the Merseyside Area Land Use/Transportation Study to act as a broad basis for future planning.
38. *Report of Royal Commission on Local Government in England* (Cmnd. 4040: HMSO, 1969).
39. The approximate financial deficits of the commuter services in 1971 were: SELNEC (Manchester) £5 million; Merseyside (Liverpool) £2 million; West Midlands (Birmingham) £2.5 million; Tyneside (Newcastle) £1.5 million. Up to the beginning of 1972 the total subsidy for the rail commuter lines was paid by the Central Government, but thereafter the PTEs were due to pay an extra 10 per cent of the loss every year, with obvious implications for rate support.
40. op. cit., p. 12.
41. The injunction is in any case paradoxical since the PTEs are instructed not to practice cross-subsidization within their own undertakings (*Public Transport and Traffic*, p. 7).
42. Joint Statement of Merseyside PTA and PTE, 1970, p. 12.
43. In one instance, North Western Road Car, an NBC subsidiary, has been partly taken over by the SELNEC PTE, with the other part being distributed among other NBC companies. However, it is not yet clear what will happen to other NBC services in PTE areas.
44. op. cit., p. 13.
45. ibid., p. 6.
46. Inevitably the various services try to show that their subsidies are good value for money by comparing themselves with other public expenditures. Thus the NBC, in its 1970 Report, showed a map of Cumberland

illustrating the wide range of routes for which its subsidiary, Cumberland Motor Services, was seeking £13,000 subsidy and comparing these with the Carlisle–Barrow railway line, for which the railways receive a subsidy of £365,000. The railways for their part, have compared the relatively 'low' cost of their subsidy with the spiralling costs of the Concorde project.

INDEX

Advanced Passenger Train, 30, 118, 155, 191, 206, 330, 333
Affinity charter, 39–40, 84, 85
Aircraft industry, 42, 62–3, 82, 99, 115
Aircraft procurement, 60–6, 72, 73, 82, 88–9, 91, 116
Aircraft utilization, 95–8
  in BEA 54–5, 57, 74
  in BOAC, 75, 76
Air fares, 102–12
  advanced purchase, 84–5, 108–9
  difference between domestic and international, 60, 66–9, 121n
  'open-rate' situation, 84–5
  regulation of, 43, 45, 51, 66–72, 84–5, 106
Air freight, 51, 55, 75, 85
Air safety, 42, 45, 114
Air Transport Advisory Council, 45
Air Transport Licensing Board, 45, 52–3, 60, 84, 114, 115, 117
  on cross-subsidization, 69–70
  regulation of domestic tariffs, 66–70, 102
Air trunk routes, 38
Airways Board, 52–3, 91, 93, 100
Aldcroft, D. H., 207n
Alexander, N. J. B., 210n
Allen, G. F., 211n
Ashfield, Lord, 9

Balance of Payments, 62, 83, 89, 114
  civil aviation contribution to, 37
Barnes, Alfred, 10
Baumol, W. J., 209n

Bayliss, B. T. (and Edwards, S. L.), 259n, 262n
Beeching, Lord, 135, 136, 138, 139, 144, 149, 181, 183, 191, 194, 200, 201
Beesley, M. E. (and Politi, J.), 299
——— (and Foster, C. D.), 211
Bermuda Agreement, 42–3
Boeing 747 (see also Jumbo jet), 46, 48, 52, 77, 89, 95, 96, 97
  BOAC delay in introduction of, 83, 91
Briggs, G. W., 262n
British Air Services, 53, 71
British Airways Board (see also Airways Board)
  functions of, 100–1, 114
British Caledonian Airways, 53, 60, 80, 86, 115, 122n
  restrictions on service frequency, 67, 70
British Eagle, 60, 67, 121n
British Electric Traction, 269, 270, 307
British European Airways (BEA), Chapter 2 *passim*
  aircraft fleet, 56–8, 73
  compensation for loss of revenue, 63–4, 65, 72
  cross-subsidization, 343
  financial performance, 56–61
  labour force, 57–8, 74
  loss on domestic services, 59–60, 66–67, 69, 70–1, 120n
  operational characteristics, 54–61
British Overseas Airways Corporation, Chapter 2 *passim*

British Overseas Airways Corporation, (cont'd)
  aircraft fleet, 77, 89
  Boadicea, 30
  competitive indices, 80-6
  financial crisis, 77, 87, 116
  financial performance, 77-80
  financial reconstruction, 79, 83, 86-7
  formation, 8, 11
  labour force, 77-8
  operational characteristics, 75-80
British Rail, 2, 29, 30, 255, 258, 297, 335, 337, 338, Chapter 3 passim
  cost structure, 176-9
  costing and pricing in practice, 164-73
  efficiency, 181-200
  financial performance, 140
  future prospects, 203-7
  history, 124-40
British Road Services, 268, 337, Chapter 4 passim
  economies of scale, 234-5
  financial performance, 251-2
  formation, 219
  impact on industry, 255-6
  markets, 230-1
  pricing policy, 244
  structure, 227-8
British South American Airways, 44
British Steel Corporation, 23, 28
British Transport Commission, 15, 16, 25, 131, 132, 134, 135, 218, 270, 271, 278, 327, 328, 337, 343
British United Airways, 53, 60, 67

Cabotage routes, 84, 91
Campbell, J., 209n
Cartwright, W. F., 208n
Caves, R. E., 119n
Central Electricity Generating Board, 149, 187
Charter services, 44, 81, 84, 85
Cheap Trains Act, 1883, 126
Chester, D. N., 15, 277

Chicago Convention, 39, 42
Chisholm, M., 262n
Civil Aviation Act (1971), 36, 100, 114
Civil Aviation Authority, 53, 103, 114-15
Civil Aviation Industry,
  description, 37
  licensing in, 45
  reasons for regulation, 41-5, 107
Civil Aviation (Licensing) Act 1960, 45
Cole, G. D. H., 5, 9
Committee of Inquiry into Civil Air Transport (Edwards Committee), 36, 41, 43, 48, 50, 52, 66, 71, 92, 93, 100, 117, 119n, 120n, 121n, 122n
  and the 'Buy British' policy, 63-4
Company trains, 187
Competition
  between airlines, 40, 42-4, 51-2, 55, 59-60, 67-70, 74, 80-86, 92, 106, 110, 112
  between airlines and surface operators, 38, 42, 60, 67-8, 106-107, 156
  between bus and private car, 283-5
  between road and rail, 127, 144-153, 258
Concorde, 29, 80, 118
Containers, 188, 247-8
Cook, W. R., 152
Coombes, 32n
Cooper, M. H., 119n
Co-ordination in transport, 24-5, 42, Chapter 6 passim
  The concept of co-ordination, 316-17
  Factors inhibiting co-ordination, 317-24
  Co-ordination in practice, 324-42
  Future of co-ordination, 342-5
Corbett Report on BOAC, 83
Corporate Plan (Railways), 169, 189, 190, 196

INDEX

Costs
  airlines, 48, 49, 103–5, 122n
  operating, 41, 46, 48, 56–6, 76–9, 94–5
  fixed, 56
  capital (of aircraft), 46, 49, 56, 95, 98
  seat-mile, 56–7, 66–8, 83, 94, 97, 106
  marginal, 102–9
  introductory, 57, 82
  on railways
    in principle, 158–62
    in practice, 164–71
    sources of cost, 178
    permanent way, 179
  in road goods transport
    sources of cost, 239
    allocation of overheads, 242
  in bus transport
    allocation of costs, 290–2
    allocation in transport, 318–19
Crosland, C. A. R., 13, 29
Cross-subsidization, 15, 19, 21, 327
  as a social welfare policy, 22
  airlines, 65, 69–70, 71–2, 102, 104
  railways, 128, 161, 162, 170, 193
  road haulage, 244–5, 256
  road passenger transport, 266, 278–9, 293, 296–7, 307, 309
  as a problem in demand forecasting, 320–1
Crossley, J. R. (and Devons, E. and Maunder, W. F.), 212n, 314n

Dalton, H., 6
Deakin, R. M. (and Seward, T.), 151, 181, 238, 301
Dear, D. M., 208n
Demand
  for Air Travel
    growth, 36, 55, 72, 120n
    types of, 38, 40, 46
    fluctuations in, 47, 79, 82
  for Rail Transport
    changing factors, 141–3

    freight, 144–53
    passenger, 153–57
  for Road Haulage, 236–8
  for Road Passenger Transport
    factors in long-term decline, 281–5
    peak, 285–7
    rural, 287
    problems in estimation of, 317–18, 320–1
Devons, E. (and Crossley, J. R. and Maunders, W. F.), 212n, 314n
Dieselization on Railways, 134, 191
Domestic Air Services, 39
  and BEA, 54, 59–60, 66–9
Durbin, E., 6

'Earlybird' fares, 84, 85
Economies of scale
  airlines, 50–1, 92–3, 94, 96, 100, 107
  road haulage, 233–6
  road passenger transport, 275–6
Economies of standardization (air), 49, 92, 99
Edwards Committee Report (*see* under Committee of Inquiry into Civil Air Transport)
Edwards, Sir Ronald, 36
Edwards, S. W. (and Bayliss, B. T.), 235, 246
Efficiency (see also Productivity)
  Airlines
    problems of measuring, 109–12
  Railways
    standards of, 181–2
    asset utilization, 182–6
    new methods of operation, 186–92
    through investment, 192–6
    labour and management, 196–200
  Road Haulage, 245–8
  Road Passenger Transport, 300–2
Electrification on railways, 134, 191, 192
Exchequer Dividend Capital, 78, 79, 87, 90–1

INDEX

'Fifth-freedom' operations, 81, 122n
Financial and Economic Obligations of the Nationalized Industries, 1961 (White Paper), 17–19, 79, 202
Financial objectives, development of, 15–17, 18–19
  Airlines
    in BEA, 60–1, 64–5, 70
    in BOAC, 79
    for British Airways Board, 114
    merits of, for air corporations, 101–12
  Railways, 138–9, 202
  Road Haulage, 221–2
  Road Passenger Transport, 270, 298
Financial Problems of BOAC (White Paper), 92
Forecasting
  Air, 47, 55, 112
  Railways, 168–9, 193
  In general, 318, 320–1
Foster, C. D., 160, 345n
——— (and Beesley, M. E.), 211n
——— (and Joy, S. C.), 185
Freight Integration Council, 222, 235, 337–9
Freightliners, 138, 187, 188–9, 221, 227, 230, 248, 337, 338

Garnett, H. C. (and Johnson, K. M.), 211n, 263n
Gas Council, 30
Geddes, Sir Eric, 207n
Geddes Committee on Carriers Licensing, 180, 223–226, 233, 251, 255, 329, 337
Griffiths, Eldon, 213n
Gwilliam, K. M., 119n, 207n

Hall, J., 315n
Hanson, A. H., 33n
Harrison, A. J., 235
Herman, P. S., 262n
Heyworth Report, 10
Hibbs, J., 279, 309, 312n

Highlands and Islands (air services), 60, 70, 96, 121n
Huckfield, L., 313n
Hurcomb, Sir Cyril, 260n

Imperial Airways, 8
Inclusive tour (IT), 39, 51, 68, 73–4, 80, 81, 86, 108, 117, 121n
Independent airlines, 44, 45, 52, 53, 117
  restrictions on competition, 67–8
Industrial Relations Act 1971, 250
Industrial Reorganization Corporation, 29
International Air Transport Association (IATA), 39, 43, 68, 115, 119n
  Fares Conferences, 52, 66, 67, 83, 84–5, 102, 109
International Civil Aviation Organization (ICAO), 119n
Investment
  In general, 11, 16–17, 18, 320
  Test rate of discount, 20
  Airlines, 101, 104
    BOAC financing of, 86–90, 116
    appraisal, 105–6, 110
    Ministerial control of, 113
    test rate of discount and, 111
  Railways
    Modernization Plan (see also), 133–4
    development in 1960s, 191–6
    future, 205
  Road Haulage, 253–5
  Road Passenger Transport, 299–300

Jack Committee, 287
Johnson, Sir Henry, 184, 204
Johnson, K. M. (and Garnett, H. C.), 211n, 263n
Joint costs, problems in allocation of,
  Airlines, 70, 104–5
  Railways, 159–61, 164–5
  Road Haulage, 242
  Road Passenger Transport, 290–1

INDEX

Joy, S. C., 161, 179, 184
—— (and Foster, C. D.), 185
Jumbo jet (see also Boeing 747), 80, 83, 85, 118

Keith, Kenneth, 58
Kolsen, H. M., 345n

Lee, N. (and Steedman, I.), 276, 303
Licensing (see also Quality and Quantity Licensing)
  in airline operation, 45, 119n
  in road haulage, 222–7, 259
  in road passenger transport, 268, 276–81
  as a reason of regulation, 324–6
Licensing Authorities, 217, 224, 226
Little, I. M. D., 16
Load factor (airlines), 38, 39, 40, 49, 95, 108
  in BEA, 54, 55–6, 60
  in BOAC, 82
London Passenger Transport Board, 7, 130–1, 326, 339

McGowan Report, 10
McKinseys, 200
MacLeod, W. M. (and Walters, A. A.), 260n
Macmillan, H., 9
Management structure
  in BEA, 51, 73, 74
  in a merged airline, 100
  in railways, 199–200
  in road haulage, 219, 221, 249, 255
  in road passenger transport, 278, 306, 307
Mance, H. O., 345n
Marginal cost pricing
  in development of policy, 16, 20
  in airlines, 103–8
  in railways, 162–4
  in road haulage, 242–3
  in road passenger transport, 290–1
  in general, 319–20
Maunder, W. F. (and Devons, E. and Crossley, J. R.), 212n, 314n

Maynard, A. K., 119n
Merger
  of BEA and BOAC, 52, 92–101, 117
  advantages of, 94–100
Merry-go-round train working, 187
Milward, Sir Anthony, 43, 121n
Modernization Plan (Railways), 24, 133, 134, 176, 184, 189, 191, 193, 194
Molson, Hugh, 261n
Morrison, H., 5, 8, 130
Moses, L. W. (and Williamson, H. F.), 313n
Munby, D. L., 171, 208n, 209n, 259n, 322

National Board for Prices and Incomes, 21, 23, 28, 29, 74, 100, 112, 121n, 168, 171, 173, 198, 199, 233, 240, 243, 244, 248, 250, 252, 257–8, 280, 291, 295, 296, 304, 305, 306
National Bus Company, 2, 343, Chapter 5 *passim*
  origins, 271
  structure, 271–272
  and rural routes, 287–8
  financial performance, 298–9
  relation with PTAs, 340–1
National Carriers Ltd, 227, 230, 237, 239, 248, 251, 253, 258, 338
National Coal Board, 2, 16, 29, 31
National Freight Corporation, 138–139, 187, 204, 335, Chapter 4 *passim*
  origins, 221–2
  holdings, 227–8
  cost structure, 239
  financial performance, 252–3
  reorganization, 257–8
  relations with BRB in Freight Integration Council, 337–9
National Joint Council for Civil Air Transport, 74
National Travel Survey 1965, 286
Nationalization, Chapter 1 *passim*
  origins, 1–9

Nationalization, (cont'd)
  rationale in nationalization Acts, 9-14
  economic rules developed, 14-26
  position in 1970s, 26-9
  Airlines, 107-8, 115-18
  Railways, 130-2
  Road Haulage, 218-19
  denationalization, 220
  Road Passenger Transport, 269-70
  As a means of co-ordination, 326-7
Nationalized Industries: A Review of Economic and Financial Objectives (1967 White Paper), 19-21, 22, 158, 173, 202
Nationalized Transport Advisory Council, 328, 337
North Atlantic routes, 80-6
  components of, 81-2

Osborn, H. E., 262n, 263n

Pan American Airways, 78, 81, 83, 122n
Passenger Transport Authorities, 173, 206, 271, 272, 281, 307, 332, 335, 339-42, 343
Peaks in demand
  Air, 50, 102, 104
  Railways, 156-7
  Road Haulage, 236-7
  Buses, 285-7
Politi, J. (and Beesley, M. E.), 299
Ponsonby, G. J., 312n
Pooling, 43-4, 46, 49, 80, 102
Post Office, 2, 3, 5, 7, 13, 14, 338
Pricing Policy (see also Marginal Cost Pricing)
  development of, 16, 19-20
  Air Corporations, 101-12
  Railways, 166-73
  Road Haulage, 241-5
  Road Passenger Transport, 292-6
Productivity, 111
  Performance of nationalized industries, 30

Airlines
  in BEA, 56-8, 74
  in BOAC, 78, 91
Railways, 181
Road Haulage, 247
Road Passenger Transport, 300-2
Productivity Bargaining, 199, 250, 304
Profit
  Airlines
    in BEA, 58-60
    in BOAC, 79
  Railways, 134, 140
  Road Haulage, 251-3
  Road Passenger Transport, 296-9
Profit centres
  in BEA, 73
'Provision One', 39, 68-9
Pryke, R. W., 30, 31
Public Dividend Capital (see Exchequer Dividend Capital)
Public Transport and Traffic (1967 White paper), 276, 294, 302, 340-1

Quality of Service
  civil aviation, 67, 71, 106
  railways,
    freight, 151-3
    passenger, 154-5
  road haulage, 238
  road passenger transport, 284-5
Quality licensing, 225
Quantity licensing, 139, 204, 225, 226, 335-7, 343
Quarmby, D. A., 285
Quick Smith, G. W., 215, 262n

Railway Act 1844, 126
Railway and Canal Traffic Act 1894, 126
Railway Policy 1967 (White Paper), 196, 206
Railway Staff National Tribunal, 198
Railway Trunk Routes, The Development of Major, 135, 137, 139, 185
Railways Act 1921, 128, 129, 133

INDEX

Rate of return on net assets,
  BEA's, 58, 60, 61
  BOAC's, 79
Redfern, R., 207n
Regional air services, 47, 53, 66, 71–2, 118
Regional policy, 21–2
Reid Committee, 11
Reorganization of the Nationalized Transport Undertakings (1960 White Paper), 207n, 220, 261n
Reshaping of British Railways, The (Beeching Report), 134–6, 156, 175, 178, 179, 182, 186, 188, 190, 194, 197, 329, 337
Richard Thomas and Baldwin, 2, 13
Ridley Committee, 16, 25
Road Goods Survey, 1962, 231, 237
Road Haulage Association, 216, 225, 229, 230, 233, 234, 240, 243, 249, 251, 252, 255, 325
Road Haulage Executive, 219, 327
Road Passenger Executive, 269
Road and Rail Traffic Act 1933, 130, 217, 222, 249, 323, 325
Road Traffic Act 1930, 130, 249, 268–9, 274, 276, 280, 287, 292, 307, 323
Road Traffic Act 1967, 225
Route density (airlines), 48, 94–7
Route structure (airlines), 47, 48, 49, 50, 94–9, 120n
Royal Commission on Local Government, 266
Royal Commission on Transport 1928–30, 128, 130, 216, 268, 324, 325

Salaries in nationalized industries, 26, 74, 100, 121n
Salter Conference, 216, 224, 325
Sargent, J. R., 345n
Savage, C. I., 207n, 260n, 311n
Scheduling (air craft), 46, 47, 49, 50, 72–3, 97–9, 104–5, 121n
Scottish Bus Group, 269, 271, 275, 284, 307
'Second-force' airline, 52–3, 80

Select Committee on Nationalized Industries, 17, 21, 22, 27, 28, 61, 66, 134, 135, 144, 171, 183, 191, 195, 202, 328
Service frequency (airlines), 40–1, 43, 46, 67, 70, 95, 96, 99, 105–6
Seward, T. (and Deakin, B. M.), 151, 181, 238, 301
Sharp, C., 262n, 346n
Shinwell, E., 6
Smith, J. H., 261n
Social service obligations
  In general, 10–11, 22
  Airlines
    in BEA, 70, 121n
  Railways, 126, 137, 139, 205–6
  Road Haulage
    absence of, 256
  Road Passenger Transport, 278–9, 310–11
Standards of service (air), 51, 107
Stedeford Committee, 134, 328
Steedman, I. (and Lee, N.) 276, 303
Straszheim, M. R., 119n
Stratford, A. H., 119n
Strauss, G., 33n
Subsidies
  Airlines, 44, 64–5, 71, 107
  Railways, 139, 172, 204, 205–6
  Road Passenger Transport, 287–9, 309–11
Swingler, Stephen, 203

Thesiger Committee, 270, 276, 278
Tilling Group, 269, 286, 290, 307
Traffic Commissioners, 268, 273, 276–81, 293–5, 298, 341
Traffic in Towns (Buchanan Report), 283, 330
Transport Act 1947, 131, 218–19, 226, 269, 323, 326
Transport Act 1953, 132–3, 220, 224, 270, 323, 328, 343
Transport Act 1962, 134, 135, 137, 145, 199, 220, 221, 235, 255, 270, 323, 328, 329
Transport Act 1968, 124, 138–40, 144, 153, 173, 175, 196, 200, 203,

Transport Act 1968, (*cont'd*)
 214, 223, 225, 228, 241, 255, 268, 270, 272, 280, 287, 302, 304, 307, 316, 323, 324, 329–42, 344
Transport Costing Service, 164
Transport Development Group, 229, 234
Transport for Industry, 145–52, 238
Transport Holding Company, Chapters 4 & 5 *passim*, 135, 328
Transport Needs of Great Britain in the Next Twenty Years (Hall Report), 143
Transport of Freight, The (1966 White Paper), 153, 208n, 336
Transport Policy (1952 White Paper), 270, 327–8
Transport Policy (1966 White Paper), 225, 331, 341

Transport Tribunal, 16, 132, 133, 165
Transport Users Consultative Committees, 132, 309
Trans World Airlines (TWA), 78, 81, 83, 122n
Trunk services (airlines), 47, 59–60, 67–8, 71, 100
Tugendhat, C., 265n
Tyson, W. J., 314n

United Transport, 229

Walker Gilbert, 241, 262n, 270
Walters, A. A., 235, 245, 262n
——— (and MacLeod, W. M.), 260n
Wheatcroft, Stephen, 41, 119n
Williamson, H. F. (and Moses, L. W.), 313n
Wilson, Sir Reginald, 257